Just Enough Web Programming with XHTML™, PHP®, and MySQL®

Guy W. Lecky-Thompson

Course Technology PTR

A part of Cengage Learning

COURSE TECHNOLOGY
CENGAGE Learning™

Australia • Brazil • Japan • Korea • Mexico • Singapore • Spain • United Kingdom • United States

COURSE TECHNOLOGY
CENGAGE Learning™

Just Enough Web Programming with XHTML™, PHP®, and MySQL®
Guy W. Lecky-Thompson

Publisher and General Manager, Course Technology PTR: Stacy L. Hiquet

Associate Director of Marketing: Sarah Panella

Manager of Editorial Services: Heather Talbot

Marketing Manager: Mark Hughes

Acquisitions Editor: Mitzi Koontz

Project/Copy Editor: Kezia Endsley

Technical Reviewer: Matt Telles

PTR Editorial Services Coordinator: Erin Johnson

Interior Layout Tech: ICC Macmillan Inc.

Cover Designer: Mike Tanamachi

Indexer: Sharon Shock

Proofreader: Andy Saff

Library of Congress Control Number: 2008921609

ISBN-13: 978-1-59863-481-5

ISBN-10: 1-59863-481-X

Course Technology
25 Thomson Place
Boston, MA 02210
USA

Cengage Learning is a leading provider of customized learning solutions with office locations around the globe, including Singapore, the United Kingdom, Australia, Mexico, Brazil, and Japan. Locate your local office at: **international.cengage.com/region**

Cengage Learning products are represented in Canada by Nelson Education, Ltd.

For your lifelong learning solutions, visit **courseptr.com**

Visit our corporate Website at **cengage.com**

Printed in the United States of America
1 2 3 4 5 6 7 11 10 09 08

This book is for my wife, Nicole, who was the first person I taught "Just Enough" HTML to, when she needed to set up Web pages.

ACKNOWLEDGMENTS

A big thank you once again to my ever-supportive family, for keeping me sane through the trials and tribulations of yet another book. It's never a routine matter, even if we all get used to the process from concept to the final edit.

Of course, the final product would not look as good as it does without the help of the copy editor, Kezia Endsley and the technical editor, Matt Telles. Once again, they have done a sterling job of making sure that my point is both linguistically and technically correct.

Mitzi Koontz also deserves a thank you for helping behind the scenes, so to speak, along with the rest of the publishing and support team.

Last, but not least, my children—Emma and William—deserve a special mention for reminding me that there's more to life than getting a book out. Like learning how to jump rope or play soccer . . .

About the Author

Guy W. Lecky-Thompson holds a BSc. in Computer Studies from the University of Derby, UK, and has written articles and books on a variety of subjects, from software engineering to video game design and programming.

A technical all-rounder, he brings all aspects of his professional life and personal views to his writing, injecting personality into technical subjects. In his books, this often translates into giving the readers the vital information, while cutting away anything that isn't immediately relevant or useful.

When not writing books, Guy enjoys family time, video gaming, writing opinion pieces, and creative programming.

CONTENTS

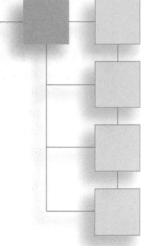

x   Contents

INTRODUCTION

Welcome to *Just Enough Web Programming*, part of the *Just Enough* series of books, where the author's aim is to equip the readers with accurate information that is immediately useful, rather than trying to make them an expert overnight. In particular, *Just Enough Web Programming* will provide:

- An understanding of Web publishing

- A build-up of useful information over time ✓

- Reference chapters for later use, whenever you get stuck in the real world

- Examples using real-world services that would otherwise be difficult to leverage... without the added context.

You should be able to get started very quickly, by taking the basic outline principles and shading in the detail as they progress. A newcomer to the World Wide Web and online publishing can start at the very beginning, and work right through to the end, whereas those who already have some experience can pick up additional tips and tricks at the appropriate point. for reference,

The book begins with the "Getting Started" chapter, where you learn about tools that you can use to deploy Web applications and services. This chapter also points out some useful paths through the rest of the book for those needing specific guidance—for college courses, work-related problem solving, and so on.

For those who might not be completely at ease with all the terminology associated with the Internet, Chapter 2 contains an Internet recap. Here, the main idea is to just run through all the things that you might think you know about the Internet and World Wide Web, just to make sure that you understand the basic principles.

Of course, some readers might want to skip this part, but Chapter 3, which covers the basic language of the Web, HTML, moves along quite quickly, and uses the principles laid out in the "Internet Recap" chapter. It also covers XML and XHTML in order to illustrate some of those principles in action.

Ch 4
Text/
Graphic
Styling

Chapter 4 then contains a discussion on CSS and styles, which are ways of presenting guidelines on how the information is presented. In other words, they tell the computer how to display the text, graphics, and other pieces of information that you want to share with the Web user.

Ch 5 *Ch 6*
The next two chapters cover client side and server side scripting. This is where the bulk of the actual programming information comes in. The build up to this point has all been about presentation, and these two chapters are the first time that I mix that with the flow of document creation.

Integral to that discussion is Chapter 7, "Web Databases," where you look at the ways in which the data shared with the Web user is stored. In fact, the vast majority of dynamic Web pages use databases in order to store information in a way that can be easily indexed, retrieved, and cross-referenced.

Ch 8
Part of the power that this mixture of presentation, flow, and information storage allows us to leverage is in creating Content Management Systems. Chapter 8 presents some of the popular existing CMS that are deployed on the Internet, in an aim to show you how they work underneath the outside presentation layer.

*Ch 8
Creating
or
deploying
a
Content
Management
System*

I do this so that you can then deploy your own customized versions of these CMS, or even start to create one of your own. This is not as daunting as it might first sound, and having followed the discussion in the book thus far, you will be adequately equipped to make your own CMS, which follows your own specific needs.

Ch 9
Part of this customization can also be shared with the Web users, which is where the Web 2.0 concept comes into play. In the Web 2.0 chapter, you look at what the approach entails, and how you might benefit from it in your own projects. It

draws on all the other chapters to this point, as Web 2.0 is not so much a technology as a way to deploy existing technology in a changing environment. *This is what it is*

The last part of this is the "Setting Up with Open Source" chapter, where you learn the various stages of setting up, from getting a Web host, to downloading and installing the software that you need in order to make all this information work. Having read this, you'll be fully able to get an interactive Website up and running in hours, rather than weeks.

Part of the "Setting Up with Open Source" chapter shows you some useful technologies that are built around the concepts that the Internet has made famous, and that this book teaches. It serves as an illustration of what you can do with your newfound knowledge in providing new services to the Internet community. *More Information*

Finally, the "Web References" chapter is exactly that—a collection of annotated references to places on the Internet that you will find useful. In a here today, gone tomorrow publishing environment such as the Web, I have tried to list only those that are likely still to be there in years to come.

Absorbing everything the first time around is unlikely, even for the most dedicated Internet hack. On the other hand, there are several ways that the book can be read, and it is designed to be continually useful. In other words, I fully expect that you'll pick up the book and thumb through it, and I have arranged the information with this use in mind.

The place to begin is with the "Getting Started" chapter, where you will be able to plan your way through the rest of the book—whether you decide to just plough through all the material or want to pick off bits and pieces to fill possible knowledge gaps.

Either way, it is likely to be an entertaining ride, and I hope you'll enjoy the journey.

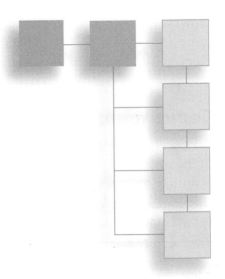

CHAPTER 1

GETTING STARTED

Before you can begin to experiment with your own Web pages and scripts, you need to look at a few general points pertaining to the way that the book is written. As I don't wish to overcomplicate the process of learning the ins and outs of Web programming, I have trimmed down the information that you need to remember.

Nonetheless, there are certain conventions that I use to convey meaning in a low impact way, as well as some standard pieces of software that I encourage you to have at your disposal.

This chapter is structured around the following appropriate points:

- Conventions used in this book—Some typographic conventions explained.

- How to use this book—Some paths through the book.

- Choosing the right tools—Tools you need to create Web pages and write scripts.

- Using Open Source resources—Code, tools, and libraries, for free.

these can be grouped

After you work your way through this chapter and make sure that you have everything you need to get started, you'll find that your own experiments will be that much easier. One of the best ways to learn is through doing, and in doing, you can make mistakes and ask questions in a way which mere reading might not allow.

1

However, in order to ask the right questions, and get the right answers, you need to be sure that you all understand the way that those answers will be presented. Hence, you need some conventions.

Conventions Used in This Book

A book on Web programming would not be complete without some examples of how specific concepts are applied in real pieces of computer code. For instance, pages are delivered as documents coded using HTML, the special language of the Web. But, you can write such pages as long as you understand HTML, use a special application (that also understands HTML), or employ a piece of programming code.

So, you can generate pages using a server side language such as PHP. In addition, the presentation can be changed using styles, and even dynamic layouts can be applied using JavaScript, which is interpreted by the browser. Naturally, the book gives just enough of these technologies so you can apply them in the real world.

HTML for presentation

Coupled with the presentation language (HTML), a specific set of scripting languages (such as JavaScript) can be used to modify the output displayed by the browser. In essence, this is the programming part of the Web programming process. Although you'll learn about the basic presentation language first, at some point you will actually have to write scripts as well. *When, Chapter 2/3?*

Javascript for dynamic output

This will become clear as you go along. However, you must understand that using scripting requires knowledge of two important items:

1   ■ Syntax: How specific scripting commands are to be used.

2   ■ Semantics: Where these script statements are to be used.

E.g. Programming with Javascript or PHP

In other words, you need a generic template description that shows how to form the scripted command, as well as showing how it is used alongside other bits and pieces of Web scripting or presentation layer information. Each important facet of Web code (HTML, PHP, XML, and so on) will be presented according to these two important aspects.

Conventions

To distinguish something that you should type in and use as a script or Web page definition, the book uses a specific font. Whenever text is shown in a fixed font like this, it is something that you are expected to type in. Of course, the typing in is optional, but the book uses the font to show the difference between code and the textual description of the script or code.

Sometimes the text needs to show, in the generic template for a piece of script or presentation language, some items that are either:

- Optional, in that the users can choose to include them

- Mandatory, in that the computer expects them to be there

Besides these rules, the actual values can sometimes be chosen freely, or from a list of allowed values, so you need to be aware of these cases. Whenever I want to indicate that you can *choose* a specific value from a list of possible allowed values, I show a list separated by the pipe symbol, |. For example:

One | Two | Three | : or symbol

This example means that you can use One, Two, or Three wherever this list is specified. I will, however, usually enclose the list in one of two sets of symbols in order to indicate whether the value is optional or mandatory. To show that the value is mandatory, I enclose it in chevrons:

< One | Two | Three>   < > MANdATORy
(at least one item mandatory)

This indicates that any of the values in the list can be used, but that at exactly one must be present. Conversely, to indicate that there is both a choice of value, *and* choice of presence, you'll see the list in [and] symbols, thus:

[One | Two | Three]   ← None necessarilly. Optional.

These are all examples where you're given a list of values from which to choose and the value is optional; so you need only choose one if it is really necessary. This might sound like an unnecessary complication, but it can be very useful and is much easier to understand once you look at some concrete examples.

If there is no list to choose from, the value can be freely chosen, with some restrictions that will be explained when the specific item is introduced. It will usually look something like this:

< *number* >

This indicates that any number can be used, but that a number of some kind must be provided, because the chevrons (< >) indicate that this is a mandatory value. On the other hand, you might see:

[*number*]   ← optional value, must be in form of number if included.

This indicates that while any number can be chosen, its presence is optional. Notice that the value is in *italics* to show that it is a value chosen freely. I might also indicate that a specific constant value (one that does not change, and is imposed on the reader) should be used by specifying a list with a single item:

< 1 >

Again, this indicates that the digit 1 must appear in the piece of code, whereas the following indicates that the digit 1 might appear, depending on the specific needs:

[1]

This last use is not very widespread in the various examples, but is included here to complete the picture. It is more usual that a specific value required to be used in the code will just be specified as part of the generic template itself, as a constant value, without any indication as to whether the programmer has any choice over its inclusion.

How to Use This Book

This book is designed to have a certain shelf life, and as such, the way that you use it will change as you gain experience through experimentation. The book is also designed for technicians and non-technicians alike, and so covers the material at various levels. However, you're not expected to have any knowledge of:

- Web design

- Website creation

- Programming

Different readers will have different needs (following their competences), so there are different paths through the material depending on individual circumstances. Along with your changing circumstances over time, the following general categories can be defined:

- Beginner: No exposure to Web design or development

- Some knowledge: Some exposure to Web design

- Intermediate: Current Webmaster wanting to extend current knowledge beyond HTML

- Learning reference: Ongoing study

- Professional reference: Off-the-shelf solution seeker, with some exposure to HTML and related technologies

The book has been written in such a way as to offer a good solution for each of these reader types. The material is presented in an order for those needing a professional reference guide. However, I can give some guidance for the other three categories of readership.

As a Web programming course text, this book enables you to follow a path that introduces the Web, moves on through presentation of Web pages, and finishes up with advanced scripting and presentation techniques such as Web 2.0 and content management systems.

Those readers with no initial agenda, with the time to dedicate to reading and understanding, can just read the book from cover to cover and try out the various ideas and snippets as they go along. Some readers will likely benefit from more structure to the process, and so I can give some guidance that will help group similar topics together.

Study Areas

To help course developers and those looking for a professional reference work, I have grouped the chapters according to three principal areas:

- Client Side Web Programming—Ways to present information in the browser, allowing it to render the content. *Rendering in a browser*

- Server Side Web Programming—Scripting on the server allowing dynamic content, databases, and so on. *Dynamic data e.g. from a DB*

- *Other* Applied Topics—Ways that you can leverage the client and server side programming techniques to provide useful technologies ranging from Web 2.0 content to CMS and games. *Web 2.0 and more databases (CMS)*

Some topics can be skipped, depending on personal requirements; however, I recommend that you at least skim through topics that you think you have already mastered. The final aim of the book is to provide enough information that you can create dynamic Web programming applications of your own, or leverage other people's applications as easily as possible. *Why? How?*

Client Side Web Programming

This study area is aimed at providing you with enough knowledge of the languages used to describe the way in which Web pages should be rendered (HTML, XML, XHTML, CSS, and so on) along with some techniques for dynamic content generation in the browser itself. *(Javascript)*

I also introduce some vital topics relating to the way that the Internet and World Wide Web are used in presenting content to the end user. The idea is to give a thorough basis, without going into detail with respect to the more esoteric possibilities that Web programming offers.

Internet Recap

Here I discuss the way that the Internet and World Wide Web are organized, and review some of the core technologies and frameworks.

HTML, XML, and XHTML

examples? of frameworks vs. technologies

This chapter deals with the way that you can communicate the content and description of its rendering (the way it should be displayed) to the browser.

How does HTML and XHTML work?

CSS and Styles

Following on from the previous chapter, styles allow more control over the exact rendering possibilities offered by the standard rendering languages used on the Web.

Then, same for CSS.

Client Side Scripting / *Programming*

Scripting.

Collecting together the material from the first three chapters, and adding the use of scripting within the Web page, this chapter is the first introduction to programming for the Web. It is the culmination of the client side Web programming study area and a first look at dynamic and interactive Web design and development.

Server Side Web Programming

In this study area, you'll look at the various technologies that allow you to offer interactivity, storage, and associated services on the Web server itself. These result in the delivery of content to the client using the channels established in the previous study area.

This includes aspects relating to the commercialization of the Website, such as online catalogs, search engines, dynamic rendering of relevant content, tracking, and so on. It is an extension of the client side programming that allows a deeper user experience and higher value service than using client side programming alone.

Server Side Programming

This chapter offers an introduction to PHP, one of the best established and most popular languages used for cross platform server side scripting. The chapter covers the key language core concepts and the most commonly used libraries and extensions, but without going into the full details of what is a complex subject— you're given just enough to be able to build practical Web applications.

Web Databases

Following on from learning about server side Web programming, you'll then learn about the way that data can be stored and retrieved in a Web connected database, using the ever-popular MySQL implementation. I introduce the SQL language, as well as the interfaces offered by PHP, and bind the two together using server and client side scripting in a technology known as AJAX.

Applied Topics

Having prepared you with knowledge of client and server side scripting techniques and technologies, the final study area deals with the implementation of common services that use these technologies. In doing so, I also cover how you might go about creating a site from scratch using only customized Open Source solutions.

These examples pull together all the techniques and technologies and prepare you for their deployment in the real world. Here again, you'll also learn about the commercial implications of being able to leverage these technologies.

Content Management Systems

The CMS chapter looks at the available implementations, features that are required, and how you might implement your own. These systems relate not only to content delivery, but also to content generation such as that needed in gaming and other interactive applications.

The knowledge that is required to understand this chapter includes Web page presentation, server side scripting, and databases. Some knowledge of client side scripting will be an asset, but is not required to understand the examples.

Web 2.0 Features

With the advent of social networking and associated services, Web 2.0 will play an increasingly important part in the future direction of content creation on the Web. This chapter deals primarily with user content creation and personalization.

This is just a verbose way of stating that you'll want to allow the end user to customize his or her experience and contribute to the service and the content that it delivers. Web 2.0 requires knowledge of client and server side scripting and content presentation.

This chapter can be understood without specific knowledge of databases; however, it would be an asset to have an understanding of the interaction between the server and databases in a CMS environment.

Setting Up with Open Source

The final chapter in this study area takes you through the steps required to set up your own Web server, using only Open Source components. You'll look at two scenarios: establishing your own hosted server and a remotely hosted service.

Reference

Parts of the book are written in a way so they can be used for off-the-shelf reference. In Chapter 11, I make a note of where these are so that you can access them quickly.

Experienced IT users might want to start with Chapter 11 in order to look up specific information that they have a current need for. In doing so, they will be able to cross reference with the explanatory text as well as apply the knowledge immediately in the solutions they are currently deploying.

Choosing the Right Tools

It is important, before reading the book proper, that you put together a series of basic tools that will allow you to use the examples from the book. These tools fall into two principal areas:

- Client tools
- Server tools

The first area deals with tools that are of use to you when working with single pages of static content. The second is important when you move away from those constraints and into the realm of Web programming for interactivity.

Those readers unconcerned at this time with server side processing (although it never hurts to understand what goes on behind social networking and publishing sites) can stick with the client tools. These tools are generally always available in a very basic form as part of the operating system, as you shall see.

Readers who have their eyes set on server side programming will need the server tools also; again, though, most of these are available out of the box for server operating systems. In both cases, Open Source solutions will be available for those who are not exploiting these techniques within a corporate environment.

Client Tools

Client side tools include those tools that you'll use for editing the pages that you create as part of the examples, as well as editing the various pieces of code throughout the book. To display the pages, a browser will be used, which is another client side piece of software.

You also need to bridge the client and server environment in order to test your newly learned skills on the Web at large. Some Web host providers offer a "through the browser" upload facility, for others a special piece of (freely available, Open Source) software will be required to transfer the files. This software is known as FTP (File Transfer Protocol) software.

Editor

The editor is used to construct the Web pages. When choosing an editor, generally speaking, the simpler the better. In fact, many Web page designers work with a simple text editor.

One feature of many editors that is highly useful, however, is known as *syntax highlighting*, which colors pieces of text that have a special meaning. In this case, this includes certain keywords that are not part of the Web content that the end user will see, but which have relevance to:

- The browser
- The Web designer
- The Web programmer

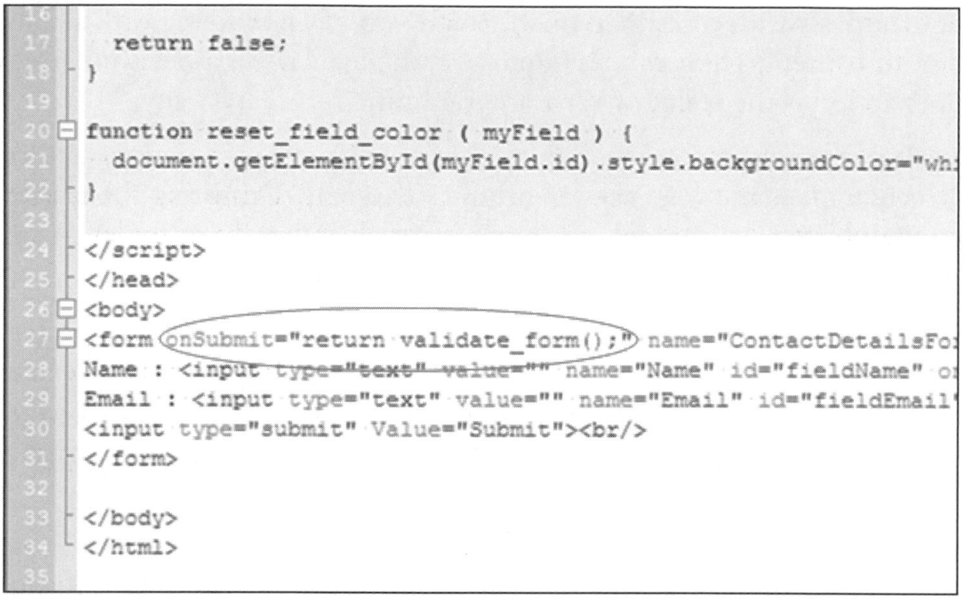

```
16
17      return false;
18   }
19
20 □ function reset_field_color ( myField ) {
21       document.getElementById(myField.id).style.backgroundColor="whi
22   }
23
24   </script>
25   </head>
26 □ <body>
27 □ <form onSubmit="return validate_form();" name="ContactDetailsFo
28   Name : <input type="text" value="" name="Name" id="fieldName" o
29   Email : <input type="text" value="" name="Email" id="fieldEmail
30   <input type="submit" Value="Submit"><br/>
31   </form>
32
33   </body>
34   </html>
35
```

Figure 1.1
Syntax highlighting in SciTE

The highlighting allows the designer or programmer to edit the content more easily, but is not carried through into the final content. A good editor will offer configurable highlighting that can be adjusted depending on the code being edited (HTML, XML, PHP, and so on) either by the editor's developer or the end user.

In Figure 1.1, you can see syntax highlighting in action. The circled area, for example, shows part of the HTML code that is used to create a Web form, highlighted along with many other pieces of code. Regular text is in black, HTML is in aqua, and JavaScript is background highlighted (shaded), too.

In addition, this highlighting can be extended to include *error identification*, which alerts the designer or programmer to potential errors in the code. Again, this is specific to the content that is not designed to be seen by the Web surfer, but that's vital to describing the way that this content must be presented.

Part of generating this code might include a certain amount of *automation* or *scripting* built into the editor. This is quite advanced, but many recent editing tools now support the possibility to program buttons that fill code in on behalf of the designer or programmer.

Specific editors designed to create specific types of coded content (HTML, XML, PHP, and so on) extend this even further to provide menu items that can be used to start wizard style interfaces that help create specific pieces of content. It's better not to use such features until you are completely comfortable with Web programming.

The reason for this is that, quite often, these kinds of editing solutions can produce code that is impossible for the designer to edit. This being the case, if there is a problem with the code (if the server does not have the assumed configuration), the designer or programmer will be unable to fix it.

Therefore, I recommend for readers of this book that they find a basic solution—something that is similar to Microsoft Notepad—with the possibility to use syntax highlighting for HTML, XML, PHP, and so on.

The high-end editors offer some additional flexibility, but they can be cumbersome for beginners, and I recommend them only for programmers who have had some exposure to similar tools in the past. For example, a programmer used to a specific environment that offers the possibility to add an HTML module for syntax coloring and error checking (such as the Eclipse IDE) might find that advantageous.

All just enough readers should stay away from all-in-one solutions like Microsoft FrontPage for the time being. As mentioned, you should first understand the code you are creating, and be aware that such tools often hide too much of it in potentially incompatible extensions.

Upload

At some point, after having put together the pages that make up the Website, designers or programmers have to transfer the files from their own machine to a Web server. Unless they have put together their own local server (rare, but possible), they will need to do this to share their works with the surfing public.

The way that you do this is using a protocol aptly named FTP—File Transfer Protocol. You'll look at this in more depth in the next chapter; for now all you need to remember is that you use FTP to put a file on a remote server. To do this, you use a piece of FTP software.

As with editors, FTP applications come in various shapes and sizes—from the simple command-line FTP application provided with Microsoft Windows, to sophisticated file transfer applications. Some readers may have used them before, others will not have.

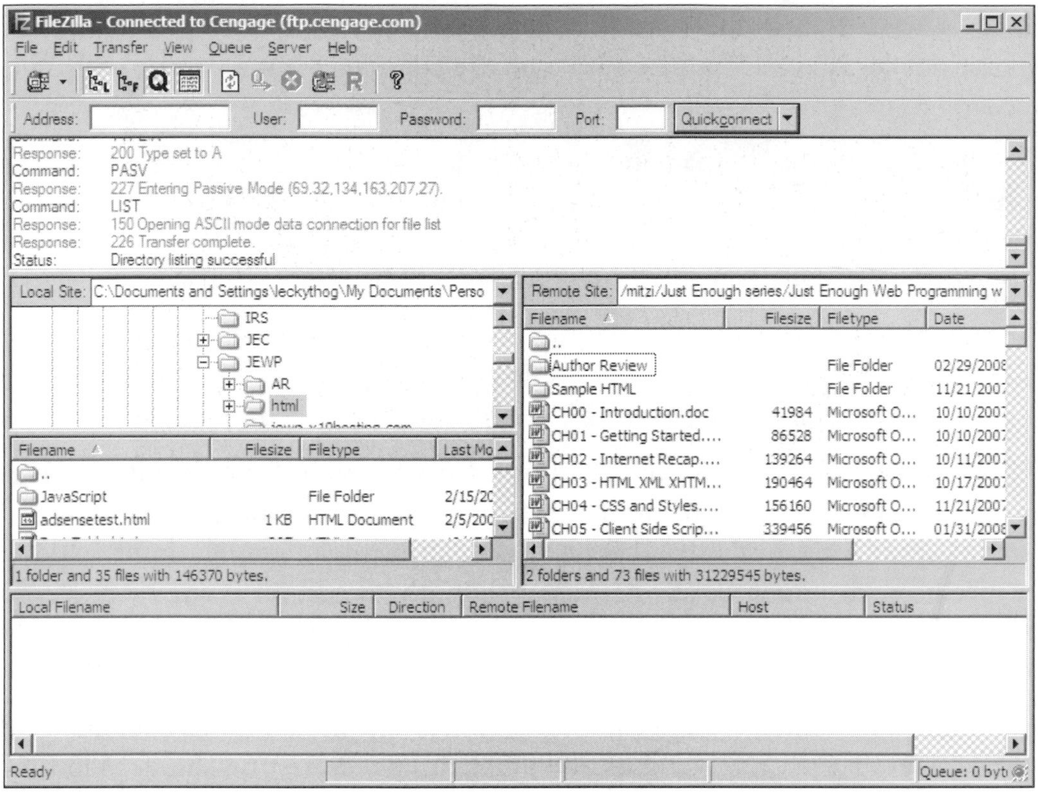

Figure 1.2
FileZilla FTP application

Figure 1.2 shows the popular FileZilla application, which is available as Open Source, and allows drag and drop between the local site and the remote site, as well as many other useful features. This is the application that I personally use, and have never had cause to complain.

Linux users are usually well served by having FTP functionality delivered as part of the tools that come with the operating system. Of course, those users will have already used FTP to download updates and new packages so they will be familiar with the options available to them.

Windows users also have a command-line FTP application available to them through the FTP application. It is basic, but it works. More recent versions of Internet Explorer can also be used to FTP files, but it might be a better option to download one of the many Open Source FTP applications that sport a Windows Explorer style interface and take advantage of a drag-and-drop interface.

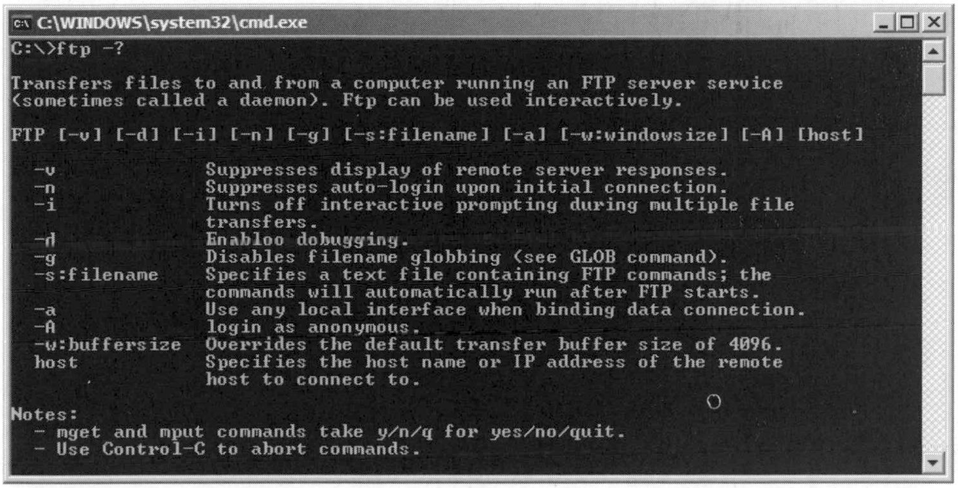

Figure 1.3
Windows command-line FTP

Figure 1.3 shows the help screen from the Windows command-line FTP application. As you can see, it is not the most user friendly environment, and most readers will benefit from the GUI offered by tools such as FileZilla.

Those using the Apple Macintosh might also need to find a low cost or free Open Source solution, given that they may not have access to the UNIX style command-line tools. This is version dependent, but those users may also benefit from a friendlier user interface that does not rely on users typing commands through an obscure interface.

Another FTP package is called CuteFTP, which works well and is available for both Mac and Windows platforms. Finally, there is a goodly collection of freeware FTP packages that run on all three, such as NcFTP.

Browser

To test static pages, and take a first look at the dynamic pages that you'll be creating as part of the learning experience behind this book, you need to use a Web browser. Most readers will be aware that this is an area where there is a slightly bitter competition in process between three principal suppliers of free browsers.

Although you are of course free to test your creations using your favorite browser, I have limited the testing of the book's examples to the three tried and tested main contenders:

- Firefox

Figure 1.4
The Mozilla Firefox Web browser

- Opera

- Internet Explorer

Figure 1.4 shows the landing page for Firefox, inside the Firefox Web browser. Later screenshots in the HTML chapter show comparative displays from both Firefox and Microsoft Internet Explorer.

For those with a penchant for more esoteric browsers, as well as those developing for third-party and mobile platforms, I have limited the presentation layer examples to the W3C (World Wide Web Consortium) implementations. Again, this topic is covered in the next chapter, but you need to be aware that some browsers offer different interpretations and facilities to the Web designer or programmer.

Wherever possible, this book tries to respect the principle that as long as the browser respects the W3C guidelines for presentation, the examples will work, except where noted. These exceptions are usually in the area of scripting or specific plug-ins (such as Adobe Flash, Microsoft Silverlight, and so on).

Part of the client side scripting interface uses JavaScript, hence the browser must be JavaScript capable, and JavaScript must be enabled for the examples to be tested. If this all sounds unfamiliar, don't worry, all will be explained in the next chapter.

Server Tools

You'll read about the setup of the server and the role that it plays later on. However, you do need to be aware that at some point, to get the most out of the book, you need to upload some server side scripts to a remote site and test them.

This can be a Windows, Linux, or Apple Macintosh based server, as long as it offers several key facilities. Amongst those, PHP must be available for the server in question, and if you're using a remotely hosted Web server, this may come at a price premium.

However, you can also use a local server for test purposes, and there are also some low cost and free Web host providers that can offer facilities that meet the requirements of this book. In other words, in return for a small hosting fee, or perhaps the agreement to post adverts in return for the Web space, you can experiment to your heart's content.

Because Apache and PHP are both freely available and well-supported, it is assumed that these are being deployed on whichever platform you decide to host your practice (or even real) sites on.

Database

One specific tool that might not be offered by the Web host is the ability to create, manage, or run third-party applications. Among the ones that I regularly refer to in this book, there is a specific need for the more advanced topics to use a database.

The database that I use is the relational database MySQL; it is Open Source, well-supported, and integrates with the various tools, services, and scripting languages introduced in the book. Your Web hosting service should either provide this as standard (which is reasonably common) or provide the facility to install MySQL or a similar relational database.

Those readers unable or unwilling to do this may use other solutions, ranging from Oracle (arguably the industry leader) to PosgreSQL (another popular Open Source alternative). However, be aware that some of the examples may need to be adapted accordingly. In the "Web Databases" chapter, you'll find some examples of implementations for these three databases; the emphasis is, however, on MySQL.

There are many versions of MySQL, and because different hosts will provide different versions, the book concentrates on ensuring that all the examples will work with as many MySQL implementations as possible. None of the more advanced features of recent versions will be used, and where incompatibilities arise, they will be appropriately marked.

Where the integration of the Web services with the database might differ from database to database, I use SQL, a standard language, so the examples usually work with any database. When there are SQL differences between database implementations, they are highlighted.

Part of the issue is that you need a link from the Web scripting language (PHP) to the database implementation. In other words, you need to establish communication between the two, and it is in this interface that most of the differences will be apparent.

If this sounds a little advanced right now, rest assured that, over time, it becomes second nature. You will be interfacing in a variety of ways; however, each one can be adjusted for each database that could be used on the server.

Using Open Source Resources

One of the closing chapters in the book deals with pulling together a collection of Open Source resources and using them to set up a whole server environment, script it, and deliver a variety of different example applications—from an online shop to a basic game.

Open Source chiefly means one thing—that the code used to create an application is freely available to the general public, and that it, and derived works, must adhere to the same principle. Of course, the text of the Open Source license is more complex than this, but the overriding philosophy is that Open Source software is created and distributed for the greater good.

However, as you will now be aware, during the learning process, you will need to have some resources at your disposal. The concept of Open Source provides you with many excellent resources:

- Applications

- Sample source code

- Server solutions

- Libraries

The first of these relates to the various editing, browsing, and other associated applications already listed in the start of the chapter. These can be freely used, for profit or personal use, with very few limitations. The license that is affixed to each usually only prohibits something called "derived works," and selling the application to someone else and passing it off as your own.

The concepts of derived works and selling basically prohibit the user from making a new application out of the Open Source application and making it available without respecting the license conditions or selling the existing or derived applications for a profit.

Sample source code can be useful as a learning exercise; whether it can be used in a commercial application thereafter is usually a question of common sense. The usual restrictions of copyright and intellectual property will likely apply, and you might want to seek legal advice if you are at all unsure.

Server solutions and libraries fall into the same category as applications. Use of the solutions is usually acceptable, but selling them or deriving works might not be. The most prominent exceptions to this are libraries covered by a specific license that allows the developer to derive a work as long as the library remains intact.

Again, however, you need to check the license and seek advice for any points that you are not completely sure about.

I feel adequately equipped to make a few recommendations regarding the use of Open Source solutions alongside this book. For example, most Linux boxes have server capabilities and make a good choice for testing many of the coded examples.

Despite some bad press, setup can be easy, if the right Linux is chosen for the reader's technical capabilities. The best way to explore Linux is to download a Live CD, which can be booted from the CD and will be able to access network, USB, and other devices.

For users of Windows or Linux (and Apple Macintosh), the Open Source PHP is the standard Web-side scripting language, and binaries exist for most platform variations. The same goes for the MySQL relational database.

Beyond this, there are also many frameworks that are customizable that I introduce along the way. These can usually be deployed and customized with very few restrictions, and you can fully deploy them using the knowledge gleaned from this book.

For creating the various Web pages, scripts, and other pieces of useful code, there are also Open Source tools, editors, and applications that can be used freely. You'll want to find your own favorites, but we have listed some in Chapter 11, "Web References."

Also in that chapter are the free Web hosting services that have been made possible by the provision of Open Source solutions. In addition, most cheap hosts will also use Linux-based Open Source solutions, which is why I have dedicated an entire chapter to these services.

Before moving on, I do need to mention Microsoft Windows and ASP (Active Server Pages). This is an excellent technology, but not conducive with a low-impact entry to the Web programming field. The server space tends to be more expensive, harder to customize, and usually only applicable for high-end Web applications hosted by corporations, on their own premises with dedicated support technicians.

However, given that Windows is one of the most prominent operating systems, and that many, many Open Source tools (including PHP and MySQL) are also available for Windows variants, for local practice and experimentation, this may well be a great solution for many readers.

Recap

You are now well prepared. If you follow the book through from the start to the end, you will first need to assemble some tools—just for editing and client side display in the first instance—and then you can dive right in with the first real chapter: an Internet recap.

Following that, you will need to learn about the way that Web pages are described, and how you can cerate interactive Web pages, before moving on to server side scripting. At this point, you'll need to decide how to set yourself up to continue the learning process.

Once you have learned how to deploy your first set of Web services, Chapter 10, "Setting Up," will point you in the right direction. Of course, Chapter 11, "Web References," will be helpful in putting the plan that you create into action.

That is what the book is about—preparation, planning, and execution. Whether it is a simple case of putting an interactive CV on the Web or creating a Web store, this book is the key to kick starting the learning process. Everything is explained, without unnecessary detail, and will leave you in no doubt as to how you should implement that piece of the jigsaw.

To understand what all the pieces are, however, you should start your journey at the beginning—with a recap of the Internet and World Wide Web, as seen through the eyes of the programmer, and not just a Web surfer.

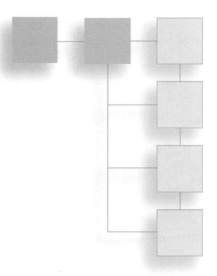

CHAPTER 2

INTERNET RECAP

This chapter is designed to put the book into the context of the Internet as a whole, and the Web in particular. In case you're not familiar with some of the concepts and technology, or if you classify yourself as a consumer and look at the Web browser and the content behind it as just another application on your computer, the topics will be key in understanding the remainder of the book.

The principal topics covered in this chapter are:

- The Internet—An introduction to the various parts of the Internet.

- The World Wide Web—A look at the components that make up the Web.

- Presentation layer—An introduction to the separation of content and presentation.

- Data exchange—The way in which clients and servers communicate.

- Client side scripting—Dynamic control over the browser.

- Server side programming—Dynamic control over the content.

The first two sections of the chapter look at how the Internet has evolved from its humble beginnings, and introduce the way that people interact with it. The second section, in particular, deals with the relationship between the users and the World Wide Web, from both the consumer and producer aspects.

Then you read about the way that presentation of the content is described, followed by a discussion of some of the mechanisms that allow the exchange of information between the computer displaying the content and the one serving it. This is covered only from a high level—leaving out the actual network implementation—in the interest of staying within the principle of giving just enough information to allow you to make sense of the topic.

Finally, the last two sections dissect the framework of the World Wide Web by splitting it into two component parts—the client (browser) and the server (host). In doing so, these sections set the stage for the discussions of the topics that follow.

You need to be aware that this separation between the client and server exists if you are to make the most of the remainder of the book. It is only when the client and server work independently to achieve a unified goal that the Web truly comes alive.

It all begins with a look at the application of information technology that has made it all possible—the Internet.

The Internet

The Internet is basically a collection of computers, all connected together in a big network. This topography provides a delivery mechanism in which a piece of information can take multiple routes from one point to another. These multiple routes make the network fairly robust—if one part is missing, information can still travel as long as there are alternative routes.

This information typically takes the form of:

- Requests for information or service

- Responses containing that information or the result of a service

- Informational responses, that is, reasons why the service or information could not be delivered

The information is exchanged in a client/server model; in other words, clients (users) connect to servers on the Internet and use their resources by placing requests with or without data. Typically, many clients can connect to each server at the same time—concurrently—and cause it to carry out operations on their behalf. As long as the server has capacity, that is.

Capacity is measured in two ways—the power of the server and the amount of network resources (bandwidth) available to it. Both of these factors will affect the number of users who can connect at the same time while still being able to deliver the services required of it.

In the beginning, the Internet was powered by less capable servers than are available today, both in terms of network capacity and computing power. Subsequently, most of the content was text only. The servers were not capable of delivering anything more complex, and the interconnected networks were neither fast enough nor reliable enough to allow for the transfer of anything other than plain text.

Email was one of the first Internet applications to be made available to the general public, and was text only. It revolutionized communication possibilities; it had the immediacy of a phone call, but was asynchronous, like a letter. It was also cheap, something that mass mailing companies, and less scrupulous individuals, quickly took advantage of.

Other text interface services included Gopher, which offered hierarchical menus of information. These were accessed through a text-only interface, the precursor to the browser, called a Telnet client. Telnet, in this case, is the protocol used to communicate between the client and the server.

This allowed for some level of interactivity, but response times were slow. This became known as lag among early Internet users. Lag is the time between the request and response. In other words, when using one of the first kinds of chat rooms, lag was the term used for the time delay between the user typing the command and receiving confirmation of the command being executed.

Network performance bottlenecks were also reflected in the time that it took to download files—images, documents and software were all downloaded in this way. The resources were referenced in the text-only interfaces, there were no links per se, and no document-embedded artifacts.

As network performance increased, along with computing power in general, the first wave of innovations brought the concept of hypertext. Hypertext is a way of linking documents together using references that contain the location of other documents and binary resources.

Alongside the possibility of referring to, and downloading, binary resources such as pictures came the idea of embedding the resources in documents. The program that was used to render (display) these pages became known as a browser;

among the first wave of such applications was NCSA Mosaic, which later became Netscape Navigator.

The hypertext concept morphed into HTML (HyperText Markup Language, also referred to on occasion as HyperText Meta Language), an open, governed, standard for exchanging information. As a mark-up language, HTML left the actual details of how the page should look to the browser, but provided a structured way to display the documents and link them together.

The actual documents are encoded in plain text. Any graphical elements have to be downloaded inline; they are resources that are referred to in the document, and then displayed rather than just saved.

HTML also put the possibility to publish information to a very wide audience into the hands of the users. This newfound freedom gave rise to a "web" of documents and other resources, all connecting to each other—the World Wide Web.

The World Wide Web

The World Wide Web (WWW or just Web) is a collection of linked resources. Documents (called pages), images, videos, interactive applets (mini applications), and music (MP3s, for example) are just a few of the resources available to surfers.

However, it doesn't work by magic, and it is useful to have a handle on the underlying technologies to better understand how Web programming works in practice.

Servers and Protocols

The Web is still a client/server environment, based on requests and responses. These conversations between the browser and the server needed a standard framework for communication, and some protocols were established in order to provide a standard way to exchange information.

The two used most frequently in this book are:

- HTTP (HyperText Transfer Protocol)

- FTP (File Transfer Protocol)

There is also a standard, MIME (Multipurpose Internet Mail Extensions), for the exchange of emails. The protocols also provide for a set of standard responses that allow the browser to display appropriate information in the event that the requests cannot be fulfilled.

An HTTP server, for example, provides facilities for storing and retrieving documents and other artifacts based on their URL (Universal Resource Locator). It can reply to a request in a number of ways, usually with a numerical code.

The most common of these codes are:

- 200—Everything okay, usually followed by the information requested

- 404—Resource not found, usually an incorrect URL

- 500—Server error, a problem on the server

The Web server itself is just a piece of software that runs on the machine and processes the requests through the network interface. Usually, the Web server software (Apache, Microsoft IIS, and so on) and associated applications are the only things running on the server.

Other applications might include an email server and an FTP server. FTP (File Transfer Protocol) is used for browsing the file system of a remote store and downloading from or uploading items to that store. FTP client applications can be graphical (looking like Windows Explorer) or text based.

Before you learn how information is indexed and located on the Web, note first that there are secure variants on the HTTP and FTP protocols, called HTTPS (HTTP Secure) and SFTP (Secure FTP). These allow the exchange of information through an encrypted channel rather than the plain text usually employed between the client and server applications.

Given the sheer volume of documents and artifacts on the Web, it became imperative that users had a way to find out what was available. This required that there was some kind of service capable of both indexing and retrieving locations for information based on their content. These became known as search engines.

Search Engines

A search engine is a Web based service that allows consumers to locate artifacts on the Internet as a whole. You will be familiar with names such as Google, Yahoo, MSN, Altavista, and so on, which are all examples of search engines.

Historically, searching the Internet started out as a way to search through catalogs of possible information based on the filenames and directory entries in the Gopherspace, which was based around hierarchical menus. In the beginning, searching relied on the descriptions given by the authors.

When full-text search was introduced, the search mechanism become a little more accurate, allowing everything from library catalogs to documentation repositories to be searched by anyone with an Internet connection.

Finally, Web searching became more sophisticated: searching deeply in sites by indexing them in their entirety. This allowed consumers to find information based on the content, rather than just a loose description of what the author intended the page to contain.

Given the volume of information available on the Web, the search engine has become a vital part of the producer-consumer relationship. Search engines are the only way that surfers (the consumers) can often locate information that interests them.

Ideally, you might want these searches to happen in real time, but since this is not really feasible, searches results are based on pre-indexed copies. Each indexing session builds a database that can be searched on demand, with pages returned that fit the query made by the surfer—based on the evaluation of an algorithm usually proprietary to the search engine itself.

In order to keep the database fresh, search engines need to update their databases from time to time. This is either done automatically, by a robot that trawls the Web for changes (the Google approach), or when producers informs the search engine that they have added something to the collection of pages that make up the Web.

This is known as site submission, and has grown from being a formality into something of a commercial opportunity. SEO (Search Engine Optimization) consultants can charge a premium fee to help individuals and companies obtain a good ranking in the results pages.

These rankings are based on the evaluation of the algorithm with respect to the rules that the search engine applies to evaluate the relevancy of the information contained in the database. With such a large number of pages, honing the submission and content submitted has become somewhat scientific.

With the popularity of the Web, getting found has become increasingly difficult; more often than not, pages find themselves pushed down the search engine result pages (SERPs) and therefore not immediately visible to consumers. So, search engines are important.

However, visibility in the search engines is only part of the marketing strategy that gets the page the attention it deserves. Marketing Web pages also includes creating other ways to attract traffic, if that is the aim of the site. Unsurprisingly, it usually is—the Web is, for many people, first and foremost a business opportunity.

The first to really benefit from the opportunity might arguably have been the ISPs, or Internet service providers. Without them, there would be no email, Web hosting, or even Web surfers to try to attract.

Internet Service Providers

The ISP's role is to give Web surfers the possibility to access the Internet using equipment that is available off the shelf. Running a network capable of tapping into the Internet is an expensive proposition; not many people can afford to run a network connection directly to their home.

Without getting too technical, the backbone of the Internet relies on connecting ISPs and other entry points together using a variety of different networking solutions. ISPs provide an entry point as well as, usually, a routing point for network traffic.

Originally, the role of the ISP was just to provide basic connectivity and email. The ISP would run an email server (receiving and storing email), and possibly offer a gateway into other services. For example, Usenet newsgroups were among the first mass communication and publishing platform (or forum).

ISPs would copy the contents from a central point and provide dial-in users the possibility to download messages and email. The very first connections were over the plain old telephone system, with simple modems providing the possibility for users and servers to exchange data over the phone line.

As the line speeds increased—from slow dial-in, to faster broadband connections— so did the sophistication of the information services provided by the ISP. ISPs began to offer out-of-the-box solutions: customized Web browsers, dialers with pre-programmed numbers, and so on.

Partly this was required because connecting to the Internet used to be a difficult proposition. The first mass-audience versions of operating systems like Microsoft

Windows did not offer the possibility to connect to Internet services as part of the retail package.

This gave ISPs an opportunity to give away CDs (or even diskettes in the very beginning) which would automatically configure the PC to connect to their services. These services were expensive in the beginning, but rapidly gave way to local call rate services as the use of the Internet expanded.

Fueled by this popularity, ISPs gave way in importance to other services, such as Web hosting. Consumers began to express a wish to participate in the production of information beyond posting to Usenet newsgroups, and the Web hosting service was born.

Web Hosting

Web hosting providers (Web hosts) provide a place for consumers to store pages designed to be consumed by the Web surfing public. ISPs often offer Web hosting services along with their standard connectivity packages.

The kind of package that you will receive will be, as a minimum, an all-in-one HTTP and FTP server with email. In other words, HTTP gives you the possibility to offer Web pages over the Internet, and FTP gives you the possibility to upload pages to the server so that they can be shared with the Web at large.

What the ISP might not offer is the registration of your URL. This is the Web address where your site can be found (for example: http://mysite.com). Early Web hosts (or Web space providers) such as Geocities.com often subdivided their Web space into longer addresses such as:

```
http://www.geocities.com/CapeCanaveral/Lab/1888
```

This approach is still often taken by ISPs wanting to offer Web hosting to their clients. In the early days, having a domain name (the bit commonly ending in .com, .net, or .org) was an expensive and technically challenging proposition. However, the price and ease with which the domain can be registered and used has reduced dramatically.

Domain names are centrally managed and distributed under license. Different countries have different policies and registrars, all working to set rules, but all charging different fees for the privilege. All that you need to make sure of is that the registration happens in your name, and that you have the right to update the DNS record at will.

The DNS record points your domain name to your Web hosting provider. The DNS system is a distributed database that is updated automatically by propagation. This means that specific servers (DNS servers) maintaining lists of domain names and IP addresses are propagated across the Internet, thus allowing traffic to be correctly directed.

Without the IP address (a number such as 193.169.137.5), it is impossible to correctly send data to, or receive data from, a server on the Internet. But a dotted number is not very user friendly, so we also need some way to connect a friendly name—the domain name—to the IP address.

That is the role of the DNS (email has a similar mechanism known as MX—mail exchange) and the final IP address that the domain name resolves to is the address of the Web host. One host can have many domain names pointing to it; that is all part of the service.

It is important to realize that, under normal circumstances, one server hosts many different sites. This helps to keep the price reasonable, while providing a good range of services.

Client machines then connect to the host either to download or upload files. Downloading is usually associated with browsing the Websites, and uploading is, as mentioned, the act of placing those files (pages) on the server for others to browse. Static pages make up a large proportion of the content available on the Web, but increasingly producers are taking advantage of other Web hosting services that allow for interactive sites to be built.

Web hosts vary enormously in terms of interactive services provided and the quality of those services. For example, this book is all about Web programming; the aim is for you to learn how to create an interactive (dynamic) Website using a combination of HTML, PHP, and database programming.

Not all of these facilities will be available on all Web hosts. Even where they are, there are different levels of service that are provided. Some might limit the bandwidth (amount of data that can be transferred in a given month), others might allow only a single database of a limited size, and many don't provide scripting or databases at all.

To get a good mix of services that can be used in a production environment—in other words, expecting to have a certain volume of data transfer and a robust service—it is often necessary to pay a monthly fee. This can range from $3.95 per month right up to $60+ per month, depending on bandwidth and plug-in services offered.

Free Web hosts exist, usually requiring that the user suffer some form of advertising, which is perfectly acceptable for learning purposes. Advertising is as much a part of the Web ethos as search engines are, and worthy of further discussion.

Advertising

Advertising on the Internet started out as a way for people to try to attract traffic, or at least to alert other users, through banner adverts, to the existence of their site. Over time, it became clear that advertisers would pay money for their banner to be shown more frequently than others, and paid advertising was born. *on the internet.*

Displaying adverts on behalf of advertising networks and even direct advertisers used to be a good way to make money from a Website. Over time, however, the *Impact* impact on surfers has been reduced. Most learn to ignore banner adverts quite quickly, which lessens their impact.

This forced advertisers to move from a pay-per-impression model to a pay-per-click model, which is still in force today. These days, it is therefore more difficult to make money from advertising, but still possible. *because of pay-per-click model of generating income from ads.*

The pay-per-impression model meant that advertisers paid the Web content producer to display adverts on their site. This was open to abuse—faked impression rates—as well as being hard to justify. As advertisers saw less and less return from their investment—fewer clicks per thousand impressions—they decided to change the model.

The pay-per-click model pays the content producer only if the advert that has been displayed generates a click from the surfer. In other words, the content producer gets paid only if the visitor clicks the advert, leaves the site, and spends time at the advertiser's site.

The obvious disadvantage with this is that you have spent so much time trying to make sure that the visitor can find the site that asking them to click on an advert and leave the site seems to run against common sense. The model, however, does work, if only because a proportion of traffic to your site were looking for something else that they might just find among the adverts that you display.

Advertising supports many services on the Internet—from free email to free Web hosting and mailing list services—and it works because there is power in the volumes. The Internet and Web are so popular that even if only a small percentage of visitors to, say, Yahoo click on a banner, it still generates enough income to support the underlying service.

Of course, it would be logical to assume that the big service providers such as Google, Yahoo, MSN, YouTube, MySpace, and so on actually attract bigger advertising dollars than the rest of us. They might even still be being paid on the basis of just displaying the adverts, and not by click.

However, some of the big article repositories, such as About.com and Suite 101.com, earn their income through PPC (pay-per-click) advertising. In the case of Suite101.com, it is shared with the writers in order to compensate them for the right to print their articles.

Social networking sites also use PPC income to support themselves, so clearly it pays off. Of course, it helps to have a site that is centered around the kind of traffic that will generate clicks for advertisers and that attracts high paying advertisers. Generally speaking, the more technical the subject, the less likely a visitor is going to be to click on an advert.

Advertising suppliers include Google (through AdSense), as well as various brokers (such as Commission Junction) that link advertisers and content producers. The latter example caters to both advertising and affiliate schemes. The difference between the two is that advertising only alerts and attracts the visitor to the advertiser's Website, whereas affiliate schemes actually generate income for the content producer as a percentage of the sales generated.

In other words, Commission Junction might list a collection of advertisers all offering a specific product. Content producers can pick the advertisers that they are attracted to (usually on the basis of a high commission rate) and advertise the actual products on their site.

The visitor will then be enticed (you hope) by the product or offer, and proceed to the advertiser's site where the sale is affected. The content producer gets nothing for redirecting the visitor, which makes it more risky than the pay-per-click model. However, the rewards are bigger, as is the threat of losing the visitor to the affiliate site altogether.

Again, it is a balancing act between attracting a wide enough spectrum of visitors that you don't care if some of them click through to other sites, and providing value to those who you want to stay. Part of the reason you want them to stay is that you have something of your own to sell or give away.

Finally, there are actual product suppliers that offer affiliate schemes (such as Amazon.com, eBay.com, and so on) where money can be made by selling their products directly. These outlets are actually making more of an effort to integrate with the content producer's sites, eschewing the usual approach of capturing the traffic for themselves.

After all, when the box from Amazon arrives, the receiver is going to be well aware where to go next to get a similar product. The advertising is all over the packaging and inserted into the package itself. However, given the opportunity for good Web content producers to profit from selling their goods, one can hardly blame them.

So, advertising generates income that supports services, including free Web hosting and content production. That helps you, the Web programmer and content producer, because it means you can get a lot of services that you will need for free.

For example, many free Web hosts support the provision of their services by advertising revenue, meaning that you get a whole setup, with PHP, MySQL, email, Web space, and a large monthly quota for no cost. Or, Web 2.0 services such as Google Documents provide a state-of-the-art, Microsoft Office-compatible suite of tools to users of the Web for nothing.

You may also want to take advantage of advertising and affiliate selling to supplement income made from the site or your own products. To do this, you will need to customize the offerings as closely as possible to the consumer using client/server programming.

Client/Server Programming

In Web programming, people use the client/server model to deliver content to the visitor in a dynamic fashion. In other words, they move away from serving up static Web pages of the kind that were produced in the past, and provide information that is customized to the needs of the producer-consumer relationship.

There is a split between remote and local processing, where both work together to produce the end result that helps to realize this. For example, the Web browser is a piece of client programming that requests information from the server and displays it to the user. The browser can also process scripts that form part of the response that is delivered to it, making it possible to offer additional features to the end user.

As an example, you can use scripts on the side of the browser to detect the kind of browser being used and reflect that in the services offered (or perhaps the way that they are offered) to the end user. You can also ask for information (in forms) from the end user and use that information in a request to the server to elicit a certain response.

These are all ways in which the client/server relationship can be used to enhance the producer-consumer relationship. These kinds of interactions are at the core of the Web programming paradigm, which is based on a request and response mechanism.

This request and response mechanism is largely synchronous. It happens in a fashion that is prescribed by the protocol being used. You cannot have a response without a request, even if a single request elicits multiple response packages. A server does nothing until the client asks it to.

This can leads to infuriating waits for the whole page to be loaded before the browser can display the content that has been requested by the end user. This is much less of a problem since the advent of fast connections between servers, but at peak times the lag is still very noticeable.

Some tricks such as interlacing can be used for graphics—in these cases, the client/server model relies on the browser supporting this feature. Interlacing works because the image is downloaded in parts; in other words, the file contains a collection of smaller parts of the whole.

The browser can display one part of the image while the next is loading, with the result that the image appears to materialize rather than appear. The first few frames allow a reasonably low quality image to be displayed, which is built upon as the data is downloaded by the browser.

Text and other information such as the layout of the page on the screen cannot be interlaced in this way very easily. For content, this means that the whole page has to be downloaded before the page can be displayed. For the layout, is also important that as much information is conveyed with as little overhead as possible—this is called the presentation layer.

Presentation Layer

The presentation layer is the term given to the information that allows the browser to display the content. It controls the way that the content is presented, in terms of the font, colors, layout, interactive elements, and so forth. In order to keep some semblance of order, the presentation layer is structured according to specific standards.

Managing the standards is a body known as the World Wide Web Consortium, or W3C. The role of the W3C is to make sure there are standards for the presentation layer, and that these are communicated, formulated, and extended appropriately according to the needs of its members. To quote the mission statement from the W3C site:

> "To lead the World Wide Web to its full potential by developing protocols and guidelines that ensure long-term growth for the Web." W3.org

The standards, called recommendations, make up the open, non-proprietary standards that all Web authors should stick to when creating content. There are more than 400 members of the W3C, covering almost every company with a vested interest in the Web and the technology that drives it.

These companies—from Apple to Yahoo, Google, Microsoft, the BBC, Dow Jones & Company, several educational establishments, telecommunications operators, consulting companies, and many, many more—all work together to make sure that the Web continues to work for everyone. They do this through their work on standards consulting, mainly through the W3C Technical Team, which "contributes to and coordinates the W3C's activities."

These standards are important, because you need to be sure that the layout can be communicated effectively to all client systems that might request the content. The standards make sure that everyone—from producer to consumer, developer to Web service provider—are all using the same basis to develop the functionality that is required.

However, despite the standards, each user agent (browser or something else) remains free to render the presentation layer differently. You see, the presentation layer is not there to dictate how the resulting page should look, but rather the hierarchical relationship between the elements on the page.

One example of this is the heading hierarchy—the presentation layer allows the content producer to designate headings of different levels. It is assumed that the levels adhere to strict rules:

- They cannot overlap

- They have to nest in order

- They need to be presented with diminishing visual importance

The exact choice of rendering—bold, italics, large font, small font, the font itself—is left up to the browser or other client software application. There are other non-hierarchical elements which provide possibilities to exert more control over the rendering of the content, but by and large the presentation layer provides a fairly abstract level of control.

The definition of the presentation layer takes the form of an abstract language (meta-language, or mark-up language) that allows one to describe the presentation without the content, as holders for the content without prescribing exact appearance. A top-level heading on one browser might be different from another in appearance while having the same hierarchical weight.

The mark-up language also allows for you to specify exact rendering instructions so that it is possible, with some work, to make the content appear in the same way (within a margin of error) on multiple different browser platforms. The caveat is, of course, that in order to do this, you often need to know the platform (browser) and give slightly different mark-up in order to obtain the same result.

This is the flexibility and power of the mark-up principle on the one hand, and possible disadvantage, as you need to test the implementation on many different platforms to be sure that the appearance is the same. Or, you can just trust that the browser developer has respected the philosophy of the mark-up laid out by the W3C.

This also extends across non-visual and alternative rendering platforms. For example, if the user agent was a Braille device, that would render the same presentation layer and content mix differently than a text-only interface (such as Lynx) or a fully graphical one (such as IE, Firefox, Netscape, and so on).

The mark-up abstracts you away from the implementation details so that you can use the exact same presentation layer definition (within reason), no matter the target rendering platform. There are different flavors of mark-up, but the main language that people use to describe the presentation of content is called HTML.

(As a side note, and for those who are interested, HTML was not the first standard that the W3C tried to establish. In fact, HTML is a kind of subset of something called SGML which tried, in vain, to define *any* possible mark-up language as a self-contained definition. This concept has since become XML, or eXtensible Markup Language, which is a less complex rendition of SGML.)

Introduction to HTML

HTML (HyperText Mark-Up Language, sometimes also called HyperText Meta Language) is the lingua franca of the World Wide Web. All pages are encoded in some form of HTML, whether it be a version from 1994 or 2007, and Web browsers tend to maintain as much compatibility as possible.

Part of the responsibility is shared with the producers of the Web content. If you use esoteric tags, which are not part of the standard, but which look as if they might follow it and which are only supported by a minority of browsers, you can expect your page to look a bit strange on some platforms. On the other hand, the simpler the use of HTML that is made, the fewer problems the page is likely to have in the longer term.

So, there is a balance that you have to strike between elaborate presentation and maintainability of the code. This job is made easier by the fact that browser application providers tend to be somewhat looser in their adherence to standards than in the past, coupled with techniques such as server side scripting that generate much of the HTML at the same time as the content is presented.

This is the key to HTML—it provides a standard definition for the presentation layer which is robust and well-defined by open standards maintained by the W3C. As a mark-up language, it contains information that is not designed to be interpreted as content (that is, the user never sees the HTML itself) but as presentation information that enriches the actual content.

The page content is enclosed in a mechanism known as *tags,* which tell the browser how the designer intended the content to be rendered in an abstract fashion. Each tag contains specific information relating to the way that the browser is to begin rendering the content that follows it.

Usually, there is a starting tag and ending tag (although there are exceptions). You might like to think of this as turning formatting on and off, because this makes it easier to conceptualize some of the principles. So, a starting bold text tag tells the browser that, until the ending tag is reached, the content is to be rendered using a bold font.

However, the end result might not always be the same on all platforms, including that of the designer—it is only there to give details of the *intention* of the designer with respect to the content that is being presented. Bold text on one platform might be of a different size, weight, or font depending on the browser being used.

When the Web was in its infancy, these tags were all put into each document individually, because the pages were static. In other words, once they were created and uploaded to the Web host, they did not change. They might have been linked to (and interlinked) to give the effect of navigating through a dynamic document set, but each page was a single document, edited by hand.

This meant that changing some of the elements required multiple changes on the page; if the designer wanted to insert new levels of heading, that would have knock-on effects through the rest of the page. Some headings would have to be promoted and others demoted.

For example, there might have been ten headings on a page, each denoting a piece of information of diminishing overall hierarchical importance. Heading 1 might have been the page title, heading 2 a section title, heading 3 a sub-section, and so on.

Each heading would have to be detailed separately in terms of size, color, and decoration, and HTML provides a set of relative hierarchical tags (H1, H2, and so on) that you can enclose the heading text in to provide decoration. This takes some of the pain away, but not all.

You still had to change all the H3 tags to H4 if you wanted to insert a new heading item. For menu management especially, this became a painful experience. It meant in some cases that you would have to go through a search and replace exercise whenever you wanted to insert a new menu item.

In addition, once HTML became more precise and offered the possibility to create very detailed tags to specify the exact font, size, and color, as well as discrete position of content on the page, designers became ever more ambitious. In the main, they were still manually editing the pages.

They had tools that made the management of the HTML itself easier, but few tools to maintain congruence between multiple pages if the style of the content had to change. Let us assume, for example, that a company had a Web page where regular content was in green text and menus in black.

Each piece of text has to be marked up as being in either black or green. What happens when the company decides that green is no longer in vogue and wants to change it to red? The Web designer has to go back and change all the mark-up on the static pages so that the content is in red.

A far easier solution is to use a standard tag to describe the content in an abstract fashion (as either Content or Menu text) and then define the fact that Content text is in green and Menu text is in black in a single point. This mechanism is known as defining a *style*, and the place that it is usually defined is in an external *style sheet*.

The separation of the positioning and flow information and the actual style details allowed designers to change the individual artifacts with a single change to the style sheet rather than making multiple changes to static pages. The pages could still be static, but it was possible to change the look and feel by simply swapping the style sheets.

This is a trend that has been further enhanced by server side programming, allowing for users (visitors or browsers) to select style sheets dynamically so that their experience is customized accordingly. You shall look at the mechanics of this in later sections; for now, let's examine how a style sheet works.

Introduction to Style Sheets

A style sheet is a concretization of style information referred to in a page of HTML; each tag can be customized by changing its style. Style sheets give guidelines for the style of all the classes of elements in a page, where the Web designer has determined that they should be different from the default.

Physically, a style sheet can be a separate document, downloaded along with the HTML, or it can be part of the HTML itself. The style information enhances the way that the standard HTML tags are displayed, and is downloaded to the client.

You might give styles for headings, general text, paragraphs, shading, tables, and so on that override the defaults that are chosen by the browser application manufacturer. You will remember that the W3C does not actually mandate any rendering information, but provides a comprehensive framework to support almost any rendering possibility.

In addition to enhancing standard tag styles, you can name element classes. A class, in this case, is a specialization of an element, to which you give a name that is meaningful to you. So, you might create a collection of named classes and have different kinds of tables, paragraphs, headings, and textual elements. For example, you might decide to have a different colored background for certain types of paragraphs, and enclose these with the standard paragraph tag, but with a named class for each kind of paragraph.

These new classes then become specializations of the default. You can change the default independently of the new classes, making it a very powerful mechanism for altering the style of the pages from a central point. This is still static presentation, however.

Dynamic presentation layer generation is also possible, on two fronts. Firstly, you can generate style information and attach it to the page that is being downloaded. This requires server side scripting and is not overly complex.

Secondly, you can write a script that is part of the downloaded page, but that changes the style information dynamically within the page. The difference might not be apparent at first, so an example might help envisage the two mechanisms.

Let's assume that you want to allow visitors to change the layout of the page so that it matches more exactly their screen size. You do this by attaching a style sheet to the page that contains layout information. This layout information will include discrete positioning for the various elements (menu bars, navigation and advertising sections, and so on) using named tags.

To keep the example simple, assume a vertical MenuSection that is 25% of the screen width, a middle ContentSection that is 50%, and an AdvertisingSection that is 25% of the available screen width. The user has a small screen, and the ContentSection is unreadable, so you want to change the proportions to 15%, 70%, and 25%.

You have two choices—you can generate a collection of styles that meets these proportions using a server side script, or you can create a client side script that does that for you. Either mechanism is acceptable in this case, but each requires a different set of scripts.

In the first case, you dynamically generate the content specifically for each visitor; in the second, you manipulate the styles using a script that is written once for all users. In reality, you will most often use a combination of the two approaches.

This level of dynamic generation is also often a result of data exchange with the server, and again, it can be either the client or server that generates the resulting HTML. So, you might write a script that can dynamically detect the resolution that the user is using and adjust the page accordingly.

This is where the first implementation is weaker. You would need to communicate with the server to tell it what kind of screen the user has, and only then download the correct layout information. In the second case, you could detect and update the layout locally.

You can also change styles dynamically, and asynchronously, as you communicate with the server, usually in reaction to something that the user has done. So, if you have detected that the screen resolution is 640 × 480, and rendered the page accordingly, you could allow the user to change that by selecting a different rendering style.

If there were more items to change than just the layout (the color, for example), you could also handle that by regenerating the page or dynamically altering the styles. The locally scripted solution is the only possible solution in cases where the Web host does not offer support for server side scripting.

So, style sheets allow more control over the rendering, with the possibility to group rendering information into collections, which can then be dynamically altered. Again, this is via an open standard mechanism that is maintained by the W3C.

In the same way that you need a standard way to describe the documents, you also need a standard way to exchange the data that they contain.

Data Exchange

I have mentioned that the communication between the client and server is essentially a series of requests and responses. This is the same for all protocols that are used to access the Internet, be it a Web protocol, FTP or email and other messaging systems.

The actual protocol name that is used for data exchange between the client and Web server is called HTTP (HyperText Transfer Protocol), and is the reason that all Web addresses start with the `http://` stanza. It is, as mentioned previously, a mechanism for requesting services of a server and displaying the results of those service requests.

Essentially, each request that you have considered until now has been simple enough, and with little actual payload. In other words, you have made a simple request for an artifact, without giving more data than the URL.

The response to this HTTP request then contains a status code, and then the data that represents the page content, and links to various artifacts such as images and style sheets that are external to the page itself. It all happens asynchronously—the

Web client first is given the page and is expected to request any of the additional items separately.

The data flow is more or less all downstream towards the client. There is more data received than submitted. The HTTP protocol, however, allows a user agent (browser, client, and so on) to send information to the server as well, in a structured manner.

HTTP provides two mechanisms, called GET and POST. The difference between the two is a regular discussion point for those learning Web programming. Technically, the difference is that a GET request contains data that is part of the URL, whereas a POST request sends the data as part of an independent message.

You might have seen URLs such as:

```
http://search.live.com/results.aspx?q=Web+programming
```

In this URL, everything after the ? indicates an HTTP GET request and that the name-value pair represented by q=Web+programming is data destined for the server in order to allow it to perform some kind of service. In the case of this line, it is a search.

Decoding the previous example still further, all data that is destined for the server in this scheme is split into pairs. In this case, q is the command, and Web+programming is the value associated with that command. All data must be in this command=value pairing. The plus sign is used in place of a space, because spaces cannot appear in URLs, and special encoding is needed for this, along with some other characters.

The superficial difference between this and the POST mechanism is that you do not see the data that is being posted to the server as it is part of the payload data that follows the HTTP request.

There is a philosophical difference too. The W3C indicates that the GET request should be used to retrieve information stored on the server, and that the POST request should be used to cause some form of permanent change on the server.

So, if you were in the process of adding a URL for the search engine to index, along with the title, a description, and a category (for example), you would use an HTTP POST request. This makes sense, as there is usually more data connected with giving information to the server than just requesting some data from it.

The resultant data can come back from the server in the form of a dynamically generated Web page, as you have already seen. This is usually generated by the server where the content contains result of the query made via the GET/POST request.

It could be a page of results—like a search engine—or it could be simple confirmation that the data has been received and will be processed. Some interactive sites (such as Web games) take this a step further and provide some visual feedback to the effect that the POST has had an immediate and lasting effect on the state of play.

Aside from the aforementioned Web gaming interfaces, the mechanism on the client side for allowing the user to prepare and submit information is known as a *form*. It is again something that this defined by the W3C as part of the HTML standard.

Form Processing

The simplest kind of form is a collection of input areas, with a button marked Submit, and is aimed at providing a way for the user to input information to be sent to the server. Common input areas include:

- Text boxes (single and multi-line)
- Radio buttons and checkboxes
- List and drop-down list boxes

In Figure 2.1, many of the available controls are shown. For example, the first is an example of a single line text input area, which is followed by a multi-line version. There is a drop-down list box and a simple checkbox control. Finally, there is a set of option buttons, of which only one in the group can be selected. At the bottom is a Submit button, used to send the result to the server.

Although it is possible to allow the simple interaction with these elements to cause some processing, it is more common to provide a Submit button. The Submit button explicitly sends the form for processing at the server side via a GET or POST request, depending on how the form has been coded by the Web programmer.

There may also be a Reset button, which will reset all the data input areas back to their default values. This is a standard mechanism that is provided by the

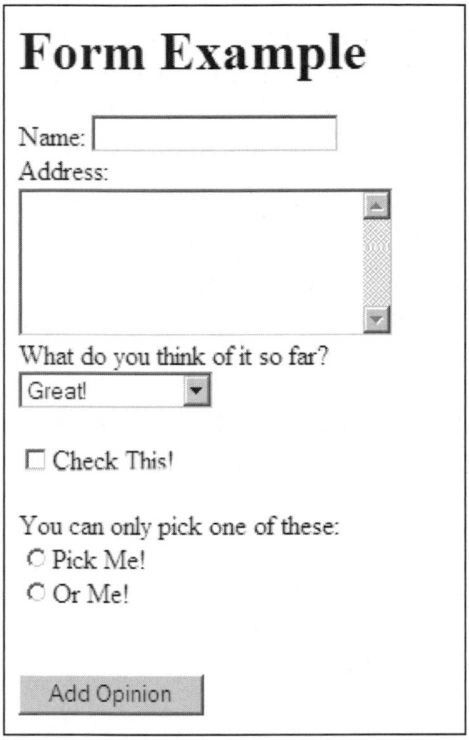

Figure 2.1
Form example

HTML specification, and the result of the form submission is usually an HTTP response directing the browser to some data.

However, some data may come back in structured fashion that is not designed to be actually displayed to the user but translated by the browser. In the same way that HTML is a holder for content, you can also retrieve data that is used by the client to display content that is also contained in a structure that you define.

Put more simply, there might be a control in the form that is designed to be used to submit information to the server, but which can also be updated by another control that updates its contents dynamically. You need a way to communicate with the server "behind the scenes" and add this new information to the form.

This is known as asynchronous data exchange—you do not have to reload the page in order for it to become apparent, but the data that is retrieved from the server has a direct effect on the contents of the page. This is affected through client side scripting.

An example of this is the Google suggest service (http://suggest.google.com), which provides a text entry area and a dynamically changing list box that contains suggestions retrieved from the Google database. The list box contents are updated with respect to the value being entered by the user in the text entry area.

Here the form is being updated—the drop-down list box is populated with data that is exchanged with the server—asynchronously to the page being loaded. The data being returned is not HTML, because that would cause the page to be reloaded and this is not appropriate in this case.

On top of which, the HTML standard is well defined, and does not allow you to casually start inventing tags that can contain the data that we need. Instead, you need to have the data returned in a way that allows you to extend the basic definition by adding your own definitions.

One such mechanism for data exchange is called XML, which is an open standard for data exchange that allows for the creation of data elements and attributes. Others include JSON, which requires special handling in most browsers and is not usually decodable by the platform itself. The book uses XML, as it is widely supported and understood.

Introduction to XML

You'll learn the actual definition of XML and its various rules in the next chapter, when you look at these languages in detail. For now, you just need to know that it is a mechanism by which data can be exchanged with a server.

This data can be used in a variety of different application areas, and is not just used for Web programming. The widest use, until recently, was as a way for bloggers and other information, content, and product providers to inform their fans when new items were available.

For example, RSS (Really Simple Syndication) is based on XML; these are feeds of data that are designed to be read and displayed. If you open an RSS feed in a Web browser, the structured XML is laid bare, as shown in Figure 2.2.

Clearly, this is not designed to be directly viewed by the users, so you need to use other mechanisms to allow it to be rendered correctly. Feed readers exist that will monitor the feed (by loading the XML from time to time) and inform the users of an update.

```
<?xml version="1.0"?>
<rss version="2.0">
  <channel>
    <title>Liftoff News</title>
    <link>http://liftoff.msfc.nasa.gov/</link>
    <description>Liftoff to Space Exploration.</description>
    <language>en-us</language>
    <pubDate>Tue, 10 Jun 2003 04:00:00 GMT</pubDate>
    <lastBuildDate>Tue, 10 Jun 2003 09:41:01 GMT</lastBuildDate>
    <docs>http://blogs.law.harvard.edu/tech/rss</docs>
    <generator>Weblog Editor 2.0</generator>
    <managingEditor>editor@example.com</managingEditor>
    <webMaster>webmaster@example.com</webMaster>

    <item>
```

Figure 2.2
RSS XML example

Where a link to an artifact is provided (such as an MP3 podcast), some feed readers will actually download the content on behalf of the user. This is known as subscribing, and is one of the many non-Web programming applications of XML currently in use.

You'll look at some more uses later on in Chapter 9, when you read about specific Web 2.0 features of Web programming. The important point to note is that the data is structured and adheres to a specific format. That is, RSS is a specialization of XML (or an application of XML).

A mixture of client and server side technology is needed to allow a user to display feeds in a browser. For example, the server can offer the feeds, but the client needs to be able to display the elements that are contained in each entry to the user in a way that enables them to look at them in a meaningful manner and possibly click on links that are included as part of the feed information.

Part of the browser scripting language has to allow one to manipulate the XML data that is returned—building something that has meaning from the structured data stream. This requires some clever client side programming, because XML manipulation is not an innate part of the HTML specification.

However, it is a part of some standard scripting language implementations that allow the Web programmer to make a request using a special kind of HTTP request—XhttpRequest—and process the data that is returned. Like all areas of Web programming, the client side programming languages (scripting) have to be reasonably standardized to allow producers to be reasonably certain that consumers all experience the same effect regardless of platform.

Client Side Scripting

Just as a reminder—client side scripting is a way to extend the functionality of a Web page beyond static data by requesting that the user agent (the Web browser, for example) do some additional processing on behalf of the Web programmer. This can be for the purpose of making the Web page interactive, dynamic, or just animated in some way.

The content, layout, and other features used in the rendering of the page can all be manipulated using client side scripts. This makes them very useful for displaying items that are platform-, browser-, or user-dependent.

Client side scripting allows you to validate forms, change the document with respect to interaction with the user, and manipulate style information dynamically, as well as generating new content.

Like all programming languages, the client side scripting mechanism usually allows for selective execution (decision making), flow control (loops), and other programming constructs. The script interpreted is either built into the browser (JavaScript, for example) or is interpreted via a plug-in that has to be downloaded from the manufacturer (Flash, for example).

This book's scope is limited to those solutions that are available to all Web programmers, so I have chosen to use JavaScript as the basis for all discussions of client side scripting. This doesn't mean that I ignore common plug-ins that can be used with JavaScript to provide extended functionality, just that I assume that browsers have the ability to process JavaScript natively.

If plug-ins are defined that extend the scripting language, you can communicate with them provided that the developer has given you an API that is integrated with the object model of the browser and underlying operating system. In other words, the JavaScript standard gives you an object model that you can use to manipulate the HTML document, and this mechanism is inside the scope of this book.

The discussion of other object models and how to communicate them is outside the scope of this book. Where necessary, I will give code fragments that illustrate how such a plug-in (for example, Microsoft's Silverlight) can be communicated with, but the exact definition of the object model mechanism itself is an advanced developer topic.

However, it's worth noting that it is also standardized, but relies on co-ordination between the browser and operating system. Each plug-in is installed as a part of the system software, and HTML allows you to embed an object of the required type in a document.

The browser needs to support the object, through the plug-in, and supply an interface (API—application programming interface) that enables you to use JavaScript to communicate with the plug-in. Some do not have this kind of API, which makes them more or less self-contained.

In order to make the Web programming examples as relevant as possible, the book examples are limited to ones where the plug-in is freely downloadable and provide a standard API or XML interface for communication.

The XHttp mechanism that allows you to do Asynchronous JavaScript and XML (AJAX) is an example of such a case; Microsoft Silverlight is another. In both of these, standard JavaScript and XML programming can be used, and the relevant plug-ins are either freely available or built into the browser.

You will look at both of these in detail later on, but they are both made possible by the use of a standard client side scripting language—ECMAScript, which is a standardization of JavaScript. For the purpose of this book, I treat JavaScript and ECMAScript as equivalent, and avoid areas where they might be differently implemented.

A quick recap—client side scripting lets you manipulate the rendering of the page by adding some logic to be processed by the user agent (browser). The implementation of the scripting language lets you access the content and layout information through the document model. This lets you communicate with objects—be they built-in (like HTML tags) or external (like third-party plug-ins).

This document model also lets you find out information, programmatically, about the client environment (browser, platform, user, and so on) that can help you to generate relevant content on the server side. For example, you might detect that the user is running Windows, and therefore only display advertising that is relevant to Windows users.

Or, you might use a cookie to store information about the user's last visit to the site and use that to try and help the user navigate through the site when he or she returns. Both of these examples will require a certain amount of server side programming, which allows you to generate content selectively to be sent to the browser.

Server Side Programming

As you will have realized, server side programming powers the bulk of Websites on the Internet today. From the actual HTTP server (such as Apache or IIS) which handles requests and delivers data, to the various Webmail, interactive applications (such as Facebook, MySpace, YouTube, and so on, without some logic on the server none of these services would be possible.

Before you delve into this subject more deeply, you need to remember that there is a difference between a server side application, such as the Web server, and a server side script. Server side scripts are interpreted by a server side application. I don't cover applications that can be written to run on the server, but do cover scripted Web applications.

In order to make Websites more interactive, dynamic, and customized, some form of server side programming was required. You have seen how the first pages were static text, and this gave way to style sheets and client side scripting. As the technology expanded, however, Web programmers saw the need to go a step further.

Programmers started to make little programs that were designed to run in the background and generate content. They ran natively as applications capable of interfacing with the Web server and provided functionality from databases to content presentation.

This not a good solution, however, as all operating systems are different, so there was a need to find a standard scripting language which would work everywhere a Web server was present. The reasons for this were many, but the chief features are that:

■ The scripting language can be mixed with HTML

■ The scripts run on, and have access to services provided by, the Web server

A scripting language is also interpreted. This means that the manufacturer can distribute an interpreter built for a given platform—a Windows version, a Linux version, a MacOS version, and so on—and all users can exchange scripts without having to build them for each platform.

This is another advantage of using a scripting language rather than building little applications that run on the server—code can be written once and run everywhere. Over time, the community has settled on three possible contenders—ASP (for Microsoft, mainly), Perl, and PHP, which are multiplatform.

Given the target of this book to try to deliver the most relevant information possible, I have chosen to cover PHP as the server side scripting language. This choice is based on the fact that it works on the largest number of platforms (at the time of writing) and is available as freeware.

I might have chosen Perl, but this is a rather daunting language to a newcomer. PHP has the benefit of being slightly easier to understand due to its roots. It is a hypertext processor, and is designed to be embedded in HTML as well as able to stand alone. So the script can be in the Web page or a separate file.

The difference between a client side script, such as a JavaScript which is also embedded in the page, is that the Web server will interpret the PHP that it encounters and send the result of that processing to the client rather than the text of the script itself. So, if you wanted, you could have PHP code to generate JavaScript (or HTML, or style information) which is then delivered to the client.

This might sound complex, but I will only give you as much as you need to get started. You will learn the basics, but will, over time, add to your knowledge as you become more familiar with Web programming. Using PHP, JavaScript, and HTML to make your own projects will be a useful learning exercise in itself—this book gives just enough to get the ball rolling.

So, server side scripts have the advantage of being invisible to the user as the server interprets them at the same time as it serves the Web page. Because they are interpreted on the Web page, they can also be quite lengthy and complex; assume that there is more processing power available to the server than the client.

Being able to build complex applications, coupled with the Open Source philosophy of the PHP community, means that many frameworks have been implemented. Some of these are application frameworks and extensions, and some of them are complete Web content delivery systems, made available to the general public.

The key advantage of using them is that it gives a good starting point for code of your own. Provided that it is Open Source, and provided that the license permits it, you can customize the PHP scripts to your own needs. There are many frameworks that actively encourage this.

In the main, these are CMS (or Content Management Systems), which allow you to create complex document delivery systems. Blogger is an example of a fairly simple CMS implementation. More complex ones allow for categorization of documents, advertising placement, dynamic menus, and other features.

You'll look at some of the main freely available CMS frameworks in Chapter 8 of the book, as these will be the ones that you come across most frequently. I have chosen ones that allow you to add functionality easily through the use of plug-in modules that you can create, and which can become part of the CMS reasonably seamlessly.

Sometimes, the integration of client and server side scripting leads to very sophisticated user interfaces. Web 2.0 features, for example, rely heavily on the possibility to mix client and server scripting, along with databases and external services such as XML.

Some of the best examples come from the Google Labs—I've already mentioned Google Suggest, but they also have Google Sheets (a spreadsheet application) as well as a word processor. All of these rely on server side scripting to provide the back-office functionality—saving, storing, sharing, and so on—and client side scripting to edit the actual information in the document or spreadsheet.

Another good example is the Yahoo Pipes application. This also uses dynamic client side HTML and style sheets mixed with server side programming, which provides data feeds and storage of the user's account and Pipe information.

The Pipe service allows the user to build up expressions for filtering RSS feeds based on XML and a simple scripting language that is built through the browser. The results are small applications that run as a mixture of client and server side programs, communicating through XML.

These can then be shared with the general public. The end user just sees a resulting XML stream that can be viewed through a feed reader. Yahoo even provides such a reader to display the results; so a general news feed can be filtered and combined with (for example) and Amazon.com product feed to create a valuable revenue generating Website plug-in.

This kind of possibility is part of the definition of Web 2.0, which is the latest trend in Web programming. Key to Web 2.0 is allowing the consumer to become the producer—YouTube, MySpace, Facebook, and Flickr are all examples of Web 2.0 applications.

The ability to create and share information is what powers the Web 2.0 concept, and it is made possible by the integration of client and server technologies over the Internet. This is then combined with other server side applications such as databases to provide the complete package.

So, part of the purpose of server side scripting is to link server applications (databases, for example) with front-end interfaces. The resulting interface may be modified as a result of the data that has been retrieved, or the logic that has been implemented in the script.

Recap

The Internet is a collection of interconnected computers, split into client and server roles. The clients access the servers and display the result to the end user (the surfer). The exact nature of the result (appearance and content) is a function of the following:

- Client side scripts

- Server side scripts

- Content stored on the server

All of these are governed by standards. Despite the work of the W3C, the presentation layer definition language is not always as standardized as it might seem. Different browsers might have extensions (such as some Microsoft Internet Explorer text decorations) that are not supported on other platforms, or they might evaluate scripts differently.

In this book, I try to respect standards and give code that will work on all browsers without changes. This is necessarily done by avoiding some of the areas where contentions exist.

However, this might be impossible in some cases, and I give appropriate guidance in these examples to illustrate certain points. Luckily PHP is a stable standard, as is SQL, so this is less of an issue on the server side.

You now understand the underlying philosophy of Web 1.0 (static pages and dynamic content) and Web 2.0 (social networking and user created dynamic content) and are ready to begin learning the underlying technology that drives Web programming.

In Chapters 5 through 9, you will steadily progress through the languages that you need to create the applications that enable you to write Web applications. These will all generate, towards the end user, various flavors of HTML.

So, before you can begin, you need to cover the basics, and you will start with an introduction to HTML, the language of the World Wide Web.

CHAPTER 3

HTML, XML, AND XHTML

HTML is the language of the World Wide Web. It is the basis for all the content that you see, hear, and interact with on Web pages. The language itself gives the producer the ability to define the look and feel of the content (layout and presentation) as well as the actual content—text and multimedia—itself.

Without HTML, all you would be able to exchange on the Internet would be the individual content pieces themselves. This is quite adequate if all you need to do is read plain text, look at a picture, or watch a video in isolation, but not sufficient if you want to be able to navigate, search, and interact with the Web pages.

HTML is based on a standard called XML, which allows you to define your own content delivery specifications. In short, HTML is an application of XML, but formally, the new standard of the Web is XHTML. XHTML is a formal redefinition of HTML under XML.

This makes the HTML code easier to validate, as it adheres more closely to the XML standard for data exchange. You will learn, in due course, how to form an HTML document correctly so that it adheres to the XML standard (XHTML) to make your Web applications as future proof as possible.

You will learn about the Document Model, how the parts relate to each other, and what each section is nominally for. HTML breaks each page down into a set of parts, each with their own function, and it is vital to know what goes where.

You will also learn about the relevant HTML tags that you will use most frequently for formatting content. It is important to understand them before you learn about styles, because the attributes that the tags have can all be changed using style information. If you do not know what attributes can be used with each tag, and what effect they have, it is difficult to apply styles.

HTML can be used without styles, especially if it is generated, but the addition of style sheets in Chapter 4 makes the dynamic presentation of content easier. This chapter will also be useful as a reference in its own right once you start building pages of your own.

Although it was designed to be easy to deploy, the HTML tag collection is *large*, and it is unlikely that you will be able to remember all the tags at a single sitting. Over time, of course, you will gain experience that will allow you to both hand-create HTML documents as well as techniques to enable you to build HTML documents using scripts.

The Document Model

When people want to refer to the collection of elements that make up a Web page, they refer to them in terms of the Document Model. Of course, this term means much more than just a Web page—it is the core technology behind sharing information using standards such as XML and computer programs.

As far as this chapter is concerned, the HTML Document Model consists of layered containers:

FIRST Container
- The physical HTML document (or file)

- The document information (title, keywords, and so on)

- The layout information (formatting and presentation)

- The content items (text, hyperlinks, videos, pictures, add-ins, and so on)

The physical file contains the plain text that makes up the HTML logical document. Inside that, there is document information that tells the browser more about the actual HTML (including the version and character set), as well as the title of the document, usually displayed in the title bar of the browser.

Also inside the logical HTML file there is the layout information and content, collectively also known as the *body* of the document. The content can be contained inside tags (formatting or layout), and tags can contain tags (nesting).

Before you look at a document, you need to know how to construct the basic unit of definition used in XML and HTML—the tag. The basic usage, all you need right now, is as follows:

```
<tag_name>Content inside tag</tag_name>
```

You almost always need a start and end tag (the end tag being the one that has the tag name preceded by a forward slash, /), and whatever is in between is considered to be the target to be modified by the tag. Tags are always (in HTML, XML, and XHTML) contained within chevrons (< and >).

Bearing this in mind, let's look at how an HTML document is constructed.

Anatomy of the Document

An HTML document consists of three parts:

- Definition section

- The HEAD

- The BODY

In the Definition section, which you'll read about in a moment, you put information that has nothing to do with the content to be passed to the browser, but defines that content. It is outside of the HTML section, which contains the HEAD and BODY.

In the HEAD section you put all the content that is information to the browser (W3C calls this the user agent), but which is not intended to be displayed to the end user. In the BODY section, you place all the content that is designed to be rendered.

Outside of the HEAD, and something that many Web creators leave out, is the aforementioned Definition section. In this, you tell the browser what version of HTML you're using:

```
<!DOCTYPE HTML PUBLIC "-//W3C//DTD HTML 4.01 Transitional//EN"
    "http://www.w3.org/TR/html4/loose.dtd">
```

The DOCTYPE in this case is HTML 4.01 Transitional. This is allowable under W3C guidelines, but includes some features that have been replaced by style sheets. In essence, if you are creating a document that doesn't use style sheets, Transitional offers some features for controlling attributes that the strict version of HTML 4.01 doesn't.

(Each document that the server serves that follows the standard ought to have a DOCTYPE—named types exist for all flavors of HTML and XML, for example. If a proprietary standard were to be used to transmit information, the DOCTYPE could be used to tell the user agent what kind of information to expect.)

Although with experience you will work out which to use between the two, the examples for now stick with Transitional, because it gives you better control over the tags that you want to deploy. As long as you include the DOCTYPE information, along with the reference to the Document Type Definition (DTD) file, the browser knows where to find the exact definition of the version you are using.

The Strict DOCTYPE statement looks like this:

```
<!DOCTYPE HTML PUBLIC "-//W3C//DTD HTML 4.01//EN"
   "http://www.w3.org/TR/html4/strict.dtd">
```

The changes have been placed in bold text to set them apart. It might look complex, but all you really need to do is copy the text for the Transitional DOCTYPE into a text file and copy and paste it into future HTML projects.

The remainder of the document framework then looks like this:

```
<HTML>

   <HEAD>
   </HEAD>

   <BODY>
   </BODY>

</HTML>
```

Again, you might find this a bit alien at first, but all you really have here is a container HTML with a HEAD and BODY container inside it. Again, copy it to the text file, which is going to be your HTML skeleton file, underneath the DOCTYPE, and keep it handy.

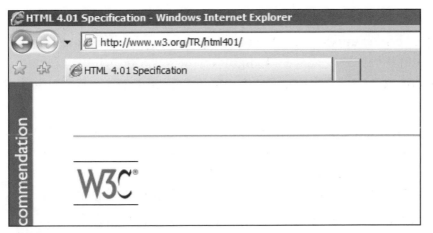

Figure 3.1
Browser with title in application bar

These stay more or less static for every page. The first section that you'll learn to customize with each different Web page is the HEAD.

The HTML *HEAD Tag*

The TITLE tag contains the title of the page, which is usually displayed in the title bar of the browser. Figure 3.1 shows the W3C HTML 4.01 page.

The title appears, in this case, next to the Internet Explorer icon in the title bar and is followed by the application name (Windows Internet Explorer). The HTML source for this would be:

```
<TITLE>HTML 4.01 Specification</TITLE>
```

This is another tag that you can store in the skeleton file that you are building, and should be inserted in the HEAD section. You will need to change the actual content, of course, to match your own page content.

Another set of tags that can be present in the HEAD section are known as *meta tags*. These tags contain information that might not be relevant to a browser, but that could be relevant to another user agent application. The most common example, and the one that I'll use to illustrate the use of meta tags, is in SEO (Search Engine Optimization).

You read in the previous chapter that search engines power the Web. Without them, your page will never be found. But, you can tell a search engine to index a page and give it some help in categorizing the information you're providing.

Meta tags provide one way to do this and are often used by search engines and other information broker applications to construct an entry in their database that can be displayed to the users. For search engines, you want to include a meta tag with keywords, for indexing purposes, and a meta tag with a description of the page, to display to the end users.

The SEO (search engine optimization) meta tags for a page about this book might look like this:

```
<META NAME="keywords" CONTENT="HTML, book, tutorial" >
<META NAME="description" CONTENT="Just Enough Web Programming, a book about..." >
```

You will note that the META tag, unlike the other tags you have met so far, does not have an end tag. This is because all the information that you need is contained within the tag, in something called *attributes*. The NAME is one attribute and CONTENT is another. You will look at these in more detail when you come to the short reference section.

Of course, here again, you will need to copy these tags to your skeleton text file, for later use. Feel free to split the tag definition across multiple lines—the browser will not mind, or indeed notice any whitespace, which is part of the XML flexibility.

Tip

If you want to test out your file, *copy* it to a new name and add the extension .html. So, if your skeleton file was called html-skel.txt now, it should be called new-html-skel.html, thereby preserving the original. You can now open the .html file in your browser.

The final item that you might put in the HEAD of the document is a section containing any client side scripts that are needed for the page. Now, these can also be put in the BODY of the document, but Web programmers tend to collect any common functionality in the HEAD section for clarity.

You will see this in action in Chapter 5, when you look at client side programming. For now, let's look at the BODY of the HTML document in more detail.

The HTML BODY Tag

The BODY is where you place the actual content that you want the browser to render, along with the mark-up that determines what it will look like. The content might be rendered as it is read, or the browser might read the whole page in and then render it.

This makes a difference, because if the browser does not intend to wait before rendering the page, it has no way of knowing what the final layout will look like. This means that, from the point of view of the content producer, you need to make sure that you give the browser enough information.

For example, browsers typically render images last, because they need to be downloaded separately. So, if you do not tell the browser what dimensions the images are, it cannot arrange the content appropriately. The more information about content you can give the browser up front, within the confines of HTML, the better.

Part of this information includes the logical layout, of which the default unit is the paragraph. Each block of text should be contained between paragraph tags that delimit the block. Within each paragraph, you can introduce tags that modify the style of the text. So, you contain the text between <P> and </P> tags, denoting the start and end of a paragraph.

This is achieved with specific tags (such as <B> for bold) or by using the SPAN tag, which allows you to name an inline block of text and apply discrete style attributes to the text. The SPAN tag may not cross paragraphs, nor contain them.

If you want to do that, paragraphs can be entirely contained (one or more of them, in fact) within a DIV (or division). Similar to the SPAN tag, the DIV tag lets you apply both a name and a collection of attributes to format the text (and paragraphs) more precisely than with individual style tags.

The next section looks at these style elements in more detail.

Style Elements

There are many style elements in HTML. You have come across two in the preceding section—SPAN and DIV—that offer a way to change both the flow and the appearance of the content that they contain.

HTML also offers nested headings to give titles varying levels of importance. These headings can be specified in a hierarchy from one to seven, with one being the most important. The HTML designer should not try to circumvent the strict hierarchy; if text is to be given a specific visual aspect to set it apart, but is not a heading, a heading tag should not be used.

Instead, you must find a way to set the text apart using other visual style formatting. Similarly, headings must not be skipped; otherwise, future browsers or other user agents may have problems parsing the HTML code and rendering the page.

If you need to create collections of items, line by line, HTML offers two kinds of lists. A numbered list, for example, allows you to list items with a number in front of them. The numbering is automatic, so there is no need to worry if you want to add items at a later date. The accompanying list, without numbers, is an unnumbered list.

HTML also provides ways in which tables can be constructed, complete with headings in a separate style, and the possibility to add borders. Besides using tables to arrange collections of data, you can also use them to lay out the page.

A common use for tables is to set all the content in a single table, with a left column for the menu, and a right column for related content, advertising, or product sales. The middle column contains the content proper.

The remaining style elements fall into the text-formatting category. These range from simple bold and italic text to decorations such as underlining. They do not generally allow you to change the behavior through the use of attributes, so they are designed to be used for very discrete textual effects.

If you need more flexibility, HTML allows the possibility to manipulate fonts—changing the style (face), as well as the size and color. With the advent of style sheets, the specific font handling tags have become deprecated, but you still have the possibility to use them, and they can be easier in many cases to deploy than style sheets.

Hyperlinking

The power of the Web, of course, is in being able to link content together. Whether it is a page, an image, a video, a sound, or a zip file containing a software release, hyperlinking is a vital part of the HTML standard.

Besides links to resources (covered next), you will encounter two kinds of reference within an HTML page. These are called anchors:

- Internal anchors

- External anchors

An *internal anchor* is a reference within the current document—you can, for example, specify a table of contents at the top of a page, and allow the users to click each one and be directed to a different part of the page. If you want this reference point to be accessible from another document, you need to refer to it using an external anchor.

Calling these requires that you construct something called a URL.

URLs

A URL (Uniform Resource Location or, sometimes, Uniform Resource Locator, depending on who you talk to) consists of:

```
<protocol>://<location>[/path_to/resource.type]
```

So, for example, you could create an URL that points to a simple Website:

```
http://www.w3c.org
```

However, you could create one that points to a specific page:

```
http://www.w3c.org/TR/html401/index.html
```

HTML gives you a variety of ways to introduce these into your pages, all of which are covered in the HTML Short Reference section. You need to remember, however, that the http:// protocol is only one of a collection. You could equally have:

```
ftp://        FTP file download (usually done in the browser)
mailto://     Shorthand for "please open my mail application and start an email"
telnet://     Command-line remote Internet services
```

No doubt in the future there will be more protocols to contend with, but for now these are the four (along with http://) principal ones.

(Systems programmers will also be aware that you can define your own protocols and register them in the operating system or Web server configuration, but most readers will never have cause to do this!)

Interactivity

The principal way in which a page offers interactivity to the end user is through clickable images (maps) or forms. The HTML Short Reference contains the actual HTML tags and appropriate codes.

A clickable image simply allows the users to click on a part of it and be directed to a new resource. It can also trigger a script, which should be reasonably transparent to the end users. The image can be part of a form.

The form offers, as you have seen, text entry areas, buttons, and other user interface elements. It is usually posted to the server, as discussed in the preceding chapter, but it can also be processed locally if the data is not designed to be relayed to the server, and the result displayed in the browser using client side scripting.

HTML Short Reference

HTML 4.01 is the current standard for Web documents. It is not the most recent incarnation of HTML; the W3C actually suggests that you adopt the XHTML standard as soon as possible. However, well formed HTML 4.01 is compatible with the XHTML standard, and is well understood by content producers and Web application developers alike.

It is also likely to remain usable by browsers for the foreseeable future, largely due to its stability and wide acceptance. It is also very helpful, even if you are going to develop content in XHTML, to understand the way HTML is constructed, as most of the principles carry through.

Before looking at the actual tags that will enable you to create marked-up content, you need a grounding in the basics, as well as some of the rules for using the tags in practice.

Deprecated Usage

You should be aware that some of the usage that is referred to here is what the W3C calls *deprecated*. Deprecated usage includes things that remain in the standard, but which have been superseded by other, more recent, innovations.

Using deprecated HTML carries a very minimal risk that the content will not be correctly rendered in the years to come. However, following the principle that the content is designed to be around for a given period of time, and also taking into account the fact that browsers will try to remain as backward compatible as possible, for commercial reasons, I am quite content to include deprecated usage where such is useful.

Deprecated usage is pointed out as it is encountered, and the advised replacement, as offered by the W3C, is given. Often, items become deprecated with the addition of style information, which is covered in Chapter 4. This is, despite the stance of the W3C, often taken as a separate topic, and I have also adopted that approach.

So, the following gives perfectly valid HTML 4.01; however, if you are building more than a couple of static pages, it is advised to take this as introductory matter, and use inline styles and style sheets instead of some of the deprecated usage mentioned here.

Syntax

The syntax of HTML is very easy; each element consists of a tag, possibly some attributes, bracketing the content that the tag is designed to alter. Anything in the document that is between chevrons (< and >) is considered to be an HTML tag, and will be evaluated as such.

It need not even be correct; the robust parsing of most browsers will just ignore tags that are invalid or improperly formed. This is a double-edged sword, of course, as it can mask poorly formed HTML as well as providing for unofficial extensions.

One set of tags that needs special mention is for inserting comments into the HTML. Comments are things that are intended for the human reader, and not the browser. It's a good habit to get into: making sure that the comments that you write into the HTML give a clear indication of the intent of the code.

For example, you might implement a page as a table with three columns. At the start of each column, you might want to place a piece of text that indicates what the column is for: Menu, Content, Averts, and so on.

So, the HTML comment for a menu might look like this:

```
<!--This is the Menu Bar -->
```

The starting tag <!-- indicates to the browser that the following text is a comment and can be ignored. The closing tag --> marks the end of the comment. This technique is equally useful for footers, copyright notices, and the like. It has the advantage that you can then search for the text when you open the source and jump straight to it.

Tags and Attributes

Information designed to be treated as mark-up for the content is expressed in terms of a tag and some attributes. The generic form for a tag is:

```
<tag attribute="value">content</tag>
```

The tag tells the browser what kind of mark-up is being introduced, and the attributes can be used to change the exact rendering of the mark-up. Depending on the tag, the attributes might be optional.

The content to be marked up is contained between the start and end tags. The start tag switches the formatting "on" and the end tag "off." The tags and attributes can have any names you like, but only a certain collection is recognized as valid HTML.

Minimized Tags

A minimized tag is one where there is no start and end tag, just a single instance of the tag. Line break tags, for example, need no end tag. The HTML specification allows for them to be written as follows:

```
<tag>
```

or:

```
<tag/>
```

Note that the second variation is the one preferred by the XHTML standard and is also implemented for HTML 4.01 browsers. Unless backward compatibility with other standards is a concern, it is the preferred form.

Nesting and Overlapping

There are two other small usage matters to clear up—nesting and overlapping— that must abide by fairly strict rules to be correctly interpreted and rendered by the browser. Nesting means including tags inside other tags, and overlapping means extending the inner tag past the outer tag.

Many tags can be nested, provided that the sense of the document is retained. In other words, you can specify italic text inside bold text in order to have bold, italic text. You can also nest containers such as tables inside other containers (inside cells of tables, in the case of tables). On the other hand, although nesting a `<B>` tag inside another `<B>` tag might not be rejected by the browser, it makes no sense as it will not create a doubly bold result.

In other words, you can put one set of tags inside another to add to the mark-up being applied to the content. This is called nesting, and should be complete.

```
<tag_one>Content <tag_two>Other Content</tag_two> More Content</tag_one>
```

In the previous example, `Content` has the `tag_one` applied to it as does `More Content`. Because `tag_two` is nested inside `tag_one`, `Other Content` has both `tag_one` and `tag_two` applied to it.

The nested tags should be completely contained within the outer tags, which means that the inner set of tags should be within the start and end tags of the outer set. In fact, there are some sets of tags that can be overlapped, which means that there is an area that is common to both tags, as well as two areas outside:

```
<tag_one>Content <tag_two>Other Content</tag_one> More Content</tag_two>
```

In the previous example, if you assume that `tag_one` turns on bold text, and `tag_two` italics, you would expect `Content` to be in bold, `Other Content` to be in bold italics, but `More Content` to be in italics only. This not only looks confusing, but is arguably incorrect.

```
<B>Bold <I>Bold + Italics</B> Italics only?</I>
```

The result of this example can be seen in Figure 3.2.

Here, in Firefox, you can see that the result is exactly as expected. However, this might not always be the case, because some user agents might have trouble rendering the overlap. In a trivial example such as this one, that might not matter, but the more complex the Web document becomes, the more the end results begin to matter.

My own advice is to avoid nesting wherever possible, and never use overlapped tags. It is too easy to lose track of exactly what the original intent was, even if there are some tags that will allow overlapping within the HTML standard.

Overlapping Tags **Bold** *Bold + Italics* *Italics only?*

Figure 3.2
Overlapping tags

Text Formatting

The first three tags you will learn are the easiest. They typically have no attributes, and are used on their own, or nested, in order to render specific effects—bold text, italicized text, and underlined text. The bold text tag is <B>:

```
This will be <B>in bold</B>.
```

If you want italics, use the <I> tag, as follows:

```
This will be <I>in italics</I>.
```

Finally, for underlined text, the appropriate tag is <U>, which follows the same pattern:

```
This will be <U>underlined</U>.
```

You can nest these tags, giving the following HTML fragment:

```
<HTML>
<HEAD>
  <TITLE>Bold, Italics and Underlined</TITLE>
</HEAD>
<BODY>
This is <B>bold text</B>.<BR /><BR />
This is <I>italicized text</I>.<BR /><BR />
This is <U>underlined text</U>.<BR /><BR />
This is <B>bold +<I>italicized +<U>underlined</U></I></B>.
</BODY>
</HTML>
```

The nested code example will be rendered as shown in Figure 3.3.

You can add a little more finesse to text by using the FONT tag. Although this has been deprecated by the addition of style sheets, it remains a popular way to manipulate textual content without all the additional complexity that style sheets entail.

By itself, the font tag doesn't actually do anything, it only provides a vehicle for the attributes that allow you to specify the font, color, and size of the text that you want to be displayed. Let's take these attributes one at a time.

The FACE attribute allows you to select a font by name. Of course, you need to be sure that the font that you choose has a good chance of being available on the target system. Not all systems have all fonts, but luckily most platforms are

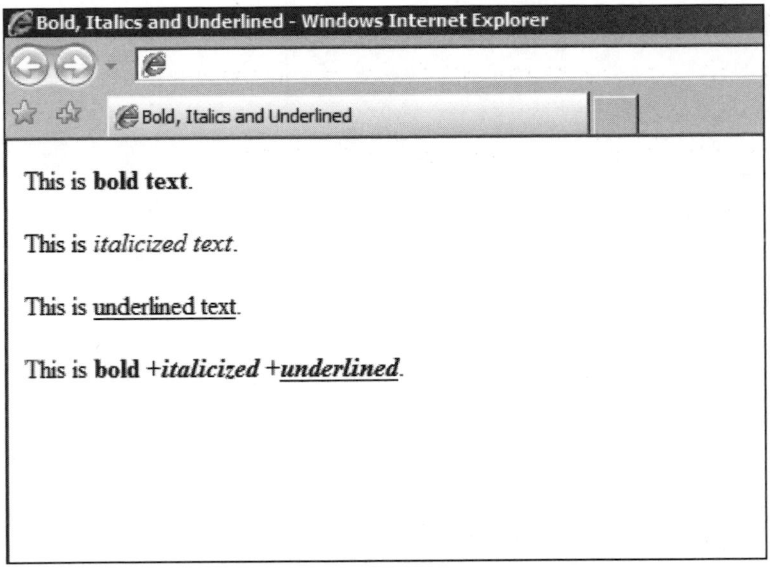

Figure 3.3
Bold, italics, and underlined tags in a nested format

capable of selecting replacements (substitutions) in case the ones you choose are not present.

However, you can also specify a list of font names (faces) to choose from. So, if you do know what platforms support what fonts, you can at least give the browser a list of suitable names. Some of the common ones are Times, Courier, and Verdana.

To apply an attribute, you simply add it as part of the starting tag. For example, the following HTML fragment selects first Courier, and then Times, and finally Verdana faces:

```
<HTML>
<HEAD>
  <TITLE>Times, Courier and Verdana Text</TITLE>
</HEAD>
<BODY>
<FONT FACE="Courier">This is Courier text</FONT><BR /><BR />
<FONT FACE="Times">This is Times text</FONT><BR /><BR />
<FONT FACE="Verdana">This is Verdana text</FONT><BR /><BR />
</BODY>
</HTML>
```

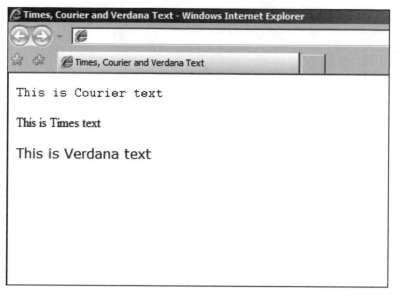

Figure 3.4
Courier, Times, and Verdana text

Now the system will try to render the fonts that are specified, but if they are not available, the browser will try to substitute a font that ought to work. This means that different results might be obtained on different systems. The result of this on my system, for example, can be seen in Figure 3.4.

In addition to specifying the font face with the FACE attribute, you can also specify the size using the SIZE attribute. This is not a discrete font size, as it would be if you were specifying it in a word processor in points. Rather, it is a proportional measure—2 is bigger than 1, 3 is bigger than 2, but there are no guarantees as to the actual size in points.

The following HTML fragment illustrates all seven possible values for the SIZE attribute:

```
<HTML>
<HEAD>
  <TITLE>Font Sizes</TITLE>
</HEAD>
<BODY>
<FONT SIZE="1">This is Size 1</FONT><BR /><BR />
<FONT SIZE="2">This is Size 2</FONT><BR /><BR />
<FONT SIZE="3">This is Size 3</FONT><BR /><BR />
```

```
<FONT SIZE="4">This is Size 4</FONT><BR /><BR />
<FONT SIZE="5">This is Size 5</FONT><BR /><BR />
<FONT SIZE="6">This is Size 6</FONT><BR /><BR />
<FONT SIZE="7">This is Size 7</FONT><BR /><BR />
</BODY>
</HTML>
```

To have an idea as to the actual result that this brings, Figure 3.5 shows the previous HTML code loaded into a browser.

The last FONT attribute that you'll look at here is the COLOR. Color values in HTML are a little odd at first glance. For a start, there is actually a list of named colors in the HTML standard, and these have been designed to fit into most display palettes.

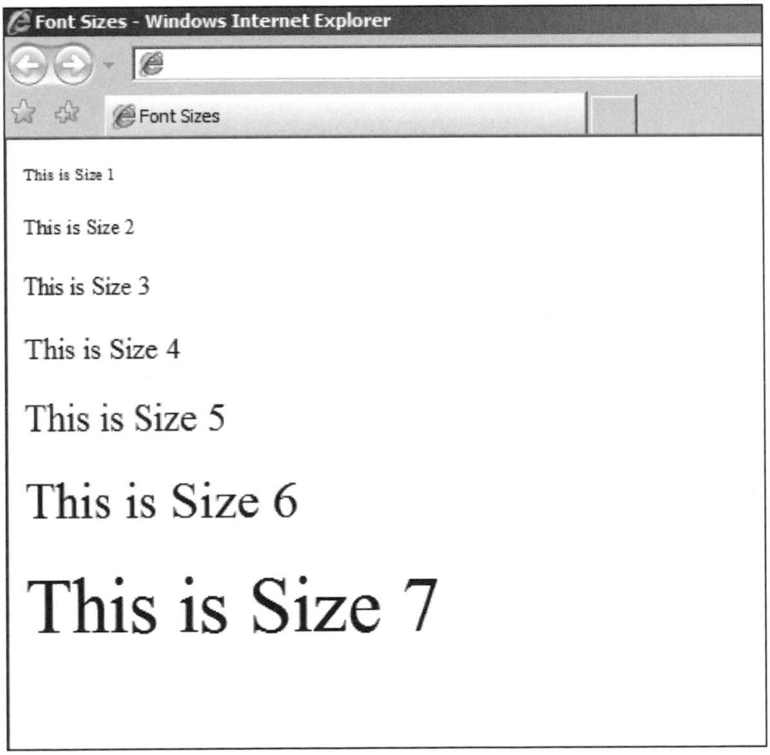

Figure 3.5
Font sizes

The standard HTML colors are:

Black	Silver	Gray	White
Maroon	Purple	Fuchsia	Red
Yellow	Olive	Green	Lime
Navy	Teal	Blue	Aqua

These are used in the same way as the previous FONT attributes:

```
<FONT COLOR="Red">This is Red Text</FONT><BR /><BR />
```

However, there is another way to specify the color, by using a series of hexadecimal numbers. If you're not familiar with this color coding scheme, rest assured it is not terribly complex. Let's start at the beginning.

The numerical value that can be specified instead of the standard color name is split into three parts—red, green, and blue. These colors are therefore called RGB colors. Each component is specified as a number between 0 and 255 representing the relative intensity of the color.

So, 0 is black (zero intensity) and 255 is maximum intensity. The following table shows some basic colors:

Red	Green	Blue	Result
0	0	0	Black
255	0	0	Red
0	255	0	Green
0	0	255	Blue
128	128	128	Gray
255	255	255	White

You can also combine the red, green, and blue components to give any shade in the spectrum between black and white, by varying the independent components. If this was all there was to it, it would be easy enough. However, you will remember that the color components are in hexadecimal, and not decimal as in the table.

Hexadecimal is a counting system where numbers are represented by values between 00 (decimal 0) and FF (decimal 128). Without going into too much detail, all that you have to really remember is that you probably have a tool

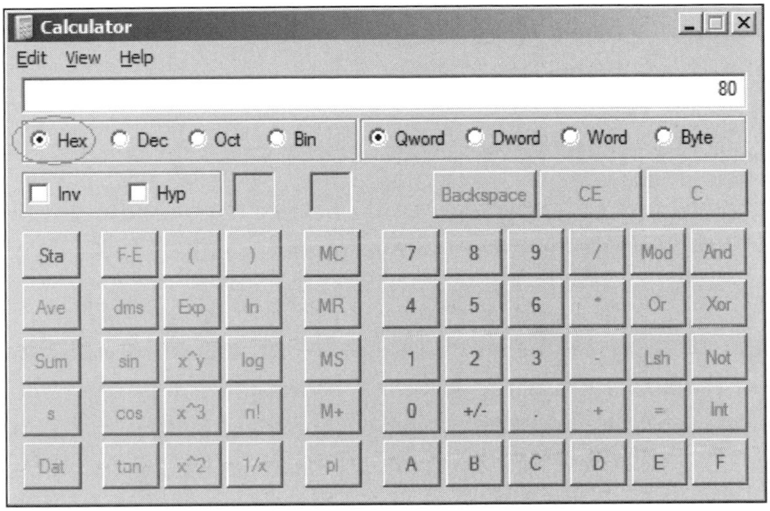

Figure 3.6
The Windows Calculator

to calculate hexadecimal values—the calculator supplied with your operating system.

Figure 3.6 shows the Windows Calculator application, with the Hex button circled. If the user then selects Dec, the value changes back to decimal. In order to access this mode, it may be necessary to select the Scientific mode. This is shown in Figure 3.7.

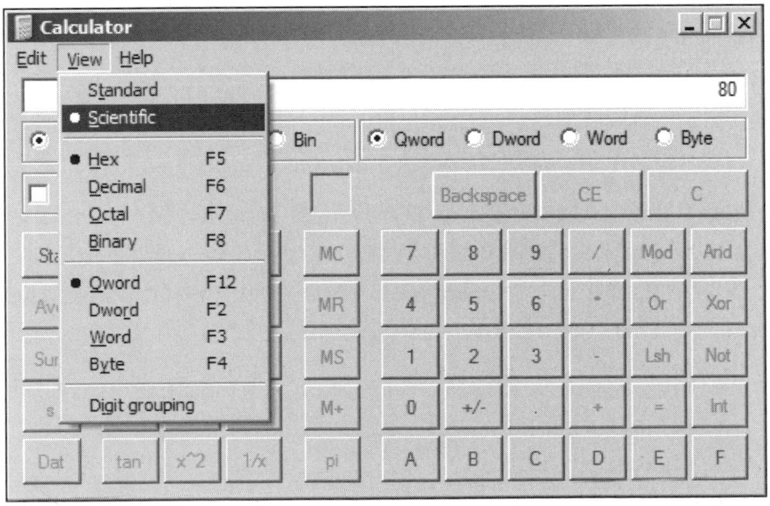

Figure 3.7
Selecting the Scientific mode

Having calculated, for example, that the color gray is made by mixing 80 red, 80 green, and 80 blue (having converted from 128, 128, 128), you can then introduce this into the color attribute as follows:

```
<FONT COLOR="#808080">Gray Text</FONT>
```

Now, all this is looking to be quite abstract, so it would be nice to have something to play around with. Luckily, there is an excellent resource called the Color Schemer, available at http://www.colorschemer.com/online.html.

The Color Schemer comes in two versions—online and downloadable—and helps you to select colors based on an intuitive interface. It is designed such that the resulting colors work well together, and should be the first place you go when designing a color scheme. It is also handy for converting RGB decimal to hexadecimal values, as well as picking colors from a selected set of HTML safe possibilities.

Rather than using the FONT tag, there are some standard HTML tags that allow you to structure blocks of text according to some predefined layouts. Although different browsers will likely interpret these in different ways, the advantage is that you can later change the layout to something more specific using styles.

This might not be immediately apparent, but in Chapter 4 you will see how using styles with HTML text formatting tags (or elements) can help reduce your workload when creating and changing HTML pages. For now, you need to know that these elements exist and how they make your life easier.

For example, the <PRE> tag allows you to pre-format a section of text:

```
<PRE>
  This text
    is preformatted.
</PRE>
```

The browser should render this <PRE> tag exactly as it is typed. However, the HTML standard does not prescribe any formal rules as to how it should look. Guidelines exist, though, and usually a browser will create a text block where the layout is unchanged, and in a fixed font (such as Courier).

Although many people use the <B> tag (bold) and <I> (italics) to identify text that should be emphasized, HTML actually provides <EM> and <STRONG> for this very purpose. They are used in the same way as <B> and <I>, that is:

```
This text is <EM>emphasized</EM>.
This text is <STRONG>strongly emphasized</STRONG>.
```

Browsers are free to render these as they wish; however, you can be certain that they will both be emphasized over the appearance of normal text within the same block, regardless of the underlying style chosen for that text.

There is also a collection of tags aimed at programmers:

- CODE—Computer code excerpts

- SAMP—Sample output from programs

- KBD—Text to be entered by users

This last would be equally useful for an online user manual. Each one must have a start and end tag and can be adjusted with style information. Other useful text rendering tags include handling abbreviations and acronyms:

- ABBR—For an abbreviation, such as Mr.

- ACRONYM—For an acronym, such as WWW

These also require a start and end tag to enclose the abbreviated text or acronym. Citations are handled through the <CITE> and </CITE> tags, whereas quotations are inserted as a block with <BLOCKQUOTE> and </BLOCKQUOTE> or inline with the <Q> and </Q> tags.

For all of these additional text rendering tags, there may be some variation on how browsers handle the exact layout and fonts chosen. They are incredibly useful for organizing the text, however, and the general flow of the page will be respected. Tighter control through styles is possible, of course.

The last two HTML tags that you need for text formatting are:

- SPAN

- DIV

The purpose of these tags is very similar—to provide bulk formatting for a section of text, which can be adjusted using nested tags such as <B>, <I>, and so on, to enhance the base formatting specified in the <SPAN> or <DIV> tag. You'll revisit these tags when you look at styles in the next chapter.

The <SPAN> tag is used in conjunction with inline content. In other words, it cannot break across paragraphs (see the following section called "Flow Formatting") or divisions (defined with the <DIV> tag).

The <DIV> (division) tag defines block content—one that can contain any other tag, including paragraphs and <SPAN> content. Divisions can also be nested, but I would advise against it, based on experience with the way that some browsers render the content.

You'll see how these tags can be used for formatting the flow of the content in the next section.

Flow Formatting

Anything that changes the flow of the content around the page, as well as (optionally) specific color and style information, I have chosen to place in this section. These tags are usable on their own, but can also be combined, as you shall see in the next chapter, with specific style information to enhance them.

The first of these tags is the heading tag. HTML supports up to six levels of headings, with heading 1 as the most important, and 6 as the least. Browsers are expected to use appropriate fonts, sizes, and decoration to put across this hierarchy. However, in some cases, the lower level headings may not be all that different from normal text.

For example, consider the following HTML fragment:

```
<H1>Heading 1</H1>
<H2>Heading 2</H2>
<H3>Heading 3</H3>
<H4>Heading 4</H4>
<H5>Heading 5</H5>
<H6>Heading 6</H6>
This is normal text.
```

You might expect that all the headings would be rendered in a suitable fashion such that they would all be more visually important than the normal text. This is not the case in all browsers. For example, in Internet Explorer, headings after <H3> are rendered in a way that makes them smaller in size than the normal text.

This can be seen in Figure 3.8.

It is advisable to avoid skipping levels, as there may be some browsers that add a number to the start of the heading, and this would cause them to skip numbers. In addition, you should not nest headings, as this is both illogical and might not be rendered consistently.

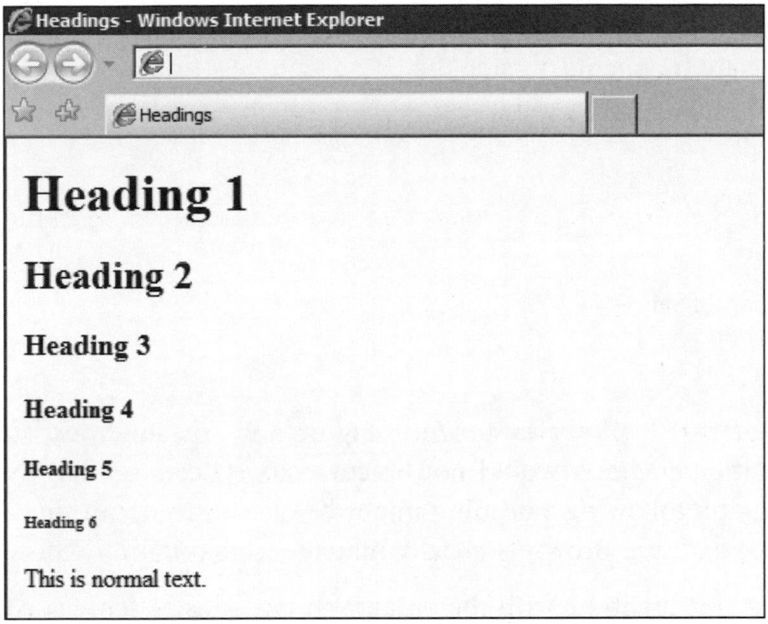

Figure 3.8
Headings in Internet Explorer

As you can see from Figure 3.8, extra line breaks are also added to make sure that the heading stands apart from the rest of the content. The heading tag accepts a number of attributes, some style related (discussed in the next chapter) and others not. Of the non-style related attributes, the only one of particular use is the ALIGN attribute.

For example:

```
<H1 ALIGN="RIGHT">Right Aligned Heading</H1>
```

This HTML code would place the heading text at the right side of the current content block. Other possible values for the ALIGN attribute are "CENTER" and "LEFT", producing centered and left aligned headings, respectively.

The next flow formatting tag is the paragraph tag. This is used to separate a block of text into a nominal paragraph of content. This implies inserting line breaks appropriately and choosing a default font.

The basic use of the <P> tag is as follows:

```
<P>This is a
paragraph of text.</P>
<P>This is another paragraph.</P>
```

You can combine this with the heading tags, and the browser will usually keep the flow, even when there are fragments outside the paragraph tags, and when there are paragraphs directly following heading tags. For example:

```
<BODY>
<H1 ALIGN="LEFT">Heading</H1>
<P>This is a
paragraph of text.</P>
This is not inside a paragraph.
<P>This is another paragraph.</P>
</BODY>
```

This is rendered by Internet Explorer as shown in Figure 3.9. You might expect that the text outside the paragraph would not be correctly spaced, or that the act of placing a paragraph following a heading might be over-spaced, but this is generally speaking not the case. Browsers usually manage to maintain the flow.

You can also use the ALIGN attribute with the paragraph tag. This is deprecated, having been superseded to a certain extent with style information. The following is perfectly valid HTML:

```
<P ALIGN="CENTER">
Centered paragraph text.
</P>
```

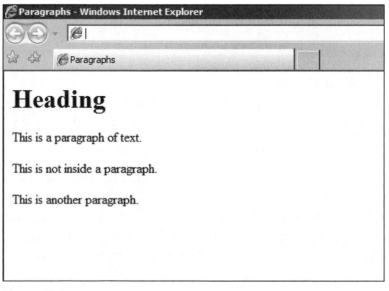

Figure 3.9
Paragraphs

This ALIGN attribute will cause the whole paragraph to be centered. Although its use is deprecated, the use of the ALIGN attribute with the DIV tag is not, and so you could group a collection of paragraphs within a division:

```
<DIV ALIGN="CENTER">
<P>This is centered.</P>
</DIV>
<P>This is not.</P>
```

The alternative is to use a style (see Chapter 4) that centers the text, or to use three very useful flow control tags:

- `<CENTER>`

- `<RIGHT>`

- `<LEFT>`

As you would expect, these will center-, right-, and left-align text in the vast majority of browsers. However, only the CENTER tag is supported in the HTML standard and is part of the Transitional definition. In other words, under strict HTML 4.01, it should not be used.

The paragraph tag makes a paragraph by inserting line breaks at appropriate places. If you want to force a line break, either within a paragraph or because you're just not using paragraphs, you can use the `<BR>` tag.

Prior to XHTML, it was accepted just to use the short form:

```
Line break<BR>
new line.
```

Since the introduction of XHTML, it is generally regarded as bad practice to ever use a minimized tag in this fashion; instead, you should get into the habit of using the proper XML minimized tag form:

```
Line break<BR />
new line.
```

A double line break will insert a blank line. Often, this will be rendered by the browser as if it were the close of a paragraph. It is not, however, a good idea to rely on this, and you should use proper paragraphs rather than line breaks.

If you need to have lists of items, there are three kinds of lists provided by HTML:

- Ordered list

- Unordered list

- Definition list

An ordered list has numbered items (nominally 1, 2, 3, and so on, but this can be changed), where an unordered list just has bullets. A definition list is slightly special in that each item is rendered in two parts: the item title and the actual definition. These will usually be rendered in different styles in order to make the meaning plain.

The various lists can be seen in Figure 3.10.

You construct the ordered list by enclosing it in <OL> and </OL> tags. Each item must begin with an <LI> tag; however, a closing tag is not required. Many Web programmers choose to include it, if only to disambiguate the usage for those

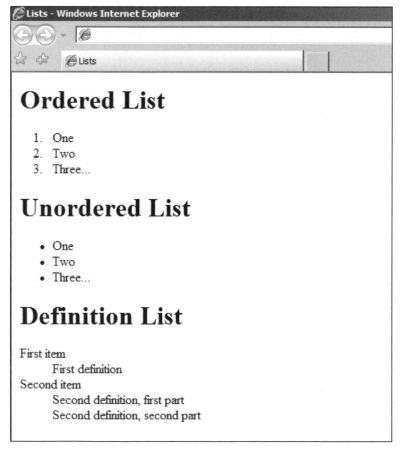

Figure 3.10
Lists

browsers that might not correctly display list items that do not have both a start and end tag.

Because it does no harm to the correctness, you may prefer to leave the closing tags in place as a matter of course, but I do need to mention that the HTML standard leaves them out. The closing </OL> tag is, of course, required.

Another deprecated feature of the <OL> is the TYPE attribute. This has been superseded by the use of styles (see Chapter 4); however, it is still part of the HTML 4.01 Transitional standard and in widespread use.

The TYPE attribute can be used to change the numbering scheme used. So, specifying "i" will cause the list to be rendered using successive roman numerals (i, ii, iii, iv, and so on), and specifying "a" will cause the list to be rendered using lowercase letters (a, b, c, d, and so on).

This can be useful in nested lists, as in:

```
<OL TYPE="1">
<LI>This is the first item
  <OL TYPE="a">
    <LI>This is sub-item one
    <LI>This is sub-item two
    <LI>etc.
  </OL>
</OL>
```

This example should be rendered as in Figure 3.11, but you should remember that other browsers may do so differently. You will also notice that I have left off the closing LI tags by way of illustration.

The counterpart to the ordered list is the unordered list. Here, there is simply a bullet or other illustrative element in front of the item rather than a number

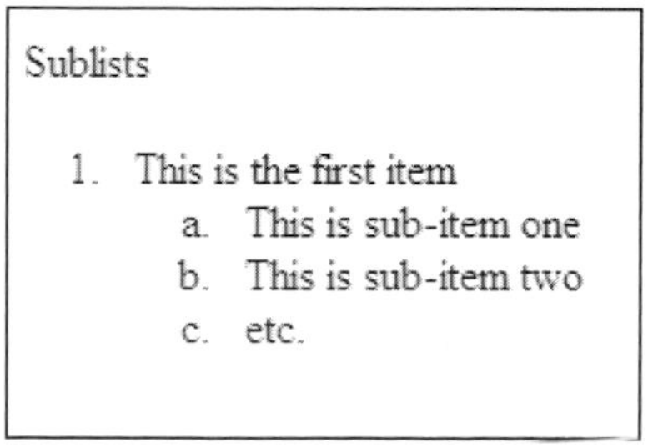

Figure 3.11
Sublists with the TYPE attribute

(letter, numeral, and so on). Otherwise, the unordered list works in the same way as an ordered list, except that you use the tags `<UL>` and `</UL>` rather than `<OL></OL>` as before.

Nested lists are also possible:

```
<UL>
<LI>This is the first item
  <UL>
    <LI>This is sub-item one
    <LI>This is sub-item two
    <LI>etc.
  </UL>
</UL>
```

Note in these two HTML fragments I have indented the list items so that it is clear what the structure of the list is. HTML indenting keeps the code neat and readable and is a must for easy maintenance. There's nothing worse than picking up an HTML page and not remembering how the flow translates into the rendered page, and being unable to determine that from the HTML itself.

The graphical element used to indicate the list bullet can be changed through the `TYPE` attribute in much the same way as the `TYPE` attribute is used to change the ordering style for the ordered list. There are three allowable values:

- DISC

- SQUARE

- CIRCLE

Although these are accepted under HTML, and defined as part of the standard, some people consider their use to be deprecated by the introduction of styles (see Chapter 4). However, they remain very much in the fore, and while you will learn in due course how to change the bullet using styles, the `TYPE` attribute remains very popular.

You can use bullet types to separate sub-lists:

```
<UL TYPE="DISC">
<LI>This is the first item
  <UL TYPE="SQUARE">
    <LI>This is sub-item one
```

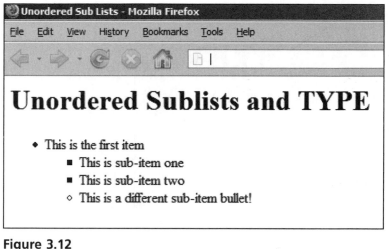

Figure 3.12
Unordered list bullet types in Firefox

```
    <LI>This is sub-item two
    <LI TYPE="CIRCLE">This is a different sub-item bullet!
  </UL>
</UL>
```

However, you cannot always rely on different browsers treating this fragment equally. As an example of how rendering can change between platforms, Figure 3.12 shows the HTML fragment as rendered by Mozilla Firefox.

By contrast, Figure 3.13 shows the same fragment rendered by Microsoft Internet Explorer.

Neither is incorrect; it is part of the flexibility of HTML, and the accepted norm that different browser application developers will make different rendering decisions. Until you use styles to dictate exactly what kind of rendering you want, the browser is free to decide for itself what makes a logical graphical representation.

This interpretation philosophy is equally applicable in rendering the final kind of list—the definition list. A definition list is just a structured list that contains items and their definitions. The definition block is usually slightly indented from the item to which it refers, and when the line wraps, the indent is kept.

You can see an example of a definition list in Figure 3.10. It is rendered more or less the same way in any browser, but you cannot change the aspect of it using the TYPE attribute. Instead, styles must be used to change the rendering.

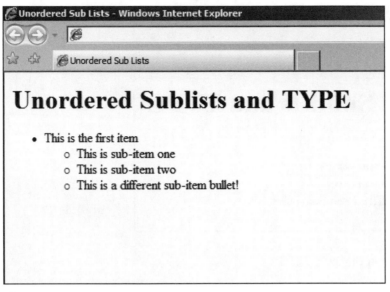

Figure 3.13
Unordered list bullet types in IE

The following HTML fragment is the one that produced the example in Figure 3.10:

```
<DL>
 <DT>First item</DT>
  <DD>First definition</DD>
 <DT>Second item</DT>
  <DD>Second definition, first part</DD>
  <DD>Second definition, second part</DD>
</DL>
```

You will also note that you can have multiple definition lines in each item; if the line wraps around due to the width of the available area, this will cause the new definition line to be rendered with a carriage return, much as you would expect.

Other ways to organize content include tables. Like lists, tables are examples of HTML elements I call structured flow control containers. These are elements that are built up from a structure where nesting is an integral part of the HTML code. Care has to be taken so that someone reading the HTML is aware of where the various parts of the container start and end.

A table consists of a start tag `<TABLE>` and end tag `</TABLE>`. Between these, it is build up from a series of rows, which have a start tag `<TR>` and an end tag `</TR>`.

Inside *those,* there are a number of columns, or cells, each with a start tag <TD> and end tag </TD>. The browser will not render the table until it has entirely loaded.

The basic structure of a table might look like the following HTML fragment:

```
<TABLE BORDER="1">
 <TR>
  <TD>Row 1, Cell 1</TD>
  <TD>Row 1, Cell 2</TD>
 </TR>
 <TR>
  <TD>Row 2, Cell 1</TD>
  <TD>Row 2, Cell 2</TD>
 </TR>
</TABLE>
```

An example of how it might be rendered is shown in Figure 3.14.

You will have noticed that I have introduced the BORDER attribute to be sure that the border is shown ("0" can be used to force the border to be invisible). Otherwise, you would not have been able to see the separation between cells. In addition, the browser has rendered the table such that it is exactly the right size to contain the content.

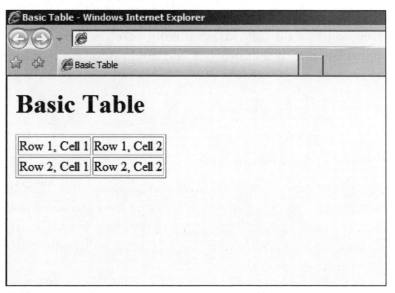

Figure 3.14
Basic table

This might not be the effect that you want, so you can control the width that the table is supposed to take up by using the WIDTH attribute. The value for the WIDTH attribute can be presented as a percentage of the available block or as a discrete value, in pixels.

So, to create a table that has three columns, two of 25% and one of 50%, you would use HTML such as:

```
<TABLE WIDTH="100%">
 <TR>
  <TD WIDTH="25%">
  </TD>
 </TR>
<TR>
  <TD WIDTH="50%">
  </TD>
 </TR>
<TR>
  <TD WIDTH="25%">
  </TD>
 </TR>
</TABLE>
```

Note that this example has specified that the entire table will take up 100% of the available width, and that each column width is specified in terms of the total width, and not the table width. I do not advise mixing pixel and percentage widths, because experience has shown that browsers do not always render tables in the same way. For example:

```
<TABLE WIDTH="640">
 <TR>
  <TD WIDTH="25%">
  </TD>
 </TR>
<TR>
  <TD WIDTH="50%">
  </TD>
 </TR>
<TR>
  <TD WIDTH="25%">
  </TD>
 </TR>
</TABLE>
```

In this example, you might assume that the browser is clever enough to spot that you want the first column to measure 25% of the available 640 pixels that you have specified as the total width of the table. However, browsers might not always render this in the same way, and instead choose to use a value that is equal to 25% of the total document width rather than the 640 pixels that is use for the width of the table.

Naturally, if you want to center the table, you can enclose it in <CENTER> and </CENTER> tags. This is a common approach for a newsletter style Web page, where you would like the content to appear in the center, in columns divided (like a blog) between the navigation, advertising content, and main article text.

There are also a few tricks that you can use to add, for example, a row that spans the whole table width, regardless of the number of columns. This is very useful for creating headers (banners or navigation strips) or footers. For example, assume you want to create a page layout such as that in Figure 3.15.

Now for the longest HTML fragment that you have yet seen, and which generated the page rendered in Figure 3.15.

Figure 3.15
Sample layout with a table

```
<TABLE WIDTH="600">
  <TR>
    <TD COLSPAN="3" VALIGN="BOTTOM">
    <CENTER>
      <H1>Banner Would Go Here</H1>
      [ Home | Latest Blog | About Us... ]
    </CENTER>
    </TD>
  </TR>
  <TR>
    <TD WIDTH="150" VALIGN="TOP">
        Menu<BR/>
         Sub-menu<BR/>
    </TD>
    <TD WIDTH="300">
    <!- - An empty paragraph to space it out,
        with a double line break - ->
    <BR /><BR />
    <P>This is where all the glorious content
       would go, if we actually had any.</P>
    <P>Instead, we've put in this wonderful placeholder
        that is more original than the fake Latin that most
        people use instead of real text.</P>
    <!- - An empty paragraph to space it out,
        with a double line break - ->
    <BR /><BR />
    </TD>
    <TD WIDTH="150">
    <CENTER>
    Sample<BR/>Advertising<BR/>Here<BR/>
    </CENTER>
    </TD>
  </TR>
  <TR>
    <TD COLSPAN="3" VALIGN="BOTTOM">
    <CENTER>
      <I>Copyright Statement, privacy statement,
         perhaps an additional menu here...</I>
    </CENTER>
    </TD>
  </TR>
</TABLE>
```

I have introduced a number of interesting attributes in this HTML fragment, all of which are vital in laying out the page properly. Firstly, the COLSPAN attribute allows you to create cells that span several columns. This is used in the header (banner and menu strip) as well as the footer (copyright statement).

You can only span as many columns as are available in the table. If a larger number is used, the results are probably going to vary wildly between browsers. Next, I have used the VALIGN attribute to make sure that the vertical alignment is correct for the various cells that contain less content than the calculated cell height.

The browser decides the cell height, and sometimes (as in the advertising pane) the content will not be as large (in height) as the entire column. The default behavior of browsers seems to be to center the content. So, to prevent this happening for content that you *want* to be aligned otherwise, you can specify a VALIGN value of:

- TOP

- CENTER

- BOTTOM

As you are probably starting to appreciate, leaving the default behavior (or assuming any default behavior at all) for layout is inadvisable, so you should get into the habit of always specifying the layout (alignment in this case) for HTML where it is of importance.

Cells can also be aligned horizontally, using the ALIGN attribute, although it is deprecated. Instead, I have chosen to use the <CENTER> tag to center the content where appropriate.

There are three other attributes that I might have made use of to further break up the visual appearance of the table.

The BGCOLOR attribute is used to set the background of the table or a particular cell inside the table. Now, it has been deprecated, and you are encouraged to use styles instead; however, often it is simply more convenient just to insert a BGCOLOR attribute when only a single instance is required.

Although this is quite acceptable by most people for the time being, if you want to try to make sure that your content is XHTML compliant (see the next section) or want to prepare for full XHTML rendering, you should get into the habit of using styles for setting the background color.

The CELLSPACING and CELLPADDING attributes are used in the <TABLE> tag to set the space between cells (spacing) and the inside margins (padding). You could have used this to introduce whitespace in the previous fragment if, for example, the left menu items began to creep towards the main content.

The CELLPADDING attribute, in particular, has to be used with a degree of caution, as it can cause unintended line breaks to appear as the table will not be extended with reference to the border or padding that is used. In other words, you get less space for your content, and subsequently if the content extends beyond the new edge of the cell, it will be wrapped automatically.

Of course, tables can also be used to display data sets. Arguably, this is what they were designed for, and with this in mind, the last tag that I present here is the <TH> tag. This allows you to specify that a cell contains heading information, and the browser will usually render it in a way that is more visually important than the regular table data.

The following HTML fragment employs this tag:

```
<TABLE>
 <TR>
  <TH>Col 1</TH>
  <TH>Col 2</TH>
  <TH>Col 3</TH>
 </TR>
 <TR>
  <TD>Cell 1</TD>
  <TD>Cell 2</TD>
  <TD>Cell 3</TD>
 </TR>
</TABLE>
```

Like all tags, the collection of table elements can all be manipulated through the use of inline styles or style sheets (see Chapter 4). This includes the headings as well as the cells themselves.

Images

A vital part of the multimedia communication possibilities offered by HTML is the ability to include images inline with the other content. This includes non-interactive pictures as well as images that can be given a clickable user interface—anything from a map to a navigation bar can be created using a simple image and some tags.

Firstly, you need to know how to insert an image into a Web page. This is broken down into two stages—first you need to tell the browser that you want to insert an image, and then you need to tell it where to find the image itself.

Assuming that the image is in the same place as the Web page, the generic form for an image element is as follows:

```
<IMG SRC="image_name" WIDTH="width" HEIGHT="height" ALT="Image Text">
```

Note that there is no end tag—it is not allowed under the HTML standard. You have several attributes, with the first being the location of the image—its URL (see Introduction and Chapter 2).

The next two are the width and height of the image. If you don't know the width and height, load the image into an image editor (such as Microsoft Paint, Ifran-View, or Adobe Photoshop) and use the Image Information option to find out.

It is a good idea to tell the browser what the width and height of the image are so that it can render the page correctly before loading the image and determining the dimensions for itself. As an aside, you can also force the image to be resized in the browser, with varying degrees of quality, by specifying a size that is bigger or smaller than the original.

The ALT attribute allows you to supply a textual description in case the browser is unable to display the image or is not a visual user agent. For example, if the interface is vocal, the image's alternate text will be read out, because the image itself cannot be displayed. The best practice, in order to be compliant with standards on accessibility, is always to provide an ALT attribute. Plus, it makes for better SEO—a search engine cannot index an image if it doesn't know what it displays.

Finally, there is an optional BORDER attribute that can be used to specify a border around the image, or "0" for no border. Using "0" also means that if you turn the image into a hyperlink (see the "Document Linking" section), there will be no blue border around it.

To turn the image into a client side imagemap, you need to specify the USEMAP attribute and insert a reference to the <MAP> element that contains the specific information relating to the areas of the image that can be clicked. You will find a concrete example at the end of this section.

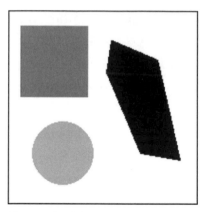

Figure 3.16
Sample image

However, before you can go on, you need to know a little bit more about how the imagemap works. The HTML code is designed to divide the image up into areas that can refer to other documents. In the "Document Linking" section, you will read how this works in more detail; for now, you just need to be aware that the mechanism exists.

The areas of the map can be rectangular, circular, or irregularly shaped. In order to be able to tell the browser what the shape is, you need to know the coordinates. To get these, you need to load the image into an image editor and use it to determine exactly where each corner (or the center of a circle) is located.

Figure 3.16 contains a sample imagemap that has a rectangle, circle, and polygon.

Next, you need to load your image into, for example, MS Paint. I've used that for illustrative purposes because it is part of nearly every Windows system and suits the needs here perfectly. Figure 3.17 shows where the coordinates can be found.

In Figure 3.17, you will note that the image is zoomed in to help with accuracy. The next step is to locate each corner of each shape and write them down. So, for the image that I have used as an example, the coordinates would be:

Rectangle	13,16	83,90	(Top-Left and Bottom-Right)
Circle	58,147	32	(Center and Radius)
Polygon	108,31 158,51 181,155 139,147 103,65		

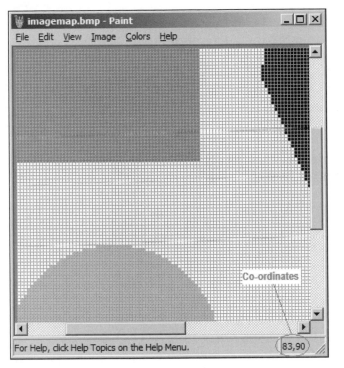

Figure 3.17
Sample image loaded into MS Paint

For the polygon, you have to note each point on the perimeter, because it is irregularly shaped. All that is left now is to encode the image and its map into HTML. This is fairly repetitive, but straightforward:

```
<IMG SRC="imagemap.jpg" WIDTH="200" HEIGHT="200" USEMAP="#image_map">
<MAP NAME="image_map">
 <AREA HREF="index.html" SHAPE="RECT" COORDS="13,16,83,90">
 <AREA HREF="page2.html" SHAPE="CIRCLE" COORDS="58,147,32">
 <AREA HREF="page3.html" SHAPE="POLY"
    COORDS="108,31,158,51,181,155,139,147,103,65,108,31">
</MAP>
```

This HTML fragment has introduced a lot of new information, some of which is unfamiliar. Firstly, you will note that I refer to the image_map by putting a # in front of it in the IMG tag's USEMAP attribute. This is an example of an internal reference to an element, which is covered in the "Document Linking" section that follows.

Next, you will note that the NAME attribute of the MAP tag, which is used to contain the map element itself, does not contain the # reference. There is then a new tag <AREA> with no end tag, which allows you to specify a clickable region.

The HREF attribute is an example of a reference to a document, its URL. It tells the browser where to find the resource once the user has clicked inside the area to which it refers. The SHAPE attribute tells the browser what kind of COORDS it can expect: the shape of the area.

The three values that SHAPE can take are:

- RECT: Rectangle

- CIRCLE: Circle

- POLY: Polygon

The final note is that the COORDS just contain the list of corner locations that you worked out using the MS Paint (or similar) application previously. The polygon contains identical coordinates in the first and last slots so as to close the shape to provide a filled area that can be clicked.

Because this is an example of document (or resource) linking, now is a good time to look at this topic in more detail.

Document Linking

As you saw in Chapter 2, the World Wide Web is an interlinked collection of documents and other resources. In order to navigate between them, HTML defines elements called *anchors*. These anchors point to other resources, and when the user clicks them, they open that resource in the browser.

There are two kinds of links:

- Link with an external target (external link)

- Link with an internal target (internal link)

Assume that you have a collection of pages where the first one is an index into the others. Each of the other pages in the collection is a single subject, broken down into sections. Using external and internal links, you want to build up navigation between the topics covered in the collection of pages.

The generic form for an external link (which will be in the index page, linking to other pages) is as follows:

```
<A HREF="target_page.html">Link Text</A>
```

This is known as the anchor tag. The HREF attribute, like in an imagemap <AREA> tag, refers to the location of the page. In the previous example, I have assumed that it is in the same location as the source page. This is known as a relative URL.

You can also specify a link to a page that is in a different folder, relative to the one that the source page is in:

```
<A HREF="target_folder/target_page.html">Link Text</A>
```

If the target page is on a different server altogether, the final possibility is:

```
<A HREF="http://www.mycom.com/target_folder/target_page.html">Link Text</A>
```

In this last example, the target folder might not be required, depending on the URL to the page being linked to. In each example, the browser will render the link text (between the <A> and </A> tags) in a specific way that indicates to the users that the text can be clicked. This can be changed through the use of styles (see Chapter 4).

The next kind of link that you need in order to be able to use a small table of contents at the start of each page is an *internal* link. These consist of a named anchor within the page that provides a location that can be linked to. The general form for this is as follows:

```
<A NAME="internal_ref_name">Anchor Text</A>
```

This snippet creates the named area that an internal link will point to, but it does get rendered as a link by the browser. It is just a reference point. This kind of anchor can be referred to from inside or outside the document. To refer to it from inside the document, the following form can be used:

```
<A HREF="#internal_ref_name>Link Text</A>
```

Note that the # symbol is used, as it was in the client side imagemap, to create the proper reference to the anchor. If you need to link directly to this point in the page from outside the page, the external reference form can also be used:

```
<A HREF="http://www.mycom.com/target_folder/target_page.html #internal_
            ref_name"> Link Text</A>
```

This anchor will be underlined and highlighted in the same way as any other anchor, and when clicked, it will jump to the appropriate place in the target document.

This is all that there is to creating hyperlinks, for the time being. I will expand upon the basic form through the book as I discuss different aspects of site and content management systems. For now, you need to look at another kind of interactivity—the form.

Forms

This section is only designed to give you the basics about forms. You will look at how a form is constructed and what the basic parts are, but not what to do once the data has been submitted. The two different methods (Get and Post) were discussed in Chapter 2, and you will look at how to process form data in Chapters 5 and 6.

A form is created by using the `<FORM>` and `</FORM>` tags to contain the form elements. Each element is designed to offer some form of data capture to the user, which can be relayed to the server (or pressed by the client, using client side scripting).

Typically, a form has two attributes filled out—the `ACTION` and the `METHOD`. The action is the location of the script that will process the form contents, and the method indicates the method that will be used in sever side processing (`GET` or `POST`).

In order to specify the elements that are to be used to allow the users to enter data, the `<INPUT>` tag is used. This needs to be accompanied by the `NAME` and `TYPE` attributes. The `NAME` gives the name of the field that will be used by the script on the server (or client) to retrieve the data associated with the field.

The `TYPE` attribute can be one of a variety of different data entry types, of which the most common are likely to be:

- `TEXT`
- `RADIO`
- `CHECKBOX`
- `SUBMIT`

The `TEXT` type is a single line text entry field. The `RADIO` type is usually a group of items, of which only one can be selected. Thus, each item has the same `NAME` attribute, but with different VALUE attributes so that the server can be told which one has been chosen by the user. Only one of the group can be selected at a time.

The HTML for a set of RADIO input types might look like:

```
<INPUT TYPE="RADIO" NAME="SET_1" VALUE="OPTION_1">Option 1<BR/>
<INPUT TYPE="RADIO" NAME="SET_1" VALUE="OPTION_1">Option 2<BR/>
<INPUT TYPE="RADIO" NAME="SET_1" VALUE="OPTION_1">Option 3<BR/>
```

The CHECKBOX type provides a simple checkbox that can be selected. The SUBMIT type provides a button that is used to submit the form data to the server. Putting some of these together, you might construct an address entry form as follows:

```
<FORM ACTION="http://mysite.com/scripts/addaddress" METHOD="POST">
Name: <INPUT TYPE="TEXT" NAME="NAME"><BR />
Address:<BR />
<TEXTAREA NAME="ADDRESS" ROWS="5" COLS="25"></TEXTAREA><BR />
<INPUT TYPE="SUBMIT" VALUE="Add Address">
</FORM>
```

This HTML fragment might be rendered as in Figure 3.18.

Notice the new tag here—<TEXTAREA> and </TEXTAREA>—it allows the users to enter freeform text in a multi-line control. The ROWS attribute specifies the number

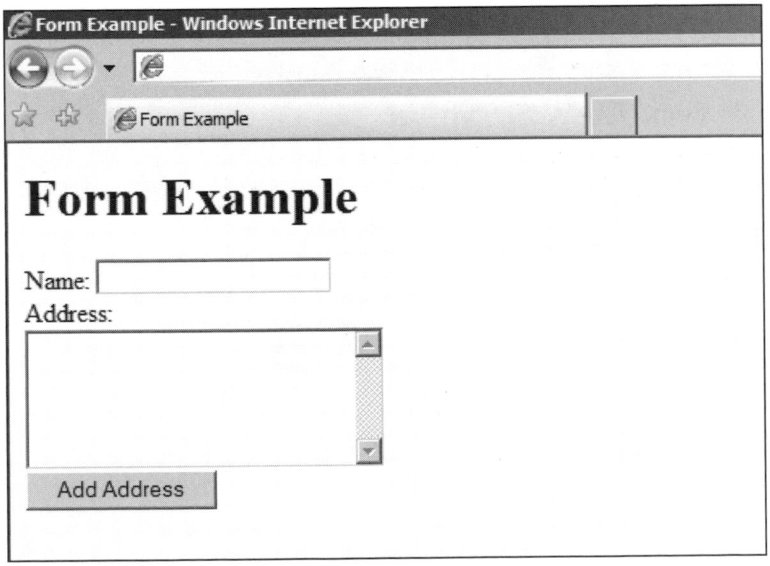

Figure 3.18
Sample form

of lines, and the COLS attribute specifies the number of characters across each row. You will also note that it requires an end tag, unlike other form elements.

Finally, the HIDDEN type is special. It allows you to enter data into the form that the user cannot see without looking at the source of the page. Even then, it is usually designed for innocuous data (that is, data which has no value, such as step information in a wizard) or is heavily encrypted or safeguarded to render it useless to anyone else but the site owner.

In addition to specifying the TYPE attribute (containing "HIDDEN"), you should also specify the NAME and VALUE attributes. The VALUE attribute, in this case, contains the vale that you want to be returned to the server.

Common Symbol Codes

As you will now be aware, there are certain characters that have special meaning in HTML: the two chevrons, for example < and >, as well as quotation marks. Luckily, the HTML standard offers a good solution, by combining the & symbol and a short code that is replaced, by the user agent, by the character that it represents.

The generic format for these short codes, which the W3C calls Character Entity References, is:

&code;

The full list is available from the W3C, but here are the some of the most common:

Code	Symbol	Code	Symbol
<	<	>	>
"	"	©	©
®	®		

There is one other code of particular importance and function, the non-breaking space. The code for this is:

The purpose of the non-breaking space is to insert a space character. You will recall that HTML is parsed as a stream of tokens, separated by whitespace. This whitespace is then discarded, as it is essentially meaningless. Of course, single spaces are retained because they are part of the content.

However, if you actually want two spaces, you need to use the ` ` code to insert a space that cannot be discarded. Why would this be useful? There are many reasons, but one of the most common is to indent child items in hierarchical menus.

The following is an example, with the layout on the left, and the HTML on the right:

Home	`Home `
Services	`Services `
Email	`  Email `
Website	`  Website `

In order to indent the Email and Website items, I have inserted two non-breaking spaces in front of each item. If I had simply used a double space, the items would be lined up along the left side, one above the other.

The entire list of character entity references can be found on the W3C Website at `http://www.w3.org/TR/html401/sgml/entities.html`.

It is also part of a specific set of ISO standards, ISO 8879, which are available from your local ISO office at a price. For the technically minded, you can actually use a direct reference to the Latin-1 character set (also known as ISO 8859-1) by inserting the appropriate character code.

This is done in a similar manner as the character entity name:

`&#number;`

If, for example, you want to insert the character code for a non-breaking space, it would be:

` `

Note the use of the # in this case to signify a decimal number. The last time you saw it was in the definition of color codes, where the numbers were hexadecimal. From this you can deduce that # just denotes data of some kind. Anchors also used it to reference a named section inside a document.

To look up other character codes, you can use your system character map application. Under the Windows operating system, it is located in:

Start→Programs→Accessories→System Tools→Character Map

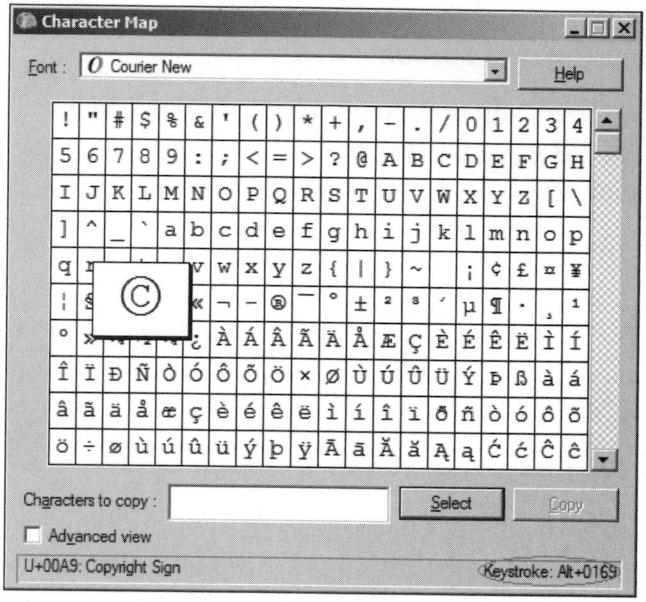

Figure 3.19
The Windows Character Map application

Usage is simple—just pick an appropriate Latin-1 encoded font (Courier New, for example), and select the character that you want to use in your HTML. In Figure 3.19, I have selected the copyright symbol.

In Figure 3.19, you will see that the bottom right corner has been circled in red—this is the code that you need to insert in the HTML, using the &# notation. In this case, it is keystroke Alt+0169, which is how you would access it if you were typing a document. Because you're creating an HTML code, you only need to retain the number:

©

This character reference system can be used with any of the characters in the Latin-1 character set, and is more fully discussed in the aforementioned W3C reference. It is helpful when writing HTML for content publishing frameworks that filter out the character entity names.

XML and XHTML

Now that you know all about HTML, it is time to discuss the newer standard, XHTML. You will find that some of the statements are a little general, but all will become clear as soon as you start deploying HTML in the field.

An HTML document can be seen as a specialization of an XML document. In fact, HTML is based on the SGML standard, and for more detailed information on this, you should consult the W3C Website.

In essence, XML gives you the framework and standards by which you can create documents that contain marked-up content: tags, attributes, and content. It is a standard for data exchange, as discussed in Chapter 2.

It tells you that you need tags, that there must be start and end tags, and that tags can nest but not overlap, along with specific rules for how you inform people what the standards are. One particular rule that you've already seen is in processing end tags.

In HTML, the document definition itself is responsible for telling the user agent whether a tag is allowed to have an end tag. It is assumed that if no end tag is specified, it is forbidden.

However, XML takes a different view. It says that only minimized tags are allowed in cases where no end tag is necessary. Thus, you will see that, when you use the line break tag, in HTML, <BR> was allowed. In XHTML (based on XML), the correct form, and the one you will see here, is <BR />. This is just one example.

XML also allows for attributes (in an extensible way, to refine elements) and standardizes the way that you can present data. In other words, the document can be parsed by knowing how XML works, without needing to know what the document represents. This makes it easy to validate for correctness, but gives no information about rendering.

HTML tells you what kind of tags and attributes you can have by name and usage, whereas XML documents are self-defining. XHTML constructs HTML documents, based on XML principles.

The W3C currently offers XHTML 1.0 as a replacement for pure HTML for those who wish to adopt it. Because these standards are all open, there is no compunction to migrate towards XHTML, especially since HTML 4.01 plus styles and style sheets is more or less stable and well recognized.

There are good reasons for using XHTML, however, and these are explained on the W3C Website. Without going into too much detail, XHTML provides a much more easily adapted and flexible approach to document exchange and allows for better interoperability between agents accessing the content.

This means that, by definition, XHTML documents must be well formed. In other words, the reasonably lax approach to validation used by modern browsers is supposed to be replaced with more strict adherence to XML principles.

In addition, element and attribute names (tags and attributes) must be in lowercase. I have generally used uppercase for HTML 4, as it is more readable and easier to identify the tags from the content.

You have already seen how empty tags are treated, for example, using `<br />` and not `<br>` by itself. Furthermore, elements that are designed to be empty but which may have content should not be used in their minimized form. In other words, you must write `<p></p>` and not `<p/>`.

Even if not using XHTML, Web programmers must get into the habit of producing correct documents, and this starts with respecting these differences. In addition, you should consult the XHTML specification provided by the W3C if you want to write XHTML; because if you say that it is XHTML, it will likely be validated as such in the future.

Part of this, as you have seen, is providing a valid `DOCTYPE`. This is the bare minimum, and should be used to identify the fact that you are providing content that is HTML or XHTML in nature.

Many current sites (Google, Yahoo, and so on) do not actually follow the standards at all, at the time of writing. If you want to check, you can use the W3C validator service at `http://validator.w3.org/` which can tell you of probable standard violations in your HTML.

Browsers obviously want to be as open as possible to all implementations; to do anything different would make them incompatible with a lot of existing content. So, they don't usually adhere 100% to the standards proposed by the W3C, and can sometimes even provide unauthorized extensions.

On top of which, the open nature of XML allows you to extend the mark-up and still remain correct with respect to the XML principle. This means that specific application vendors and providers can process information provided in documents in a special way.

These extensions are another reason why XHTML is a step up from HTML; it allows for you to have these extensions in a more graceful manner. If the user agent does not support a given feature, they can still validate the document, display those elements that are relevant, and leave out those that are not.

XHTML, then is a more correct implementation of HTML (which is an SGML) using the XML standard. Very few new functionalities are in fact added at all, and the work of the W3C is more in line with bringing the existing standard into the XML world.

Recap

This is essentially a reference chapter, in that you have looked at a collection of the most useful HTML tags, seen how you can correctly form your HTML so that it is acceptable in an XHTML world, and learned the key concepts of Web programming.

These are the basic fundamentals upon which you need to build your knowledge to turn the reasonably plain looking HTML documents that the basic tags can produce into something more visually pleasing, using styles. But, before you read the next chapter, please be sure that you have experimented a bit with the examples, and perhaps even created some local Web pages, to test your newfound knowledge.

CHAPTER 4

CSS AND STYLES

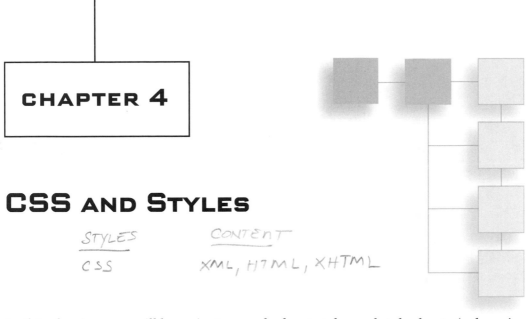

STYLES   *CONTENT*

CSS   *XML, HTML, XHTML*

In this chapter, you will learn just enough about styles and style sheets (otherwise known as CSS) to be able to deploy them on a daily basis. There is enough information to achieve something concrete, but not so much as to cloud what should be a simple issue—you want the content to reflect the design, but be able to change it on a whim without recoding everything from the ground up.

Not everything in the CSS standard is covered, because that would not be helpful; naturally you will learn more about CSS and its applications as you use it in real projects. The W3C maintains an excellent repository of detailed and interlinked information that can be referred to if esoteric code is encountered: for the most part, everything you need is here.

Style sheets solve a very specific problem—how to attach specific information pertaining to the rendering of HTML while remaining within XML and HTML guidelines. Moreover, you might want to define that information separately from the actual content, to facilitate maintenance or just a change to the look and feel.

This is part of the principle of separating content from layout, something you'll meet again in Chapter 8, when you look at Content Management Systems (CMS). If you want to build a CMS that is as future-proof as possible, you need to be able to separate the style (colors), the flow (layout), and the content as far as possible.

future-proof ;
does not risk becoming outdated
too quickly ?

Styles solve this very easily—they provide an addition to the Web programmer's toolbox that's XML compliant (styles can be used with both HTML and XML/XHTML) and provides an interface to set any of a number of properties, as well as a way to create named variations (classes) of specific tags.

So, if you want a purple heading, you can create a named derivation of the `<h1>` tag and adjust the text color in the style. Then, whenever you use the new class (`<h1 class="PurpleText">`), the browser knows what to do with it. This makes styles very easy to apply and keeps them separate from the HTML.

Styles are created using the `"text/css"` language (remember that you learned in the last chapter that HTML is specified as `"text/html"`). Style *sheets* are an external implementation of styles. You can introduce styles in three places:

Inline = at the same time as tag

- Inline (at the same time as the tag, such as `<h1 style="color: purple;">`...)

- Internally, as part of the `<head>` of the document

- Externally, in style sheets

External style sheets are a good idea if you need to be able to swap between styles (think of the different Blogger.com layouts, for example) without changing the actual XHTML that defines the content. If the content is generated, you can benefit from an external style sheet because you simply need to give the browser the reference to a different sheet, and the style change is reflected through the content.

There are actually two flavors of style sheet languages—CSS and XSL—which exist to perform slightly different functions. Generally, you will use CSS throughout this book, but in future projects, you may find that XSL becomes necessary.

The difference between CSS and XSL is that where CSS just adds style to existing content, XSL actually provides the possibility to transform the content into something different—be it CSS and HMTML, XHTML, or XML. Therefore, XSL is a *transformation* language, defined in XML (so as to be self-validating and self-referential).

XSL takes XML and transforms it into HTML

CSS does not transform the content, allowing the browser only to display the existing content in a specific way having interpreted the style information. If you need to take one data format (say XML) and transform it into something else, like HTML, XSL provides a way to do that.

You'll look at XSL briefly when you read about Web 2.0 and XML processing, as it is just one way in which you can deploy XSL in a Web 2.0 environment. However, many things can be achieved with client side processing of incoming XML data (the main reason for using XSL is to transform it into HTML), which you look at in Chapter 5.

Remember that CSS (styles) just manipulate the properties of existing items in the page, it does not change the content. This means that the rendering of any object can be updated by the browser, either statically or dynamically, with client side scripting and *without* changing the content itself.

Ref. to Client-side scripting

It also means that the presentation of generated content can be changed without updating the content itself. As mentioned, an example of this is in a CMS, where the content is stored in a database. At the storage point, the content is just text, which is then rendered (converted from database entries into an HTML page) by a server side script.

CMS Changes presentation only

An application of CSS to Databases

DATABASE → script → render → HTML

That style information is used to tell the browser how to display the content. If the style information is stored outside the script generating the page, as a style sheet, the generated content need only refer to it. The server side code can then remain the same, even if it is necessary to change the style used to render the content.

So, to change the look and feel, you need only to update one small item in the database; this means that users can change between predefined styles as well.

To do this, you need to manipulate the Document Model that you last saw in Chapter 3, attaching style information to the elements rendered by the Web browser.

Caution

Note that because styles are designed to be used with XML as well as HTML, I have presented all the code in XML standard: with the tags in lowercase, rather than uppercase. If you want your style information and HTML to be XHTML compliant (as noted in Chapter 3), it *must* be in lowercase no matter how hard that makes the resulting document source to read!

The Document Model, Revisited

In the previous chapter, I talked about the Document Model. All that it is, is a way to describe a document that contains more than just text. A plain text file has no real Document Model, as it is just flat text with no real style information. A

Word document has style information for bold headings, plain text, and so forth, called "Styles."

Each one of these Word Styles can be adjusted to taste, and is reflected through the Word document. So it is also for HTML—each object (element) in the page has properties, and you refer to each one through the Document Model. The Document Model can be seen as a tree, where the document is at the bottom, and each block element (<div>, <p>, heading, table, list, and so on) can be a branch, or leaf, on that tree.

Each element has properties, but in HMTL most of these are hidden because they have default behavior that is well understood. For example, the <b> tag makes whatever text is enclosed in it bold. The <font> tag has no default behavior, and so you can attach properties to it:

```
<font face="Arial">This is Arial Text</Font>
```

Styles give access to all properties, so that they can be changed, but to prevent collisions with existing definitions, you can give any derived styles new names, much as you can in Word.

Tags and Styles

Each tag in an HTML document can be altered with the application of a style, and that style will override any default behavior (or augment it) that the tag might have had. The W3C actually defines a style sheet for XHTML 1.0, which gives the default style information for the tags that are defined in that standard.

Using styles means, for example, that you can change the meaning of the bold tag to use a different color or some other text decoration. The published W3C default style sheet for HTML 4 (http://www.w3.org/TR/CSS21/sample.html), for example, describes the styles for each of the defined tags.

The trouble with overriding those tags so that they reflect the kind of styles that you want to display is that doing this makes the changes document wide. If you define the bold tag as being green and bold, that will be applied each time you use the <b> tag. This might not be convenient.

For example, if there is some black text on a green background, having a single color (green) defined for bold text is clearly not going to work. Now, you could use HTML tags such as the font tag to change that color, but this means inserting specific style related information directly in the HTML, which is exactly what you are trying to avoid.

The CSS way to achieve this is to separate your tags into *classes*. Each class becomes a specialization of a tag, with a user-defined name, thus keeping its definition apart from other tags with similar meanings. These objects are *derived* from the basic HTML elements.

So, to create a specialization of the h1 class, you would write:

```
h1.my_heading { color: "blue"; }
```
← element class

This would turn all the text in h1 tags, which were indicated as belonging to the my_heading class, blue. To access this, you would then write:

```
<h1 class="my_heading">H1 In Blue</h1>
```

This might need some more explanation, so let's look at how to use derived objects in detail.

Derived Objects   (accessing special objects)

Deriving objects means that you can create special versions of tags and assign them a *class* name. You can use any of the HTML tags for this purpose and attach style information to them. The default properties defined for the derived tag will not change unless negated by a specific piece of user-defined style information.

So, you typically override those bits that you want to be rendered differently, and leave the rest alone. There are exceptions to this, which you'll see soon. It is also not possible, except under special circumstances, to alter the behavior associated with a tag—a <ul> for example, will always be a list, and a <table> will always be a table.

You can change the flow, layout, position, and size, and even adjust the parameters so that the resulting rendering might not look much like a list or table, but the behavior will remain the same: the content in the <ul> must be contained within <li> tags, for example, and each row of the table (<tr>) must still contain cells (<td>).

To derive your own version of a tag, you simply name the class in the tag:

```
<h1 class="my_heading_1">Heading 1</h1>
```

Then, you create a style for my_heading_1 that reflects the way that you want the browser to render it. So, as before, you create a statement such as:

```
h1.my_heading_1 { color:"blue"; }
```

Using css

Exactly where this is done is the subject of the next section of this chapter entitled "Setting Up Style Sheets." Before you look at that, let's review two common, powerful, and easy-to-use tags: <div> and <span>. These are commonly derived to provide some great visual effects, using exactly the same syntax as in the simple heading example.

The <div> and <span> Tags

Branch/ Leaf property

The <div> is a block level element. In other words, in a Document Model tree it can be either a branch (containing sub-blocks) or a leaf (containing only text to be rendered). It is almost a document within the document.

A block defined with the <div> tag can have specific borders, background, margins, text styles, and so on. The default text formatting for content inside is inherited from the <div> tag, so a list, for example, will have the same font as the other content.

→ acts like <p>

Leaf property only

The <span> is an inline element. Therefore, it cannot have all the properties of a block level element like <div>, but can have specific a background, font, and text decoration. It also does not separate itself from other blocks, like <div>, which adds space between itself and the next block level element, much like the <p> tag does. <span>, on the other hand, does not interrupt the flow of text.

The <div> and <span> tags can both be used to make classes. The mechanism is much the same as for the <h1> tag that you saw previously:

```
<div class="sidebar_menu">
  <span class="sidebar_menu_item">Item One</span><br/>
</div>
```

From this snippet, you will note that I have started to lay out the code in a more readable way. This is purely so that you can see where the tags are and how they are defined—there is no relation between how you write the code and how the content is rendered in regard to whitespace. A carriage return does not start a new line without the <br/> tag.

A final note about the `<div>` and `<span>` tags is that they have very few default properties set. So, they are blank canvases for you to apply style information to. To do that, you need to know how to set up style sheets.

Setting Up Style Sheets

A style consists of three parts:

- The selector—The object, or part of the HTML document
- The property—The attribute (property) of the object
- The value—A valid value for that property

The style mechanism works in the following way. When you create a selector, you do so using a dotted notation to select a tag and name a new class (if you are deriving your own class). Then, in curly brackets (`{` and `}`) that I shall call *braces* from here on in, you specify each property and value, separated by a colon and terminated by a semicolon.

The layout of the notation can be quite varied, there being no set standard, but the book uses one of two possible variants:

```
tag.class { multiple properties; }
```

or   *"Selector object"*

```
tag.class {
    property: value;
    property: value;
        }
```

Programmers will note that the closing brace does not have a semicolon. The class may not be required, which results in notation such as

```
tag { multiple properties; }
```

or

```
tag {
    property: value;
    property: value;
      }
```

[handwritten margin note: tag.class { property: value }]

In all cases, tag (or tag.class) is the selector and the property: value combination or combinations that set the actual style data are always contained within braces. This only changes when you use *inline styles*, something that I cover later on, but which I do not recommend, for a number of reasons.

Where a single line is used, the multiple properties must be supplied with semicolons splitting them, just like with the multi-line variant. It actually makes no difference to the Web browser, unless either the colons, semicolons, or braces are missing, because it will remove any whitespace from the code layout, as it does when parsing HTML. *[handwritten: NO WHITESPACE in its final form.]*

So, the layout mentioned here is purely for human convenience. *[handwritten: ✓]*

Setting multiple properties at once also has a shorthand where single properties can be combined. In other words, there are certain properties that can be grouped into a single statement, thus negating the need to be long-winded when defining a object that has multiple possible properties that can be set, or multiple components.

For example, a border has four sides, and there are often four variants of the border property, for example:

```
border-top    border-left    border-bottom    border-right
```

[handwritten margin note: tag.class]

To set the style (say dotted or solid), you can specify each property independently:

```
div.odd_borders { border-top-style: solid; border-bottom-style: dotted; }
```
[handwritten annotations: prop1, val1, prop2, val2]

These can also be combined in a specific order (top, right, bottom, and left) into a single property setting: *[handwritten: Conventional order for Border properties to be applied]*

```
div.odd_borders { border-style: solid solid dotted solid; }
```

This is rendered in Figure 4.1.

As mentioned, these styles can be set in different places in an HTML document, and the notation changes slightly accordingly. There are:

- Inline styles—As a tag property

- Internal styles—Defined along with the head of the document

- External style sheets—As separate documents

Like so many of the aspects of HTML and CSS, these are purely human conveniences. The rendering will be no different if you use an external style sheet or

Figure 4.1
Odd borders

an inline style, but there are big implications for maintainability and updatability of the style information.

or the way it gets stored

Inline Styles

Inline styles are defined where the HTML is actually introduced, as if they are properties of the tag that they are creating a specialization of. For example, you can set a new kind of heading style with the following:

```
<html>
<head>Example Inline Styles</head>
<body>
<h1 style="text-decoration: underline overline; font-weight: bolder;">
Heading 1
</h1>
</body>
</html>
```

This goes inside the tags of HTML code...

< > style = " property : val; " < />

Inline Style

This code is rendered as in Figure 4.2.

The convenience of this is that specific style information can be attached to each element separately. It cannot, however, be easily changed in multiple places. If you want each heading to be defined as in the previous example, you would need to attach the appropriate style to each one, as evidenced in Figure 4.2.

Changing it difficult

So is replacing.

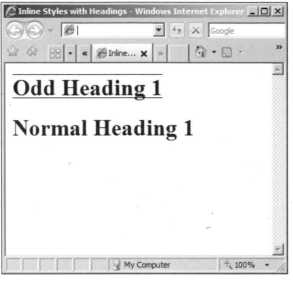

Figure 4.2
Odd headings

This is the inconvenience of inline styles. A side effect is that you would need to recode all of the HTML pages to change the style, say to change the text color or remove the overline. This might be massively time-consuming. *(or it might not be)*

Part of this can be mitigated if a server side script is being used to generate the HTML and inline styles. However, if the style data is to be generated by a server side script, it will still be a lot of work to change both the content generation and the style generation because it is intertwined in the code. You'll look at this in more detail in Chapter 6.

A better approach, if you want to use styles that are local to a specific document, is to put the style data in a single place in the file, using an internal style sheet.

Internal Style Sheets

Located in <head> sort of like a script would be

Internal style sheets are defined in the <head> section of the document, along with elements like the <title> and <meta> tags. Scripts also go in here, as you'll see in Chapter 5, so it is a good place to embed some specific style information.

The style sheets are embedded inside a special style tag that is part of the <head> section, and has a property that defines the type of style sheet that is being used. For example:

```
<head>
  <title>Example Style Placement</title>
```

```
<style type="text/css">
  <!-- style statements here -->
</style>
</head>
<body>
  <!-- page content here -->
</body>
```

[handwritten: embedded style]

[handwritten: Watch out it is not replaced/overwritten by a script output]

The disadvantage with this approach is that if the page is to be generated by a server, you again need to provide code to write the style information as well. At least, using this approach, you only need to change the code that generates the <head> section and the style with it. All the style information is in one place and applied to the document in question.

This might not be convenient, though, especially if you have multiple pages with similar style information (you need to generate the style for each one, wasting bandwidth), or if you want to be able to use the same specialized classes, but with different styles, depending on the circumstances.

[handwritten: Don't]

To do this, you need to use external style sheets.

[handwritten: WHY? Doesn't make sense]

[handwritten: New classes are easily made so no need to repeat use them]

[handwritten: (Preferable for)]

External Style Sheets

[handwritten: scalable]

External style sheets are defined in a file that is external to the HTML page itself, but that is referenced from the HTML document via a special kind of tag in the <head> called <link>.

```
<link href="mystyle.css" rel="stylesheet" type="text/css" />
```

Without going into too much detail, the href simply gives the URI for the style sheet—a location—just like you do with images, other Web pages, and so on in regular HTML objects. The URI contains the location of the style sheet, expressed here as being in the same location as the Web page.

[handwritten: Location of sheet]

However, as you'll see in the CMS chapter (Chapter 8), many systems group style information in specific places. So, you might equally well end up with URIs such as:

```
href="http://myserver.com/cms/styles/default/blue.css"
```

The rel gives the relationship between the page and the resource, in this case a style to be applied to the HTML document that contains the link. The type, as before, tells the browser that the file contains text of the CSS language.

The external style sheet file itself (with the .css extension), with no preamble, can go straight into the style data. It is just a plain text file that begins with the first style and ends with the last one. It can contain comments, too, just like in HTML.

Properties

Firstly, a quick reminder about how properties are set in styles. They can be done explicitly, property by property, for example:

```
tag.class { property: value } i.e. h1.inverted { color: white; }
```

They can also be set in a shorthand, by compiling a list of multiple property settings, attached to a single named property. There are two types of this kind of named property.

The first is for setting multiple properties for a tag or class, the second is for setting properties across common components, like the sides of a box that has a border. So, you can set all the borders to be dotted, red, of width 10 pixels in a single statement:

```
div.dotted_borders { border: 10px dotted red; }
```

This example groups style statements and applies them to multiple elements. The properties need to be given in the correct order, although if you miss one, the browser will figure it out and render the result appropriately. Of course, if an invalid value is used, and the browser cannot decide what it represents, and the results will vary.

It is also possible to group style information and apply it so a single element that makes up a collection. So, you can apply the shorthand style to a single border, with the following:

```
div.dotted_sidebar { border-left: 10px dotted red; }
```

This is shorthand for:

```
div.dotted_sidebar {
  border-left-width: 10px;
  border-left-style: dotted;
  border-left-color: red;
   }
```

With this in mind, let's now look at some different kinds of properties.

Positioning Properties

Most of the following needs to be understood with respect to the viewport—the bit of the document currently visible—and how it relates to the document. In essence, the viewport is like a window on the document: different browsers display different parts of the document in the viewport.

This is because different users have different screen resolutions, or different browser window sizes. Toolbars, for example, encroach on the available screen real estate for the document to be displayed in. So, the bottom of a document that coincides with the bottom of the viewport on one platform might not share that relationship with other users' platforms.

In order to help get around these differences, different kinds of positioning modes are permitted.

Positioning

First, there is *absolute positioning,* which allows an element to be placed on the document surface (canvas) at a precise location. This location is an offset from the elements containing block. So, if the containing block has a left edge that is 50 pixels from the left side of the screen, and you define a new block with a left edge of 50 pixels, it will end up 100 pixels from the left side.

A containing block is just a block level container, such as a `<div>`, which can be positioned. Spanning tags such as `<span>` cannot be accurately positioned in this way as they are not block level.

The following properties are allowed:

```
left  right  bottom  top
```

These can be specified as either percentages or pixel values, depending on the way that the content author chooses to lay out the document. If a percentage is used, it is with reference to the containing block.

Within the category of absolute positioning, *fixed positioning* does not allow the item to move when the page is scrolled; it becomes fixed at the absolute point that it has been set with reference to the viewport. Anything that is behind the fixed items can be scrolled as normal using the scroll bar, but the fixed items will remain fixed in their places.

Caution

Internet Explorer 7 handles absolute and fixed positioning in the same way, and does not fix them to the viewport as defined by the CSS2 standard. Firefox, however, interprets fixed as being fixed to the viewport, and absolute as being absolute with reference to the document itself.

In both cases, content that extends beyond the specific height of the box will cause it to extend itself, unless fixed is specified. Naturally, this only works for Firefox, as IE seems to ignore the fixed value.

To be cross-browser compatible, it is wise only to use absolute positioning, based on the flow of the document. To define fixed items, you can use client side scripting instead.

To specify an absolute position for a box, for example, you might find a style:

```
div.inside_box {
    position: absolute;
    border-top: 1px dotted black;
    text-align: center;
    width: 100px;
    height: 100px;
    top:100px;
    right: 0;
    bottom: 0;
    left: 25px;
    background-color: white;
      }
```

The result of this is Figure 4.3.

The alternative is relative positioning, which is the default. Position information supplied is considered to be an offset from the containing block, so if a value of 10px is supplied for the left property of a contained paragraph, the paragraph will be offset by 10 pixels from the left side of the containing block.

When positioning is used, quite often you will find that the text "underneath" does not quite flow around the objects that you position. This can be changed using floating positioning, which useful because it specifies a box (image, division, and so on) that is shifted to the left or right of the current line and allows text to flow around it using the float property.

For example, suppose that two styles are defined:

```
div.outer_div {
  width:200px;
  background-color:gray;
```

```
  color:white;
  }
p.floating_para {
  float:right;
  width:50px;
  border:2 dotted white;
  text-align:right;
  background-color:silver;
}
```

In the floating_para, the float: property has been set to right. This style information was used to create the layout shown in Figure 4.4.

In Figure 4.4, no matter the size of the viewport, the text will always be made to flow around the paragraph. This is useful for resource boxes, or sidebars containing additional, separate, but related information. They can be further separated from the flow of text using margins, padding, and borders.

Margins

All block level elements have a margin, which gives the offset of the content of the containing block from the outside edge of the inner block. This applies equally to

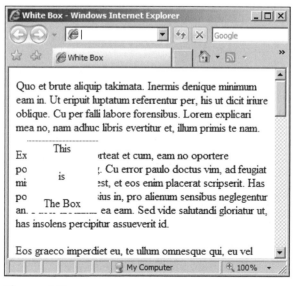

Figure 4.3
White box

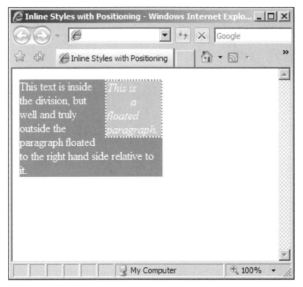

Figure 4.4
Floating paragraph

divisions, paragraphs, table cells, and so on, which all contain content inside a formatting box.

Another way to look at it is that a margin is outside of the block to which it applies. For example, if you redefine the floating paragraph from the previous example as:

```
p.floating_para {
    float:right;
    width:50px;
    border:2 dotted white;
    text-align:right;
    background-color:silver;
    margin: 25px;
}
```

This yields the result in Figure 4.5 that you can compare with Figure 4.4; the top-rightmost edge of the floating paragraph is offset by 25 pixels from the outer edge of the containing division.

Margins can be set explicitly—`margin-left/right/top/bottom`—but also as a group margin, as in the previous example. If you wanted to get rid of the outer margin, leaving only a gap between the left and bottom edges, you would use:

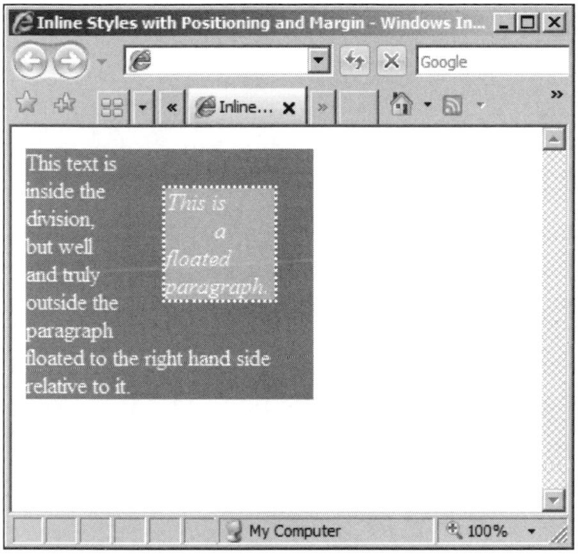

Figure 4.5
Floating paragraph with a margin

```
margin-left: 25px;
 margin-bottom: 25px;
```

To create a gap around the inside of the paragraph, you need to use padding.

Padding

Padding is applied inside the block, in the same way that a margin is applied around the outside. Again, this effect applies equally well to all kinds of block level elements, this time creating a gap around the inside of the bounding box. For example, you could add padding to any of the previous examples:

```
div.outer_div {
    width:200px;
    background-color:gray;
    color:white;
    padding: 5px;
    }
  p.floating_para {
    float:right;
    width:50px;
    border:2 dotted white;
    text-align:right;
    background-color:silver;
```

```
    margin: 5px;
    padding: 5px;
}
```

The two `padding` properties keep the text away from the edge, but do not create gaps between the content and any inner floating blocks of content. Hence, to retain the gap around the floating paragraph, you need to retain the `margin`. The result is as shown in Figure 4.6.

Like margins, padding can be set explicitly—`padding-left/right/top/bottom`—or as a group, as in the code that produced Figure 4.6. Note that I have added padding to both the division (`outer_div`) as well as to the floating paragraph.

One feature of the floating paragraph is the border, something not yet covered.

Borders

The preceding examples have used a border to show you the effect of the formatting. For example, there is a dotted border around the floating paragraph in Figures 4.4 to 4.6, to separate it from the content inside the outer division block. The border is, by default, positioned between the margin and the padding (if there is any of either specified).

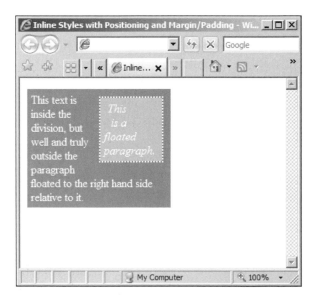

Figure 4.6
Floating paragraph with a margin and padding

As with other box-based parameters, borders can be set explicitly or as a group, as you have seen on previous occasions. There are three basic parameters that each border can be set with:

- Width—The width, in pixels, percentage, or relative measurement

- Style—For example, solid, dotted, and so on

- Color—The color

You'll look at the actual values later, in the short reference, because there are many settings that can be applied. There are three ways that the parameters can be specified. You can group a border by edge, for example:

```
border-top: width style color;
```

The parameters can be grouped for all edges, by property, for example:

```
border-width: width;
border-style: solid;
border-color: red;
```

Finally, they can be set explicitly for a specific edge-property combination, for example:

```
border-top-width: 5px;
border-bottom-style: dotted;
border-right-color: blue;
border-left: 10px solid red;
```

Adding this to the floating paragraph in place of the existing border code yields the output shown in Figure 4.7.

You will note that (although you cannot see the colors) the style information for the top and right borders has not been applied. This is because there is style information missing. This is a good lesson to learn—it is better to over-specify the styles so that all possible parameters are covered and not rely on any automatic handling on the part of the browser.

Pseudo-Classes

So far, all of the examples have concentrated on elements that have a specific place in the document model (tree). Style information is then attached to them on the basis of their named occurrence or the default class attached to them.

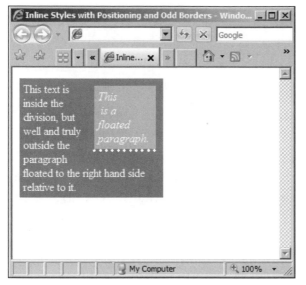

Figure 4.7
Floating paragraph with odd borders

However, there are some elements that do not fall into this framework, or do not have specific default classes attached to them. For example, actions such as hovering over or clicking on a link can be applied to multiple elements, and their style information is contained within *pseudo-classes*.

CSS allows you to create pseudo-classes of properties, and pseudo-elements to give you objects to refer to, for those things that are not included within the basic document model or are not explicit properties or elements under the HTML element definition.

This is quite advanced use of CSS, but can be very powerful, and is mentioned here because that power can be useful. It is better to know about and have to refer back to it rather than try to remember all of the techniques. There are some pseudo-classes that you will use quite often and others that you will never see again.

Link Pseudo-Classes

These pseudo-classes are attached to any anchor (that is, an `href`) that refers to a resource that can be clicked to from the document. A URL that points to another HTML page, for example, has some properties that are part of the `link` pseudo-class.

Typically, these are underlined and colored in blue or purple, depending on whether the link has been visited. The colors that are applied are potentially browser-dependent, but the standard appears to be blue, underlined, and purple, also underlined.

The browser will reset the color after a period of time, as the link moves from being recently visited to just another link. Now, the color and decoration is applied as a style that can be manipulated using style information.

To change the link and visited link, for colors and decoration that are different from the default, style information such as the following could be used:

```
a:link { color: green; }
a:visited { text-decoration:overline; }
```

This changes the color to green and adjusts the decoration, but all other text-formatting properties (see the section entitled "CSS Objects and Properties Short Reference" that follows) can also be used. Also, certain box formatting such as borders and backgrounds can also be applied.

However, these are more commonly used with the dynamic pseudo-classes that are activated as a result of interacting with the mouse. Dynamic pseudo-classes work in much the same way as the link pseudo-class.

Dynamic Pseudo-Classes

When the mouse pointer moves into range of a clickable element (link, button, and so on), it generates a dynamic event that can be trapped. There are three such events, each of which is mapped to a dynamic pseudo-class. The three events are:

- Hover: When the mouse is over an item

- Active: When the user clicks the button, but before it is released

- Focus: When the element can accept keyboard input

So, to change the background color, when a user hovers over a link, for example, code such as the following could be used:

```
a:hover { background: gray; }
```

When the user clicks the item, it is activated, and the resulting style can be changed with code such as the following:

```
a:active { color: white; }
```

Finally, for those elements that accept input from the keyboard, such as tabbed over links and form controls, their style can be changed with code such as:

```
a:focus { border: 1 dotted red; }
```

The properties that can be changed will differ from one element to another. Form elements such as buttons, for example, may have different formatting possibilities that lead to different style options.

Pseudo-Elements

Finally, there are elements that have no corresponding tag in HTML. In other words, they might be contained within a tag or just be outside the document model. They are, however, quite browser-dependent, and so I will cover only two of them here.

The two pseudo-elements that I do cover, as they are interpreted in the same way under Internet Explorer and Firefox, are:

- The first line of a block (div, p, and so on)

- The first letter of an inline or block element (span, block, p, and so on)

Note that the first line might not be as long or short as you think, depending on the way that the users have positioned and sized their browsers. It is possible to make sure (using specific font sizes in points and bounding boxes in pixels) that the text takes the same space on every platform, but often this is not desirable.

In such cases, the browser will break the line according to the space available and the formatting options (margins, padding, and so on) that are applied at the time that the line is rendered. Without using precise measurements in the styles, the only way to guarantee that the line meets your needs is to include a <br /> tag.

(This might have other undesirable effects, such as a too-short first line, so it is better to leave the line break decision to the browser.)

Bearing these caveats in mind, the first-line and first-letter pseudo-elements can be used to set formatting styles and are quite useful. If the first letter of each work of the first line of a block should be in uppercase (for example), you can use:

```
div.article:first-line { text-transform: capitalize; }
```

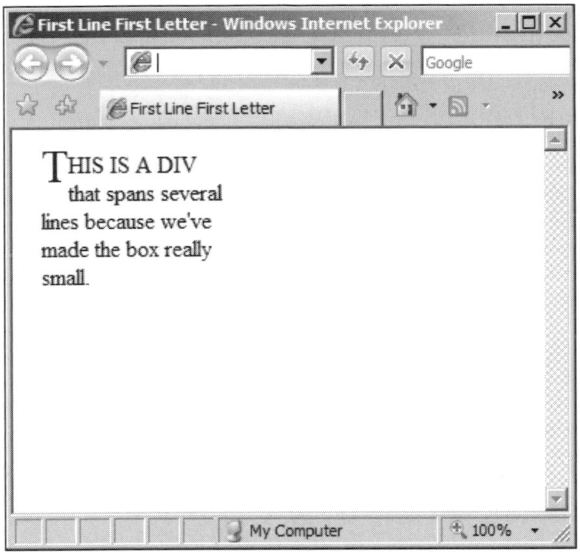

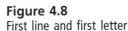

Figure 4.8
First line and first letter

If you assume that the very first letter should be given extra importance, you can add the following:

```
div.article:first-letter { font-size: 14pt; }
```

Sometimes, you will need to add other properties to make the text flow better, which is where having better (more precise) control over the box formatting comes into play. For example, you can use the following:

```
div { width: 150px; margin:10px;}
div:first-line { text-transform: uppercase; }
div:first-letter { font-size: 200%; float:left; }
```

This gives the result in Figure 4.8.

Without the float specified in the division, the effect is not quite the same, and you might like to experiment with different floats for the first letter to see how the text flows around it with different settings of float.

CSS Objects and Properties Short Reference

This section contains a rundown of the most useful combinations of objects and properties that can be defined in HTML with CSS. Not every possible combination of tag and style is covered, because this would be inappropriate for those trying to obtain a working knowledge of the topic.

It is therefore not designed to replace the W3C official appendix to HTML CSS (Appendix F: `http://www.w3.org/TR/1998/REC-CSS2-19980512/propidx.html`) but it is a useful application of some of the objects and properties.

In essence, this chapter provides an overview of the most common uses for HTML and CSS, and those sticking rigidly to "Just Enough" principles will find that it suites their needs perfectly. There is no extraneous detail, just the most commonly used objects and styles.

Background

Background properties can be used with practically any element, from divisions and table cells to the document body itself. It is most useful with the body itself, as well as tables and divisions, to set the background color or possibly to add an image.

The background color can be set with styles such as:

```
background-color : red;
background-color : #f00;
background-color : #ff0000;
```

So, to set the background for a division, code such as the following can be used:

```
div.warning_text {
  background-color: red;
    }
```

It is also possible to specify a background image, using an URI to point to the image on the server, with code such as:

```
background-image: url("http://www.server.com/myimage.jpg")
```

The image will scroll with the rest of the content, but it can be fixed to the viewport by specifying fixed as a value for the `background-attachment` property. For example:

```
body {
  background-image: url("http://www.server.com/myimage.jpg");
  background-attachment : fixed;
}
```

If the image is smaller than the allotted space (canvas), it is also possible to make it repeat to cover the available space. This is known as *tiling*, and is typically performed by the browser by starting in the center of the horizontal or vertical axis and repeating the image from the center out towards the edges.

The `background-repeat` property is used to set this behavior. There are four possible settings, from which one may be chosen:

```
background-repeat : repeat repeat-x repeat-y no-repeat
```

If `repeat` is specified, the image is tiled throughout the background, starting from the center of the background. If `repeat-x` or `repeat-y` is specified, the image is repeated in either the horizontal or vertical axis, working from the inside out.

Borders, Margins, and Padding

Box formatting styles generally contain properties for individual borders and styles as well as supporting grouping of properties and styles. For example, you can set the border color (or width, style, and so on) for the box using the appropriate selector with a named parameter:

```
div.warning_text {
   border-color: black;
   border-width: 2px;
   border-style: solid;
    }
```

On the other hand, you can also set specific border colors using one of two methods—first by using the specific `edge-color` property:

```
border-top-color: black;
```

The second method for setting a single color (or width, style, and so on) is through grouping values, such as:

```
border-color: black red blue white;
```

Remember that the order is important—top, right, bottom, left—so the previous example will assign black to the top border, red to the right border, blue to the bottom, and white to the left side. The last kind of property grouping can be used to set all the borders to specific width, color, and style using code such as:

```
border: 2px black dashed;
```

Like background settings, borders can be applied to many kinds of elements, including block and inline elements. They can be combined with the dynamic pseudo-classes, too, to provide additional visual clues and interactivity.

They are best used with the `div` tag to provide areas of the screen that are naturally separated into areas, as a way to highlight the different uses of each area. When used with absolute positioning, borders can make a page that has specific areas like navigation and advertising that are in appropriate places.

The width can be set as a number or as a relative size. The relative sizes include a predefined value (thin, medium, or thick) or a percentage. The relative sizes can be unreliable, so leave the choice of width to the user agent—be it a Web browser or something else.

However, for a Web browser, you should generally use pixel measurements for the best effect (they offer the most control), resorting to percentages when you are unsure as to the actual screen resolution of the user's browser platform. The obvious advantage of using percentages is, of course, that they minimize the chance that a navigation or advertising pane will be in an area of the screen that must be scrolled to in order to make it visible.

So the border width can be set as a number:

```
border-width: 25%;     For a relative percentage
border-width: 2px;     For a pixel value
```

Or, it can be set as a predefined relative thickness:

```
border-width: thin;
```

The border color can be set using standard HTML named colors, or #RRGGBB values. These are identical to the colors and hexadecimal values discussed in Chapter 3 and follow the same rules.

There is also an additional possibility, the #RGB setting, which allows the designer to use single digit 0-F values which are then multiplied to fill the #RRGGBB hexadecimal values traditionally used. So, #FAB becomes #FFAABB, meaning that #FFF is white and #000 is black.

Therefore, the following are all equivalent:

```
border-color: blue;
border-color: #00f;
border-color: #0000ff;
```

The case of the color specifier does not matter. However, XHTML convention, based on XML, would suggest that lowercase is possibly the default choice for those working with XHTML, and that uppercase is normally used by those who have a background in HTML.

In addition to the width and color of the border, there are many styles that can be set. These are set with code such as:

```
<div style="border-style:groove; text-align: center;">
<p><b>Groove Border</b></p>
 </div>
```

This is a snippet from a longer piece that produced the image in Figure 4.9, showing the currently supported options (dotted, dashed, solid, double, groove, and ridge).

The borders in Figure 4.9 were set as inline styles as div element properties inside a borderless table (covered in Chapter 3). They could equally well have been set as table borders, with the additional caveat that this would have merged them, as all the cells share the same walls in a table.

So, the different types of borders can be set with statements such as:

```
<div style="border-style:dotted; text-align: center;">
```

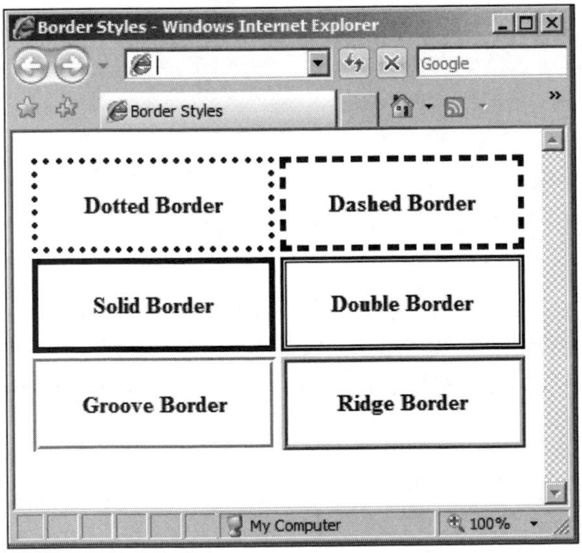

Figure 4.9
Border styles

The available styles—`dotted`, `dashed`, `solid`, `double`, `groove`, and `ridge`—can all be set per side or for the element as a whole (as in the example). As noted, they can be combined with the other elements and specified per side:

```
border-top: 2px double red;
```

And, each of the properties can be set individually, again either per side or for the whole element border at once. This gives very precise control over the styles, while also offering the possibility to create short forms of the style to set the properties quickly and easily.

Finally, blocks can have margins and padding, which can also be set side by side or applied to the whole block. Examples of this have been introduced already, but to recap, the margin is the distance from the outside formatting box to the border, and the padding is the distance from the border to the content inside the block.

Experimentation will often be your best guide to get the right look, especially because the margin and padding values *add to* the width of the element. The best way to think of this is to imagine that the width value specified is the width of the content and that the margins and padding then add to that measurement.

So, to specify a ten-pixel margin all around, you would use the following:

```
margin: 10px;
```

To specify only the top and bottom margins, you would use a style such as:

```
margin-top: 5px;
margin-bottom: 5px;
```

Padding might be inside the border, but otherwise works in the same way as margins, so you can specify the padding for the whole block level element as:

```
padding: 10px;
```

You can also set the individual padding side by side:

```
padding-top: 5px;
padding-bottom: 5px;
```

Typically, you use margins and padding with the `body`, `div`, and `table` elements as a way to lay out the page in conjunction with borders and shading.

Text and Fonts

Any text block or span can have its text and font properties set; this includes the div, p, table, and span elements. The font, color, spacing, decoration (under-lining, for example), line height, weight (bold, for example), and alignment (center, right, and so on) can all be specified using styles.

In addition, href elements (like the <a href... tag) as well as others can also have their text style settings specified. This allows for specific colorization or customization of the font properties for different kinds of links (inline, menu, image, and so on) within a document, above and beyond those asso-ciated with the dynamic pseudo-classes mentioned in the "Pseudo-Classes" section.

The most basic setting is the only one that doesn't have a text- or font- prefix, and is used to set the text color:

```
color: <name> or value
```

As before, and as with all color settings, you can use #RRGGBB, #RGB, or the accepted XHTML names. So, for example, the following are identical:

```
p.red_text { color: red; }
p.red_text { color: #F00; }
p.red_text { color: #ff0000; }
```

all produce
identical result or output, visually.

To change more than the color, you can assign values to properties in the same way as for other elements using style statements. The first of these is the font-style property, which allows you to select among the following:

```
font-style: normal, italic, or oblique
```

In most browsers, italic and oblique are rendered in the same way, as are the different weights that can be set with font-weight. This is clearly shown in Figure 4.10, which gives various styles and weights alongside normal text for comparison.

The weight is set with the following style statement:

```
font-weight: normal, bold, bolder, lighter
```

However, as Figure 4.10 shows, the only font style and weights that are rendered any differently tend to be italic, normal, and bold. This gives bold, italic, and

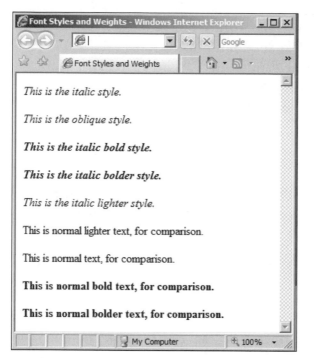

Figure 4.10
Font styles and weights

bold italic text as the three principal variations to remember. In effect, these are equal to using the `<b>`, `<i>`, and `<b><i>` tag combinations.

In addition, you can set the text (font) size, as a relative or actual value, using:

```
font-size: pt size or percentage
```

So, you could have style statements containing either of the following (which are not equivalent):

```
font-size: 14pt;
font-size: 200%;
```

The effect of these is shown in Figure 4.11.

In Figure 4.11, it would have been helpful also to set the `line-height`, which is generally used to ensure that in a mixed font block, the lines are the correct distance apart. For example, if a paragraph consists of text in several sizes, a line containing a smaller size only will be spaced with reference to that text size.

Figure 4.11
Font sizes

To make sure that all the lines are spaced with reference to the largest font used *in the entire paragraph,* and not space each line according to the size of the text contained within, you must set the line-height property:

```
line-height: pt size, multiplier or percentage
```

The pt size is the size in points. The multiplier is a simple number, and, like the percentage, is calculated with reference to the font size of the element to which the style property is being set. The following are equivalent:

```
<div style="line-height: 1.2; font-size: 12pt;">
<div style="line-height: 120%; font-size: 12pt;">
<div style="line-height: 14pt; font-size: 12pt;">
```

The next style property you'll read about is the font-family, and is possibly the most complex to remember and apply. The basic generic form is quite simple:

```
font-family: name
```

or

```
generic name
```

Using this form, you can identify an exact font, with a generic alternative:

```
font-family: Times New Roman, serif;
```

 alternative

This first example would choose an appropriate serif styled font, if Times New Roman were not available on the system in question. This is important, because not all platforms will have all font styles available, and to avoid viewers having to download custom fonts, it is better to stick with well-known font families, backed up with "best guess" generic system fonts.

[handwritten note: generic is best]

The generic families are:

- Serif—Times New Roman, Garamond, and so on

- Sans-serif—Arial, Verdana, and so on

- Cursive—Script, Corsiva, and so on

- Fantasy—Anything goes. . .

- Monospace—Courier New and so on

These are all shown in Figure 4.12.

Note that you should always try to provide explicit guidance with the real name and the generic family as a fallback to help the system choose the right font. It is inadvisable to specify only the specific font name unless you are certain that all

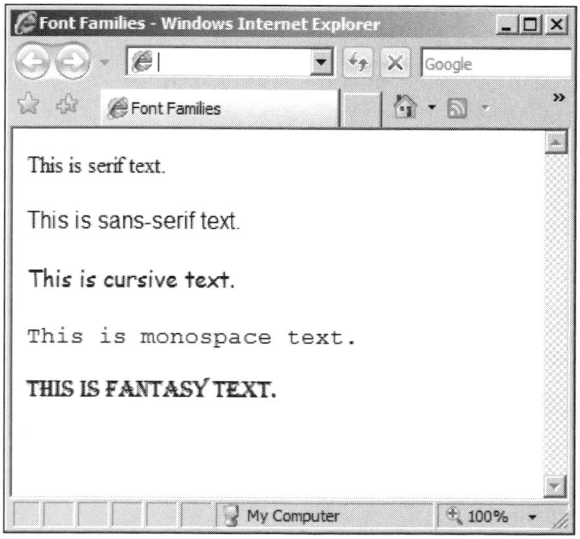

Figure 4.12
Font families

systems support the font in question. If the exact family is not important, stick to the generic families.

The font property can also be specified as a compound property statement:

```
font: style + variant + weight + size + line-height + family
```

So, you could set a font as:

```
div.article:first-line {
    font: normal small-caps bold 12pt
    14pt Times New Roman, serif;
    }
```

The result of this code is shown in Figure 4.13.

I have not really discussed the variant setting in any great detail, because there are only two settings—normal and small-caps. The small-caps setting is as in the first line of Figure 4.13 (which is also in bold).

There are also possibilities to exclude certain items, but it is better to set them explicitly rather than try to create a minimum compound property setting. One property that cannot be combined is the decoration property, which allows you to add additional formatting:

```
text-decoration: underline, overline, line-through, none
```

First → STYLE normal, italic, oblique
VARIANT normal, small caps
lighter WEIGHT normal, bold, bolder
SIZE in pts or %
LINE HEIGHT pts, % or X
Last → FAMILY specific or generic
• SERIF
• SANS-SERIF
• CURSIVE
• FANTASY
• MONO-SPACE

← *text decoration cannot be combined*

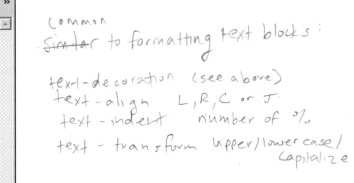

Figure 4.13
Font styling

Common
~~Similar~~ *to formatting text blocks:*

text-decoration (see above)
text-align   L, R, C or J
text-indent   number of %
text-transform Upper/lower case/ Capitalize

These can be combined with any of the other formatting properties, of course, so you can, for example, indicate changed text by striking it through and making it blue (for example) with:

```
div.changed_text {
    text-decoration: line-through;
    color: blue;
    }
```

Any block level element can also have its text alignment set with:

```
text-align: left, right, center, justify
```

Single line elements like h1 can also be set with the text-align property, but for some inline elements it makes no sense. Because the rest of the rendered block will not be affected, browsers may not implement this uniformly. The values for text-align work as you expect, save that the justify value does not always create a justified text block. It is platform-dependent and best avoided.

In addition, the indent can be set using a number (in pixels) or a percentage with:

```
text-indent: number
```

or

```
percentage
```

Finally, you can apply transformations to blocks or inline elements:

```
text-transform: uppercase, capitalize, lowercase
```

The uppercase option sets every letter to uppercase, whereas capitalize just sets the first letter of each word to uppercase. The lowercase option forces lowercase.

Lists

Lists are quite specific, because they have many options that can be set, including all the various text and font settings. For example, they can have various bullet types, borders, backgrounds, and layouts, as well as many variations of counted lists, including special character sets and numbering schemes.

If block level formatting is used, care has to be taken, as the first property you see shows. The list-style-position indicates where the bullets (or numbers, letters,

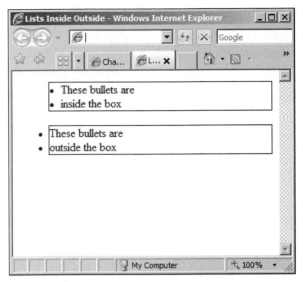

Figure 4.14
Inside and outside lists

and so on) should be placed in relation to the list item text and formatting box. It is specified as follows:

```
list-style-position: inside, outside
```

If `inside` is set, the list bullets are contained inside the formatting rectangle; if `outside` is set, the formatting affects only the text and not the bullets themselves. This is best illustrated with an example, as in Figure 4.14.

The code for the Figure 4.14 is as follows:

```
<ul style="list-style-position: inside;border: 1px solid black;">
  <li>These bullets are</li>
  <li>inside the box</li>
</ul>
<ul style="list-style-position: outside;border: 1px solid black;">
  <li>These bullets are</li>
  <li>outside the box</li>
</ul>
```

You will note from Figure 4.14 that the border in the `outside` list runs between the text content of the items and the bullets. The style of the bullets can be set with the `list-style-type` property, which has different variations depending on whether you are using an ordered or unordered list (`<ul>` or `<ol>`).

For unordered lists, there are three main variations:

```
list-style-type: disc, circle, square
```

These are little discs, circles, or squares, and are rendered according to the whim of the browser creator. For ordered lists, there is a choice between several possible styles:

```
list-style-type: decimal, alpha, roman
```

These are shown in Figure 4.15.

The decimal style can be seen in the top-left and is just a numerical scheme. The alpha style must be used in conjunction with the word lower- or upper-, indicating the case of the alphabetical scheme used. These can be seen in Figure 4.15.

Similarly, the roman variant must be used in conjunction with an upper- or lower- prefix, and examples of these can be seen in the second row of lists in Figure 4.15. There may be other fonts and systems supported, but because they are not guaranteed between platforms, it is wise to stick with the more common variations.

It is also possible to specify an image using the following statement:

```
list-style-image: url(http://mydomain.com/image_file.png)
```

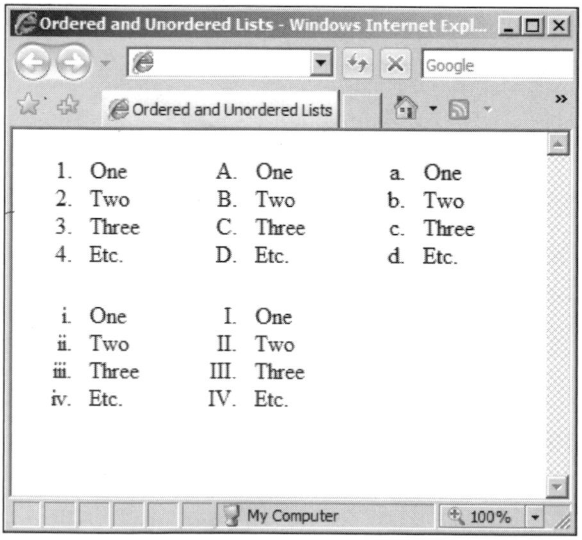

Figure 4.15
Ordered lists

This is useful if you need control over the images used for the bullets, and the browser will lay out the list with respect to the image size. Finally, you can group these into a single compound statement:

```
list-style: type + position + image
```
— for use as bullets   *E.g.* ⊞ or ◇ or ☺

This code might be useful when the image may not be available, as it allows you to specify the type as well as the image. That way, if the image cannot be found, the browser can substitute a suitable bullet type. For example:

```
<ul style="list-style: disc inside url (http://domain.com/image/image_file.jpg;">
```

Of course, ordered lists are not particularly useful when you specify the image variation, because the numbers will be overwritten.

Recap

The HTML defines where the content should be in the layout, as well as the actual content itself. It gives the general look and feel of the document without being specific about the details. A browser can render the page in absence of any style information, because the actual page is defined using standard HTML tags that are well understood.

So, styles do not generally add new tags to the HTML set, they just give you a way to customize the default behavior of the browser in rendering them, as well as giving you precise control over the positioning of individual elements. These styles can be placed inside the page or as separate documents.

It is a good idea to abstract the styles into named extensions (classes) of existing tags so as not to include the style information inline. This has many advantages, such as being able to update the styles in all pages that link to the style sheet rather than having to edit each one individually.   *within designated location on web*   *Classes*

The visual formatting model is based on discrete pixel measurements, or percentages of available space. This is known as the box formatting model and allows block level elements (and some inline elements) to have borders, backgrounds, padding, and margins.

The flow of the content around the page is then defined by the measurements given by the designer in either absolute or relative terms. Absolute positioning allows the designer to give the precise location for elements, whereas relative positioning uses a parent-child relationship to determine the layout of elements that are contained inside other (block-level) elements.

CHAPTER 5

CLIENT SIDE SCRIPTING

The purpose of this chapter is to give you just enough knowledge about client side scripting so you are able to understand the technologies that are behind them and deploy JavaScript with HTML in real projects. In essence, the aim is to put you in a position to be able to:

- Learn from scripts that you might see

- Create your own scripts

- Learn new scripting languages and techniques

The Web and associated technologies are moving so fast that new languages and techniques are appearing all the time. Understanding the basics behind client side scripting, and the purposes and mechanics, will prepare you for the future.

Most advanced techniques are based on the same underlying principles, and, in a sense, they are all based on one of two technologies—JavaScript and XML—sometimes working together (as in AJAX) to achieve the final result. JavaScript is the client side scripting language, and XML provides a communication layer between the page and the server.

So, this chapter teaches you the basics of JavaScript and also gives you a good reference section. This part of the chapter is very information dense, but feel free to use it whenever you need to look something up. Essentially you will first learn how to program, and then how to program with JavaScript, before finally applying it in an HTML and CSS context.

It is important to separate the reference section from the explanations that precede it. There is no (or very little) overlap in actual content—the reference is there to show you individual parts of the language, with examples, that you will only understand if you first understand the concepts behind the JavaScript language.

Generally speaking, when you include a client side script within the Web page (or as an external script), it is to perform one of the following functions:

- Improve navigation

- Provide special effects

- Provide contextual highlighting

- Validate forms or data

- Provide dynamic content

- Communicate within pages (inter-page communication)

Examples of improved navigation include drop-down menus that take the visitor straight to a given section without having to click through a hierarchical system of pages. These so-called jump boxes attach a small script to a drop-down selection box that is more commonly found as part of an HTML form, as in the last chapter.

Special effects include inline calendars or image selection (from thumbnail examples), which layer CSS (styles, such as div elements) on top of regular HTML. These are also manipulated using JavaScript, coupled with something called *events*, which are triggered by the browser underneath.

Contextual highlighting includes offering topic expansion or inline help. This can be in the form of cue cards hinting at the content behind, as well as floating sign-up boxes or splash screens. Again, these are previously invisible div elements (for example) that are brought to the front when a particular event is triggered.

Form and other data validation should be self-explanatory but allows the page to return data to the server that is pre-validated. This gives a better experience for the end users and reduces bandwidth usage in cases where the user has made a mistake. It also reduces the complexity (as you'll see in the next chapter) of the server side scripts that process the results of the form.

Dynamic content includes the ability to switch between content without loading another page (that is, like a tab control), as well as retrieving and displaying information from the server based on data that the user is entering (as in the Google Suggest service). This last uses a technique called AJAX that combines JavaScript and XML, and is covered in Chapter 7.

Finally, inter-page communication includes the use of JavaScript as a shopping cart or questionnaire (survey) platform for multi-page questionnaires. This is a convenience more than anything else, but the Sun JavaScript documentation notes that the original intention of JavaScript was to provide just this functionality.

This chapter spends a lot of time on these topics because you will usually be creating more client side scripts than server side in order to reduce server load, and because server side scripting might not be available on the host you choose to use at first for your Web creations.

To do all of this, you first need to understand the role of client side scripts in the client/server model. Specifically, you need to be able to create small programs (scripts) in the special cross-browser language that is JavaScript (and which they understand).

Before you go on, there is an important distinction to make between something called the DOM (Document Object Model) as separate from the language, and the objects that it provides to manipulate the way that the browser displays the page. The DOM is provided by the browser and is specified by the W3C.

If you look into the specifications provided by the W3C, you will find that the Document Object Model is a set of objects and methods that define the way that a document and its contents can be manipulated. It is only a *specification* and not an implementation, and it is left up to the browser vendors to add libraries that support the DOM and its operations.

However, in the case of JavaScript, there is a substantial amount of something called *mirroring* that makes it look as if you are addressing the objects directly, when in fact you are manipulating the JavaScript mirror of those objects. If you bear this in mind, everything should be a lot easier to follow.

So, it is not the document itself that is being manipulated, but an abstraction of it. The changes are reflected thanks to the link between the JavaScript language and the browser. Different languages and environments have different abstractions, and the JavaScript choice is to use mirroring with built-in objects.

You should not rely on these objects being mirrored the same way in other environments; although the DOM might be present, it might be manipulated in a slightly different, but compatible, way.

Introduction to Client Side Scripts

Client side scripts are executed by the client (the browser) as if they are extensions to the HTML page that is being displayed. Logically, the browser must have support for the scripts that the Web page is asking it to display. There are a few of these scripting languages, and each one has separate support requirements.

Sometimes these scripting and content rendering languages are built in (like JavaScript, HTML, and, in some cases, XML). These are part of the browser, and as such, they can be activated or deactivated (in the case of JavaScript) and have a certain relationship with the underlying rendering model.

Then, there are add-ins (otherwise known as plug-ins) such as the Adobe Flash player for Flash movies, Microsoft Silverlight, VRML, and so on. These add-ins enable the browser to display special kinds of files that they download. In much the same way that your operating system must have a browser in order to display an HTML page, so your browser must have a special piece of software to display a Flash movie.

(These add-ins can also sometimes communicate with the Internet, and even the browser, using a variety of interfaces like XML.)

This book concentrates on the scripting and communications interfaces that are built in to most browsers—JavaScript, XML, and HTML—and not specific technologies that are added on to the browser by the users in order to do something specific.

However, you should not confuse these add-ins with things like applets and other drop-in elements that some Web 2.0 sites provide you with: these should be cross-browser too, even if they have been compiled into Java class files. These are out of scope for the book, but an interesting technology nonetheless.

Like CSS (style sheets—see Chapter 4), scripts can be included inline or as externally loaded, separate files. The Web server can serve scripts in the same way that it can serve image files and external style sheets—they are just another reference to be loaded as part of the page.

JavaScript can also be created by the server when it serves the pages, allowing for mixed-mode processing, which you'll look at in the next chapter. In this kind of solution, the server side script delivers a Web page to the browser, with HTML, inline scripts, and references to external styles and scripts, and the browser then has to request the resources that it needs.

One thing to remember is that the whole page must load, and that includes the scripts, before anything can happen. This is because if an executing script references an HTML object in the page, that object must be loaded before this can happen. To avoid a chicken-and-egg situation, the browser generally tries to make sure that it has all the information it needs before executing scripts.

This does not extend to the resources such as embedded document objects (images are just loaded as placeholders, for example) might use, and so an image object might be accessible and loaded but it will not necessarily have an image in it. Instead, it might just have a reference to the place where it will appear. On the other hand, it means that you can do something called image preloading, which uses a client side script to load the images that a page needs before they are needed.

Inline Scripts

Scripts can be placed in the head section of the HTML document and will be accessible for all the HTML document. Anything that is defined here is visible to the rest of the page, as if it were style information.

```
<script>
// Code lines go here...
</script>
```

Typically the script section is a good place to put named blocks of code, called *functions*, which you'll look at later in the chapter, and variables (temporary data storage boxes) that need to be used by the rest of the page. Usually, as you'll see, the type of script should also be mentioned in the script tag, but most browsers will try to detect the scripting language being sued.

Also, inline scripts can be placed within the body of the page, by using the `script` tag. This is frowned upon by some Web programmers as it very much reduces the maintainability of the resulting page. If something needs to be changed, it is much more useful to have all the code in the same place.

Finally, scripts can be used as actions in, for example, form controls. This makes use of the events that are part of the HTML DOM and defined by the W3C. Any script language or action could feasibly be used in these event triggers. There are also a few cases where they can be used when other actions take place, such as the loading of a page or resource.

For example, `onClick` is an event that can be triggered by an HTML interactive object (such as a button or link). This can then be used with a piece of scripted code to perform a specific action when that object is clicked, called the *event handler*.

External Scripts

Scripts can also be linked to from the head of the document as an external resource, in much the same way that style sheets can be. This implies that the browser has to be able to request the resource from the server—which is either a fully qualified path or a relative path—in exactly the same way that other resources are referenced.

You do need to tell the browser what kind of script you are referring to, however, so that it knows what kind of interpreter to use. Again, if you don't, most browsers will try to guess from the file extension or the content. It's best not to rely on this, however.

The advantage of using external scripts is that they can be shared across multiple Web pages. In addition, there is a certain amount of hiding of the script that takes place because it is on a server and not directly in the page. The user cannot look at the script simply by selecting View Source from the menu, and downloading it might not enable them to see it either.

But make no mistake about this—scripts are never going to be safe from prying eyes unless you take additional steps to protect them by using a tool that makes them unreadable. This can also be a compiler that turns the script into an embeddable object (such as a Java applet), but this is beyond most, even intermediate, Web designers and Web programmers.

Most people won't bother because they never put anything in the scripts that would give someone a competitive advantage. The kind of code that is scripted in is not usually proprietary; its inclusion is just a matter of convenience.

For example, simple code that preloads document images so that rollover menus work correctly or form validation scripts are things that are scripted in to make the whole interface hang together better. On the other hand, an on-the-fly encryption algorithm would be better off encoded as a separate object not directly viewable by the end users.

Mixing Scripted Approaches

Most often the approach will be mixed, with functions (named blocks of code) defined in the head section and called from inside the HTML. These will be called from event handlers or directly from script blocks.

This approach will usually be interlaced with separate scripted modules outside that provide functions that are common to all Web pages in a set. These modules usually carry code that is abstracted across many pages—like generic form validation operations or interface code such as pop-up information boxes.

Then, functions which are only valid for the current page are kept in the head section; these might specialize the form validations or change the colors, text, or appearance of pop-up information boxes. These functions are called from the HTML page and they use the external modules that provide the actual functionality.

This keeps good organization because the objects and page that use the localized functions are kept separate from the code that provides the actual generic functionality. Sometimes this is referred to as object oriented programming.

The modular style makes the scripts easier to read, modify, and even share (or sell) than if the code was all in multi-line statements within the HTML objects. The advantages become more easily grasped the further you examine the role of JavaScript in Web programming and design.

Introduction to JavaScript

It is not the aim of this book to give an in-depth guide to the JavaScript language; there are many books—offline and on—which detail the language. And it is just that—a language which can be used in browsers, compiled into applications, and used on the server.

In this book, the aim is to offer just enough information for you to get started and do useful things with JavaScript, by mixing it with HTML, XML, and other Web programming technologies. More than that, it's treated as a client side (browser) scripting language only, which is arguably its strong point.

Much of the actual learning that you do will be online—through examples and probably other people's scripts and tutorials—as well as using the official reference texts. The grounding that you receive here will make this process much easier and give you something useful to refer back to when you encounter something that you do not understand completely.

If you want to become a proficient JavaScript developer—to the extent that you can make a living doing it, for example—you will need to get a good in-depth guide to the language. This chapter is, however, an excellent start.

Using JavaScript in HTML Pages

As mentioned, there are three ways to use scripts in Web pages, and there is no exception to this rule when using JavaScript:

- Inline

- External

- Mixed

All the examples here are compliant with version 1.1 of the JavaScript standard, owned by Sun Microsystems, and as such ought also to be compliant with ECMA Script. There are variations between browser platforms such as Mozilla (Firefox) and Internet Explorer, but these should be few and far between.

The HTML DOM that is used by the browsers ought to be standard as it is defined by the W3C, but because the standardization is a relatively recent innovation, there may be some older browsers that still have issues in this respect. The reason for this is that the mirroring is not always correctly implemented and some specific objects might not be available under some browsers.

The samples have all been checked, however, and should work as is. As an aside, there are techniques for detecting which browser is running, but because these are changing as fast as new browsers are being released, there being no standard way to detect browser versions, you'll have to do your own research.

Inline

An inline script must be contained within a matching pair of `<script>` tags, as in the following example, which also identifies the language and version:

```
<script language="JavaScript1.1">
// Code lines go here...
</script>
```

This is the same whether it is in the `head` section or within the HTML itself, except where it is provided as an event handler. In such cases, the `script` tag is not necessary, and the language and version identifier is omitted. For example:

```
<input type="submit" value="Submit" onClick="document.myForm.name.style =
            'background-color:red'">
```

However, if it is ever used as a target in a clickable entity (anchor, link, or suchlike), a special usage is generally applied. This is to identify the target of the link as JavaScript as opposed to something else such as a Web page (prefixed with `http://`) or other resource.

This inline usage then becomes:

```
<a href="javascript:history.go(−1)">Back</a>
```

These are the three ways in which JavaScript can be identified and used inline. In all cases, multiple statements could theoretically be used, but, generally speaking, the JavaScript statements for event handlers and link targets tend to be single function calls or object references.

External

External JavaScript documents must have the extension .js and must be specified by the Web server as a type of document that it can serve. This can require special configuration on the part of the server administrator, and in some cases, special permission to host the .js files must be sought (especially on free Web host providers' domains).

The reason that the configuration is required is so that it can pass the correct MIME type to the browser; without it, the browser might not know how to process the included file. Again, though, as with many client side functions, as long as the browser receives the resource, it will try to figure out how to process it for itself.

Tip

Including an external script is very similar to the method used to include an external style resource:

```
<script src="my_functions.js" type="application/x-javascript">
```

The `type` attribute is often omitted, because it is assumed that the server will supply the correct MIME type to the browser. However, because this is not guaranteed, I prefer to give the browser all the information that it might need in advance.

The `<noscript>` Tag

Sometimes it is necessary to do two things when using JavaScript, or any other scripting language, where support is optional, to prevent the browser becoming confused. The two possibilities are as follows:

- Hide the script in HTML comments

- Provide alternative rendering instructions

The first is used to mask the script from those browsers that do not process the `<script>` tag at all. Because rendering HTML requires (or at least encourages) that browsers ignore tags that they do not understand, the problem is not with the `script` tag itself. Rather it is with the JavaScript code that is contained within it.

A browser that does not process JavaScript (or the `<script>` tag) will not be able to do anything more than ignore the information that it does not understand. To this end, you just put those commands in HTML comments, thus:

```
<script language="JavaScript1.1">
<!-- Use HTML comments to hide the code
// JavaScript commands go here...
// ... this line ends the hiding here -->
</script>
```

This is the first of two possible options provided for those browsers that understand the `<script>` tag, but whose authors have chosen not to implement script processing. The second approach is to display some other content that does not rely on scripts to be displayed by the browser.

For example:

```
<noscript>
Your browser does not seem to support JavaScript!<br/>
```

```
(Perhaps you need to enable it?)
</noscript>
```

The browser is expected to render the content contained in the `<noscript>` tag as if it is regular HTML. This gives the author of the page the possibility to redirect the users to a download page for an updated browser that might support scripting. It also allows the users to enable the scripting engine if they have disabled it for security reasons.

Although it is becoming less and less necessary to do either of these options, it is still polite to attempt one or the other to make sure that all users have a consistent experience. They can even be used together, and there are no hard and fast rules about which is more appropriate. As a rule of thumb, if something viable and sensible can be displayed on platforms that have no script support, the `<noscript>` tag can be used. Otherwise, it is best to comment out the script commands and leave it at that.

Things to Remember

Before you go on to the first part of the language discussion, there are a few basic things that you will need to remember. These form part of the underlying rules that govern the language and must be respected at all times.

First, in your experiments, you will note that JavaScript rarely fails noisily. Often the only clue that you have that it is not correctly written is that it fails to do anything. At this point, you need to use the reporting function of your browser.

In Internet Explorer, this is indicated by a little error flag in the bottom left of the status bar. Double-clicking it will result in a dialog box containing the nature and location of the JavaScript error, as shown in Figure 5.1.

In Firefox, you need to access the error console via the menu. This is shown in Figure 5.2. The console can also be used to execute simple JavaScript statements and display the result.

Many of these errors will stem from the fact that JavaScript is case-sensitive—`thismodule` and `ThisModule` are not the same. This means that if you define something as `thisModule` and then try to access it as `ThisModule`, JavaScript will assume that you are trying to create a new item called `ThisModule`.

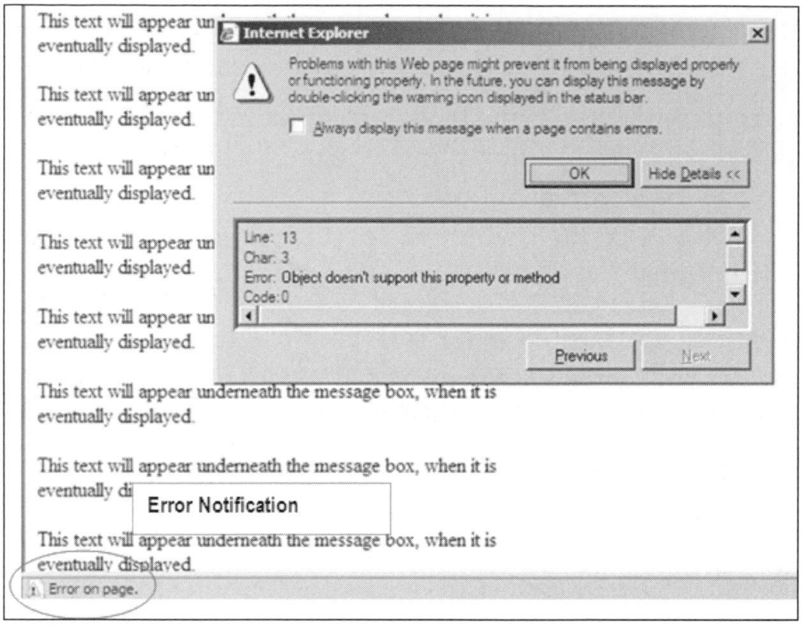

Figure 5.1
Internet Explorer error handling

Figure 5.2
The Firefox JavaScript console

You can't put quotes inside quotes. Sometimes, however, it is necessary. This usually happens when you're trying to use a piece of JavaScript inside an event handler (such as `onClick`), where the code needs to refer to the name of something. In such cases, you need to use a single quote inside the double quotes. An example of this is as follows:

```
<input type="button" onClick="document.src = 'new_page.html';">
```

All statements must end with a semicolon (;). Sometimes, programmers leave them out in cases where the statement is an obvious end to a program, or in an event handler. This is not good practice for the novice, however, and is a bad programming habit to get into.

Comments are pieces of code that are not supposed to be executed by the browser, in the same way that HTML comments are not meant to be rendered. In JavaScript, comments are usually contained after `//` and inside `/* */`, which should be very familiar to C programmers. The following is a valid comment:

```
2 + 2; // This will not be evaluated
```

The `/* */` usage is for multi-line comments:

```
/* Nor will this
   be at all */
```

Bear in mind that if something is inside a comment, it will be discarded. So, everything from the `/*` to the `*/` will be ignored, even if it is, itself, a comment. This means that it is not possible to use the `//` single comment token to end a multi-line comment that has been opened with `/*`.

Names of things in JavaScript cannot start with numbers or other special characters (although they can start with underscores, _, if you so wish). If you stick with a to z and A to Z or possibly an underscore, this is the correct approach. In addition, JavaScript names cannot contain spaces; an underscore is an acceptable substitute.

JavaScript is also not type-sensitive. As far as JavaScript is concerned, the number 42 and the string "42" are identical for numerical operations. JavaScript converts values by itself based on the target type or chooses the most appropriate type for a literal provided by the programmer.

This last point might be a little confusing right now, so it is a good time to discuss variables and types.

Variables and Types

A variable is a place to put information—a named box, if you like. The information can be inserted, temporarily, and retrieved again. It is only in existence for as long as the script is in focus. As soon as the user moves away from the page, the variable is lost and any information that was in it is destroyed.

Each box contains information that has a given *type*. This means that it is treated by the script engine (the part of the browser that runs the script) in a certain way. A number is different from a string; a `true` or `false` value is different again.

But JavaScript is not type-sensitive and will freely convert—usually managing to get it right. In JavaScript, there are only four data types that you really need to be concerned with:

- `null`, `undefined`—nothing, empty, and undefined (these are not the same)

- Numbers—Integers or floating point numbers

- Boolean values—`true` or `false`

- Character strings—`"a"` or `"a string"`

That really is it; there are no long integers or double-precision floating point numbers to worry about, and for the most part, you won't need them. Most scripts will get by with processing very simple pieces of information, usually strings.

Before you can do much with these data types, you need to define a variable to put the data in. Only when a variable is defined can any data be stored in it. This is done either implicitly or explicitly, at the time that the data is needed, locally to a specific part of the script, or globally for the whole page and all the scripts within it.

An implicit declaration just requires that a variable be assigned a value, and the JavaScript engine will try to determine the data types from the values that it is passed. For example, you can write code such as:

```
myString = "a string";
```

However, because JavaScript is not strongly typed, it is also possible to write code like the following:

```
myString = "a string equals " + 42;
```

These values are called `literals`, and the built-in JavaScript type processing equates the two as best it can in the absence of any other reference point. The result of this is that `myString` now contains `"a string equals 42"`, which is logical enough.

But what happens if you write the following:

```
myString = 42 + 42;
```

JavaScript will again try to match the type as closely as possible to the operation that is being performed. In this case, the result is that `myString` now contains 84 as a numeric value. Similarly, the following ought to have the same effect:

```
myNumber = 42 + "42";
```

Caution

A variable is usually assigned the data type of the first piece of data to be stored in it. Do not try to mix literals or variables and hope that JavaScript will make the right decision—it is better to ensure that your code does not assume anything.

A variable can also be declared explicitly with the `var` keyword:

```
var myString = ""; // an empty string
```

For the sake of clarity, in the examples in this book, I always declare variables explicitly. Note, however, that I do not assign a type to the variables at the time of declaration, unlike in other programming languages. It is also possible to declare a variable without putting any data in, as follows:

```
var myVariable;
```

In this case, the undefined value is automatically assigned to `myVariable` until such a time as some information is put into it. This value can be tested for, so the programmer can check to see if the variable has been *initialized* and take appropriate action.

Before you learn how to manipulate variables and test for the values that they contain, you need to look briefly at arrays, which are special kinds of variables.

Arrays

A string is often viewed as an array of characters. Therefore, an array is a place where multiple pieces of data can be stored. You can think of it as a row of boxes that can contain individual pieces of data.

An array can contain any data type that can be defined in JavaScript, including the objects that make up an HTML page. They can also be mixed, meaning that different types of data can be stored next to each other in the array. There is a slight issue with this—as the programmer, you have to remember what order you put the data into the array so that when you take it out, it has the meaning that you expect.

Arrays that mirror the DOM are special objects in JavaScript because they follow the HTML model and give you access to parts of the HTML document. So, each element becomes a container (an array) for the elements that are logically stored inside it.

You'll look at this in more detail later on, when you start to manipulate the Document Object Model (DOM). For now you just need to know that the paragraphs, headings, forms, and their various fields and buttons are all objects, and they can all be accessed using JavaScript arrays.

So, the document has an array of paragraphs, divisions, spans, layers, and other HTML elements inside it. A form contains an array of the controls that are used to provide the interactive content to the users.

Similarly, the document has an array of forms, and so on.

All of these objects can be referenced by their index in the page. The first form, for example, is contained at the first position of the forms array, which mirrors the DOM collection of forms inside the HTML document. This index is zero-based.

This means that an array of ten pieces of data is referenced by numbers 0 to 9. The type of the data will be assigned when the first value is stored at a referenced position inside the array. So, to access the first element in an array, you would use code such as:

```
myArray[0] = "element one";
```

An array can be declared by either filling it with values or reserving a certain number of items in advance. To set up an initially empty ten-element array, you would write:

```
var myArray = new Array ( 10 );
```

You access an element in the array using the square bracket notation:

```
myArray[0] = "banana"; // This is the first element
```

Up until this line is executed, `myArray[0]` had the special value undefined as did the rest of the array. This special value can be tested for to see if an array has already been initialized. This is a technique that you'll look at later on.

There is an easier way both to initialize and declare the array, at the same time filling it with an initial set of values. This uses the `new` keyword, along with the correct object type for an array, which happens to be `Array`. The code looks like:

```
var myFruits = new Array ( "apple", "orange", "banana" );
```

There are other objects that can be created in this way, such as strings, and the JavaScript short reference (the Core Objects) covers a useful subset of the objects and the various operations that they support (also called *methods*).

There are many such operations that can be done on an array, such as adding and removing elements from it, sorting the array, and so on. These methods are all covered at the appropriate point in the short reference section.

Before leaving the topic of arrays for the time being, note that the previous examples are of one-dimensional arrays. Multidimensional arrays are also possible and used quite frequently in JavaScript programming. For example, if you want to store a table of integer values, you would first set it up using a declaration such as:

```
var myTable[10][10]; // 10 x 10 array
```

It is only when you begin to assign elements to the array that you begin to tell JavaScript what the elements are that should go into it. For example you could write code such as:

```
myTable[0][1] = 3;
myTable[1][1] = "three"; // [0][1] still contains 3
```

So far, you have looked at a lot of data storage and manipulation without looking at the operators in any detail. This would be a good time to do that, before you start putting the pieces together.

Operators

An operator performs some kind of operation on a set of values, be they variables or literals. An operator typically takes two arguments, although there is something called the conditional operator that takes three.

- Assignment—Assigns a value to a variable

- Comparison—Compares one or more values

- Mathematical—Performs simple mathematical operations

- Logical—For use with Boolean (true and false) values

- String—Specifically for use with strings

One thing to remember when using operators in JavaScript is that it will automatically translate a literal or a variable (that contains a literal) into an object before operating on it. This is part of the underlying mechanisms provided by JavaScript that make it flexible and easy to program with.

Assignment   The simplest form of an operator is the assignment. You have already seen this in many of the small code examples. Formally stated, it takes a variable on the left side, and puts everything on the right side, once evaluated, into it as a literal value.

For example:

```
x = x; // Possible
x = "42"; // Put a string literal in x
"42" = x; // odd, doesn't do much
x = x + 1; // add 1 to x, put result in x
```

There is also something called the assignment operator, which allows you to perform the last operation with a single operator rather than the slightly clumsy long form. The generic format for the assignment operator is as follows:

```
operation=
```

where *operation* is any possible binary operator (+, -, /, and so on). The following is therefore equivalent to the x plus 1 example:

```
x += 1;
```

Other examples of the assignment operator are as follows:

```
x /= 2; // x = x / 2 (division)
x -= 7; // x = x - 7
```

The next operator you'll look at is the comparison operator.

Comparison   The purpose of the comparison operator is to test whether two values are the same or not, whether one is bigger than the other, and so on. You can compare two variables, a variable and a literal, or even two literals (although this might not make much sense). The == operator is used to compare two items. For example:

```
x == y; // will be true if x equals y
```

If the two values are not of the same type, the JavaScript engine will attempt to convert one of them so that they are. So, the following should be valid:

```
var x = 3;
var y = "3";
x == y; // will still be true
```

By a similar token, the != operator determines whether two values (or variables) are not exactly equal in value. Again, conversion will take place in an attempt to make sure that the types of the two arguments are correctly evaluated:

```
x != 1; // will be true if x is not equal to 1
x != true; // will be true if x is false
```

There are also two operators to test for whether one side is greater than or less than the other. These are the familiar mathematical symbols > and <. These can also be combined with the = operator to test for equality (that is, greater than *or equal to* and less than *or equal to*).

The following, for example, determines whether x is greater than y:

```
x > y; // true if x is greater than y
```

In addition, the following determines whether x is greater than *or equal to* y:

```
x >= y; // true when x is greater than or equal to y
```

The less than operator works in exactly the same way:

```
x < y; // true if x is less than y
x <= y; // true when x is less than or equal to y
```

The same rules hold as for the == and != operators when the values to be compared are not of the same type—that is, conversion. However, you should not rely on the automatic conversion and try specifically to convert values using the appropriate methods as discussed in the JavaScript short reference section.

Mathematical, Logical, and String Operators The four mathematical operators are the familiar +, −, /, and *. These do exactly what you expect (add, subtract, divide, and multiply) and usually operate on numerical data except in certain cases (strings). For completeness:

```
var x = 42 + 1; // x = 43
var y = 100 - 1; // y = 99
var z = x / y; // z = 0.43 or thereabouts
```

However, the logical operators are a little strange at first glace, especially for non-programmers. They operate on Boolean values, which can be either `true` or `false`. These two keywords represent the Boolean values as literals. The result of a comparison can also yield a `true` or `false` value.

The logical AND operator, `&&`, tests two arguments to see if they are both true at the same time. These arguments can be literal Boolean values, the result of a comparison or other operation, or a mixture of both. By way of example:

```
x == y && a == b; // statement is true if x is equal
                  // to y and a is equal to b
```

On the other hand, the logical OR operator, `||`, determines whether one of the arguments is `true`, whereas the other one might not be. In other words, it determines whether A *or* B *or both* A and B are `true`. Therefore:

```
x == y || a == b; // true when x equals y or a equals b, or both
```

There is also a `!` operator, called NOT, which returns `true` when the operand is `false`, or `false` when it is `true`. It effectively inverts the meaning. The following example might need to be read a couple of times before it is clear what it does:

```
!(x == y) || !(a == b); // true when x != y or a != b, or both
```

Finally, when used with strings, the + operator changes in meaning slightly. If both arguments are string literals, it converts them to string objects, concatenates the two strings, and then returns a single literal. This is easier to show than to explain:

```
"a " + "b"; // returns "a b"
```

The assignment operator works in exactly the same way:

```
var myString = "a ";
myString += "b"; // myString now contains "a b"
```

There are also some other useful operators that provide some additional functionality when dealing with various data types. Take a look at these next.

Other   The new and delete operators are used to create and destroy objects, as you have already seen in the discussion of arrays. This book uses new and delete mainly in relation to arrays and other complex objects (such as Date or String objects). For example:

```
var myAddress = new String ("some text");
var myArrayOfNumbers = new Array ( 1, 2, 3, 4, 5);
```

The delete operator discards the object. You should be careful not to discard an object that you might need later, and always to test for the creation of objects that might not be instantiated at the time you try to access them (by testing against the special literal undefined). The delete operator is simple enough:

```
delete (myAddress);
```

After execution, the variable myAddress is no longer populated and cannot be used.

However, delete can also be used to delete a specific item from an array, rather than the whole array at once. For example:

```
delete myArrayOfNumbers[0];
```

This example would empty array element 0 (the first one) and set its value to undefined. If you delete an item in the middle of the array, it is set to undefined and the rest of the array is left untouched.

Next, the conditional operator, ?, is the only one to take three operands and is a shorthand evaluation of a condition that must evaluate to true or false. It allows you to perform code statements conditionally depending on the result of a condition. The generic form is as follows:

```
condition ? if_true : if_false
```

In this generic form, if condition evaluates to true, the if_true expression is evaluated; otherwise, the if_false expression is evaluated. This allows you to create simple expressions that do something in a limited number of possible outcomes.

For clarity, the condition should be placed in brackets. For example:

```
(y == 3) ? x = 0 : x = 1;
```

This expression compares y with 3, and if it evaluates to `true` (that is, if the variable y contains 3), x is set to 0; otherwise, x is set to 1. There is another way to perform this operation, as you'll see later, using the `if` statement.

The next operator you'll look at, `this`, is special in that it returns the object that is currently being referenced. This will usually be in the context of an event handler coupled with an HTML object.

You'll meet objects later when looking at the JavaScript interfaces to HTML and internal, core objects. For now you should just be aware that the whole environment that JavaScript operates under is called *object oriented,* comprised of individual objects.

The String is an object, the Number is an object, and Arrays are objects. They all have specific functions that can be called (called *methods*) to make them perform specific actions on their contents (otherwise known as their *value*). Notice that I have used a capital letter at the start of the object names to differentiate them from literals that have not been created with the `new` keyword and an object name.

In the definitions of those objects, there might be a call to manipulate one or more of their assigned values. This is most often used in conjunction with processing HTML objects, so an HTML `form` might have an action defined that validates its data:

```
<form action="submit.php" onClick="validate_form(this);" method="post">
```

In this snippet, the named function `validate_form` will receive the special object `this`, which will refer to the `form` created by the HTML statement (you'll learn about named functions later on). You say that the object `this` is *passed* to the function `validate_form`. This enables `validate_form` to be written to validate *any* form, as you can reference the exact form to be validated as needed.

Finally, the special operator `void` is used when something must be evaluated, but no value is returned or processed. In the previous example, you could use the code:

```
<form action="submit.php" onClick="void(validate_form(this));" method="post">
```

In the previous line of HTML, the function `validate_form` would still be called, but its result would be discarded and the form never submitted. In reality, `void` is not used very often.

Expressions

An expression is a collection of valid JavaScript literals (1, "a string", and so on), objects and their operators, or logical operators and valid values that all result in a single value. Any collection of the such objects that are combined in a single statement to be evaluated is known as an expression.

For example, all of the following are valid expressions:

```
x + 27; // assuming that x exists
y = x + 3; // result is assigned to y
myBoolean = (x > 42) ? true : false;
```

Where expressions become very important is for testing in *conditions* that allow the programmer to execute code conditionally (if a given expression is true, do this; otherwise do something else). You say that you are evaluating the expression.

Also, expressions are very useful in *repetition* statements (also called *loops*) where an action can be performed multiple times inside a code block. It is the evaluation of the expression that dictates when the loop can be terminated.

Functions can also be used as part of expressions, as long as they return a value that is of some use in the context of the expression being evaluated. You have not yet met functions, so now would be a good time to introduce them, as they are an integral part of client side JavaScript programming.

Functions

A *function* is a named piece of code that is executed by name. It can receive a list of arguments that it can operate on and possibly returns a value. Typically, when using JavaScript for client side scripting, all the functions that the HTML document needs are stored in one of two places:

- In the head of the HTML document

- In a separate .js file

The reason for this is simple—to be sure that all the functions are available when the HTML document objects are instantiated (loaded and rendered) by the browser. If they were stored in the HTML document, it would be harder to maintain and they might not be loaded at the time they were needed.

(Functions can be defined inline, at the point at which they are needed. However, in my opinion it is better style to keep the HTML and JavaScript as separate as possible, because it makes for much easier debugging and problem solving, as well as cleaner code.)

There is also a set of useful built-in functions, but the vast majority of work in JavaScript is done via the methods associated with built-in objects and not standalone functions.

So, all the functions that an HTML document uses are likely to be user-defined. They can be called from anywhere in the HTML document by using the `script` tag or by assigning them to *event handlers*.

Calling Functions

A function is called by name, giving any arguments in the parameter list enclosed in parentheses. For example:

```
myFunction ( "string", 1 );
```

The same naming conventions apply to function names as for other names in JavaScript. All the parameters are passed by value. This means that they cannot be changed, even if they are passed as variables. An example of passing variables (as opposed to the previous example, which passes two literals) is as follows:

```
myFunction ( myString, myNumber ); // myString and myNumber passed by value
```

The exception to this is when an object is passed (such as an array). In such cases, if the value contained in the object is modified, that modification stands even outside the function. This method of passing entities is called passing by *reference* instead of by *value*.

There are several built-in functions that can be used for a variety of tasks, which you'll read about now.

Built-In Functions

You'll read about these in more detail later on, because there are many different functions used for various tasks. Here is a brief summary of the most useful ones, which you need to understand in order to grasp some of the other examples in the book.

The first are the conversion functions—`Number` and `String`—which turn an expression that is not a string or number into a string or number. This is an alternative approach to allowing JavaScript to do the conversion for you.

This sounds reasonably straightforward, and it is. There is a particular example, where the String function can be used to render strange objects like a Date object into readable text. So, the following snippet can be written:

```
myDate = new Date (); // make a new date object, set to Today
myDateString = String (myDate); // convert to a string
```

Having evaluated this code, myDateString now contains:

```
"Sun Jan 27 2008 10:52:41 GMT+0100 (Romance Standard Time)"
```

Next, the eval function allows you to evaluate a string as if it were a piece of JavaScript code. The result of the eval function is, therefore, the result of the code that was executed. Clearly, this is very powerful for building expressions in a string with input from the user and then letting the JavaScript engine perform the relevant actions.

(Imagine, for example, entering a string of JavaScript into a text box in a form and having JavaScript evaluate it as if it were code.)

If the string to be evaluated contains statements or function names, eval will even call the functions and perform the statements. Some examples:

```
myNumber = "1 + 3"; // myNumber contains "1 + 3"
myNumber = eval ( myNumber ); // myNumber now contains 4
```

The last really useful pair of functions is escape and unescape. These are very useful in client side Web programming because they allow you to encode a URL by escaping the special characters. These characters are not allowed by the HTML standard; for example, you cannot pass characters in search strings to a search engine. For example:

```
mySearchString = escape("first second third");
    // mySearchString contains "first%20second%20third
```

You will meet these two again when you look at some client/server scripting for use in the Web environment.

User-Defined Functions

The programmer can also define functions as long as they do not conflict with any functions that exist in the JavaScript namespace, and as long as they follow the aforementioned naming conventions.

It is good programming style to differentiate user-defined functions sufficiently that they do not become confused with pre-existing JavaScript functions.

Although JavaScript will complain only if the functions are identical—name and parameter list—reading back the code is made much easier if there are no naming conflicts.

A user-defined function is declared as follows:

```
function myFunction ( myParameter, myParameter ) {
// My code statements
}
```

The code between the braces (`{` and `}`) is executed when the function `myFunction` is used by name with the correct number of parameters in another code block. This is called *calling* the function.

You call the code between braces a code block, in this case a named code block. Other constructs for decision making and looping (repetitive statements) also use code blocks contained in between braces.

A function can also return a value, which can be used for ongoing processing. An example of a function that returns a value is as follows:

```
function myFunction ( myParameter, myParameter ) {
  // My code statements
  return myReturnValue;
}
```

The type of `myReturnValue` can be anything that JavaScript supports, even objects. It can be denoted as a variable, as in the previous example, or as a literal. So, an equally valid return statement might be:

```
return true;
```

Other functions that have been defined within the scope of the function being defined can also be called. As long as the function has been defined before it is called, it can be called from inside another function.

A function can also be defined as *recursive;* in other words, it can call itself. This is quite useful for processing lists (arrays) of objects in a similar fashion. If you use recursion, it is important to make sure that the exit condition is defined; otherwise, it will call itself forever.

Recursion is used in Web programming when the objects in a Web page must be traversed when looking for a specific item. The classic textbook example of a recursive function is the factorial function (for positive, non-zero numbers). It looks similar to this:

```
function my_fact ( n ) {
  if (n <= 1) return 1; // is n less than or equal to 1?
    else return (n * my_fact(n-1) ); // if not call myself
}
```

The book covers conditional processing later on; for now, all that you need know is that the `if` clause evaluates the expression in brackets and performs a specific function—in this case, exiting the recursion—if it evaluates to true. You will probably recognize the alternative:

```
(n <= 1) ? return 1; return ( n * my_fact(n-1) );
```

A function can also be called with a variable number of arguments.

Using Variable Arguments

It is perfectly possible to define a function that does not have exactly one named parameter for each piece of information that it needs to process. Instead it has only one named parameter, and the rest are implied and can be accessed from the function code implicitly.

Parameters that are passed and not named can be accessed through the `arguments` property of the function. A function is, in this case, being treated as an object. The following example shows access to the parameter list, using the `this` object:

```
function myFunction ( parameter_0 ) {
  return parameter_0 + this.arguments[1];
}
```

The `this` variable is special in JavaScript, and it refers to the current object. Inside a function, that object is the function itself. Outside functions, it can refer to the page, an HTML form, or an object inside the form (when called from a handler).

This example assumes that the function will be passed more than one argument, otherwise `arguments[1]` will be `undefined`. You can obtain the number of arguments by using the `length` property of the `arguments` collection (which is just an array of argument strings):

```
for ( var arg = 0; arg < this.arguments.length; arg++ ) {
```

```
// process this.arguments[arg] here
}
```

This example uses a counted loop, which you'll look at later on. Here, all that is necessary is to be aware that, inside the braces, the code is executed as many times as there are arguments, adding 1 to the `arg` counter each time. When the `<` expression evaluates to false, the loop stops.

The collection of values in the `arguments` array are accessed via a zero-based index, like all array processing.

Strings and String Processing

There are two types of string in JavaScript programming. There are literals like `"a string"` and `String` objects. As noted previously, JavaScript will freely convert between real objects and variables that happen to contain string data.

So, the following examples are all equally valid:

```
var myString_1 = "My String";
var myString_2 = new String ("My String");
```

In order to determine the difference between the two programmatically, you can use the `typeof` function. When you use `typeof` to determine what kind of type these are, the difference becomes clear:

```
typeof myString_1; // returns string
typeof myString_2; // returns object
```

In reality, because JavaScript converts between a value and an object, there is no difference between the two when it comes to practical matters of their application.

JavaScript provides many powerful string-processing methods, which can be accessed either from an object or a literal. You'll read about the basic string processing in the JavaScript short reference, which includes methods for splitting strings, determining length, extracting characters, and so on.

There are also some specific methods covered in the "The JavaScript Web Function Library" section of this chapter. These are methods that allow you to process strings with added HTML awareness—making automatic bold text, for example:

```
<script>
var outText = new String("Bold");
```

```
document.write(outText.bold());
</script>
```

The effect of this code is to make the text bold, before it is written into the document. This amounts to the same as the following HTML code:

```
<b>Bold</b>
```

T i p

Remember that when you look at the document source, only the JavaScript will be visible!

Another way to use this feature is in conjunction with the `eval` string processing function which will execute a piece of JavaScript code. For example:

```
var evalString = "outText.italics()";
evalString = "document.write(" + evalString + ");";
eval (evalString);
```

The effect of this code is to put the text in italics. This would be useful in a design application, for example, where it would be possible to select the formatting from a drop-down list box in a form and apply the chosen formatting in a generated block of HTML.

Note also that the application of the `bold` or `italics` method does not change the content of the string (the string does not become "Bold"), but does change the way that it is rendered by the browser.

Assuming that the HTML exists in a named `<div>` block, and that `outText` has been set to something that is static, a function can be created that adjusts the formatting as required. This might look like this:

```
function applyFormatting ( formatting_code, div_id, output_text ) {
   new_output_text = "<" + formatting_code + ">" + output_text;
   new_output_text = new_output_text + "</" + formatting_code + ">";
   document.div_id.innerHTML = new_output_text;
}
```

The other side of the equation is to have a list box that causes the formatting to be applied whenever the contents are changed. To create one that selects either bold or italics, the HTML would look something like this:

```
<select OnChange="applyFormatting(this.options [this.selectedIndex].value,
                  targetDiv, targetText); ">
<option value="i">Put in italics.
```

```
<option value="b">Make bold.
</select>
```

The OnChange handler calls the formatting function with the appropriate tag, which is then added to the text to affect the required change. It is assumed that the variables targetDiv and targetText exist and are appropriately populated.

Conditional Processing and Repetition

JavaScript provides a number of features that can be used to execute blocks of code selectively, either based on a condition or in a repetitive fashion. These two mechanisms allow you to have precise control over how the code is executed, which is vital to being able to create code that serves a specific purpose.

Decision Making

JavaScript has two basic decision-making mechanisms, allowing for both binary decisions and testing for one of a set of values. These are similar to those provided by other programming languages:

- if .. else—If a condition is met, execute a code block

- switch—Execute a code block depending on a discrete value

The first is for use when a condition needs to be evaluated that resolves to a binary condition—yes or no, true or false. The second is used when an expression could evaluate to one of a known discrete (finite) set of values.

The simple form of the if construct is as follows:

```
if ( a == true ) { // assuming a is Boolean
// execute this code
}
```

If the code to be executed consists of a single statement, the braces ({ and }) can be omitted. For example:

```
if ( a == true )
  // do this
```

If there is an alternative piece of code to be executed when the condition evaluates to false, the following construct can be used:

```
if ( a == true ) {
  // do this if a is true
```

```
} else {
  // do this if a is false
}
```

Again, braces can be omitted in cases when there is only a single line of code (a single statement, in reality) to be executed. The expression in parentheses can be any expression that is valid in JavaScript and evaluates to a single true or false value. So, for example:

```
if ( a == "my string " + myNumberAsString ) {
  // do this if a is true
} else {
  // do this if a is false
}
```

In cases where one of a known set is the result of the expression, the switch construct is used. This is often preferable to a whole slew of if statements, all testing for a specific value against a predefined set.

This mechanism has two parts: the switch with an expression, and a list of case statements that test a range of values. A simple example might be as follows:

```
switch ( colorNumber ) {
  case 0 :
    colorString = "#ff0000";
  break;
  case 1 :
    colorString = "#0000ff";
  break;
  default:
    colorString = "#ffffff";
}
```

Again, the expression in parentheses can be any valid JavaScript expression. All it needs to do is evaluate to a value that can be tested in the case statements. Unlike other languages, it can be a string as well as a numeric value.

The break keyword is used to make sure that the evaluation stops when a case has been satisfied. However, multiple case statements can be grouped if they should have the same meaning attached to them. So, for example, to group values 1 and 2:

```
switch ( colorNumber ) {
  case 0 :
    colorString = "#ff0000";
  break;
  case 1 :
  case 2 : // do the same as for 1
    colorString = "#0000ff";
  break;
  default:
    colorString = "#ffffff";
}
```

The `default` keyword indicates what should happen if none of the `case` statements can be satisfied. It should be the last statement in the `switch` block, and does not need to be followed by a `break` statement, as no more processing will take place after it.

Loops

A loop is a construct that allows you to execute a set of statements in a code block a specific number of times. The loop can continue either until a condition is satisfied (uncounted loop) or a set number of times (counted loop). The difference between the two is that you use a counted loop when you know in advance how many iterations there should be.

The JavaScript language uses the `for` loop as a counted loop. A generic form is shown here:

```
for ( var counter = 0; counter < total_iterations; counter++ ) {
  // statements to execute
}
```

The three parts of the statement in parentheses are the initial value that is assigned to the variable that is used in the loop (`counter`, in this case). The second part is the condition that must be satisfied for the loop to continue (in this case less than `total_iterations`). The final part is the operation that should be used to change the variable—simple addition in this case.

This last is the equivalent to:

```
for ( var counter = 0; counter < total_iterations; counter = counter + 1 ) {
```

The shorthand is known as the post-increment operator. Post-decrement is also possible, as is a loop that counts backwards. For completeness, the following is possible, but note the different condition based on the reversal of the meaning of counter:

```
for ( var counter = total_iterations; counter > 0; counter-- ) {
```

Any complexity of expressions can be used in these three places, as long as they satisfy the criteria, but they should be kept as simple as possible. Once the condition in the middle is satisfied, the loop exits and execution continues on the line following the closing brace.

The do ... while loop allows you to specify that a set of code statements is executed at least once, and continually until a condition is satisfied. So you can rewrite the previous for loop code as the following:

```
var counter = 0;
do {
  // statements to execute
  counter++;
} while ( counter < total_iterations );
```

The first line just sets the value for counter to 0, just as the initial setting section of the for loop example did. Everything in the braces will be executed *at least once* including the counter increment, which, again, is shorthand for counter = counter + 1. Apart from the syntactic differences, this new loop does exactly the same thing.

The while clause gives the expression that is evaluated at the end of each loop— in this case, counter is tested against the variable total_iterations, which you can assume has been set elsewhere in the JavaScript program. Again, this is fairly self-explanatory.

One thing to note is that the counter should be updated at the end of the code that uses it; otherwise, the initial value that is used to do the work, inside the loop, will be 1 and not 0, which is perhaps not the intended behavior.

The next kind of loop that JavaScript supports is the while loop. This kind of loop is only different from the do ... while loop in that the loop might not execute the first time because the evaluation is carried out at the start of each iteration and not the end. Like many JavaScript tasks, this is easier to understand than it is to explain.

Rewriting the previous example, you have the following example:

```
var counter = 0;
```

```
while ( counter < total_iterations ){
  // statements to execute
  counter++;
}
```

Aside from the small difference noted, it is identical in function to the for loop and do ... while loop.

The break and continue Keywords   When using loops, the break and continue keywords let you test for conditions inside the loop and then perform special processing. They can be helpful if some of the work code inside the loop need only be executed under additional circumstances.

The break keyword that you met in the discussion of the switch decision-making construct has roughly the same meaning for a loop—it allows you to terminate the loop prematurely if a condition has been met. Execution will then continue after the closing brace. The following is an example:

```
var counter = 0;
while ( counter < total_iterations ){
  // statements to execute
  counter++;
  if ( counter * 2 > target_value )
    break; // leave the loop
}
```

In this example, it is assumed that target_value has been declared elsewhere as a value at which to abort the loop. The break keyword causes the loop to be exited, as described in the preceding paragraph covering the break keyword.

On the other hand, the continue statement allows you to skip the processing between it and the end of the loop, with execution starting again at the top of the loop, rather than exiting the loop altogether. Be careful not to skip any statements accidentally that update variables that are used in the condition, though, or the loop might never end.

A simple use of the continue keyword is as follows:

```
for ( var counter = 0; counter < total_iterations; counter++ ) {
  if ( counter % 2 == 0 )
    continue; // Only execute the following on odd iterations
  // statements to execute
}
```

In this example, the modulo 2 of `counter` is taken and tested against zero. This has the effect of testing whether `counter` is even or odd. If it is even, the statements following the `continue` statement are not executed, and execution begins again with the next iteration following the rules of the `for` statement.

Both `continue` and `break` can be used with any of the loop constructs.

The JavaScript Web Function Library

The reason for the introduction to JavaScript was to prepare you for how it is used to achieve Web programming tasks. JavaScript has interfaces to HTML objects and a collection of functions that are useful in Web programming based around the document container model that you are now familiar with from the last chapter.

HTML JavaScript Interfaces

The JavaScript interfaces to HTML documents are defined here on the basis of the events that can be trapped by the user and used to trigger JavaScript code. On the other hand, you'll also look at the various objects within the hierarchy that can be manipulated. These are often mirrors of the objects contained within the DOM.

Events

The following is a list of the principal events that are of use in JavaScript programming. Those specific events that have limited application have been omitted for the sake of clarity. These are all events that are attached to specific HTML objects; sometimes multiple events apply to multiple object types.

All of the separate events are listed by Sun in its JavaScript client side reference guide (see `http://docs.sun.com/app/docs/coll/S1_Javascript_13`), and I have extracted and annotated them with examples of where they should be used, to make it easier to reuse the information from this book.

Generally speaking, each event that can be attached with any HTML object (usually the `body`, `img`, `a`, and `form` tags) has the general form:

```
<tag onEvent="code">
```

Where *tag* is the object for which the event is to occur, *onEvent* is the event that is being handled, and *code* is the JavaScript code. This code can be anything from a call to a function (recommended) to a single line of JavaScript. As mentioned, it is not recommended that you put anything more than a single command in here.

If more than a single command is required, they should be grouped in a user-defined function to be called from the handler. There are two ways to use the *code* section when creating event handlers:

```
<script>
function event_handler() {
  // function code here
}
</script>
<body onKeyPress="event_handler();">
```

This example will call the event handler directly, but will not have access to the event object parameters. To have access to any properties that are assigned to the event handler, you need to create an event handler and then reassign the event to it:

```
<body>
<script>
function event_handler(e) {
  // function has access to event properties
}
document.onKeyPress = event_handler(e);
</script>
</body>
```

Note that the event handler is different in each case. In the first, it is just a function, but in the second, it is an actual event handler. Both possibilities can be used with any event. However, an event handler is treated as an object with properties, so it is used only when it makes sense to pass more than just a set of values.

This book generally uses the first form, except in very specific circumstances.

onAbort   This event occurs when the user interrupts the loading of a page. The OnAbort event should only be trapped once for the HTML document as a whole and is used with img tags. An example of trapping this event is as follows:

```
<img src="myimage.gif"
    onAbort="if (!confirm('Stop loading document?')) { history.go(0); }">
```

This snippet will ask if the users want to stop loading the document. If they click No on the confirm dialog box that appears, the document will be reloaded.

onBlur   This event occurs when an element in a page or when the window containing a page loses focus—that is, the user moves away from it by using the Tab button. It only applies to interactive form elements and the window object.

onChange   This event occurs when the content of an interactive form element changes. This only applies to those elements that have selectable or user-entered values. For example, the Google Suggest service traps this event in order to populate the list of suggested search terms. This is used as follows:

```
<input type="text" name="keywords" onChange="updateKeyList(this.value);">
```

The snippet here assumes the existence of a functional user-defined function updateKeyList that takes the value of the named text entry field keywords as a parameter and performs some processing whenever it changes.

onClick   This event occurs when an object on a document is clicked—that is, a form button (including checkboxes and radio buttons) or a link. Because a click is a combination of a mouseDown and mouseUp event, clicks can be trapped separately with their own handlers.

An example of handling the onClick event might be:

```
<input type="submit" value="Does Nothing" onClick="return false;">
```

More usefully, this event can be used to turn an image into a clickable Submit button in a form with the following code:

```
<a onClick="this.myForm.submit();"> <img src="submit.gif" alt="Submit"></a>
```

This turns a clickable link into a Submit button, but it works equally well with plain text.

onDblClick   This event is the same as the onClick event, except that it is triggered when the user double-clicks a control.

onFocus   This event is the opposite of onBlur, that is, it is triggered when the focus moves to a control on a from.

onKeyDown, onKeyPress, and onKeyUp   These three events are triggered in response to key presses, usually trapped by a document object. However, they are also listed for event handlers for links, images, and text area input controls.

They use a number of so-called event properties, the most useful of which are likely to be `which` and `modifiers`. The `which` property tells the event handler which key was pressed and is returned as an ASCII code for the key. Luckily, the `String` object provides a useful conversion method:

```
var keyName = String.fromCharCode ( e.which );
```

This example assumes that the event handler has been assigned correctly, using a user-defined event handler rather than just a function. These properties are not available if a user-defined function is called rather than assigned to the event.

The `modifiers` property lists the modifier keys that have been held down at the same time—Shift, Control, Alt, and so on.

onLoad and onUnload   The `onLoad` event is triggered when a document has finished loading. It is usually handled in the `body` tag, thus:

```
<body onLoad="my_function();">
```

When using frames, it is best to place this event handler in the `body` tag of the document that is being loaded into the frame. Similarly, the `onUnload` event is triggered when the user navigates away from the document. It is handled in much the same way:

```
<body onLoad="my_function();" onUnload="my_cleanup_function();">
```

onMouseDown and onMouseUp   The combination of these two events causes an `onMouseClick` event to be triggered. The `onMouseUp` event can be trapped as well as the `onMouseClick` event for a given object. The `onMouseDown` event occurs when the mouse button is pressed and `onMouseUp` when it is released.

Handling these events is useful in allowing drag-and-drop style positioning of elements on a page.

`onMouseMove`   This event is triggered when the mouse is moved over a browser window, but only when the mouse has been captured. Mouse capturing is achieved with the `setCapture` method.

onMouseOut and onMouseOver   The `onMouseOut` event is triggered when the mouse is moved off an image area (that is, a client side imagemap) or link, and an onMouseOver event is triggered when the mouse first enters the area or hovers over a link. This can produce interesting graphical effects such as:

```
<img src="out.bmp"
  onMouseOver="this.src='in.bmp';"
  onMouseOut="this.src='out.bmp';">
```

This example displays in.bmp when the mouse pointer enters the image, and resets it to out.bmp when the mouse leaves the image.

onReset and onSubmit   The onReset event is triggered when the user clicks the Reset button of a form, and the onSubmit event is triggered when the user clicks the Submit button. These events are handled in the form tag:

```
<form method="post" onSubmit="validate_form();" onReset="reset_form();">
```

These methods are revisited in the "Form Validation" section later in this chapter.

onSelect   This event is triggered when the content of a text field is selected. This is useful in providing dynamic forms and support to users when they fill them out. For example, a function could be written to populate a container of city names, so the users can choose their city from the list.

Objects

The following is not an exhaustive list, but contains the most useful of the top-level objects in the hierarchy supported by JavaScript that are browser-related. Again, they are mirrors of objects in the DOM specified by the W3C.

The document Object   The document object has a number of methods, some of which you've already seen in a few examples in the previous code snippets. The most useful parts of the object are actually the properties, although there are three very handy methods that can be used for programmatic Web page creation.

A Web page can be entirely created using the following methods of the document object:

```
document.open();
```

```
document.write(HTML to write)
```

```
document.close();
```

The .open and .close methods are superfluous for cross-platform browser development because not all browsers react in the same way. For example, the following code, when used in some browsers, will clear the currently loaded document:

```
<script>document.close();
document.open();
document.write();</script>
```

However, in most cases calls to these methods are additive. So if the document has already been rendered, all that happens is the additional text is rendered underneath it. This is useful for conditionally writing text into the HTML as the document is rendered by the browser (inserting some of the document properties).

The document object has the following arrays:

- forms—An array of all the forms

- images—An array of all the images

- layers—An array of all the CSS layers in the document

- links—An array of all the link locations in the document

In addition, it contains the following useful properties:

- domain—The domain hosting the document

- cookie—Any cookies associated with it

- width and height—The width and height, in pixels

- title—The title, as displayed in the title bar

- URL—The full URL of the document

The arrays are zero-based like all arrays. In addition it is possible to identify forms by their name, provided that they have been defined with a name="myForm" attribute in the HTML document.

```
document.forms["MyForm"]
```

Generally, the properties should only be read and not modified unless you really know what you are doing. Individual objects can be altered, however. For example, to change an image source in reaction to a button press:

```
<input type="button" value="Change Image"
onClick="document.buttons[0].src='new.gif';">
```

An interesting point to note is that most objects in the document model also have a visible property. This can be used to great effect, for example, by making controls in a form available (or not) depending on the options already chosen.

You will see another use for the visible property later on, when you use it to make an entire <div> appear and disappear, like a message or pop-up box.

The window Object The window object has many properties and is the top-level object in hierarchy. This does not preclude that there may be many windows at the same level because they could just as well be frames inside a frameset.

The frames property gives you access to any frames that might be contained within the window. These are stored as an array, and each one can be treated as a window object in its own right. To know how many frames there are in that array, you can use the length property and traverse to the parent using the parent property.

The location property contains the address (URL) of the currently loaded document in the window (or frame). If this is changed, a new page can be loaded programmatically.

The status property contains a value that is displayed in the status bar (usually at the bottom of the screen) and this can be updated to change the message being displayed.

In the "Useful Top-Level Methods and Properties" section later in the chapter, I cover all the common methods that are accessed as if they were top-level methods and properties. However, there are a few specific ones that are relevant only when used with an actual window.

The back and forward methods load the previous and next URLs in the history list associated with the window. The close method can be used to close it, whereas the home method will load the URL that is specified in the user's preferences.

For example, you might define three buttons:

```
<input type="button" value="Back" onClick="window.back();">
<input type="button" value="Home" onClick="window.home();">
<input type="button" value="Fwd" onClick="window.forward();">
```

The contents of the window can be printed using the print method, which will open the standard operating system's Print dialog box. It is the equivalent of the users selecting File→Print from their Applications menu bar. (Most browsers place the Print option under this menu, although your own might differ from this standard.)

Finally, stop halts the current download, which is useful if something might take a long time to complete and you would like to allow the users to stop the process.

Programmatic HTML Generation

Using the String object, it is possible to convert a string literal to a piece of HTML code. The result will not appear as HTML in the document, but the browser will render it as if it had been generated using straight HTML code.

These are usually used with the document.write method to generate the inline HTML. Again, however, the actual HTML is not visible when the user selects View Source, only the JavaScript that has generated the HTML will be, as it is the browser that creates the rendered paged based on the script, and not based on HTML generated by the script.

Linking is achieved using the anchor and link methods, which both turn a piece of text into a piece of text that has a hypertext reference added to it. The first creates a named anchor and the second a hyperlink to another HTML document. For example:

```
var myString = "anchor text";
document.write(myString.anchor("anchor_name"));
```

This previous example is the equivalent of the following HTML code:

```
<a name="anchor_name">anchor text</a>
```

By the same token, the link method is used as follows:

```
var myString = "url text";
```

```
document.write(myString.link("url"));
```

This is rendered by the browser as if the HTML had been:

```
<a href="url">url text</a>
```

There are also three methods used to create text of different font sizes:

- `big`—Makes text that is bigger than normal

- `small`—Makes text that is smaller than normal

- `fontsize ( n )`—Makes text of a specific font size

The `big` and `small` methods cause rendering that is entirely arbitrary and the actual size will be relative to the default font size. These three methods could be used as follows:

```
document.write("Big Text".big());
document.write("Small Text".small());
document.write("Really Big Text".big(72));
```

Of course, string variables could have been used in these examples instead of literals. Also there are a some methods used to create fonts of different properties:

- `fixed`—Chooses a fixed font (like Courier)

- `fontcolor ( color )`—Specifies the color of the font, where `color` is either `#rrggbb` or `color` name, following the Web standards

Then there are some general formatting methods that are rendered in the same way as the HTML equivalents:

Bold	`<b>bold</b>`	`document.write("bold".bold());`
Italics	`<i>italics</i>`	`document.write("italics".bold());`
Strike	`<strike>strike</strike>`	`document.write("strike".bold());`
Sub	`<sub>sub</sub>`	`document.write("sub".bold());`
Sup	`<sup>sup</sup>`	`document.write("sup".bold());`

These can be used at any point in the HTML document, but note that it is not possible to change the font face (besides setting fixed font) or create headings using this method. However, by using styles, this is possible.

Useful Top-Level Methods and Properties

These are methods attached to top-level objects (such as the `window` object) that can be called as if they were functions. In such cases, the default current top-level item is taken as the owner. These methods can therefore be called without the `window` reference, as it is assumed.

This is not an exhaustive list, and the standard is changing on a reasonably regular basis, so it is better to check the actual lists online. Chapter 11, "Web References," contains locations of the pertinent documentation.

Message Boxes

Message boxes are a good way to communicate with your Website visitor, and JavaScript offers three possibilities—`alert`, `confirm`, and `prompt`.

First, the `alert` method displays a box alerting the user, with a custom string and a single OK button. For example:

```
alert("Alert! You pressed the alert button...");
```

This code snippet yields the result in Figure 5.3.

The `confirm` method displays a confirmation box from which the users can select OK or Cancel. If they click OK, `confirm` returns `true`; otherwise, it returns `false`. For example:

```
theResult = confirm("Do you really want to do this?");
```

This snippet yields the result in Figure 5.4.

The `prompt` method displays a box in which the users can type some text. If they then click OK, the text is returned; otherwise, `null` is returned. For example:

```
theResult = prompt("Please enter some text...");
```

The result of this snippet is shown in Figure 5.5.

Figure 5.3
Alert box in Internet Explorer

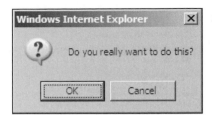

Figure 5.4
Confirmation box in Internet Explorer

Figure 5.5
Prompt box in Internet Explorer

If more complex interaction is required, you can use the `window.open` method to open a new window containing a form from which information can be obtained. Or, a custom `div` can be displayed containing the relevant HTML. This is explored later in the JavaScript examples section.

Interval Processing

JavaScript provides the possibility to execute a function after a certain length of time has elapsed in one of two ways:

- Once every x milliseconds (interval)

- After x milliseconds and never again (timeout)

The first of these models is activated by using the `setInterval` method and stopped using the `clearInterval` method. The `setInterval` method can be used in one of two ways—with an expression or with a function plus an argument list. For example, the following two usages are identical:

```
setInterval("my_function ( 1, 2, 3, 4 );", 25)
setInterval(my_function, 25, 1, 2, 3, 4)
```

In both cases, `my_function` is being called with four arguments. The advantage is that with the second, it is possible to execute code such as the following:

```
var arg1 = 1;
setInterval(my_function, 25, arg1);
```

Without this, it would be necessary to build the string explicitly, as follows:

```
setInterval ( "my_function(" + arg1 + ");", 25);
```

The number represents the timeout value that is set in milliseconds. To have the function called every second, the value should be 1000. The call to `setInterval` returns a timer identifier that can be used to access it.

So, to cancel the interval timer, use the `clearInterval` method with the timer identifier:

```
clearInterval ( timerID );
```

The `timerID` variable must be globally accessible, as there is no way to retrieve it once the timer has been set. A good way to do this is to make sure that it is specified in a section of the script in the `head` of the document.

If you want the function to be called only once rather than every so often, after a specific time has elapsed (for a timed test, for example), the `setTimeout` function can be used:

```
var myTimerID = setTimeout ( "my_function ();", 1000);
```

This will execute `my_function` after 1 second. If, however, you want to clear the timer before it expires, you can use the companion function, `clearTimeout`. Again, the `setTimeout` function returns the timer identifier. The `clearTimeout` function is called as follows:

```
clearTimeout ( myTimerID );
```

Location, Status, and History

You have seen some of these before, but there are a few things to note about the values that they return.

The `window.location`, for example, contains the URL of the document which is in focus when the method is called. If it is set by a piece of JavaScript code, it will cause the window to refresh. Remember, though, that the window might be a frame, so it is useful for refreshing part of the document set currently loaded.

By a similar token, the `window.status` property contains the current status text that is displayed at the bottom of the window. This can also be set using Java-Script, as in the following example that combines both methods:

```
<input type="button" value="Set Status"
 onClick="window.status='Current URL : ' + window.location;">
```

The `location.reload` method causes the current page to be refreshed, which is useful in conjunction with timers. This can also be attached to a button with code such as:

```
<input type="button" value="Reload" onClick="location.reload();">
```

Finally, the `history` object can be used to change the current page location based on the recent history.

For example, `history.go(-1)` has the same effect as when the user presses the back button, `history.go(0)` is the same as a reload using `location.reload`, and `history.go(1)` is the same as the user moving forward in the history. These can all be used with JavaScript handler, as in these examples:

```
<input type="button" value="<- Back" onClick="history.go(-1);">
<input type="button" value="<- Refresh ->" onClick="history.go(0);">
<input type="button" value="Next ->" onClick="history.go(1);">
```

Accessing Cookies

Cookies are small pieces of information that are stored as name, value, expiration tuples. A *tuple* is just a collection of related values—in this case, the basket of values that control the cookie.

The expiration date is optional, and the exact format of the cookie data is up to the programmer to define. JavaScript provides access to the cookies through the `document.cookie` property.

They need to be encoded (using the `escape` and `unescape` functions) to render un-supported characters (such as spaces) as data using their hexadecimal equivalents.

For example, a space is replaced by %20 with the call to escape. This is then replaced by a space value when given to the unescape function.

So, to set a cookie, it is necessary to build a cookie string (document.cookie) with three parts—the name (not encoded), the value (encoded), and the expiry date (not encoded and also optional). This cookie string can then be set in the document properties, but is stored by the browser.

The complete solution is as follows:

```
document.cookie = name + escape(value) + "; expiry=" + expiry_date; + ";"
```

To get the expiry date, you simply convert the Date object value to a GMT string using the .toGMTString() of the Date object. For example:

```
now = new Date();
expiry_date = now.toGMTString();
```

If expiry date not required, the cookie becomes a pair with just the name and encoded value.

Reading the cookie is slightly more complex as you need to examine each one in turn and see if it matches a specific name of the cookie you want to retrieve. Luckily, the .indexOf method of the String object provides the interface to get the location of the 'Name=' substring.

Because all cookies should end with the ; character, you can also extract the end location and use these two (start and end) to extract the named cookie data from the whole cookie string.

To get the start and end positions, you could use code such as:

```
startIndex = document.cookie.indexOf ( name );
endIndex = document.cookie.indexOf ( ";" );
```

Then, the value string can be extracted using the .substring method with the start and end indexes, as follows:

```
value = document.cookie.substring( startIndex, endIndex );
value = unescape(value); // decode the string
```

Of course, in cases where startIndex is −1, there are no cookies to extract (the indexOf function was not able to find a match), and if endIndex is −1, this means that there is no trailing semicolon.

Subsequently, where `endIndex` is –1, but where `startIndex` is valid, this is the only named cookie, and so the `endIndex` is effectively `document.cookie.length`. There can be multiple cookies assigned to a given domain (or document), so be sure to check that there are not already some assigned.

Finally, `document.cookie.length` returns the length of the string associated with the cookies that are part of the document data, as noted. If it is zero, no cookies have been stored.

Query Strings

Some URLs that are the result of a form submission contain data that has been submitted and that might be useful to extract from the URL. This is a good technique to use when making multipart forms.

The `location.search` property accesses the portion of the URL after the ? (question mark), which is otherwise known as the query string. The value returned includes the ?, so the first operation is to discard it. For example, from a client side imagemap click that is passed back to the page, you might have the following in the URL:

```
?x,y
```

The x is x position of the cursor in the `area` tag used for the imagemap, and y is the y position. Using the `indexOf` method of the string object, it is possible to extract the values for use in the JavaScript code.

This could also be true of a form that is passed back to the same document for processing, but the query string is likely to be more complex. For example, consider the following HTML code:

```
<form>
<input type="text" value="" name="textfield">
<input type="Submit" value="Submit!">
</form>
```

This submits the form back to the source page with the URL. If you had entered Banana in the text field, the URL would look something like this:

```
file:///test_html?textfield=Banana
```

This means that you can extract the query string, break it up, and use the value on the page by checking the index of the ?. Then, the value can be extracted relative to the = sign. The whole function might look something like this:

```
function check_form_input( queryString ) {
  if (queryString.indexOf("?") != -1) {
    var myValue =
      queryString.substring(queryString.indexOf("=")+1,
                            queryString.length);
    document.write("<b>"+myValue+"</b><br/><br/>");
  }
}
```

This code could be placed in the onLoad handler of the document's body tag. This would mean, however, that the rest of the document would not be visible. This is because the document.write statement closes the document. Care must be taken, therefore, to use the document.write method only when you know that the result will look coherent. Otherwise, the .innerHTML property can be set with most CSS tags (such as <div> tags) to change their HTML content.

JavaScript Core Short Reference

This quick reference section covers all the core objects and the most useful methods that you'll see in the JavaScript examples section that follows it. This reference is not designed to be exhaustive, but it does cover most of the pertinent core objects and their methods.

In addition there is a recap of the core language statements for conditions and loops, to act as a refresher whenever you encounter something that you do not understand in the working examples. Of course, if you need to relearn any of the language statements, you will need to refer back to the programming section of this chapter.

If you are just starting out in programming, this will be likely to be the case, because some of the more technical points take some practice to master!

Core JavaScript Objects

The core JavaScript objects are a collection of primitives that all JavaScript implementations support, regardless of the platform. It just so happens that most of the examples in this chapter relate to client side Web programming tasks, because that is the focus of this book.

Number

The `Number` object can contain any number and perform basic math operations on it. Advanced math functions, including trigonometric functions, are contained as methods of the `Math` object. However, there are two values associated with the `Number` object that might be of use:

```
Number.MAX_VALUE
Number.MIN_VALUE
```

The first is the largest number that the `Number` object can contain, the second is the smallest. Each value can only be accessed from the `Number` object; in other words, they are not properties of all numbers contained in variables in the JavaScript code that you create.

String

You should always use string literals in your JavaScript code, and never allocate a `String` object directly. The reason for this is that the `String` object sometimes works in a way that is not logical with respect to the code that you might want to write.

Specifically, when you use `eval` to evaluate a string expression, when it is a literal string, it is evaluated as if it were a real expression, but the `String` *object* is always evaluated as a string. This means that the following two examples do not yield the same result:

```
eval ( " 1 + 1 " ); // returns 2
eval ( new String(" 1 + 1 ") );
        // returns the string " 1 + 1 "
```

The JavaScript engine will substitute an object for the literal value or variable in order to perform the required operation on it. It is far more convenient to leave the variables as literals, both for understanding and manipulation.

There are several functions for extracting character sequences from strings, starting with a single character, which can be extracted by position using:

```
string.charAt ( n )
```

Next, you can extract a sequence of characters from the string using the `slice` method:

```
string.slice ( start, end )
```

The start value indicates the character offset that the method starts at, and end indicates the last character not included in the resulting sequence. It is also possible to use a negative value for end, in which case the index is counted from the end of the string and not from the beginning.

To extract a substring using a start offset and a *length* of the resulting substring instead, use the substr method:

```
string.substr ( start, length )
```

The length in this example is optional, in which case everything up to the end of the string (string.length) is extracted. The string can also be broken up into an array of strings using the split method:

```
string.split ( separator, limit )
```

By way of demonstration, you can extract a query string in two simple steps:

```
var queryString = location.search.substr ( 1 );
           // everything except the ?
var queryArray = queryString.split ( "&" );
           // split by the & character
```

Then, the individual items from the resulting array can be split in a loop:

```
for ( var arrayIndex = 0; arrayIndex < queryArray.length(); arrayIndex++ )
{
   var queryPair = queryArray[arrayIndex].split ( "=" );
   // queryPair[0] is the item name, queryPair[1] is the value
}
```

To concatenate two or more strings to produce one string, use the concat method:

```
string.concat( string_1, string_2, ... string_n )
```

So, to concatenate three strings:

```
var myString1 = "String1";
var myStringN = myString1.concat("2", "3");
```

The result of this would be "String123" in the myStringN variable.

As you saw previously, to get the index of a substring inside a string, you use the indexOf method. There is also a lastIndexOf method that can be called that searches the string from the other end. These two methods are illustrated here:

```
var firstThat = myString1.indexOf ( "g1" ); // returns 5
var lastThat = myString.lastIndexOf ("2" ); // returns 7
```

If you want to replace a substring directly with another string inside that string, you can use the replace method. This takes a string to search for in the first parameter, and the string to replace it with in the second. The strings do not need to be the same length. For example:

```
var myString2 = myStringN.replace("123", "1234");
```

Executing this code results in String1234 in the myString2 variable.

Finally, the case of the string can be changed with the two methods:

```
string.toUpperCase()
string.toLowerCase()
```

Neither of these affect the string that is being operated on, they just return the upper- or lowercase version of the string. The original data is preserved.

Array

An array is very similar to a string in that some of the methods feel rather familiar, even if some of the names are different.

For example, the concat method takes two arrays and returns a new one that contains a copy of each concatenated together. Different types can be combined within the arrays, for example:

```
var myNumbers = new Array ( 42, 84, 12 );
var myStrings = new Array ( "forty-two", "eighty-four", "twelve" );
var myNewArray = myNumbers.concat(myStrings);
```

This example results in myNewArray containing the following:

```
[ 42, 84, 12, "forty-two", "eighty-four", "twelve" ]
```

Next, the join method is the inverse of the split method from the String object. It turns an array into a string, separated with a user-defined or default separator. The default is a comma that can be changed to anything that the programmer wants. So, to add a space after the default comma, you would need to supply code such as:

```
var myString = myNewArray.join(", "); // default separator is comma
```

This snippet, operating on the existing myNewArray object from earlier on, yields a string containing:

```
"42, 84, 12, forty-two, eighty-four, twelve"
```

To extract data from the array, use the slice method. This takes two parameters: the (zero-based) start and end indexes for which the extraction should take place:

```
var newArray = myNewArray.slice ( 0, 3 );
  // newArray contains [ 42, 84, 12, "forty-two" ]
```

Again, the slice method does not after the array on which it operates—it returns a new array object. On the other hand, the splice method acts directly on the array, removing some elements and adding new ones. Its generic form is as follows:

```
array.splice ( startAt, toRemove, toAdd1, toAdd2, ... toAddN )
```

(The parameters in italics indicate values or variables that the programmer will supply in the actual call.)

In this definition, *startAt* gives the index at which to begin the splice. Similarly, *toRemove* gives the number of elements that should be removed. This can be 0 (indicating that no elements should be removed—they will only be added). Finally, the last parameter is the list of elements to add, in place of those that have been removed or inserted if there have been no elements deleted from the array.

Even the last parameter, giving the elements to add, is optional. This is, however, not the case if no elements are to be removed, in which case at least one to be added must be specified. This all sounds quite complex, but is easy to appreciate with some examples.

First, to simply remove the first three items, you could use the following code:

```
newArray.splice ( 0, 3 );
```

Because this acts directly on the array, it is different from the slice example, which just returns a new, modified, array. To add three items at the beginning, you could use the following code:

```
var newArray = new Array ( );
newArray.splice ( 0, 0, "1", "two", 3 );
```

This has the effect of building the following array:

```
[ "1", "two", 3 ]
```

Next, you can combine the removal and addition operations, as follows:

```
newArray.splice ( 1, 2, "twelve", "four" );
```

This example yields the following array:

```
[ "1", "twelve", "four" ]
```

The array is automatically resized and elements are reallocated as required.

The array elements can be reversed in order using the reverse method:

```
array.reverse()
```

This does exactly what you would expect, resulting in an array that has its elements back to front with respect to the original position. Again, it operates directly on the array.

The companion method, sort, is interesting in that the programmer can provide a compare function. This enables the default alphabetical sorting behavior of JavaScript to be overridden. If provided, the compare function must take two parameters and return one of the following values:

-1   If the first parameter is less than the second

0   If the two parameters are equal

1   If the first parameter is greater than the second

Allowing the programmer to specify the compare function allows JavaScript to sort arrays where the elements are not of the same type. JavaScript will deal quite happily with mixed arrays of numbers and strings, but the result might not be what the programmer actually wants.

The following is an easy numerical comparison function example:

```
function compare ( a, b ) {
  if (a < b) {
    return -1;
  }
  if (a > b) {
    return 1;
  }
```

```
    return 0;
}
```

The sort method can then be called using the compare function:

```
var myArray = new Array ( 1, 5, -3 );
myArray.sort ( compare );
```

The next set of functions deal with managing the array as if it were a list (or stack) of elements. In JavaScript, arrays are *self-sizing,* which means that you can do the following:

```
var myArray = new Array ();
myArray[0] = 1;
myArray[1] = 72;
myArray[3] = 27; // myArray[2] is undefined
```

In this code, the array will be four elements long, but the third element myArray[2] will be assigned the special value undefined. In addition to this useful feature of arrays, there are four other methods that are used to access the data contained in an array <space> and, crucially, which also change the contents of that array.

The syntax for looking at (and in this case copying to a variable) a single element in an array is as follows:

```
var myElement = myArray[1]; // extract the element at index 1
```

Given the previous code, the pop method performs a similar task, except that it returns the *last* element in the array and *removes* it from the array. So, taking myArray as an example, the following code extracts element [3] and removes it from the array:

```
var myElement = myArray.pop();
```

The inverse of the pop method is the push method, which places a value at the end of the array. Again, using myArray as an example, you can put the element back on the end with the following code:

```
myArray.push(myElement);
```

The new length of the array can then be retrieved using the following code:

```
var newLength = myArray.length();
```

This is much more reliable than testing the return value from the push method, which can return either the value that has been pushed or the new length of the array. Which one is returned depends on the version of JavaScript that the browser is using, and on the Web—you can never take anything for granted.

If you want to operate on the front of the array rather than the back, you can use the shift (pop from the front) and unshift (push to the front) methods. These work in exactly the same way as pop and push. For example:

```
var myArray = new Array();
myArray.unshift (3); // array contains [ 3 ]
myArray.unshift (5); // array contains [ 5, 3 ]
myArray.push (7); // array contains [ 5, 3, 7 ]
var myElement = myArray.shift(); // array contains [ 3, 7 ] , returns 5
```

These methods are very useful when processing data that has been submitted through forms or when building dynamic HTML pages based on user input.

Date

The Date object allows you to manipulate date information. This section looks at the three main classes of methods that the Date object uses:

- Date creation

- Date extraction

- Date string creation

First, you can create a date in three ways. You can create a Date object with today's date in it:

```
var myDate = new Date (); // now, today
```

Or, you can create a specific date object for a specific date:

```
var myDate = new Date ( month day, year hh:mm:ss );
```

In the previous example, *month* must be replaced with the month name (such as January), the *day* with the day of the month, the *year* on four digits, and the time as shown, using the 24-hour clock. Finally, the previous example can be specified as numbers:

```
var myDate = new Date ( year, month, day, hour, minutes, seconds );
```

The methods cannot be mixed. As before, the values in *italics* need to be substituted for your own values; in this case, you need numerical equivalents.

Extracting date data is very easy:

myDate.getFullYear()	Returns the year (such as 1900)
myDate.getMonth()	Returns the month (zero-based, with 0 = January)
myDate.getDay()	Returns the day of the week (zero-based, 0 = Sunday)
myDate.getDate()	Returns the day of the month, between 1 and 31
myDate.getHours()	Returns the hours of the time, in 24-hour clock, 0 to 23
myDate.getMinutes()	Returns the minutes of the time, 0 to 59
myDate.getSeconds()	Returns the seconds of the time, 0 to 59

In addition, each of the GET methods also has a corresponding SET method that can be used to set the values for each of the Date object components.

Math

The Math object is useful for performing advanced mathematical functions, including trigonometric operations. The built-in Number literal can be manipulated with all the familiar simple operators (+, −, /, *, % (modulo), and so on), but the more advanced functions have to be accessed through the Math object.

There are some properties which are useful, too, and these are accessed as follows:

Math.PI	Equal to PI
Math.E	Euler's constant (used in calculating logarithms)
Math.SQRT1_2	The square root of ½
Math.SQRT2	The square root of 2

There are more fixed properties, all accessed in the same way, but these are the most useful. The methods are similarly easy and self-explanatory:

Math.abs (x)	Returns the absolute of x
Math.sin (x)	Returns the sine of x
Math.cos (x)	Returns the cosine of x
Math.tan (x)	Returns the tangent of x

In addition, there are arc versions of sin, cos, and tan (asin, acos, and atan). All the trigonometric functions return their results in *radians* and not degrees.

Tip

To convert to degrees, it is necessary to remember that 360 degrees (a circle) contains 2pi radians.

Using the PI constant from the `Math` object, you can use the following code:

```
var myDegrees = (360 / ( Math.PI * 2) ) * radian_value;
```

Then, there are some basic comparison functions:

`Math.min ( x, y )`	Returns the smallest of *x* and *y*
`Math.max ( x, y )`	Returns the largest of *x* and *y*

Finally, there are some rounding and random number generation methods:

`Math.ceil ( x )`	Returns the smallest integer greater than or equal to *x*
`Math.round ( x )`	Rounds *x* up or down accordingly
`Math.random()`	Returns a random number between 0 and 1

This section lists the most useful set of the `Math` methods, which have been fairly static since JavaScript was first devised.

Core Language

For the sake of completeness, this section contains a quick recap of the three core areas of JavaScript programming used to control the flow of a program. If any of the concepts are still unfamiliar, you can check the exact usage, with examples, in the "Introduction to JavaScript" section earlier in the chapter.

Conditional Statements

JavaScript supports the `if .. else` statement for basic decision making:

```
if ( a == b ) {
  // Do this
}
else {
  // Do that
}
```

The else clause is optional, and the expression to be tested as part of the if statement can be any supported JavaScript expression. This expression must evaluate to true or false.

For non-binary decision making, JavaScript offers the switch statement:

```
switch ( myVariable ) {
  case value :
    // do this
  break;
  default:
    // do this
  break;
}
```

The switch statement supports both numbers and strings. If no match is found, the default clause is executed. In addition, multiple case labels can refer to the same code to be executed.

Loops

Both counted and uncounted loops are supported in JavaScript. Counted loops are provided through the use of the for statement:

```
for ( var myCounter = 0; myCounter < myTotal; myCounter++) {
  // processing
}
```

Uncounted loop support is provided through the do .. while and while statements. The difference between the two is that the do .. while loop is guaranteed to be executed at least once:

```
var myNumber = 9;
do {
  // This will executed at least once
  // do something to myNumber
} while (myNumber < 9);
```

Using a while loop, however, will mean that the code becomes unreachable:

```
var myNumber = 9;
while (myNumber < 9) {
  // This will never be executed
  // do something to myNumber
}
```

Using these three mechanisms, you can solve most programming problems requiring repetition. However, you can also use recursive functions.

Functions

Functions in JavaScript are named blocks of code, defined as follows:

```
function myFunction ( parameters ) {
  return value; // optional
}
```

A function is called by name:

```
myValue = myFunction ( parameters )
```

or

```
myFunction ( parameters )
```

Functions might not have parameters, in which case the *parameters* can be omitted. An example of a function that takes three parameters is as follows:

```
function myAdd ( a, b, c ) {
  return a + b + c;
}
```

In addition, functions might not have any formal parameters, but still have access to any parameters that might be passed to the function through the parameters array. To access this array, code such as the following can be used:

```
function myAdd ( ) {
  var myResult = 0;
  for ( var myCounter = 0; myCounter < arguments.length;
    myCounter++ ) {myResult += arguments[myCounter];
  }
  return myResult;
}
```

The myAdd function can be called with as many parameters as are required.

JavaScript Examples

This is a cookbook of several applied JavaScript examples, which illustrate mixing JavaScript and HTML, at the DOM level and native JavaScript level. The same results can be achieved with other client side languages and, in certain circumstances, using server side programming.

However, there are some elements of interaction with the user, through the browser, that can only be achieved with client side scripting. In addition, these techniques are useful if you don't have access to the server that supports scripting.

In these examples, you also meet a few new mirror objects available to JavaScript programmers, not to mention the very useful `getElementById` method, which allows you to retrieve the DOM mirror object relating to a specific HTML element in a page by name.

Image Preloading

Image preloading is a great technique for reducing the wait time between when a mouse enters an image and when the image is changed. This effect is called image rollover, and the following HTML snippet provides a simple example of rollover, using the `onMouse` handlers:

```
<img src="out.bmp" onMouseOver= "this.src='in.bmp';"
         onMouseOut="this.src='out.bmp';">
```

There are two problems that you'll want to solve here. The first is that, if there are many images on the page, or if the images to be used are large, the page will load very slowly. However, the second problem is that you might want the page to remain compatible with those users who do not have, or do not want to activate, JavaScript.

Image preloading is designed only to *cache* the images. In other words, the browser will download and store the images on the user's hard drive and display them only when necessary. The image preload code goes in the `head` section of the HTML document.

It is very easy, and looks like this:

```
function preload_images () {
  var myImage = new Image();
  // Do the following for each image
  myImage.src = 'in.bmp';
  myImage.src = 'out.bmp';
}
```

Note from this example that I have introduced another JavaScript object, `Image`. `Image` has a collection of properties, of which the following are the most useful:

width	The width of the image, in pixels
height	The height of the image, in pixels
border	The width of the border, or 0 for no border
src	The URL of the image's source

If you do not need to worry about the users not having JavaScript running, you can also preload the images into an array and set them directly using (for example) buttons. To do this, the initial script in the `head` section of the HTML document becomes:

```
var myImages = new Array();

function preload_images () {
  // Do the following for each image
  myImages[0] = new Image();
  myImages[0].src = 'in.bmp';

  myImages[1] = new Image();
  myImages[1].src = 'out.bmp';
}
```

Note that I have made the `myImages` array globally accessible by moving it outside of the `preload_images` function. Once the images have been loaded, it becomes a simple matter to change an image on the document via a button:

```
<input type="button" value="In"
  onClick="document.images[0].src=myImages[0].src;">
```

The array of Image objects in the document is stored in the `document.images` property. Although you cannot directly assign an Image object from one array to the other, you can access the `.src` property and use that to change the image being displayed. Because the image has been preloaded, there should be no delay between the button click and the image update.

Form Validation

One of the key uses for JavaScript in HTML is for pre-validating a form before sending it to the server for processing. This reduces the server load and the complexity of the server side script. You might also want to make a form dynamically update itself depending on the options already chosen by the user.

Validating the form requires trapping the onSubmit handler and returning true if the form should be submitted or false otherwise. In the following example, I have left out the action and method attributes so that the form submits itself to the same HTML page. You would need to put the required method (either GET or POST) and action (URL) as required by your server side script.

The HTML code might look something like the following:

```
<form onSubmit="return validate_form();" name="ContactDetailsForm">
  Name : <input type="text" value="" name="Name"><br/>
  Email : <input type="text" value="" name="Email"><br/>
  <input type="submit" Value="Submit">
</form>
```

There are a couple of caveats that you need to be aware of:

- You want to show only one alert per error

- You don't want the form to submit before all errors are corrected

If the function called validate_form returns true, the form will be submitted. So, all the validation needs to do is return false if there is an error detected in the form data that is being checked.

A field to be checked is accessed through the named objects that are contained in the document's form object. In basic JavaScript programming, there are three ways to do this:

```
document.forms[0].Name
document.forms["ContactDetailsForm"].Name
document.ContactDeatilsForm.Name
```

All three are identical in that they return the field that has the name="Name" attribute set in the HTML code. All that is needed afterwards is to access the value property and check it. In this case, you just need to check its length property. The following code shows this in action:

```
function validate_form () {
  if (document.ContactDetailsForm.Name.value.length == 0) {
    // User has not filled out field correctly!
    return false;
  }
```

```
  // Everything is OK!
  return true;
}
```

However, this code is not very user friendly, as users do not know why their form has not been submitted. To let your users know there is a problem, you can put up an alert box, as follows:

```
if (document.ContactDetailsForm.Name.value.length == 0) {
 alert("The Name field must be filled in!");
 return false;
}
```

It would also be nice to highlight the field that is in error. This is done using the DOM (Document Object Model) and then setting the style (as if it were a basic CSS element). The book has not yet discussed the DOM in detail, so this is a good time to introduce it.

It is important to remember, as stated in the introduction, that the DOM is separate from JavaScript and is also based on a W3C recommendation. This means that it is a standard model that all browser developers should follow, and that more details can be found at the W3C site (see http://www.w3.org/DOM/).

The particular method of interest here is called getElementById. The element ID in question is the same that would be allocated using the id="id" attribute of any CSS compliant HTML element. This includes div, span, table (and also tr and td tags), and form elements.

It is possible to access the fields in the form directly using this method, as long as their CSS ids are unique. The getElementById method is part of the document object in JavaScript and is accessed in the following way:

```
document.getElementById ( fieldID )
```

To continue building or validation code, you need to change the HTML for the form element to:

```
<input type="text" value="" name="Name" id="fieldName">
```

Now that the field can be referred to by its ID, you simply need to set its style to the correct value. Because you want to change the background color (to, for example, red), the following code is inserted in the validation section of the script:

```
document.getElementById("fieldName").style.backgroundColor="red";
```

There are a few points to note. First, the getElementById method returns an object that can be accessed as if it were a CSS object. This means that it has properties that mirror the HTML, of which the following is the most useful subset:

CSS Style	JavaScript DOM Property
Color	Color
background-color	backgroundColor
border-style	borderStyle
font-family	fontFamily
font-size	fontSize

Notice that a naming pattern emerges. All style attributes that can be defined in the style statement can be converted to DOM properties in the same way. So, you would expect that the style attribute left-border-style is mirrored in the DOM property (in JavaScript) leftBorderStyle.

Any time that the programmer needs to change the style of an object, it can be accessed via the style property of that object. This, in turn, gives access to the various attributes that can be set using a plain string that represents the new style information, following the regular CSS and HTML style principles from the last chapter.

(Seemingly, however, it is not possible to put all the attributes in a single string, and apply it to [for example] a general style parameter; they must be set separately.)

Finally it would be nice to reset the field back to white once the user starts to edit it. To do this, you could build a function to reset the color for a given field, as follows:

```
function reset_field_color ( myField ) {
  document.getElementById(myField.id).
          style.backgroundColor="white";
}
```

This function expects an object to be passed to it (myField), from which it creates a new object using the ID of the object passed in. This is a roundabout way, and is just used here to illustrate how the referencing principle works. By a similar token, the illustrative code that calls it uses the onFocus JavaScript event handler:

```
<input type="text" value="" name="Name" id="fieldName"
  onFocus="reset_field_color(this);">
```

If you want to validate on the basis of the user navigating the fields (rather than as the form is submitted), this technique can also be used. This means using the onChange event handler (rather than onFocus), with validation code very similar to that which you have constructed here.

A generic form of the previous form validation process itself might do the following:

- Check that fields are not empty

- Generate an alert based on each field name

- Highlight all fields not correctly filled in

It is also possible to test a field based on its form and element index rather than using getElementById. This uses the standard JavaScript mirrored collections of objects, as follows:

```
function is_field_empty ( form_index, field_index ) {
  if ( document.forms[form_index][field_index].
                     value.length == 0 ) {
    return true;
  }
  return false;
}
```

The advantage in this method will be shown later on when you validate the whole form. The next thing to do is to be able to toggle highlighting based on whether an error was found in the field. The resulting function might look like this:

```
function highlight_field ( field_id, on_off ) {
  if ( on_off == 0 ) {
    document.getElementById(field_id).
            style.backgroundColor="white";
  }
  else {
    document.getElementById(field_id).
            style.backgroundColor="red";
  }
}
```

Finally, you need to go through the fields one by one and check that they all validate correctly. The following is for text fields only, but the same approach can be used for other kinds of fields like select controls:

```
function validate_form () {
```

```
var retValue = true;
for ( var formIndex = 0; formIndex < document.forms.length;
      formIndex++ ) {
  for ( var fieldIndex = 0; fieldIndex < document.forms
        [formIndex].length;
           fieldIndex++ ) {
    if ( is_field_empty ( formIndex, fieldIndex ) ) {
      highlight_field ( document.forms[formIndex]
                            [fieldIndex].id, 1 );
      retValue = false;
    }
  }
}

if ( retValue == false ) {
  alert("Please correct the fields marked in red.");
}
return retValue;
}
```

Now the utility of using the field and form indexes becomes clear—you can refer to them through the JavaScript arrays rather than needing to know the IDs. The code should be easy enough to understand. The only really complex bit is the double array that retrieves the form objects (controls).

The form itself might be defined in HTML like this:

```
<form onSubmit="return validate_form();" name="ContactDetailsForm"
    action="form_results.html" method="get">

Name : <input type="text" value="" name="Name" id="fieldName"
    onFocus="highlight_field(this.id, 0);"><br/>

Email : <input type="text" value="" name="Email" id="fieldEmail"
    onFocus="highlight_field(this.id, 0);"><br/>
<input type="submit" Value="Submit"><br/>
</form>
```

There are many extensions possible to the previous example, such as putting field names in the message box, adding an identifier to the name (such as _e for "can be empty"), improving validation, and also adding the box type to the name so that different actions can be carried out by the specific control type.

However, as it stands, it illustrates the key points of form validation and the use of styles to highlight specific items. One aspect where some customization might be desirable is in the way that the errors are relayed to the user—and for this you could program your own kind of message box.

User-Defined Message Boxes

First, I should note that this can be done by opening a new window, containing some HTML that defines the message that you would like to display. However, this has problems, such as pop-ups being blocked by the browser, the page opening in a new browser window or Tab, and so on.

Sometimes the basic JavaScript alert box is not enough, especially when you want to retrieve form data that is more complex than just a single line, for example. The solution is to make a piece of HTML that can be layered on top of the content and hidden or shown at will.

In the working example, the dialog box itself will be static, there being no easy way to set the title and text programmatically. This means that either the programmer must set the title and text in the HTML themselves or have it created using a server side script.

The following is a fairly straightforward example of such a message box, written in standard CSS compliant HTML statements:

```
<div id="msgBox"
    style=" width:250px;height:150px;visibility:
            hidden;left:150;top:150;">
 <table style="background-color:#000080;"
                width=100% height=100% cellpadding=5>
 <tr height=15px>
  <td style="color:#ffffff;">
    <b>>Message Box Title</b>
  </td>
 </tr>
 <tr>
  <td style="background-color:#ffffff;"
            align="center" valign="center">
  <b>Message Box Text</b><br/>
  <table>
  <tr>
    <td>
      <input type="button" value=" OK "
                onClick="close_dialog('OK');">
    </td>
```

```
    <td> </td>
    <td>
      <input type="button" value="Cancel"
                  onClick="close_dialog('Cancel');">
    </td>
  </tr>
  </table>
  </td>
 </tr>
</table>
</div>
```

The whole dialog box is contained inside a div tag, which is set to visibility: hidden so that it cannot be seen initially. The width, height, and placement values are more or less arbitrary in this code. The message box could, for example, be centered by making an outer div that takes whole screen and then centering the inner div on it with align property.

However, for the sake of clarity, I have kept it to a single div which is either shown or hidden. The close_dialog function, triggered by the onClick events of the two buttons, is just there to set the visibility back to hidden. It looks like this:

```
function close_dialog ( ) {
  document.getElementById("msgBox")
          style.visibility = "hidden";
}
```

In the same way, the open_dialog function is just there to set the visibility to visible:

```
function open_dialog ( ) {
  document.getElementById("msgBox")
          . style.visibility = "visible";
}
```

Next, in order to test the code, you need to place a button, with appropriate JavaScript code, to make the div visible. Obviously, you just use the open_dialog method, as follows:

```
<input type="button" onClick="return open_dialog();"
                          value="Show Dialog">
```

However, the function can be called from any script on the page, in response to a failed form validation or even the user leaving the page altogether.

There is an additional trick that you can use to highlight the appearance of the dialog box further and which illustrates another important set of style properties and manipulation techniques. This is to add an overlay that blanks out the original page when the pop-up message box is shown.

The overlay is defined as follows:

```
<div id="overlay"
  style="position:absolute; width:100%; height:100%;
        left:0; top:0; visibility:hidden;
        background-color:silver; filter:alpha(opacity=50);
        opacity:0.5"></div>
```

The important bit in this code is the filter:alpha(opacity=50), which sets the opacity to 50% in Internet Explorer. There is also an opacity:0.5 style attribute, which does same in other browsers. Without setting the opacity in this way, the whole page would be hidden behind a silver block. The 50% opacity level is a better solution as the page behind remains partially visible.

To use the overlay, the code just needs to set the visibility of the overlay div in exactly the same way as the msgBox div. The visibility should be toggled when the open_dialog and close_dialog functions are called.

The same div technique can be used for navigation bars that drop down. For these to work, the programmer needs to make use of the onMouseOut handler to detect when the mouse leaves the area, so the div can be rolled back up again.

A final use would be to create a tabbed control where clicking a link at the top of the control (the tab) causes other div elements to be shown that might contain different controls or information. This mimics the Windows and Mac style tabbed controls found in most standard applications.

Recap

Client side programming can be used for many tasks, depending on the purpose of the page. JavaScript is a fully implemented language that can complete very complex processing, and coupled with the rich multimedia capabilities of HTML and the standard document model, some very complex effects can be created.

These can be useful to improve navigation or present information in a way that is dynamic, allowing the users to swap between pieces of information on a page very quickly. For example, many online Web 2.0 editing interfaces (such as

Squidoo, Hubpages, or any of the Google document tools) use JavaScript and dynamic HTML to provide a rich editing environment.

Scripted pages are also good for pre-validating form data so that only data that is known to be correct is passed to the server. This both makes the server side programming easier and improves the experience for the end users.

Coupled with other client and server side technologies, JavaScript is useful for creating dynamic data collection services such as questionnaires and shopping carts. Online marketing gurus have shown, for example, that pages that include a quick analysis of someone's knowledge level increase the sign-up rate for special offers.

To do this, a modified version of the data validation script can be used for a simple approach or a tie-in with server side programming can be used for more complex setups where the server returns the result of the quick question and answer session.

JavaScript can be combined with other communication technologies such as XML to improve the flow around a Website—classic examples of this are the Google AdSense Keyword Research Tool and the Google Suggest service. They both leverage connections to an online database mixing JavaScript, XML, and server side scripting to create pages of "live" data.

CHAPTER 6

SERVER SIDE SCRIPTING

This chapter covers one of the most important topics in Web programming for those who plan to create easy-to-update sites, with dynamic content or interactive possibilities. Interaction with visitors includes the ability to offer shopping carts, vote in polls, or comment on blogs, all key parts of today's Web commerce paradigm.

Server side scripting is the ability to provide scripts to the server that it can run, in the same way that the browser can run client side scripts, to generate HTML or XML pages. Generally, the use of server side scripting is limited to these two formats, although there are libraries available that will generate other artifacts such as images or sound.

Unlike with client side scripting, the end user (visitor) never sees the code that generates the pages, so it is a useful technique if there are proprietary techniques or technologies that the Web programmer would not want to share with anyone else. All that is delivered to the browser is the result of executing the script.

In addition, the server side script also has access to all the resources on the server—databases, email, plain text files, and so on—which means that it can do a lot of local processing before proceeding to deliver the results to the browser. There will be some restrictions as to what is available locally, but you need to check with your Web host to see what those restrictions are.

The server side scripting market is quite crowded, with four main contenders:

- Server Side JavaScript

- PHP

- Perl

- Active Server Pages (ASP)

Before I start explaining why I chose PHP, it is worth spending a little time examining the other three, for the sake of completeness. There is no question of bias, but there isn't space in a book of this nature to look at *all* the possible options, and one had to be chosen that was most fit for the purpose of the Just Enough Web programmer.

Take Server Side JavaScript, for example. This does not yet have wide enough acceptances among the free, budget, and even medium priced Web hosts running Linux. Therefore, clever and reusable though the technology might be (after all, the book spends a whole chapter on JavaScript), the popularity of PHP means that it seems to be more widely available at the time of writing.

Plus, most Open Source server side software packages (such as WordPress and other popular content-management systems) are available in PHP. It is, therefore, well worth your time to get to know it a bit better.

Perl is an extremely powerful extraction and reporting language. It has a C-like syntax, which is very similar to JavaScript in some ways, but which also has the power of regular built-in expressions. This facility enables you to build quite convoluted expressions that are evaluated in a number of ways.

This ability makes Perl a good choice for the experienced coder, but for a beginner, it can make the scripts hard to read, write, and debug. Some would argue that there is no need to understand regular expressions to program in Perl, but because many of the modules that you're likely to want to reuse will be written by professional programmers, not understanding them will make it difficult to learn from code that has been downloaded.

Active Server Pages were originally based on Microsoft's Visual Basic language. This makes it a great choice for those who had already had an exposure to VB or VBScript (for browsers). With the move to ASP.Net, Microsoft opened up the languages to include most of those supported by the .Net environment, which made ASP.Net even more flexible. However, it is also a proprietary environment, and as such is not available as Open Source.

Furthermore, the price of hosting for ASP-enabled servers, running Windows, makes them prohibitive for Web programmers who are just starting out. This, combined with the commercial aspects of ASP, makes it unsuitable for discussion here. However, it is an excellent server side solution for Microsoft developers.

Which brings the topic to PHP. PHP is Open Source, has a very wide community following, is based on C styled scripting, and looks and feels vaguely familiar. It is also object oriented (or at least can behave in an object oriented fashion), meaning that Web programmers can play around with their own defined objects as if they were part of the language, which makes life much easier.

PHP also has the support of the hosting community, so any free or budget Linux host will likely support it, and there are even Windows builds available for those wanting to use that particular platform. It can connect to MySQL (a Web database, which you learn about in the next chapter) and comes with libraries for processing XML.

Above all, many if not all of the leading CMSs are written in PHP or have a PHP interface, from WordPress to Drupal, Joomla, and PHP-Nuke. These you'll look at in Chapter 8.

For all of these reasons, Web programmers should at least become conversant with the basic ins and outs of PHP and keep a handy bookmark to this chapter for reference when they encounter something that they do not understand. Also, being aware of the capabilities is as important as being able to read the code—so that if Web programmers find that they need to achieve a given goal, they can work out how, in theory, it should be achieved before using this chapter to look up the actual solution.

PHP Programming

This chapter references PHP 5, although no PHP 5 specific functions have been referenced explicitly. There is always a PHP 4 version of any function or language feature that is discussed here available to those restricted by this version.

Given the acceptance of PHP as a reasonably standard platform, there is also reason to strongly suspect that future releases will remain fairly backwards compatible, too, as one can never be sure, in this Open Source world, what version will be running at any one time.

PHP is used as a *pre-processor*. This means that it's the server has to invoke the PHP software that is installed on the server when serving the page. The PHP software then interprets the various statements that are in PHP script and ignores everything else, passing any output back to the Web server, which forwards it in an appropriate manner to the client.

These PHP scripts are written in plain text, making them easy to edit and upload to the server. Although they can be compiled (which is programmer-speak for turning them into machine code), this is not common for user-created scripts. Most of the modules, which provide additional functionality beyond the core language, are compiled from PHP scripts.

Like JavaScript, PHP can be contained inline within an HTML document, or it can be referenced from an HTML document, usually through embedded PHP code. HTML and PHP can be freely mixed so long as the conventions are followed.

The difference is that all pages that contain PHP code should have the extension .php, so that the system can send them to the pre-processor. In addition, they will probably need to have their permissions changed so that they are classified as executable. Please refer to your Web host's documentation or support forum for more details on this aspect of managing the PHP scripts.

Inline PHP

Inline PHP code can be put in an otherwise normal HTML file, which follows the usual structure, but contains, in places, specially quoted code. The correct way to break out of HTML and introduce some PHP is as follows:

```
<body>
<b>This is HTML.</b>
<?php
// PHP code here
?>
<b>This is also HTML.</b>
</body>
```

The server evaluates the PHP code by passing it to the pre-processor, which allows the programmer to write PHP code that can create HTML statements. This uses one of the built-in features of PHP, the echo statement. An example of this is as follows:

```php
<?php
echo "<b>Bold Text</b>";
?>
```

Because PHP has constructs for selective, repetitive, and conditional processing, this means that you can create blocks of code that generate HTML on the same basis. So, for example, you can choose the background color of a document based on input from the user, if you wanted to.

Note that all of this effort will be for naught if PHP is not installed on the server. In this case, one of two things will happen. The PHP code might be identified by the server as text and returned to the browser as a page of text, thereby exposing the PHP code.

The more likely outcome, in modern server environments, is that the server returns an error page, as it is not sure what to do with the PHP file, having only been set up to serve HTML, images, and some other forms of files.

There is a third option, and that is that the server treats the PHP code as a proprietary object, and the browser starts to download it by asking the user to specify the location for the .php file. Clearly none of the three outcomes is desirable, so you'll have to verify that your host supports PHP if you want to make the most of this chapter.

Like JavaScript, the convention is that all PHP lines must be terminated by a semicolon (;), although in some cases it can be omitted. Because the rules as to when this is the case are reasonably complex, it is better just to assume that every statement that is complete has to be terminated in this way.

Unlike client side scripting, the HTML code is delivered to the browser, because it is the server that evaluates the file. This means that when users select View Source from the menu, all they see is the resulting HTML code. This keeps the PHP source hidden, but does introduce an issue when trying to locate problems.

Therefore, it is going to be easier for the developer to correctly indent any HTML code that is generated. Otherwise, finding issues in a file of generated HTML will be nearly impossible.

Indentation can be introduced just by using space characters, and lines can be broken by using the special \n character. This might need some explanation, so consider the following PHP fragment:

```
<?php
echo "<table>";
echo "<tr>";
echo "<td>Table content</td>";
echo "</tr>";
echo "</table>";
?>
```

You might hope that this code would generate:

```
<table>
<tr>
<td>Table content</td>
</tr>
</table>
```

However, what the PHP fragment actually creates is all on a single line:

```
<table><tr><td>Table content</td></tr></table>
```

Now, if you are debugging a single line, this does not matter so much. But the chances are that a PHP file will generate HTML over several lines—perhaps as many as 100. If it is all concatenated in this way, it will become unreadable.

To break it up, you can use the following PHP:

```
<?php
echo "<table>\n";
echo "<tr>\n";
echo "<td>Table content</td>\n";
echo "</tr>\n";
echo "</table>\n";
?>
```

This result is easy to read as PHP, and also generates HTML that is equally easy to read.

All kinds of code can be generated inline in this way; for example:

- Conditionally included external script files (such as .js, .css, and so on)

- JavaScript

- HTML

- CSS statements

Of course, PHP files can also be used externally and imported into PHP scripts, and there are a variety of ways to achieve this result.

External PHP

The easiest way to reference an external PHP file is through the include function, and is usually inserted in a block of PHP code. For example:

```
<?php
  include 'my_module.php';
?>
```

From the point that it has been included, the code is treated as if it were part of the underlying code file. Other files can also be included from the included file as well, so that an entire application can be built and included in a single line of code.

This mechanism is often used by content-management systems (such as Drupal, Nuke, Joomla, and others) to include variables that can be set by the programmer. These variables communicate certain settings to the underlying system, allowing for easy configuration just by altering a set of variables in an included file.

The advantage is that the programmers can create their own include file to contain the relevant variables, and it can be included after the defaults to overwrite the pre-selected values. Keeping the variables together means that they do not have to be repeated for each PHP script that uses them—they can just be included by filename whenever they are required.

There is also a function require(module) offered by the PHP language itself. This is identical to the include statement, with one difference. If there is an error in loading and executing the script, it will halt the script at that point with an error.

The include statement just produces an error in such cases, and execution of the rest of the calling script continues nonetheless.

Both of the approaches also have a _once() variation. For example:

```
include_once 'my_module.php';
```

or

```
require_once 'my_module.php';
```

These variations could equally well have been written with quotes or parentheses and double or single quotes enclosing the string containing the name of the module. So, the following are equally valid:

```
include_once "my_module.php";
```

or

```
require_once ('my_module.php');
```

or

```
require ("my_module.php");
```

The _once() variations are for use when the programmer wants the file to be included (evaluated) only once for the execution of a script. So, even when it is included multiple times from different scripts, all called from the main script, it will be evaluated only once.

Preventing the reevaluation means that any variables set are kept for the duration of the script's execution, and if they are changed, they will not be reset. This mechanism is useful when multiple scripts share the same base set of functions and/or variables.

General Concepts

Before looking at the parts of PHP that make it truly useful as a language, you first need to understand some general concepts that you'll see in the various illustrative examples that make up the discussion of the more complex topics.

Readers who have made it through the client side scripting discussions will find the terminology familiar. Those who have not might like to take a moment to go to the beginning of Chapter 5 and read about variables, types, loops, and conditional structures so that you're familiar with the basics of programming.

As a reminder:

- Variables are places to store information.

- Each variable has a type associated with it that limits what can be stored in it and how it is processed.

- Decision structures are based around conditions that evaluate to true or false.

- Loops allow the programmers to repeat a specific set of instructions a given number of times or until a predefined condition is reached.

Bearing this in mind, there are some essential underlying basic concepts that you should understand before proceeding to the main programming part of the chapter.

Types and Variables

The PHP language supports eight primitive types—four scalar, two compound, and one special value, with some overlap between the mathematical types (hence there are really only seven discrete data types, but eight identifiers). A scalar type can contain one value for a (possibly infinite) set of allowed values.

PHP treats strings as scalar types, because arrays are defined as compound types, which contain elements of differing types. So, a compound type can use a single variable to refer to an object that has components that have a variety of individual types—an address might contain a street number and a street name, for example.

The four scalar types are as follows:

- `boolean`

- `integer`

- `float` (also called a `double`)

- `string`

The following sections discuss each of these types in detail.

`boolean` This is the same as a Boolean value in any other language, except that must be written as either `TRUE` or `FALSE`, in capital letters. PHP is fairly type-insensitive and will quite freely convert a `boolean` from `TRUE` to 1 and `FALSE` to 0. In addition, `FALSE` can be equated with empty strings and arrays.

`integer`   Any 32-bit number can be stored in an integer, giving a large scope of values, both positive and negative. There is no unsigned version, so there will be an architecture-dependent limit on the size of value that can be stored there.

Integers can be cast from floating point numbers, but this will cause the result to be rounded down to the lowest integer value. The `round()` function is available to round the cast properly. This would be necessary when rounding the result of an integer division:

```php
$one = 1;
$two = 2;
$my_result = $one / $two; // == 0.5
echo (int) $my_result; // 0
echo round ( $my_result ); // 1
```

The reason for the cast is that there is no integer division in PHP, so the result is always a floating point number.

`float` **(also called a `double`)**   These are equivalent in PHP, and can store a precision of roughly 14 digits, as in the IEEE standard for 64-bin floating point number representation. You can use the usual mathematical operators with both floating point and integer numbers, as you would expect.

`string`   The PHP string is a very important data type, as it is used for a variety of purposes. A string can be created by placing single or double quotes around it, for example:

```php
$my_string = "hello";
$my_other_string = 'goodbye';
```

On the face of it, these two are functionally equivalent. However, singly quoted strings do not allow for escaping of special characters, including \n (carriage return) or \t (tab). Doubly quoted strings, however, allow for this, and subsequently, they are converted properly. In such cases, a double quote may be escaped (\") to be displayed as part of a string. For example:

```php
$my_string = "\"hello\""; // "hello"
$my_other_string = '\"goodbye\"'; // \"goodbye\"
```

The reason that the second line does not work as expected is that singly quoted strings accept escaping of characters. Doubly quoted strings also allow for expansion of variables inline. So, for example:

```
$my_substring = "green";
$my_string = "The color is $my_substring.";
            // The color is green
```

This would not be possible using a singly quoted string. There is also a final way to populate strings, using the *heredoc* operator, denoted by <<<. For example, to assign a chunk of text:

```
$my_string <<<EOD
This all goes into
my string.
EOD;
```

The heredoc behaves the same as if it were assigning a string in double quotes; therefore, it allows variable expansion and quoted characters. So, the variables can be embedded in the usual way.

Conversion to numbers from strings is automatic, but the reverse is not true. To do this, the strval($value) function must be used, which will return an appropriate string for the $value offered.

Finally, to concatenate two strings, the . operator must be used, which can be combined with the assignment operator to split a concatenation over several operations. For example:

```
$end = "the" . " " . "end";
$my_string = "The beginning ...";
$my_string .= "..."; // The beginning ... ...
$my_string .= "... the" . $end;
            // The beginning ... ... ... the the end
```

Other handy string operators and functions can be found in the PHP short reference section of this chapter.

The two compound types are as follows:

- array

- object

array   Unlike other languages, an array in PHP is stored as a map of data, which includes the possibility to store arrays of arrays, where each map has a key and a value. Simple arrays with no keys are also possible, but an array of characters does not equate to a string as it does in so many other languages.

So, the following will create a simple array;

```
$my_numbers = array ( 1, 3, 5, 7, 9 );
```

Notice in this example that the array object constructor is used to build the type, which is not necessary for scalar types. The array is, as usual, indexed on zero, so accessing the first element can be done with:

```
$first_number = $my_numbers[0];
```

Here, notice the usual [ ] notation for accessing elements in the array. Of course, variables that resolve to a valid index can also be used to return the value stored at that index.

This is especially useful when creating maps of values. This is highlighted when the following code is considered:

```
$my_pie_recipe =
  array ( "meat" => "chicken", "vegetable"
  => "potato", "serves" => 4 );
```

This code creates an array that contains three values, each indexed by a key. Instead of returning a value using a zero-based index, you can now write code such as:

```
echo "Pie with meat will be a " .
          $my_pie_recipe['meat'] . " pie.";
```

This code will output the following:

```
Pie with meat will be a chicken pie.
```

In itself, this is not staggering. However, when combined with a variable, it means that you can construct code such as:

```
$pie_type = "meat";
echo "Pie with $pie_type will be a
    ".$my_pie_recipe[$pie_type] . " pie.";
```

The output of this code will be the same as before:

```
Pie with meat will be a chicken pie.
```

However, if you want to print out the recipe for the vegetable pie, all you need to do is change the $pie_type variable to access the array using a different key. In both cases the "serves" key remains completely independent of the other two. All the pies will serve exactly four people.

object The object data type is assigned to a variable that is an instance of a class and is therefore classified as a compound data type. The concept of classes in PHP programming is a reasonably advanced topic and is discussed next.

Finally, there is the NULL data type that's assigned to a variable that has had no value set or has had its value explicitly unset with the unset($variable) function. This is quite a special data type often used for testing when the result of an operation might be in question, and in database operations so indicate that no data is necessary for a given field.

All of these data types can be used to create variables of different kinds, for different uses. Some are defined for use by the system, and others can be set as constants. One set of such values are known as the superglobals, which are system predefined variables.

Predefined Variables There is a set of predefined system variables that all start with the identifier $_ and are used to store system values. These are often referred to as the superglobals, and are available to all scripts running under the PHP processor.

A global variable is available to all code within a certain scope, usually after it has been defined in a given script. The superglobals do not have to be explicitly included in this way—they are always available.

The most important for the Web programmer are the following predefined variables that allow communication with the Web browser, by way of the request that's sent from the browser to the server. The three single most important ones are as follows:

```
$_GET        The result of a form's GET request
$_POST       The result of a form's POST request
$_COOKIE     Cookie data
```

You'll learn about how to use these later on, but they are stored as arrays of key and value pairs which map on to the form or cookie that has been used to store and/or submit the data. So, if you have a form that is designed to create a search query, using the HTTP GET request, you can use the following to extract the term:

```
$query = $_GET['q'];
```

This snippet assumes that the URL that referenced it was:

```
http://myserver.com/search.php?q=search+text
```

If the search text was submitted through a POST request, you could use the companion array key:

```
$query = $_POST['q'];
```

You'll look at these in more detail later on, along with cookie processing.

User-Defined Variables   User-defined variables are all those variables that the programmer deems as necessary to store the data required to process the scripts. Each one has a name and a value and a specific set of rule governing exactly how the name should look.

A variable is declared upon use, or possibly prepared before needed, at the top of the PHP code. Variable names can start with a letter or underscore and can contain letters, numbers, or more underscores. They cannot start with a number or include any other punctuation than an underscore. Furthermore, variable names are case-sensitive and must be declared and used by prefixing the variable name by a dollar sign. This keeps them separate from other pieces of PHP code. So, to define a string, you might use code such as the following:

```
$my_string = "some string data";
$my_123 = 123;
$my_floating_double = 23.456;
```

You can also define variables as *pointing to* existing named variables by prefixing them with an & sign. This creates a reference to the existing variable through another variable, meaning that they both end up pointing to the same value in memory. This is coded as follows:

```
$pVariable = &$myVariable;
        // $pVariable points to $myVariable
```

If a value is assigned, using either of the variable names, the value in memory is altered directly (because one points to the other). Therefore:

```
$pVariable = "more string data";
```

```
echo "->" . $pVariable;
echo $myVariable;
```

This code will display "more string data" twice, because both $pVariable and $myVariable point to the same data (when combined with the preceding code snippet).

Variables are said to be in scope when they can be accessed by PHP code. This is generally dictated by the order at which the lines are executed by the PHP processor, so a file that is included at the top of the PHP code and sets a global variable will make that variable available to the rest of the lines that follow it, even if they are from different included scripts.

However, variables inside functions (named blocks of code) stay local to those functions and cannot be accessed outside, and also mask any global variables that have been set. So, for example, the following code will not do exactly what the programmer might expect:

```
$my_text = "test this";
function myFunction () { // defines a function
  $my_text = "test_that";
  echo $my_text . "\n";
}
echo $my_text;
```

The output of this is as follows:

```
test that
test this
```

The $my_text variable has been masked inside the function myFunction by the local variable with the same name. The way around this is to use the global keyword to denote that the programmer understands that the variables he or she wants to access are global. This tells PHP that when the name is used, it is the global variable that you want to access and not any local ones.

Of course, the local variables then become masked, so ideally different names should be used for global variables, such as $g_my_text rather than $my_text. Alternatively, of course, function names could be attached to local variables to set them apart from any global variables, such as $myFunction_my_text, for example.

Constants   A constant is a value that cannot be changed in the PHP script, once the value has been assigned to the named variable. The value is available to the code only after it has been declared.

The naming conventions for constants are the same as for variables. A good programming convention to follow is to use uppercase names to separate the constants from the other variables visually.

This is why superglobals are denoted in this way—$_GET, for example—because it sets them apart.

Constants are also always global and can be accessed by any part of the script. However, they are limited to containing values that must be one of the built-in scalar types—Boolean, number, and string.

Constants are declared by using the define keyword, as follows:

```
define ("MY_CONSTANT", "the value");
define ("MY_NUMBER", 42);
```

The other thing that sets the constants apart from regular variables is that they do not have a dollar prefix. So, to use the constant defined previously in a piece of PHP code, you can use the following code:

```
echo MY_CONSTANT;
```

Constants are useful when creating code that needs values that can be changed according to a specific installation—for example, in a blog system, the default number of posts to display per page might be five. Rather than using a global variable to store this, and having to include the appropriate file, the programmer might decide to define a constant to store the value instead.

Classes

Classes are self-contained object templates that contain the data definition and method implementation that processes that data. The array data type is an example of a class and is instantiated by calling something called the class constructor.

Classes are good for modularity because they allow programmers to encapsulate the behavior and data into a single place that can be easily interfaced with. This also helps to make the code that accesses that functionality cleaner.

A class can be defined using the following skeleton:

```
class name
{
  var member;
```

```
  function name() // constructor
  {
    // Instantiate the object
  }

 function method()
 {
    // Operate on the object, perhaps return a value
  }


}
```

If this appears in a PHP file, you can use the following PHP code to instantiate it and access the method that it defines:

```
$variable = new name();
name->method();
```

Naturally, wherever there is a name in italics, the programmer should substitute his or her own identifiers. So, to create an object that is designed to represent, for example, an Amazon.com product, you might create a class as follows:

```
class AmazonProduct
{
  var $ASIN;

  function AmazonProduct ( $ASIN_in ) // constructor
  {
    // Instantiate the object
    $this->ASIN = $ASIN_in;
  }

 function MakeLink ()
 {
    // Operate on the object, perhaps return a value
    // The following is entirely fictional,
    // for illustration only!
    $link = "http://www.amazon.com/books
              /$this->ASIN/aff=12345";
    return "<a href=$link>$this-7gt;ASIN</a>";
  }


}
```

Note that access to the member variables is achieved through the this variable, which is treated as a variable name in itself. This negates the need to prefix the variable with a dollar sign, as the whole stanza this->member is treated as the variable.

To use this class, programmers have to allocate it to a variable:

```
$my_book = new AmazonProduct ( "159863481X" );
```

From this point on, whenever programmers need to insert a link to the product whose ASIN is 159863481X, they can do so with a simple call to the MakeLink member function:

```
echo $my_book->MakeLink();
```

You'll see the various ways in which functions can be defined in more detail later on. Each one is just a block of named code that can be specified once and called multiple times with different sets of data to operate on.

One final note is that the programmer can only break the class definition into multiple code blocks if that is done within a method definition. This is to allow the programmer to break out of a method to use plain HTML code and then step back into the class to finish off the definition.

It is also possible to access the properties of a class from outside it; however, in the interests of modularity, I would argue that this should be kept to a minimum. Nevertheless, the same arrowed notation can be used, as follows:

```
echo $my_book->ASIN;
```

This line of code would simply output the ASIN of the $my_book object.

Clearly, if this was to be allowed between method definitions, it would be at a time when there is no executable code being evaluated, and the result would not be coherent. For example, this is perfectly allowable:

```
<?php
class myClass {
// there is no executable code here
  function myClassFunction () {
  ?> <!- out of php code ->
    <b>This is executed in myClassFunction</b>
  <?php // back in again
  }
}
?>
```

In this code, when `myClass->myClassFunction()` is called, the only thing it will do is generate the bold line of text. This illustrates the power of jumping in and out of inline PHP within a class definition, but it is also to be used with care because it is easy to lose track of the script when moving in and out of PHP code and HTML.

Operators

The PHP language has the usual complement of comparison, mathematical, and logical operators, plus a few special ones for processing strings and arrays. You can use an operator to compare two PHP expressions or to combine them. Some of those combinations result in a modification of the operands (the variables on the left or right of the operator).

Expressions that are built up using operators can also be grouped by using parentheses to override the orders of precedence built into the language. As a rule of thumb it is always better to write:

```
$var = ($a + $b) - ($c * ($d / $e));
```

rather than:

```
$var = $a + $b - $c * $d / $e;
```

Even if the programmer knows that the two expressions should evaluate to the same final value, using parentheses makes sure that there are no misconceptions and also improves the debugging (error fixing) rounds.

Comparison   The PHP language supports the usual collection of comparison operators that you can use with the basic built-in scalar types except the string. This limits their use to numbers and the Boolean data types. Of those, only the simple tests for equality can be used with both numbers and Booleans.

The basic equality test is the familiar ==, which can be used to test for equality of two expressions, which can be built up from multiple PHP elements. The result of the comparison is true if both sides of the operator are equal. For example:

```
var_dump( 1 == 1); // prints true
var_dump( 0 == 1); // prints false
$one = 2;
var_dump( $one == 1 ); // prints false
```

The companion operator, !=, tests for inequality. It returns `true` when both of the expressions are not equal and `false` otherwise. So, for example:

```
var_dump ( "1" != 1 ); // prints false after conversion to number
var_dump ( $one != 1 ); // prints true, see above
```

For all numerical types (and in some cases the other types, but that is subject to a set of complex rules for internal type conversion), the following comparison operators are also allowed:

a < b	Is a less than b?
a > b	Is a greater than b?
a <= b	Is a less than or equal to b?
a >= b	Is a greater than or equal to b?

The PHP processor will convert values according to its own logic. So, strings provided for comparison will be converted to numbers and compared accordingly. If a string contains no numerical data, the chances are that it will be converted to zero.

Similarly, the comparison of a float and an integer will return TRUE only if both are identical, so no rounding will take place. Bearing these rules in mind, you're well advised to do any type conversions explicitly, to avoid any assumptions creating invalid logic in the scripted code.

Mathematical and Logical   The set of mathematical operators includes the usual range of familiar operations:

+	Add
*	Multiply
/	Divide
−	Subtract

These can be used with any numerical data types, although there are some special meanings that these operators take on when they are combined with other data types, as you'll see shortly. Recall that when types are mixed, PHP makes some of its own decisions when it comes to producing a compatible result.

For the sake of a quick reminder:

```
$var_result = 3 / 2;
```

The result of this code is automatically assigned to a floating point value that's placed into `$var_result`, thus making the data type of that variable into a floating point representation, regardless of what it might have been before. It can be cast to an integer by using the cast mechanism:

```
$var_int_result = (int) 3 / 2;
```

However, because it will be rounded down due to PHP's cast mechanism, the resulting value will be 1. To get the correct value (1.5, rounded to 2), it is necessary to use the round() function:

```
$var_int_result = round (3 / 2 );
```

Note that the round() function does not need to be cast to an integer, because that is the value that it returns, nor does the value passed to the function need to be cast in any way.

Apart from this minor curio, the mathematical operators work in exactly the fashion that is expected. The operators can also be combined with the assignment operator (=) to assign the result to a variable. Some examples of this are as follows:

```
$result = 0;
$result += 3; // $result = $result + 3
$result /= 2; // $result = $result / 2
$result *= 3; // $result = $result * 3
$operand = 4;
$result -= $operand * 5; // $result = $result - 4 * 5
```

Many programmers will find it easier to debug code where the fully expanded version of these operations has been used, but the previous method is a useful shorthand in many cases. In addition, you can use the + and – operators in conjunction with a variable as a post-increment or decrement operation.

For example, the post-decrement operator looks like the following:

```
$result++; // $result += 1 or $result = $result + 1
```

This point applies equally to the – operator, which performs a decrement rather than an increment. The other mathematical operators cannot be used in the same way.

The logical operators are as follows:

&&	and	Returns true if both operands are true
||	or	Returns true if one or the other or both operands are true
n/a	xor	Returns true if one or the other of the operands are true
!	not	Returns true when the operand is false, false otherwise

These operators all take two operands, except the not operator, which simply inverts the Boolean value of the expression to which it relates. Each of the operands must be a Boolean value, which usually means that it is the result of a comparison, contained in parentheses to ease readability.

For example:

```
($a == $b ) && ($c == $d)        true when all are equal
```

Each of the operands can also be used as the symbol or keyword variant, so || is functionally equivalent to or. There is no such symbol equivalent for xor, which is different from other languages which use the ^ symbol.

The result of the operations can also be assigned to a variable, which will take the Boolean data type upon assignation. For example:

```
$result = true && false;
$result = ($a == $b) || ($b >= $c);
```

In the first example, $result would become equal to false, and in the second, if $a is equal to $b or if $b is greater than or equal to $c, $result will be assigned the value true. These can take some getting used to, but they are very useful.

String and Array   String operations come in two flavors—assignment and concatenation. There are other functions for operating on strings, but using these is more complex than just applying an operator. As you've seen before, assignment works for both singly and doubly quoted strings:

```
$string_one = "a string\n";
$string_two = 'another string';
```

You can concatenate these two by using a fragment such as:

```
$string_three = $string_one . $string_two;
```

This will result in $string_three taking the result of the concatenation—"a string\nanother string". However, in the final result, the two parts will be separated by a carriage return as a result of the expansion of the escape sequence \n.

Arrays can also be used with the operators that are usually reserved for mathematical comparisons and assignments; however, they take on a slightly different meaning. Not all of the mathematical symbols have an equivalent, and there are also a whole range of other array processing functions which you'll read about later in the chapter.

This chapter won't look at all the possibilities, because most of them simply aren't useful to the Just Enough programmer. The first is the == equality operator, which will return true if the two arrays have the same key/value pairs, in any order.

For example:

```
$array_a = array ( 1 => "One", 2 => "Two", 3 => "Three" );
$array_b = array ( 1 => "one", 2 => "three", 3 => "two" );
$array_c = array ( 2 => "Two", 1 => "One", 3 => "Three" );
var_dump ( $array_a == $array_b ); // false
var_dump ( $array_a == $array_c ); // true
```

The reason that $array_a and $array_c are considered to be equal is because they contain the same key/value pairs, even though they are not in the same order. In order to test for absolute equality, you use the identity comparison operator, ===.

With this in mind, if you repeat the last comparison using this operator, you get a different value:

```
var_dump ( $array_a === $array_c ); // false
```

This operator also has a companion, the non-identity comparison, !==, which tests for the opposite. Therefore, placing this in the previous statement, you arrive at:

```
var_dump ( $array_a !== $array_c ); // true
```

Naturally, there is also the inequality operator, !=, which performs the reverse check to the equality operator. Again, if you apply this to the previous example:

```
var_dump ( $array_a != $array_b ); // true
var_dump ( $array_a != $array_c ); // false
```

Like some other languages, but unlike C and JavaScript, PHP also allows you to use the greater and less than signs together to perform the inequality test:

```
var_dump ( $array_a <> $array_b ); // true
var_dump ( $array_a <> $array_c ); // false
```

So, the operators are not dissimilar in many ways, except that the array complicates the comparison process somewhat by containing a map of data. Obviously, the same process works for arrays that are not organized into a map, too.

Flow Control

One of the most important parts of any programming language, as you are by now aware, is the possibility to change the flow of the execution around the script. This allows you to conditionally include piece of code and repeat certain sections.

For example, if a list of blog entries contains some categories that should not be displayed, you might want to process each one, one at a time, and only display certain entries in the resulting page. This requires a loop to go through each entry and a decision to print the entry conditionally based on the result of a comparison operation.

To do the latter, you use decision making, and there are a variety of constructs to facilitate this.

Decision Making

As with JavaScript, the basic decision-making unit is the if construct. This can be a simple case of testing a single condition, as the following shows:

```
if ( $blog_entry->category == 1 ) {
  // print blog entry
}
```

Deconstructing the previous code, note that the code that you want to execute if the condition evaluates to true is contained in braces { and }. In the bracketed condition part, you can use any valid PHP expression that evaluates to true.

In case you need to provide an alternative operation to the one that was intended when the condition is met, the else construct can be added:

```
if ( $blog_entry->category == 1 ) {
  // print blog entry
}
else {
 // do something else
}
```

In this snippet, if the condition is not met, the contents of the else construct will be executed. There is an alternative notation for the else statement, born out of the need to break out of PHP occasionally. The generic form for this notation is as follows:

```
if ( condition ) : some code
else : some other code
endif;
```

Clearly this method is just a template, and you need to embellish it with actual PHP code, but it quickly becomes quite complex:

```php
if ( $blog_entry->category == 1 ) : $blog_entry->display();
else : $blog_entry->show_link();
endif;
```

So far, so good. However, the main reason for the new notation is to ease the possibility to break out of the PHP. In order to add the HTML that will embellish the result of the supposed $blog_entry object member functions, you can construct code such as:

```php
<?php if ( $blog_entry->category == 1 ) : ?>
Blog entry title : <?php $blog_entry->display(); ?>
<?php else : ?>
Blog link to alternative : <?php $blog_entry->show_link();
endif; ?>
```

More alternatives can be added to the basic if .. else construct by introducing the elseif keyword. This allows you to test a second (third, fourth, and so on) condition within the same decision block. For example:

```php
<?php
if ( $blog_entry->category == 1 ) {
   // category 1 logo
?>
<img src="logo_1.gif">
<?php
}
elseif ( $blog_entry->category == 2 ) {
   // category 2 logo
?>
<img src="logo_2.gif"7gt;
<?php
}
else {
   // default logo
?>
<img src="logo_default.gif">
<?php
}
?>
```

(Note that the logo_default.gif file should be present in the same folder as the PHP code in order for it to work properly.)

You can use this code example with the alternative construction as well by following the same approach as before. Note that this code breaks out of the PHP script to write the image tag straight in as HTML rather than using an echo statement from the PHP code itself.

The other kind of decision-making construct that PHP offers should also be familiar to you, and is the switch construct, which is used to avoid endless if, elseif, else nesting. If you put this into the same logic as the previous code, you see the obvious advantage of using the switch construct:

```php
switch ( $blog_entry->category ) {
case 1 :
  echo "<img src=\"logo_1.gif\">";
  break;
case 2 :
  echo "<img src=\"logo_2.gif\">";
  break;
default :
  echo "<img src=\"logo_default.gif\">";
  break;
}
```

As in other languages, such as JavaScript, the break keyword stops the evaluation and breaks out of the switch construct. Again, the default clause produces a result when the other statements all evaluate to false.

Unlike in other languages, the switch .. case construct can test a variety of data types, including numbers and, interestingly, strings.

Looping

If you need to construct a block of code that is to be executed a number of times, PHP gives you several alternatives. The first is the basic while loop, with the evaluation of the termination condition at the top of the loop:

```php
while ( $blog_entry->category == 1 ) {
  // do something
  $blog_entry = $blog_list[$entry++]; // get the next one
}
```

This construct is accompanied by a version that uses the alternative notation that you have encountered in the previous section. This looks akin to the following:

```php
while ( $blog_entry->category == 1 ) :
```

```
    // do something
    $blog_entry = $blog_list[$entry++]; // get the next one
endwhile;
```

Note that I have added the `endwhile` keyword to the end of the loop to show PHP where I would like it to end. In either case, you can break out of the PHP in the usual manner, using the `<?php` and `?>` notation in order to mix in HTML code.

The alternative to the `while` loop is the `do .. while` loop. Here, the evaluation is performed at the end of the loop:

```
do {
    // do something
    $blog_entry = $blog_list[$entry++]; // get the next one
} while ($blog_entry->category == 1);
```

The key difference between the two is that the loop will execute at least once in the `do .. while` loop, whereas it might not execute at all in the `while` loop where the evaluation is done at the top of the loop construct. Another difference is that the `do .. while` loop cannot be constructed using the alternative notation for other flow control code blocks.

The last kind of looping mechanism you are going to look at is the `for` loop. This comes in two different flavors, each providing for the alternative notation as well as the standard usage with braces. The generic `for` statement allows initialization, comparison, and alteration clauses:

```
for ( $entry = 0; $entry < count($blog_list); $entry++) {
    // process entries
}
```

This snippet uses the `count()` function to check that the `for` loop only executes as many times as there are elements in the `$blog_list` array. The alternative notation follows the same general form as the previous constructs:

```
for ( $entry = 0; $entry < count($blog_list); $entry++ ) :
    // process entries
endfor;
```

There is also a simpler way to process items that are part of a collection, such as an array, by using the `foreach` construct. This assigns a value to a temporary variable that is placed in the `foreach` statement as follows:

```
foreach ( $blog_list as $blog_entry) {
```

```
  // process entries
}
```

This block is functionally equivalent to the `while` and `for` loop constructs already discussed, but without the `$entry` counter to index into the array. The alternative notation for the `foreach` construct is as follows:

```
foreach ( $blog_list as $blog_entry ) :
  // do things
endforeach;
```

Finally, there are two important keywords for use with loops—`break` and `continue`. The `break` keyword works in the same way for loops as it does for the `switch` construct; it breaks out of the loop without completing processing. You can use this to exit the loop prematurely when a specific condition is met.

The `continue` keyword is similar in a way, except that it does not break out of the loop, but moves to the next iteration. So, if there is a specific entry that you do not want to process, you can skip an iteration. The code for this might look something like this:

```
foreach ( $blog_list as $blog_entry) {
  if ( $blog_entry->category != 1 ) {
    continue; // we don't process these
  }
  // process entries
}
```

Although the `foreach` loop was used to illustrate the `continue` keyword, it can be used with any of the previous loops, as can the `break` keyword. With these looping capabilities, you can build any data processing model.

Functions

A function is a named block of code that can be called, with or without parameters, from a piece of PHP code once the function has been defined. These functions can also return values.

The first thing to note is that function names are not case-sensitive. This is different from the rest of the PHP syntax and also most other programming languages. However, it will make programming and maintaining scripts easier if function names are treated as if they are case-sensitive.

The scope of functions is global once the function has been defined, and this means that if it is conditionally defined, using an `if` construct or similar, it is accessible only once the condition has been satisfied and the function has been evaluated. If the code never gets executed, the function will never be defined and hence will never exist.

If you remember that all PHP scripts are evaluated in a top-down fashion, and on demand as they are required, this means that, potentially, some functions will never be executed.

This is a little counter-intuitive, especially when you consider that functions are available from anywhere after the point at which they were defined. This also extends to functions that are defined inside another function.

Subsequently, you have to be very careful about naming functions correctly so that if a module is used that comes from the outside, it is useful to have a function list so that different identifiers are used. When you design code that's to be made available for wider use, it is also useful to include some kind of function identifier to keep the names unique.

An example of a simple function that takes a parameter and returns a value is as follows:

```
function getBold ( $text )
{
  return "<b>$text</b>";
}
```

Of course, functions can be defined that do not accept a value or return one. In the former case, this just means that the function name is followed by parentheses that are empty. If no value is returned, the only difference is that the `return` keyword is not used.

In addition, you can define functions that have a default in case the programmer using the function is not passing a value for some reason. To do this, the first line (where the definition is established) is as follows:

```
function getBold ($text = "")
```

Function parameters can be passed by reference or by value. Passing by value means that if a variable is passed in the parameter list, it cannot be changed by the function. To pass by reference, which will allow these changes, all that you need to do is put a & in front of the variable name in the function definition:

```
function makeBold ( &$text ) // Pass by reference
{
```

```
    // function code
    $text = "<b>$text</b>";
}
// more code here
$myText = "Title Text";
makeBold ( $myText );
echo $myText;
```

Before you develop your own functions to perform specific processing, first read through the section entitled "PHP Short Function Reference," which covers the most useful of the functions provided by PHP to help you achieve your programming goals.

There is no sense trying to reinvent the wheel, and the community support of PHP as a Web language is such that virtually every function imaginable has already been thought of, and most of them have been implemented.

PHP Short Function Reference

This section is a not a complete reference guide to PHP, but it covers, in a compact fashion, the available functions and common extensions that you will encounter when building your Web applications.

In particular, it is a good handy reference to have when you're reading the remainder of the book, which shows you how these technologies are applied in real applications. Many of the examples that are presented in future chapters draw on the knowledge contained in this short reference guide.

Common Modules and Functions

There are over 150 common modules and functions listed in the PHP manual, and the vast majority of these are available in default binary builds, or in PHP processors that have been built from scratch by Web host providers. Luckily, knowledge of these is based on a need-to-know model—if you need it, look it up.

However, there is a set of core libraries that contain some vital extensions to the basic PHP library for manipulating data types, as well as some extensions that can be compiled into the main PHP processor and offer key external functionality, such as the ability to connect to a MySQL database.

Without going into too much detail, it is better to have these compiled into the environment, because to have to run an external PHP script every time a core library or extension has to be accessed would not be very efficient. These things are also so fundamental to PHP programming and understanding PHP code that you will encounter (and perhaps want to extend) that they are worthy of closer examination here.

Core Libraries

Some parts of the PHP system are actually libraries that extend the core functionality of the language. So, for example, all the array manipulation functions (those that are prefixed by `array_`) are part of the core libraries and not the language itself.

In addition, there is a collection of functions for manipulating arrays (`count`, `sort`, `in_array`, `current`, `next`, and so on) that are listed in the function reference and that are part of the libraries and not the PHP language proper.

Array functions include anything listed as `array_` plus a collection of non-prefixed array manipulation functions such as `count`, `sort`, `in_array`, `current`, `next`, `prev`, `reset`, and `end`.

Class functions include `class_exists` and other functions that get information about a specific class and are also extensions to the core language. These functions very useful for object oriented or modular programming. The class library includes the core language constructs for creating classes.

Date and time functions, including functions for manipulating date information, are also part of the core libraries

Finally, there is a set of DOM functions that allow the handling of HTML and XML documents, both local and remote, using a well-defined API. These functions are very easy to use for basic tag extraction, for example, or when creating/validating XML feeds.

This is not an exhaustive list, but gives an overview of the most common core libraries and the ones that are used most frequently in PHP programming. In addition to the libraries, there is also a set of extensions that can be compiled into the language when it is activated within an environment.

Unlike the core libraries, the extensions might not be available from one provider to another.

Compiled-In Extensions

The `php_info()` command shows what options have been compiled in. It can be used in a simple PHP script to display the various libraries that are available. Be warned, however, that it can lead to a rather long document being displayed in the browser window.

However, the alternative is to use the `function_exists(function)` command, which returns `true` if a given function is available. Of course, by this point in the script it may be too late, but it will at least give the possibility to choose between possible graceful exits or alternative solutions.

The MySQL database extension is a common one and is used here for database-ing and so I have listed it in the function reference.

Function Reference

The following is not exhaustive. It is, however, a summary of the functions that you'll encounter when you read and write PHP code. Some of the more esoteric functions in each class have been left out: the chances are that if you need an esoteric function, you are experienced enough to know that it exists.

The functions are broken into functional areas:

- Core functions
- Math functions
- Variables and classes
- Strings
- Arrays
- Web- and browser-related functions
- MySQL functions

The last two areas pertain particularly to Web programming and will provide vital information that is built on in the "Examples" section of this chapter as well as in future chapters when you start gluing all the pieces together and making Web applications.

Core Functions

These functions perform useful tasks related to built-in features of the PHP programming language and do not have a specific entry in the sections that follow. They will probably crop up in many projects that you put together, either from components created by other people or from your own coded solutions.

The first two are system functions—`eval` and `die`.

eval   The `eval` function takes a string and evaluates it is if it were PHP code:

```
eval( "$my_var = \"a string\");
echo $my_var;
```

This code will output `"a string"`. The `$my_var` variable had not existed until the `eval` function was called. The return value from `eval` is always set to `null` *unless* the code in the evaluation part returns a value, in which case the return value is passed back as the `eval` return value.

die   The `die` function is used to do two things:

- Print an error message

- Halt the script

When `die` is encountered, no more processing will take place, and the error message passed to the function (if any) will be displayed. An example is as follows:

```
if (not_logged_in($user)) {
  die ("Error : $user not logged in.");
}
```

As you'll see in the "Examples" section, `die` is generally used to catch system errors such as the inability to connect to a database.

unset   The `unset` function unsets a variable and sets it to `null`.

getdate   The `getdate` function returns an array that contains several key/value pairs, representing the current date/time at the server:

mday	From 1 to 31 (day of the month)
wday	From 0 to 6 (Sunday to Saturday)
mon	Numeric month of year, 1 to 12
month	Textual equivalent of mon, January to December
year	The year, in four-digit format; that is, 2008

yday	The day of the year, zero-based
hours	The hour component of the current time, 0 to 23
minutes	The minute component of the current time, 0 to 59
seconds	The second component of the current time, 0 to 59

Each of these key/value pairs can be accessed through its key:

```
$today_date = getdate();
echo "The month is $today_date['month'].";
```

For UNIX programmers, it is useful to know that an optional parameter can be supplied that must be the equivalent to the value returned by the time() function.

function_exists   The function_exists function tests to see whether a specific named function has been defined and implemented in the current scope. It is useful for testing, given a possible collection of equivalent routines, which is available for use or for making sure that the function that is about to be defined does not use a name that is already taken.

func_num_args   The func_num_args function returns the number of arguments that were passed to a function and must be called from within that function. For example:

```
function variable_argument_function () {
  $num_args = func_num_args();
  echo ("I was passed $num_args arguments.");
}
variable_argument_function ( "banana", 1, 7 );
```

The output from this code snippet will be:

```
I was passed 3 arguments.
```

This function can be combined with the func_get_arg function to process functions that accept variable argument lists.

func_get_arg   The func_get_arg, when passed an integer, will return the argument passed to the current function, indexed by that integer. To process a variable argument list, you could use code such as:

```
for ( $index = 0; index < func_num_args(); index ++) {
  $arg = func_get_arg(index);
}
```

However, the limitation of this function is that it does not take into account the default arguments when a value has not been passed by the call to the function. Ordinarily, this should not matter.

func_get_args   The `func_get_args` function returns, as an array, the arguments that have been passed to the function containing the call. This allows you to simplify the previous code to use a `foreach` loop:

```
$arglist = func_get_args();
foreach ( $arglist as $arg ) {
  // process $arg
}
```

Like the other argument processing functions, it will generate a warning when not called from inside a function.

Math Functions

This section discusses a useful collection of functions that can be used with numbers. Unless otherwise noted, both integers and floating point number can be used as arguments.

max	Returns the highest of two values
min	Returns lowest of two values

Both the `min` and `max` functions accept two arguments and return one of them by value.

abs	Returns the absolute value of its argument

The `abs` function takes an argument and strips it of any negative sign, and is the equivalent to multiplying a negative number by -1.

sqrt	Returns the square root of a number

The `sqrt` function takes an integer or floating point number and returns its square root in the same data type as was supplied:

```
echo sqrt(9); // prints 3
echo sqrt(9.0); // prints 3.0
```

Previously, you had seen casting from floats to integers and learned that the system always rounds them down. However, there are also some specific functions for otherwise rounding and converting fractions to integers:

ceil	Rounds the supplied floating point number up
floor	Rounds the supplied floating point number down
round	Rounds the supplied floating point either up or down
fmod	Returns the floating point remainder (modulo) of a division

The key difference between the ceil, floor, and round functions is that the floating point argument supplied is usually rounded according to the standard that any value equal to or greater than 0.5 is rounded up. However, ceil would force 0.49 to be rounded up, and floor would force 0.51 to be rounded down:

```
$val_low = 9.51;
$val_hi = 9.49;
echo floor($val_low); // prints 9
echo ceil($val_hi); // prints 10
echo round($val_hi); // prints 9
```

The fmod function returns the remainder of a division. This is calculated as the value left over after the division has taken place, given that the division is expected to yield an integer (whole number) and a remainder. This is much easier to appreciate with an example:

```
$x = 5.7;
$y = 1.3;
$r = fmod ( $x, $y ); // remainder after x/y
```

In this example, $r will contain 0.5. The division of 5.7 by 1.3 yields 4.38..., which is rounded to 4. Next, 4 is multiplied by 1.3 to see what the result would be. This results in 5.2, which makes the remainder 0.5 (5.7 − 5.2).

There are also two functions for generating random numbers:

mt_rand	Generates a random number
mt_srand	Seeds the random number algorithm

The mt_srand function accepts a value to seed the generator with, but can be called without a parameter to generate its own seed. Once seeded, the mt_rand function can be called, with two parameters, indicating the minimum and maximum integers between which the value should be. So, to generate a random number between 1 and 100, you use this:

```
$echo mt_rand(1, 100);
```

Finally, the math library contains a whole collection of trigonometric functions. I'll not explain what each one relates to here, because those using them will know what they are for and this is not the place for a mathematical discussion of trigonometry.

pi   The `pi` function simply returns the value of pi that is assigned to the constant `M_PI`. It is called as a function with no parameters.

cos, sin, and tan   These are the three main trigonometric functions, representing cosine, sine, and tangent functions. They are also available in arc and inverse flavors, which are denoted by an `a` prefix or `h` suffix, respectively. For example—`asinh` is the arc inverse of `sin`.

They all accept their parameters in radians and not degrees, but there are two functions to convert between degrees and radians:

deg2rad	Converts the parameter from degrees to radians
rad2deg	Converts the parameter from radians to degrees

Both of these functions accept functions that are floating point or integer values and will return a floating point value.

Variables and Classes

The following functions are useful in manipulating classes and variables that have been defined by the users in their PHP programs.

The first such function, `class_exists`, tests to see whether a given class has been defined. It is equivalent to the core `function_exists` function, except that it accepts a class and not a function name.

The `get_object_vars` function takes an object, being an instance of an existing class, and returns an array of key/value pairs representing the name of each property of that object and their associated value, if set. For example:

```
class weblog_entry {
  var $title, $content;

  function weblog_entry () {
```

```
    $title = "";
    $content = "";
  }

  function weblog_set_title ( $ t ) {
     $this->title = $t;
  }
}
```

From the previous code, you can instantiate a variable from the class definition and set the title as follows:

```
$entry = new weblog_entry();
$entry->weblog_set_title ( "A Title" );
$properties = get_object_vars ( $entry );
```

The `$properties` variable now contains an array that has the following entries:

```
$properties['title']
$properties['content']
```

In case you need to see what the array contains and what the indexes are, you can use the `var_dump` function. This provides a human friendly dump of any complex type or PHP expression. It is used as follows:

```
var_dump ( $properties );
```

The previous code will yield a display along the lines of:

```
Array
(
    [title] => A Title
    [content] =>
)
```

An even more useful function is the `var_export` function, which performs an export of the data in PHP format. This means that you could use the resulting strung to recreate the object. This can be used as follows:

```
$code = var_export ( $properties, TRUE );
                        // return, don't print out
$code = "$my_array = " . $code; // prepend some more code
eval ( $code ); // run it by PHP
```

The result of the previous snippet will be that `$my_array` contains a copy of the structure *and data* from the `$properties` variable, itself derived from the weblog_entry class. The important point to note is that it is a snapshot of the actual content and can be recreated from the string that is returned through var_export by passing it to eval.

Strings

The following is a guide to the various functions that you can use to process strings. Only the most commonly used ones are detailed here. The most common, and the one that you have already seen in several occasions, is the echo function.

This function outputs a string, either with escaping and variable expansion (if double quoted) or without (if single quoted). Strings can be concatenated in the input stream, which might not be included in parentheses.

Valid examples are as follows:

```
echo "This is a string\n";
echo 'this is a string\n';
echo "this is " . " two strings";
```

To find out the length of a string, use the strlen function. It returns an integer indicating the number of characters in the string. A companion function, count_chars, returns more detailed information about a specific character occurrence.

The count_chars function takes a string as input and produces an array where each byte (character) that is in the string is the key, and the value is the number of times that that character appears in the string. The function also takes a second parameter, which modifies the result returned. The most useful values for this parameter are as follows:

1	Returns only those characters used
2	Returns all the characters not used (based on the ASCII values)
3 & 4	The same as 1 or 2, but with the result returned as a string

The following is a possible use for this function:

```
foreach ( count_chars ( "Hello World", 1 )
                          as $letter => $freq ) {
  echo $letter . " => " . $freq . "\n";
}
```

This code would yield output similar to the following:

```
32 => 1
72 => 1
87 => 1
100 => 1
101 => 1
108 => 3
111 => 2
114 => 1
```

To convert the $letter values to characters that can be displayed, you can use the chr function, which takes an ASCII value in decimal format and returns the printable equivalent.

The explode function takes a string and breaks it up into an array of strings, based on the provided separator. So, the following would break a sentence into words:

```
$sentence = "the cat sat on the mat";
$word_array = explode ( " ", $sentence );
```

The explode function could also be used to parse a CSV string:

```
$csv_row = "value, value, value";
$csv_array = explode ( ",", $csv_row );
```

The opposite of explode is implode, which takes the same arguments and returns a string as an array of separated values. So, to turn an array of values into a CSV string, you could use:

```
$csv_string = implode ( ",", $csv_array );
```

It is also possible to extract part of a string, if you know the start and length by using the substr function. This returns a value corresponding to the section of the string that has been indicated. For example:

```
$my_string = "Hello World";
echo substr($my_string, 4, 3); // prints o W
```

The final parameter is the length of string to extract, *not* the end index, and is optional; if it is missing, the whole string past the start point is taken. The start point is zero-based.

Trimming and Padding   There are a number of reasonably self-explanatory functions for removing or adding characters to strings. These should need very little explanation:

ltrim ($ string)	Removes whitespace from the left (start) of $string
rtrim ($string)	Removes whitespace from the right (end) of $string
trim ($string)	Removes whitespace from both sides of $string

One point to note is that each of these functions can be combined with a second parameter that will remove any character from a given set from the start or end (or both) of the string. The default is, as noted, whitespace.

A related function, str_pad, is used to pad a string with the contents of another string, which can be truncated if the final length would be greater than desired. The general form for str_pad is as follows:

str_pad ($input_string, $length, $pad_string, PAD_TYPE)

The function returns a string and does not modify the $input_string in any way. The $pad_string can be any sequence of characters. There are three possible values for PAD_TYPE—PAD_LEFT, PAD_RIGHT, and PAD_BOTH.

Comparison and Searching   Beyond the operators that are used with strings, there are also some specific comparison functions that work in the same way as the C or JavaScript equivalents. For this reason, I don't go into too much detail of them here.

The first function is strcmp and it returns 0 if two strings are equal, a value less than 0 if the first string is considered to be less than the second, and more than zero if the first string is considered to be greater than the second. strcmp takes two parameters—the strings to be compared.

To find the first occurrence of a substring in a string, you can use the strpos function, which takes a string and a substring, in that order. A third parameter can be added that specifies the offset at which to start the search. To start the search from the end of the string, you can use the strrpos function.

If an entire string rather than just a character is to be searched for, you can use the strstr function. This function will return the part of the string that contains the substring rather than the numeric position. If the index is required, a string can be supplied to strpos or strrpos instead. Some examples:

```php
$big_string = "Hello World";
$substring = "orl";
echo strpos ( $big_string, "H" ); // prints 0
echo strrpos ( $big_string, "o" ); // prints 7
echo strstr ( $big_string, $substring ); // prints orld
echo strpos ( $big_string, $substring ); // prints 7
```

Similar to the strstr function, there is the substr_count function that counts the number of occurrences of a substring in a string and returns the numerical count. So, based on the previous strings, the following could be constructed:

```php
echo substr_count ( $big_string, "lo" ); // prints 1
```

Finally, there are two functions for replacing portions of a string. Neither of them need to have search strings and replacement strings of the same length, so the final length of the string can change. In addition, both strings and arrays of strings can be supplied as text to search and replace, such that each is mapped on a one-to-one basis.

The str_replace function takes three parameters:

```php
$search_for = "World";
$replace_with = "PHP";
$input = "Hello World";
$result = str_replace ( $search_for,
          $replace_with, $input_string );
```

The result from this example would be "Hello PHP". The first two parameters can also be arrays:

```php
$search_for = array ( "Hello", "World" );
$replace_with = ( "Greetings", "PHP" );
$input = "Hello World";
$result = str_replace ( $search_for, $replace_with,
                        $input_string );
```

Now the result is "Greetings PHP". These two forms represent a very powerful search and replace function, but remember that the application of the function is overlapped on each iteration. This means that if the intermediate result contains a string that can also be subject to replacement, this will occur during the processing.

The following example is taken from the PHP documentation and illustrates this behavior:

```
// Outputs: apearpearle pear
$letters = array('a', 'p');
$fruit = array('apple', 'pear');
$text = 'a p';
$output = str_replace($letters, $fruit, $text);
echo $output;
```

There are other comparison and search and replace functions, but this discussion represents the most useful subset for the vast majority of operations.

HTML-Related Operations There are a few useful functions that can help you when you're writing PHP code that needs to process HTML. Besides the obvious function of breaking a document into tags (which you'll read about later on), there is a set of functions that can process individual HTML strings.

The `html_entity_decode` function takes a string of HTML, with the various entities represented as coded values (for example, "being an encoding of"), and decodes them. Like many of the string-processing functions, it does not actually change the string but returns a new one.

Likewise, the `htmlentities` function scans a string for entities that ought to be encoded and provides a string with the relevant encodings performed. It is, in a sense, the opposite of the decode function.

The `nl2br` function takes a string that contains escaped newlines (that is, \n characters) and inserts a line break (HTML tag `<br />`) in front of them. This has the effect of breaking the lines in the resulting HTML where the original author expects them to be, based on their editing.

Finally, to remove any tags from a piece of HTML, you use the `strip_tags` function. This function will render a chunk of HTML (with or without `<script>` and `<?php ?>` tags), as plain text. Anything that would not be displayed is ignored (stripped out).

Miscellaneous Operations There are a few string operations that didn't seem to fit in anywhere else, so they are expanded here.

The `str_shuffle` function returns a randomly shuffled version of the original string. This might be useful in password generation, for example. A companion function, `strrev`, returns a reversed version of the string passed as a parameter.

Finally, the two functions strtolower and strtoupper provide a way to change the case of a string. The strtolower function returns a string where all letters are converted to lowercase, and the strtoupper function returns one where all the letters are capitalized.

As a slight curio, the ucfirst and ucwords functions can convert the first letter of a string to uppercase or capitalize the first letter of each word, respectively. All of these functions receive a string and return the string with the modifications performed. Unless this result is assigned back to the string that is passed, the original is not affected.

Arrays

Although the basic array handling built into PHP that you have already seen is great for the majority of functions, there are some occasions when a little more power is needed. Luckily, PHP provides a whole suite of built-in functions to support complex array tasks.

There are many more than are strictly needed in a "Just Enough" programmer's arsenal, but the following summarizes the most useful ones.

To find out how many items there are in an array, the count function is used. It can also be used to count the properties of an object instantiated as a variable based on a user-defined class. It generally takes one parameter and returns an integer, although there is the possibility to specify what *mode* to use when counting items.

Refer to the PHP documentation if you need more advanced control over the count mechanism.

An array can also be sorted, using the sort function. Sorting is performed in an alphabetical manner, which provides consistent results so long as the types of values in the array are not mixed. One caveat is that the array keys will be reassigned and not reordered, so if there is a logical mapping between the keys and values, this will be lost, because the array is sorted on the values.

To check for the existence of a value in an array, you can use the in_array function. The parameters for this, in order, are the value to look for and the array to look in. This parameter ordering is different from that of some of the other search functions.

Another thing to watch out for is that it is case-sensitive and can be made type-sensitive by adding a third parameter, set to TRUE. This last parameter is not used often. The search is *always* case-sensitive. An example of the in_array function is as follows:

```
$my_array = array ("Top", "Middle", "Bottom");
if ( in_array ( "Middle", $my_array ) {
  echo "Found the value!";
}
```

Note that the function returns a Boolean value. The companion function, which is used in the same way but which looks for a key in the array rather than a value, is the array_key_exists function. Aside from the fact that it looks at the key, the functionality is identical.

To obtain the key from an array that corresponds to a value (rather than just a true or false), you can use the array_search function. If a simple array is populated, rather than a key/value array, the index is returned. For example:

```
$my_array = array ("Top", "Middle", "Bottom");
if ( in_array ( "Middle", $my_array ) {
  $index = array_search ( "Middle", $my_array ); // index = 1
}
```

You can use the array_merge function to merge a list of arrays, based on some simple rules. Generally, the second array is appended to the first array. If the indexes are numerical (simple arrays), no values are overwritten. However, if the indexes are user-defined (key/value pairs), any value in the first array having the same key as a value in the second array is overwritten. For example:

```
$array_1 = array ( 1, 2 );
$array_2 = array ( "one" => 1, "two" => 2 );
$array_3 = array ( "two" => 3, "one" => 4, 5 );
$temp_array = array_merge ( $array_1, $array_2 );
print_r ($temp_array);
```

This yields the result:

```
Array
(
    [0] => 1
    [1] => 2
    [one] => 1
    [two] => 2
)
```

However, if you then merge in $array_3, as follows:

```
$temp_array = array_merge ( $temp_array, $array_3);
print_r ($temp_array);
```

The final output is as follows:

```
Array
(
    [0] => 1
    [1] => 2
    [one] => 4
    [two] => 3
    [2] => 5
)
```

Note how the index continues, even when interlaced with other keys. PHP is not fussy about the kind of data or keys used to access it, so it is possible to iterate through a whole array of different types, using various keys to access the data.

A sub-array can be extracted from an array using the array_slice function. This has many wonderful options, which you can look up if you need them. The most useful form is as follows:

```
array_slice ( $input_array, $position, $length )
```

When used with correct parameters, this form returns an array that represents a sub-array starting at the zero-indexed position $position and is of $length length. The original array is untouched.

The companion function, array_splice, accepts the same parameters, returns an array that represents the items to be extracted, and removes them from the array. If you need to provide a replacement set of values, you can indicate this in an optional fourth parameter. Otherwise, the parameter list is the same as the array_slice definition.

There is also a set of functions for adding and removing individual elements to and from an array. These are as follows:

array_push	Adds an element to the end of the array
array_pop	Removes the last element of the array
array_shift	Adds an element to the front of the array
array_unshift	Removes the first element of the array

The `array_push` and `array_shift` functions take the array to operate on and a value to add to it as parameters. The `array_pop` and `array_unshift` functions generally only take the array to operate on. Otherwise, the functionality is as expected from the descriptions.

The `array_rand` function returns the key for a random entry into the array. To shuffle contents at random, you can use the `shuffle` function. Both functions take the array variable as input parameter.

Finally, the `array_diff` function compares two arrays and returns an array that contains the difference. This has no effect on the contents of the two arrays passed as parameters. Multiple occurrences of the value are considered to be equal and the keys are ignored, so two identical values with different keys are considered to be the same and are not returned.

Web- and Browser-Related Functions

Before you learn about document-related functions, there are a few functions used to process URLs in a standard way that you should consider. The first is `parse_url`, which returns an array from an URL, where each element refers to one of the components in a standard URL. This only works for complete, fully specified URLs and will *not* work with relative URLs.

Thus, the following can be written:

```
$url_components = parse_url
    ( "http://www.mysite.com/query.php?op=1");
```

The `$url_components` array will contain:

```
[scheme] => http
[host] => www.mysite.com
[path] => /query.php
[query] => op=1
```

From here, the query would have to be split into another array using the `explode` function with the & as separator. Each string in the resulting array could also be `exploded` by passing the = as separator to yield the value pairs. It is easier to use the `$_GET` superglobal, however.

The `urlencode` and `urldecode` functions simulate passing data on the URL in the same way that form processing does. In other words, spaces are replaced by + signs, and other non-alphanumeric characters are replaced by encoded versions. Such an encoded string can then be decoded using the `urldecode` function.

SimpleXML   The SimpleXML class gives a very easy way to access XML documents that have a predefined structure that is known by the programmer. Actually, the class can parse any valid XML file, but for a number of reasons, it might not prove practical to navigate the resulting object tree if the structure is not known.

For example, SimpleXML can be cumbersome to use when processing XHTML files with varying internal structures.

A SimpleXML object can be instantiated from an XML file by calling the simplexml_load_file function. So, for example, you could load the XML feed from a Website with:

```
$xml = simplexml_load_file
       ('http://leckyt.wordpress.com/feed/');
```

If you did not know the layout of this feed, the print_r function could be used to display it. The following shows the beginning of the resulting dump:

```
SimpleXMLElement Object
(
  [@attributes] => Array
  (
    [version] => 2.0
  )
  [channel] => SimpleXMLElement Object
  (
      [title] => Leckyt's Weblog
      [link] => http://leckyt.wordpress.com
      [description] => Just another WordPress.com weblog
      [pubDate] => Sun, 03 Feb 2008 13:57:02 +0000
      [generator] => http://wordpress.org/?v=MU
      [language] => en
      [item] => Array
      (
          [0] => SimpleXMLElement Object
              (
                   [title] => That tricky second post
```

The way that the XML is accessed is through the object tree. So, to return the value associated with the title of the first entry (it's the last line in the previous dump), you can use a statement such as:

```
$entry_title = $xml->channel->item[0]->title;
```

You can probably appreciate the power of this approach, but also see the issue that it raises regarding navigation. Because the properties are filled out by name, it is difficult to navigate when you don't know the names of the tags in the XML document.

You'll look at one way of dealing with this later on in the book, but simply knowing that the object exists, knowing how to populate it, and knowing a few things about PHP is enough for most cases. For example, you can loop through the blog posts very easily:

```
foreach ( $xml->channel>item as $entry) {
  echo "<b> $entry->title </b><br/7gt;";
}
```

Of course, the feed contains many other pieces of information that could be displayed as part of the previous loop. If you need more power to dig into the XML tree, you can use the following DOMDocument class instead.

DOMDocument The DOMDocument offers a powerful front end to processing XML and HTML files. Like any library that is powerful, it is also complex, so I have tried to reduce it to its bare minimum and give just enough information so you can understand the examples later in the book and also use the DOMDocument in your own projects.

A new object is created in the same way as any other class:

```
$xml = new DOMDocument();
```

At this stage, it has no data. So, to load XML, you can call the loadFile method:

```
$xml->loadFile('http://leckyt.wordpress.com/feed/');
```

Note

At this stage, it is worth noting that there is a companion loadHTMLFile function that loads an HTML rather than an XML file. Use this when the source is an HTML document (local or on the Web).

Unlike SimpleXML, the DOMDocument does not have a structure that can be output with print_r. Instead, you have to delve into the object tree using a couple of useful methods. The first, getElementById, assumes unique IDs are in force across an HTML or XML document, using source XHTML such as:

```
<div id="my_post">
</div>
```

With the XML tree, this is not true, so you use the `getElementsByTagName` method, which returns all of the tags, and their contents, in an array. The code looks akin to the following:

```
$taglist = $xml->getElementsByTagName('item');
                // get all the items
```

This results in an array that's a `DOMNodeList` object. Given that it is an array, the `foreach` method of accessing it works and it also has a `length()` member method. So, to get the number of objects in it, you can use code like this:

```
$taglist->length();
```

The object also has an `item($index)` method, which you use instead of the square bracket notation. To return the first entry in the blog list, use code such as the following:

```
$entry = $taglist->item(0);
```

The result of this operation is a `DOMNode` object. This has the following member methods:

```
->hasChildNodes()       Returns true when there are child nodes
->parentNode()          Returns the DOMNode that is the parent
->childNodes()          Returns a list of children
->previousSibling()     Returns the previous sibling of the same parent
->nextSibling()         Returns the next sibling of the same parent
```

All of these member methods allow you to traverse the object tree. However, to extract data from the current node, you can use the following:

```
->nodeName()        Returns the node's name (item, in this case)
->nodeValue()       Returns the value
```

This last returns a whole slew of data, simply because the point at which you are in the tree as a result of all this is still a branch. The data that is required is in the `title` child of the current entry in the tag list. You could use the traversal functions to locate it, but it is easier just to call `getElementByTagName` again, but this time on the node that you have selected.

Finally, to do the same as the single SimpleXML line, to print the title, you have to traverse the whole structure. This yields the following result:

```
$item_list = $xml->getElementsByTagName('item'); // pick the items
$entry = $item_list->item(0); // select the first one
// find the entry that contains the title and print its value
$title = $entry->getElementsByTagName('title')->item(0)->nodeValue;
```

You can choose for yourself which of the two classes you use, but bear in mind that the DOMDocument approach has the key advantage that it can also process HTML, which means the previous approach makes slightly more sense.

Email   The last of the Web functions that you'll look at concerns email. To send an email message, assuming that the Web host allows it, one simple call is all that is needed:

```
mail ( $to, $subject, $message, $headers )
```

In this call, the $message must be delimited by a carriage return on an empty line. This could be written as follows:

```
$message = "Dear $user,\r\n Here is a test.\r\n
                       \r\nThanks,\nAdmin\r\n\r\n";
```

The $to is a list of comma-separated email addresses, and the $subject is more or less open, within the relevant email specifications. The $headers are optional, but if you want to send HTML email, the appropriate MIME headers have to be set in this parameter. For example:

```
$headers = 'MIME-Version: 1.0' . "\r\n";
$headers .= 'Content-type: text/html; charset=iso-8859-1' . "\r\n";
```

The return value will be true if the mail could be sent.

MySQL Functions

There are many more functions than covered here. For example, the administrative functions have all been left out because the average readers are not going to be administrators of the database that they are connecting to.

The following is the bare minimum needed to get up and running with a MySQL installation, and more than enough to cope with all the examples that are used in this book. MySQL itself is dealt with in Chapter 7, "Web Databases."

Note

As of PHP 5, the MySQL functions are installed by default. Previously, this was not the case, and they had to be enabled explicitly. However, there is always room for a specific host not to include them for a number of reasons. It is always best to check.

The first function used is one of the most complex, and it establishes a connection to a MySQL database system. It takes the following form:

```
$link = mysql_connect ($server, $username, $password );
```

The $server will be the name of the server that has been given by the Web host. Usually a value of localhost will work, or the IP address of the host in question. Your $username and $password are set when the individual database is set up—this is covered in Chapter 7.

To choose a database upon which to perform SQL queries, use mysql_select_db. It uses the $link passed back from the connection function. The general form for this is as follows:

```
mysql_select_db ($db_name, $link )
```

Assuming that the database name ($db_name) is correct, the return value from this function will be true. If it is false, there has been an error. The exact nature of an error on a MySQL function call can be determined using the mysql_error function, which returns a string containing the error details. For example:

```
mysql_select_db ($db_name, $link ) or die mysql_error();
```

This example will print a simple error message if the selection of the database did not succeed. More detail would be user friendly, but this code will stop the processing and inform the users that an error has occurred.

The mysql_query function is used to execute any kind of SQL query on the database. Its general form is as follows:

```
$result = mysql_query ($query, $link)
```

The $link parameter is the same $link that was provided when the database was first opened. If only one connection has been made to the database, this can be omitted. If the query was a SELECT query (see Chapter 7), the results can be extracted one at a time from the result set using the mysql_result function. This has the general form:

```
$value = mysql_result ($result, $row_number , $field_number)
```

The $value that is returned is the cell that is referenced in the result set. If there was only one field selected, the $field_number parameter can be omitted.

If the query had an effect on the database (data was inserted, deleted, or modified, for example), you can use a separate function to determine how many rows were updated. The `mysql_affected_rows` function returns an integer representing this. It has the general form:

```
mysql_affected_rows ()
```

The function operates on the last query, regardless of how many links are open to the database. To find out how many rows were returned in a result set that is the result of a select style query, you use the `mysql_num_rows` function. Its general form is:

```
$num_rows = mysql_num_rows ($result)
```

Unlike `mysql_affected_rows`, `mysql_num_rows` is tied to a specific result set. Several result sets can be held in memory at one time, with different variables providing the link to the result set on the server.

A much better way to retrieve the results is to use the `mysql_fetch_assoc` function, which returns an array that contains all of the results in the next row of the result set. The general form is as follows:

```
$array = mysql_fetch_assoc ($result)
```

Each element can be accessed through the array by field name. Each time the function is executed, the internal row pointer moves one row through the result set. It can be reset or set to a specific index using the `mysql_data_seek` function:

```
mysql_data_seek ( $result, $index )
```

Finally, to close the database link and free up any pending resources, you use the `mysql_close` function. It has this general form:

```
mysql_close ($link)
```

It is good practice to do this when no more operations are foreseen on the database, but because establishing the link can take some time, it should not be done until the script has no more need for the database.

PHP Examples

The following two examples cover the three most used functions of PHP in Web programming projects—processing forms and cookies and accessing databases. The code does not show the only way to proceed to perform these functions, and in some cases it might not be the best way, but the solutions work as a kind of cookbook to help beginning Web programmers get started.

Form and Cookie Processing

Form processing is made very easy in PHP by the use of the two superglobals, $_GET and $_POST, which are arrays that contain the form data that has been submitted. If you've used JavaScript validation, that data will already be pre-validated, so processing it should be easy.

Assume the following HTML form:

```
<form action="/age.php" method="post">
Name : <input type="text" name="name"><br/>
Age : <input type="text" name="age"><br/>
<input type="submit" value="Go!">
</form>
```

The age.php script that is referred to in the form receives the data in the $_POST superglobal, because that is the method chosen for the form's submission process. You can extract this data in a PHP document as follows:

```
Hi <?php echo htmlspecialchars($_POST['name']); ?>.
You are <?php echo (int)$_POST['age']; ?> years old.
```

The htmlspecialchars function ensures that all of the various special characters that the users could have entered are correctly displayed as HTML and not left raw. The cast in the second PHP snippet ensures that only a number is displayed.

If a URL is submitted that has been built by an affiliate (for example) and looks something like product.php?affid=123456&product=27, you can also use PHP's own processing to extract the data.

However, the data values will be stored in the $_GET superglobal. Other than this, they are accessed in the same way.

Processing cookies is also almost as easy. The setcookie function is used to set a named cookie with a value. It's best to address cookies as if they are all elements of an array called 'cookie'. The following examples are lifted from the PHP documentation:

```
<?php
// set the cookies
```

```
setcookie("cookie[three]", "cookiethree");
setcookie("cookie[two]", "cookietwo");
setcookie("cookie[one]", "cookieone");
?>
```

This code stores the cookies as an array that can be referenced like any other array, once it has been extracted from the $_COOKIE superglobal. Again, the following is lifted from the PHP manual:

```
<? // after the page reloads, print them out
if (isset($_COOKIE['cookie'])) {
    foreach ($_COOKIE['cookie'] as $name => $value) {
        echo "$name : $value <br />\n";
    }
}
?>
```

Because the cookies have been set as, for example, cookie[one], the value can be accessed from the root identifier $_COOKIE['cookie']. You could equally have called them apple[a], apple[b], and apple[c], but this would have meant accessing them through $_COOKIE['apple'], which makes less sense.

Database Connectivity

The section on the PHP MySQL functions provided some basic information about the functions used to connect to a database. However, the code was not linked together in one coherent PHP example. The following is a complete example that shows elements of good programming practice as well as basic usage of MySQL database access.

First, you establish the link:

```
$link = mysql_connect('mysql_host', 'mysql_user',
                        'mysql_password')
    or die('Could not connect: ' . mysql_error());
```

Note that I have adjusted the die clause a little to be more informative for the end user. It is also possible to use this model to email the administrator or provide a link so that the end user can fill out a form and report the error.

With the $link in hand, you can go on to select a database to operate on:

```
mysql_select_db('my_database')
    or die('Could not select database');
```

Again, the failure clause is handled better than in the previous section. Now, because you have not yet read about databases, the actual querying will not make much sense. However, in the spirit of completeness, here is the code to execute a query on the database:

```
$query = 'SELECT * FROM my_table';
$result = mysql_query($query) or die
          ('Query failed: ' . mysql_error());
```

Assuming that the code has progressed this far, you can now print out all the results of this query. Note that this could be quite extensive, so it is better to limit the resource usage in some way by not returning every row for the result set if it can be avoided.

The code to generate the HTML is as follows:

```
echo "<table>\n";
while ($row = mysql_fetch_assoc($result)) {
    echo "\t<tr>\n";
    foreach ($row as $col) {
        echo "\t\t<td>$col</td>\n";
    }
    echo "\t</tr>\n";
}
echo "</table>\n";
```

Note the PHP looping constructs that allow the programmer to test for the availability of rows and then loop through the columns. The model that is shown here can be reused for any kind of table.

Finally, you can close the connection, which is identical to the previous example but is mentioned here just for the sake of completeness.

```
mysql_close($link);
```

That is all that you need to know about the PHP facilities for SQL. However, the next chapter covers the actual database programming language—SQL—in more depth.

Recap

This chapter set out to give you the basic knowledge that you need to be able to create PHP scripts for use on your site. The features that you have examined here will give you enough information to create a small content-management system (when combined with a database), perform Web 2.0 RSS *mashups* (combinations of multiple existing technologies that create new platforms, technologies, or feature sets that transcend the existing ones; see Chapter 9 for more), and even create Websites that pull content from all over the Internet, using SimpleXML and DOMDocument with HTML.

The things to keep coming back to are the language constructs and function reference—these are the parts that are most easily forgotten. Above all, most of the learning that you'll do will be in deploying your own solutions, usually based on someone else's starting point. There's nothing wrong with this, as long as you understand what it is you are doing.

Many of the concepts are also common to other kinds of Web programming and server side languages, so getting used to the way that the code is used is also part of the learning process. Before doing anything really useful, though, you have to learn a little about databases, and that is the topic of the next chapter.

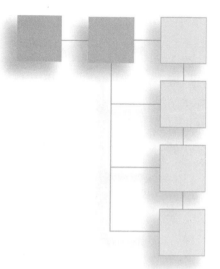

CHAPTER 7

WEB DATABASES

Behind all major Web programming efforts there is usually a database of some kind in which to store persistent information about the site and its content. This might extend to username and password combinations as well as email addresses and such.

More often than not, however, it is simply used in content-management systems, to store the text and formatting requirements for the content. This usually includes categories and tags to describe each article (or blog entry), as well as the hierarchy of pages and links between them. Using a database makes it much easier to effect changes, as you'll see.

Games, Web shops, blogs, and everything else that needs to store persistent data will likely do so using a back-end database. Prices for shops, comments for blogs, and the game state and data that describes the current game environment will also be contained in databases. The reason for this is simple: it makes it very easy to manipulate the data, both from the point of view of the setup and maintenance, and also for changing the data within Web programs (such as those programmed in PHP).

You're not expected to be a programmer or systems engineer; the people behind database systems make it very easy to get started. You already have something of a grounding in database *access*, having looked at how this is achieved from PHP in the last chapter.

Additionally, the JavaScript chapter discussed how data that is to be sent can be validated before being put in a database, which is part of the mechanism. Then, again in the PHP chapter, you saw how that data can then be sent to the Web server to generate a response.

Behind all the scripting is the database where all the data is stored, which is a piece of software (in the same way that the Web server is a piece of software), that gives a usable front-end to the collection of data that your Web application needs.

In this chapter, you'll learn how to:

- Design simple databases

- Set up a MySQL database

- Query the database to retrieve information

- Insert information

- Create tables using PHP

It is also useful to know how the database is put together and how to access it without needing scripting via a special interface. In other words, you will learn how to access the database programmatically and non-programmatically.

The reason for knowing the two access methods is that most CMSs (content-management systems) that you'll look at in the next chapter are based on a database. Sometimes, it's useful to be able to alter those databases without using actual PHP code, to reduce the programming overhead.

Points to note—the database has its own language to communicate with it, so that's the fourth language reference that the reader will have at their fingertips. This language is called SQL (Structured Query Language), and can be used for everything from managing the structure of the database to retrieving data from it and inserting or removing data.

The non-programmer will find it easy to follow, while more experienced programmers might find some of it a bit simplistic, but it's worth starting from simple foundations. You'll learn more complex techniques, of course, as you get to know the language more deeply. What you will learn here are solid foundations to build that knowledge on—and just enough of Web databases to be able to do something really useful.

Databases for Non-Programmers

A database is a place to store information in a way that can be easily retrieved. Modern systems tend to use something called *relational database systems.* The key to relational databases is that they are easy to extend, and, as long as you follow some simple guidelines, that extension will not mean changing your code or the underlying database structure.

The term *relation* comes from the fact that all the data that is stored in the database is structured around some well-defined categories. These are set by the user in advance, so clearly there is a small design component to setting up the database system.

To do that, you need to understand how the database is organized. A database contains a set of tables. Each named table contains a structure that is divided into rows and columns—each column is a category (*relation*) that defines a piece of data.

Each row in the table contains a unique combination of fields (column data) that describe that row. Data can be inserted, removed, retrieved, and modified based on this relationship among the row, column, and field.

Behind the scenes, the relation dataset system itself offers a lot of management capabilities that maintain the relations between all the pieces of data. You won't use much of the relational database management directly; instead, you'll treat the database that is behind the SQL front-end as being structured in the way shown in Figure 7.1.

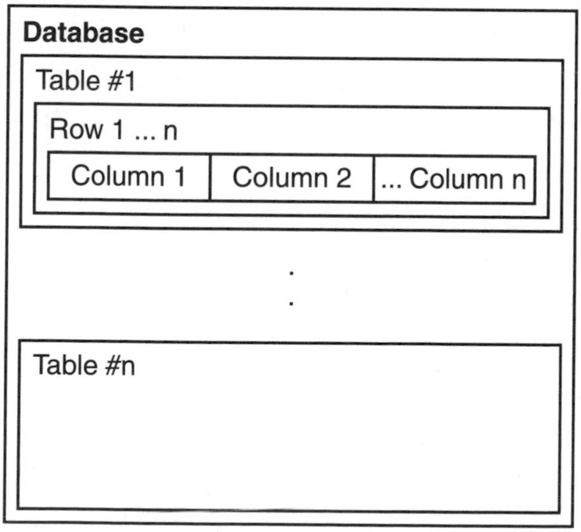

Figure 7.1
Database schematic

From the schematic in Figure 7.1, you should note the following:

- A database has multiple tables

- A table has multiple rows

- Each row is divided into columns

The database, table, and the columns have names, which is the easiest way to reference them. Rows are typically numbered, but there is never any great need to reference a row directly by number, just that it is the nth row in the current series being viewed, which is usually an interesting subset of all the rows that the programmer wants to look at.

Each of the named columns also has a set of *attributes* that defines the kind of data that you want to store in there, as well as some system attributes that tell the database what internal settings the columns should have. Without this information, it is not possible for the database system to maintain the relationships correctly between all the pieces of data.

These attributes are often called the *domain* of possible values—in other words, you might define a column as containing only numerical data, allowing the system to use it for calculations, or you might decide that it should be string data, allowing for full text search.

To help the database system further, the database design usually gives a number of *constraints* that limit the data value within a specific domain. This allows the programmer to indicate, ahead of time, whether a field is to be unique in the table—the system would reject any attempt to create two rows having the same value for a specific column. This is useful when customer IDs, for example, are used to identify uniquely customers in the system.

It is important to remember that database installations on Web hosts usually limit the number of actual databases that you are allowed to have. This is vital because each kind of add-on (such as a forum, CMS, blog, shopping system, and so on) that the Website includes must have a database all to itself (usually).

Each database, therefore, should refer to a single data domain—one for each kind of interface between the user and the system. This keeps the information conceptually separated, making maintenance easier to manage for the overall system.

Before any data can be processed, however, the databases need to be designed in a way that is logical, easy to access, and efficient, and that maximizes the potential for speedy data extraction when needed. There is nothing worse than a badly designed database for sapping system resources and slowing down the whole site.

Database Design

Before you begin this section in earnest, it's important to note that there are whole college courses dedicated to the subject of database design and management. Clearly within the confines of the book, and the "Just Enough" philosophy, this section does not cover everything that they do.

The good news is that you don't need to know everything about database design—Web databases need to be small, efficient, and manageable, so unless you're setting up a system that is the size of Amazon or Google, the database design, although important, is not the biggest single programming issue.

What is important is that the database be:

- Easy to reference (for the programmer)

- Compact and efficient

- Complete but extendable

The first of these is obvious—the database needs to have logical names for the tables and columns, the data that is stored within each table needs to be grouped logically, and building a piece of code to retrieve that data should not be cumbersome. The more difficult the database is to interface with, the harder it will be to *remember* how to interface with it.

So, the data structures have to be correct. This will also help each table be compact and efficient. Big tables take longer to access, and the more columns a table has, the more this will become apparent. Modern systems can optimize this to a certain extent, by using indexes and other methods to improve access time, but there is still something to be said for keeping a table compact.

Last but not least, the information has to be complete *now,* but structured in a way that makes it logically extendable in the future. It is highly unlikely that the requirements of the database will be static through its lifespan, so it is better to design the table with extendibility in mind, while trying to keep the data description as complete as possible.

Essentially, at some point, a line will have to be drawn, and the actual implementation begun; otherwise, an inventive mind can go on refining the data scheme almost indefinitely. This process is known as *database design*. To borrow from Wikipedia:

> "Database design is the process of producing a detailed data model of a database. This logical data model contains all the needed logical and physical design choices and physical storage parameters. . . . A fully attributed data model contains detailed attributes for each entity."
> [http://en.wikipedia.org/wiki/Database_design]

So, it's time to take out a pen and paper (or a text document) and create the database design. Again, there are whole languages and diagramming conventions given over to this topic alone, and this section skims the subject matter lightly. For a start, I gloss over the physical characteristics of the database, because, hopefully, these will not matter and will usually be beyond your control in a Web environment.

However, it is important to understand the attributes of, and relationships between, pieces of data that are stored in the database before creating a schematic of the database design itself.

Understanding Attributes and Relationships

In database design, you hear a lot about attributes (the type of data) and relationships (the position of that data within the structure). The following is a stripped–down conceptual explanation of some terms that will help you design a database.

The exact notation that you choose is, for the purposes of this exercise, entirely a question of convenience. It is better to feel comfortable with the notation than have it forced upon you. However, feel free to use a layout using boxes and lines that helps you to understand what the structure should be.

The simple table design in Figure 7.2 shows a starting point.

The Customer table contains a column for Name and Customer ID. The attributes are in brackets and show the kind of data you expect to store in them. The

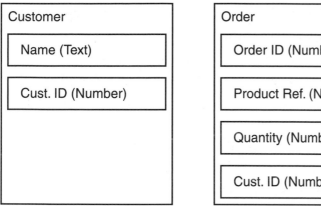
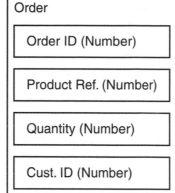

Figure 7.2
Simple table design

Order table has a similar layout. For each item there is an attribute in brackets, and each element is contained within its own box.

This simple layout allows you to see quickly what data fields are part of what tables, and this relationship is a *has-a* relationship. An entry in the Customer table *has-a* Name and ID, the Order table *has-a* row containing order details, and so on.

The relationship between the data elements and their attributes is an example of an *is-a* relationship. A Name *is-a* string, a Customer ID *is-a* number. In Figure 7.2, you can also see that there is a relationship between two items, where the tables have them in common—the Customer ID is an index that links the Customer table and the Order table.

This link hints at a relationship between the two tables. In fact, it is an example of a *one-to-many* relationship, because *one* row in the Customer table can reference *many* rows in the Order table, with each one sharing the same Customer ID.

Thus, the relationship between the Order table and the Customer table is the inverse—a *many-to-one* relationship. Many rows in the Order table can refer to a single row in the Customer table. If a customer has only placed one order, that is an example of the last relationship you'll look at—the *one-to-one* relationship.

Understanding these key concepts will be very useful when designing the structure for the database. After all, although the structure can be extended after the database has been built, the tables and the concepts *cannot easily be changed.* So, it is important to get them right from the outset.

Database Design Guidelines

There are five key problem areas that need to be addressed in order to avoid issues with the database once it moves from design to implementation (actually making it) and interacting with it. This last point is very important because creating the database is only half the story—you need to be able to talk to it as well, and this means remembering its structure and conventions.

The key potential problem areas are as follows:

- Poor planning

- Illogical names

- No documentation

- Incorrect domain splits

- Insufficient testing

The way to deal with poor planning is to create diagrams of the data structure and check that it looks logical and that all the data areas are covered. This sounds obvious, but sometimes a database design will change radically from the creators' original vision to the final diagram. To help build the diagram, it is important to stick with a convention.

Part of this convention is to avoid illogical names. A table or column name has to reflect the data stored inside it, possibly the type of data, as well as its purpose, and be easy to remember. A good naming convention will be intuitive and prevent the necessity to list the tables and their properties every time you need to refer to one of the columns.

However, to help with this, it is a good idea to solve problem number three—no documentation. Like all programming tasks, databases should be well documented so that any programmer can refer to the descriptions rather than having to look up the actual structure. Of course, for this to work, the documentation also has to be kept up to date.

Another advantage of documenting the design properly (and the initial diagrams count as part of that documentation) is that any incorrect domain splits will be found. This happens when information that should be in one domain finds its way into another. One example of this might be that the customers order IDs are listed in the Customer table rather than the Order table.

At first glance, this might seem logical; after all, for each customer, you can build a list of orders. However, it make more sense to keep the data in the order domain (in this case, an order number) with the orders and link it to the customers via the Customer ID. This is the data that both tables share.

Finally, databases, like everything else, need to be tested. The design can be tested by writing out *use cases,* which detail what data is to be stored as the result of a Web operation and where it will end up. The advantage of testing in this way is that it helps test the concept *and* feeds back into the design, so that before any concrete work is done, the database is correctly formed.

Some of these simulations will highlight the need for data *normalization,* as a way to improve the structure of the data stored in the database.

Normalization

Many of the key problem areas can be addressed by paying attention to something known as *normalization.* This can be defined as follows:

> "Normalization defines a set of methods to break down tables to their constituent parts until each table represents one and only one 'thing,' and its columns serve to fully describe only the one 'thing' that the table represents."

[http://www.simple-talk.com/sql/database-administration/ten-common-database-design-mistakes/]

An example of data that needs to be normalized is the use case that leads to customer and payment details being listed in the same table. It might make conceptual sense to have the address, phone number, and other details from the customer record next to the payment details, but this information is from two different domains.

One domain is the collection of data that relates to all the customers, and the other domain is the collection of data that relates to the payments. If you think about it, these are two different collections of data that should be stored separately. An address book and an order book, for example, in the real world, are kept apart.

The reason for this is that there will be many addresses and many payments, and although each customer might have only one set of address information, the customer might make many payments. If the data domains were mixed, it would become difficult to express these relationships, short of listing all the payments in a single table, along with the address information.

What then happens when you want to discard the payment data, or reorder the addresses, or even worse, collect all the payment data together, without the addresses as part of an accounting package? For these reasons, data domains should be kept apart as part of the process of normalization.

Normalizing the data, by finding the common element that links them (the Customer ID, for example), will lead to a better design for the data structure. Finding this relation and splitting the data up into separate tables is all part of the normalization process.

Clearly there is more to normalization than this initial overview, but the basic concept should be clear:

- Identify data in the wrong domain

- Find the item that links the domains

- Split the data into two or more related tables

This last point is important, because it may well be that the only way to normalize the data correctly is to create more than two tables and cross reference between them. For most simple databases, this will not be necessary, but it is useful to remember that it is not something that is prohibited—a table can be split into multiple domains.

Creating the Design

Once the rough diagrams have been sketched out and the first normalization is complete, it is time to create the actual design that will form the basis for the ongoing documentation. The design should include, as a minimum:

- Entity relationship diagrams

- Data dictionary

- Data relationship table

- Conventions

The entity relationship diagrams need to show the high-level relationship between the tables, leaving out the individual data elements but showing the links between tables that identify relationships between data elements. The second set of diagrams should show the structure of each individual table, and the data elements and their attributes, in a similar form to the simple table design shown in Figure 7.2.

Tip

If the relationships cannot be shown between the tables due to size limitations, this does not matter as long as the overview diagram shows where those links might be, perhaps annotated with the name of the data element (field) and attribute that links them.

The data dictionary lists the individual data elements, by name, in alphabetical order. It should list, for each data element, the following:

- The name—Following the conventions

- Table—Where the element occurs

- The type—Kind of data: text, number, and so on

- The size (length) of data—Size of number, text length, and so on

- Value constraints—Unique for the table, key value, and so on

The data relationship table lists, by entity, which tables it links, where appropriate. This is just a simple table that defines the relationships and is a text representation of the entity relationship diagrams (overview combined with individual).

Finally, any conventions used in naming and data domain normalization should be listed. This is a helpful reminder for the future when changes need to be made, and also in case the ongoing development needs to be handed on to another person or organization.

This might seem like a lot of work at first, but creating adequate documentation will help when it comes to developing the PHP scripts that will access the data. Moreover, the documentation will be invaluable should the design need to be extended.

Once the design is done, it is time to put the database together, using facilities that are available at most good Web hosts. Chapter 10 lists the items to look for when choosing a host and describes how to get the initial environment up and running.

For now, assume that MySQL is installed (by the Web host) and that phpMyAdmin will be used to manage it. Again, this is a standard setup offered by most Web hosts.

Using MySQL

Generally speaking, there are three ways to access a MySQL database system:

- Locally

- Using the MySQL command-line software over the Internet

- Through a Web interface

The first way (locally) applies only to systems that are running locally to the programmer or where an application such as Telnet is used to log in remotely to the server. This is generally available only to advanced users and those using specific packages geared towards providing a complete system that is remotely accessed.

The second interface uses the software provided by MySQL to access the database and is a command-line interface application. It can be used to run queries against the database (covered later) and interact with the system in a text-only interface. It is not as convenient for beginners as the last option.

The most common option for Web programming is through a Web interface, which uses an interface like phpMyAdmin, available on most Web hosts that use *cPanel* (an online Website management application that you'll look at in detail in Chapter 10). This is the preferred option, and the one discussed in this chapter. The advantage is that it is used through a standard browser and provides an intuitive interface for manipulating the database.

The one you use will depend on the installation that has been done on your behalf—given the choice, I would strongly recommend the last option as being the easiest, even for advanced users. Its only downside is that it's subject to the connection speed between the client and the server as well as the performance of that server.

Because of this, it is worth knowing about the MySQL client solution, in case the server on the other side cannot keep up with the phpMyAdmin load.

Local Login/MySQL Client

The application is found in the /usr/local/mysql/bin directory, on Linux/UNIX-based systems. Under Windows, the program is called mysql.exe and is located by default in the C:\mysql\bin directory.

It is a command-line package and can connect locally or over the Internet. It provides a simple interface to the database system. All the queries that you see in this chapter can be run through this text interface.

The program is invoked with the following command:

```
mysql -h <hostname> -u <username> -p
```

Valid values for <hostname> include localhost or the IP address of the machine hosting the database server. The –u option must be followed by a valid username, and the –p asks the database server to prompt for the password.

(The point is true for all databases that require a username and password to log in to MySQL. Any Web database provided by a third-party host will usually be set up this way; however, if you are running your own MySQL and Web server, you might allow local access without a username and password. Best practices, however, would *seem* to indicate that a username and password should always be used to secure the database.)

If everything goes according to plan, the users are then presented with a prompt where they may enter text, and press Return to send the command to the server. When they have finished, they should type quit to close the connection.

A similar procedure is used for remote access over the Internet using Telnet. This requires the use of a Telnet client to Telnet into the host and then run the mysql command in order to access the database locally. This is not typically offered by most Web host providers, but if you're using this book in a commercial environment, it might be available.

phpMyAdmin

phpMyAdmin is a set of PHP scripts that provide access to a MySQL database installation through a series of Web pages. There are facilities to log in to, maintain, query, and test the database installation.

The main phpMyAdmin window is shown in Figure 7.3. It displays the standard options. Different installations may differ in layout slightly, but they all follow the same basic theme.

The left panel of the screen shows the objects in the system that the user can control. At present, it is empty, apart from a system table, which should not be interfered with.

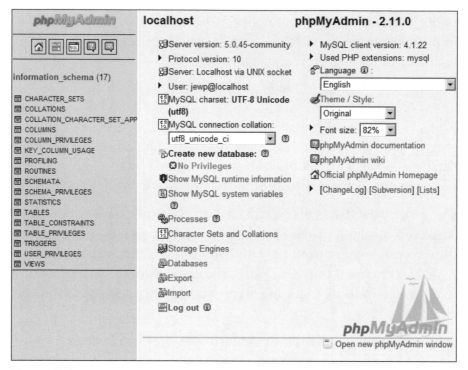

Figure 7.3
The phpMyAdmin main window

The main part of the screen shows the current options that can be performed within the context of the items selected on the left side. This screen changes depending on which database or table is selected in the left pane. When more than one set of options is available, a menu is displayed across the top of the main pane.

The phpMyAdmin tool is accessed from the cPanel databases section, shown in Figure 7.4.

Figure 7.4
cPanel databases section

You'll look at the full flow—from creating databases, adding tables, and more—later, but first take a look at the alternatives that are available apart from MySQL.

Alternative Database Packages

Considering the pace of change on the Internet, you might very well find that your Web host supports one of the alternatives to MySQL. There are quite a few on the market, of which the big four seem to be:

- PostgreSQL—Also Open Source

- SQL Server from Microsoft

- Oracle—Perhaps the biggest hitter in the commercial database world

- IBM DB2—Another commercial offering

Oracle and DB2 are for very large high-end database installations, generally speaking, and have a price tag to match. However, they have both been released in free versions that are limited in the support they give and therefore less attractive to Web hosting providers.

SQL Server from Microsoft is also a good, solid database system for medium to large Web databases and has the advantage of tight integration with the .NET Web environment. If you are using a Microsoft-based Web host, you will likely be using SQL Server.

They all support SQL and can all be connected to via PHP, but they have slightly different ways to manage them. Not all of the systems can be managed over the Web, for example. This is not the place to debate the pros and cons, but is the place to point out that there are others so you're aware of them.

PostgreSQL

In some senses, PostgreSQL is considered to be the big brother of MySQL. It is faster in some areas, slower in others. However, it is more difficult to set up than MySQL, requiring compilation from source in some cases. The difficulty level remains high, whether the platform is Windows or Linux/UNIX-based.

The new version of MySQL (5.0 at time of writing) fixes all the previous differences between PostgreSQL and MySQL that made PostgreSQL more attractive. This includes support for views, stored procedures, and cursors, which are all intermediate to advanced features.

The bottom line is that MySQL has a bigger user base and used to be less powerful. However, it is catching up, but at the same time, any issues that PostgreSQL did have are being solved, so they effectively meet in the middle.

For Web databases, MySQL is probably better and has certainly been more widely implemented.

Oracle

Oracle is for high transaction volumes with big databases and big machines, with the emphasis firmly on carrying out the transactions safely. It is a good solution for large organizations with complex data needs.

Oracle is both commercial and very expensive. Although it comes with many utilities to help put it all together, it still a pretty time consuming and painful process. The final result also requires tuning to get the best out of it, but once tuned, it is blazingly fast for high transaction volumes.

It is not used on many Web hosts because of the price, and it is very memory intensive. This means that if your system is running many other processes at the same time, they will take a bit performance hit because of Oracle's requirements. Either that, or the Oracle system itself will take a big performance hit due to scarcity of resources.

There is a free version for those who feel like experimenting, but the free version has limits on the maximum number of users and so will only be appropriate for single user installations.

IBM DB2

Finally, DB2 is again a commercial offering. It is a bit big and clunky with a lot of legacy features that make it cumbersome. However, at the top end of data storage solutions, it is still considered to be very attractive for large-scale organizations.

Like Oracle, it is blazingly fast. To get the most out of it, you must run it on a dedicated IBM server, although it does run happily, if at a lower performance, on Linux.

Like Oracle, there is a free version. The free version has no limits on users, but instead has limits on the CPU and memory that it is willing to use. This means that for all but the smallest installations, it will probably not be quite enough.

Hence, Web hosts will not tend to choose it, but for a single user local installation, it might be an attractive proposition.

Given the propensity of Web hosts (both free and commercial) to choose MySQL, this is the database platform covered in this chapter.

SQL Server

There really isn't much to add about Microsoft's SQL Server. It is commercial and was released in a kind of mini-version with several useful features missing, such as full text search, as a Desktop Edition.

Because the majority of cheap and free Web hosts tend to avoid Microsoft operating systems, chiefly because of the high requirements that the operating system places on the server and the fact that licensing is relatively expensive (especially compared with freely available OSs like Linux), MS SQL rarely gets a look.

However, if you are running a Microsoft Web server and can afford it, MS SQL is a good product and integrates well with the Web environment. Given that MySQL is also available for Windows, it might be a better route for those just getting started, for cost reasons alone.

The SQL Language

In the same way that the language for writing Web pages is HTML and that the server can be made to produce that HTML using PHP, a database has its own communication language, called SQL (Structured Query Language).

SQL is used for all manipulation of databases, from constructing tables to putting data into them and taking data out. There are also some user management functions, but the "Just Enough" Web programmer will not need these. In case you do, they are available through the much prettier phpMyAdmin interface.

The same is true for the table creation and manipulation functions, which you'll look at through the phpMyAdmin interface, because it is so much more intuitive. Before learning how to manipulate the data using SQL, though, you need to look at the theory of operation.

Theory of Operation

The reason I cover this subject first, and don't discuss creating databases straight away, is that it is useful to know how you're going to manipulate the data before you set about making the tables. Knowing how to put data in, take it out, and otherwise operate on it gives you a good idea about how to create the tables that will store it.

SQL transactions (a request and result pair) are written using *queries*. A query is just a well formed instruction that tells the database what it should do, to what table, and with what data, as well as the kind of result it should return.

To put data in the database, you use the INSERT query. This needs to specify the table, columns, and data that will be placed into the database. To see what data is in the database, you use the SELECT query, which needs to provide the database system with some parameters such as the table name and what to look for (as well as which columns to look at).

If you need to change data, you use an UPDATE query, which operates on one or more columns in a table, based on some input criteria. If you want to update only a single row, that query data has to identify that row uniquely. Otherwise, you risk running the same update on multiple rows, which is why it is useful to have a *key* value that's unique across rows.

Finally, to remove data, you use the DELETE query, again with values that should identify the data that you want to remove. The entire table can be emptied with the DROP query, but this should be done via the phpMyAdmin interface.

Inside the query values, you use *wildcards* when you want to match multiple presentations of the same piece of information. For example, assuming you want to retrieve varying entries in the Name column:

"Ban%"	Matches Banks, Ban, Bananarama, and so on
"%son"	Matches Johnson, Anderson, Jameson, and so on

The underscore character (_) can be used in the same way to match single letters. These wildcards are used very frequently in queries because you'll quite often want to return a variety of values so that the users can select one.

There is also a concept known as *joining* which allows the programmer to create a set of result rows that is a combination of two tables in a single query. The JOIN returns the columns that have been specified in the query, but only one row per result.

Finally, a very useful command is the SHOW DATABASES; instruction. It tells the system to describe all the databases that it has under its control, as well as their structure. These queries can be used within a PHP script, entered interactively via the MySQL interface, or, more frequently in this context, entered through phpMyAdmin.

A final note—a query is terminated by a semicolon, and any values are contained in double or single quotes. Groups of values (that is, column names) are contained within parentheses.

Attributes and Data Types

Before you look at how to extract data in detail, you need to understand the mechanism that MySQL provides to define the kind of data that can be stored, called data types. Different data types are supported by different platforms; what follows here is true for MySQL.

MySQL only has built-in data types and does not allow user-defined data types. Even so, there are many data types that most programmers will never use. Only the most common ones are explained here in detail.

There are a few points to remember. Once a column has a data type associated with it, it can't be easily changed. The designer must choose wisely to avoid potentially having to do a lengthy export and import operation to rebuild the table with new column types.

Part of this is choosing the correct sizing of a data type, sometimes known as an *attribute*. MySQL offers one piece of very useful functionality in this respect—the ability to resize the data type. This is called *attribute promotion*.

The process is also well documented and implemented and is simply a back up and restore process, restoring to a column with a larger data type. The data types used in this book are the basic integer, floating point, text, and date types, but there are plenty more that are outside the scope of this book.

A summary of the types follows:

- INTEGER—A normal sized integer can be unsigned to go up to 4 billion, or −2 to +2 billion otherwise.

- BIGINT—Signed or unsigned, this can represent values that are far bigger than most users are ever likely to need.

- FLOAT—Signed or unsigned, single precision, but still more than ample.

- DOUBLE—Double precision for mathematical operations, this type is not usually needed.

- DATE—The date, in a predefined format.

- DATETIME—The date, and time, in a predefined format.

- TIMESTAMP—This is an automatic stamp on a row that gives the last operation.

- TEXT—Up to 65,000 characters, doesn't need to be explicitly sized.

- VARCHAR—Up to 65,000 characters, must be sized in column description.

- BOOLEAN—True or false.

There are more, but they're not really particularly useful. Wherever possible, one should try to use native data types, that is, DATE and not a date string, or the BOOLEAN data type and not an INTEGER with either "0" or "1" in it. This is because they will take less space in the database schema when using native types.

This might not matter for one row, but Web databases are often designed to have many rows, and it will increase your data storage requirements drastically if you do not try to use *only* the space you actually *need*.

Finally, when a column is created with a data type, another attribute can be set, called the *key*, which is a unique value that identifies that row. No two rows can have the same *key* in that field. The key is often used when joining two tables, rather like the Customer ID field in the example from Figure 7.2.

Extracting Data

The basic form for the SELECT query is as follows:

```
SELECT <columns> FROM <table names> WHERE <condition>
              ORDER BY <column>;
```

This code simply states that you want the database system to select some rows, from a given table, where a certain condition is met, ordering by one of the columns. Everything except the columns and table name is optional. So, the following is perfectly acceptable:

```
SELECT * FROM Customer;
```

This query, using the design from Figure 7.2, would return all the rows from the Customer table, and all the columns therein. If you wanted only the Name column, you would use a query such as:

```
SELECT Name FROM Customer;
```

This query could then be enriched to select only those customers whose names end with o:

```
SELECT Name FROM Customer WHERE Name = "%o";
```

Furthermore, you might like to order these by the Name column:

```
SELECT Name FROM Customer WHERE Name = "%o" ORDER BY Name;
```

You can also join this result with a result from a similar table, using the *primary key* as the reference point, and using a NATURAL JOIN. If you assume that the Customer table has Customer_ID as its primary key, and that Order contains a Customer_ID column, you can issue the following SQL query:

```
SELECT * FROM Customer NATURAL JOIN Orders;
```

This query has the effect of showing only those customers who have an order (that is, the Customer_ID columns can be joined). The result displays only one Customer_ID column for each row.

The NATURAL JOIN assumes that there is a key available to join the two tables on— this key then gives the reference that allows the rows to be connected using a single reference point: the CUSTOMER_ID in this case.

There can be multiple joins performed, to access many tables, as long as they can all be held together by a series of key values. If you do not know how the data will look when it is retrieved, you can even specify the column to perform the join on:

```
SELECT * FROM Customer INNER JOIN Orders USING (Customer_ID);
```

All of these queries can be refined somewhat by the use of aliases and the ON keyword. For example, the previous query can be written using an INNER JOIN rather than a NATURAL JOIN to create the same effect.

So, the INNER JOIN lets you specify the actual column (which might not be the primary key) upon which to join the two tables. Re-writing the previous NATRUAL JOIN query to use INNER JOIN might result in the following:

```
SELECT Name, c.Customer_ID, o.Quantity FROM Customer c
    INNER JOIN Orders o ON o.Customer_ID = c.Customer_ID;
```

The ON clause is necessary because, unlike a NATURAL JOIN, the primary key is not necessarily taken into account. Without it, the query returns one row for each o.Quantity per customer. This is slightly illogical, but to get the relationship right, you either use an ON clause or specify the orders first.

Generally speaking, it is best to stick with the simple NATURAL JOIN and INNER JOIN...USING variations.

Finally, the GROUP BY clause can be useful in grouping data together. You'll see more of this in a moment, but assuming you wanted a list of all the customers who had made an order, you would do the following:

```
SELECT Customer_ID FROM Orders GROUP BY Customer_ID;
```

Deriving Data

It is also helpful to use SQL to derive data and make calculations while carrying out queries. You can, for example, count the number of entities, sum fields, and do other calculations that come back in the result table.

So, if you wanted to count the number of customers who had made an order of more than 100 units, you would perform the following query:

```
SELECT COUNT(*) FROM Orders WHERE Quantity > 100;
```

As you would expect, the WHERE clause can take all manner of different comparison operations, including all the mathematical operators and the LIKE clause for strings. These are all well documented if you get stuck, but as long as you stick to the following conventions, you should be capable of performing the majority of the queries that you will ever come across:

<, >, =, != >= <=   for numbers

%, _   for strings

Calculations can also be performed on the values of returned data. If you knew the price of a given item that had been ordered, for example, you could also work out the total value of the customers' orders:

```
SELECT Customer_ID,  Quantity * 2.50 FROM Orders;
```

This query assumes that all items have the same price, 2.50, which is rarely the case. So, it would be useful instead to be able to look up the price and use that number to multiply by the Quantity to get to the final value.

The whole query is as follows:

```
SELECT Customer_ID, SUM(Price * Quantity) FROM Orders
    INNER JOIN Products USING (Product_Ref) GROUP BY Customer_ID;
```

This is the most complex type of query that you are going to look at, so it is worth taking some time to see what it is doing. Clearly, the Customer_ID comes from the Order table, and the Price comes from the Products table.

The INNER JOIN has been specified using the Product_Ref as the pivot point for the join operation, so only the products for which there has been an order for each row of the Products table are returned. So, the first pass sees a table that contains, for each row, the Customer_ID and a Price * Quantity for each class of items that has been ordered.

However, you have also specified that you want to see the SUM of these, grouped by the Customer_ID. This causes each set of rows to be summed and grouped by the customer who ordered them. If you had chosen to group by the Product_Ref, you would have the total value ordered by product instead.

Subqueries   Sometimes it is useful to break queries down into subqueries. A subquery generally results in a single column of data being returned. For example, the following illustrates a subquery in action:

```
SELECT Product_Ref, COUNT(Product_Ref) FROM Order
  WHERE Cust_ID =
    (SELECT DISTINCT Cust_ID FROM Order ORDER BY Cust_ID)
          GROUP BY Product_Ref;
```

This query might not do anything terribly useful, but it uses a subquery to count the number of people with the same name. Of course, it can also be done with a simple WHERE clause.

It is important to note that MySQL does not allow you to mix tables and subqueries, so the following is not allowed and must be solved by the use of an INNER JOIN:

```
SELECT cName FROM Orders AS o
  WHERE cName =
    (SELECT Name FROM Customer WHERE Name = o.Name)
          GROUP BY cName;
```

This query will not work, because cName is not present in the Orders table, even though it has been defined in the WHERE subquery. The INNER JOIN looks like this:

```
SELECT Customer_ID, Name FROM Orders INNER JOIN Customer
   USING (Customer_ID) GROUP BY Customer_ID;
```

Logical WHERE Statements   It is also possible to combine conditions in the WHERE clause of the SELECT statement to filter data further. For example, a query to select only those customers who have ordered more than 100 units of a specific Product_Ref could look like:

```
SELECT Customer_ID FROM Orders WHERE Product_Ref = 456
                  AND Quantity > 100;
```

All of the now-familiar Boolean statements can be used for these kinds of queries, and parentheses can be used to separate subclauses, just like in other programming languages (JavaScript and PHP included). This allows you to build up very complex selection criteria and only return the data that you are interested in, which is very useful because it helps the processing of the data as well as reducing the memory overhead associated with the result set.

PHP and MySQL   The previous discussion represents a basic subset of the SQL SELECT statement, but, combined with programming, it is more than enough for basic tasks. As you become familiar with Web programming in general and SQL in particular, you can expand your use of these queries beyond this as projects require.

The easiest way to use SQL in Web programming is to combine it with PHP logic and keep the queries as simple as possible. When a small number of rows are returned, the efficiency gain is not much greater when performing advanced SQL queries and it is much easier to understand a comparison of two result sets in PHP than it is to create a complex inner join.

So, the advice here is to understand how to derive data from a table and how to extract data from it, but to leverage the power of PHP and MySQL *together* in creating Web applications rather than getting caught up trying to understand every intricacy of the SQL language.

With that in mind, the last piece of the puzzle is how to insert data into the database, and how to update it once it is there.

Inserting, Modifying, and Deleting Data

There are three basic commands for manipulating data in the tables, usually in the context of Web programming, and they will be issued from PHP in order to change the data following a user action of some kind.

This section discusses the INSERT, UPDATE, and DELETE FROM commands, which are used to put data into a table, change data that has been placed in a table, and delete data from it, respectively. To insert data, you use the INSERT command, as follows:

```
INSERT INTO <table> VALUES (<value>, ...);
```

The ellipses indicate that there are multiple value entries possible. In fact, there must be a single value, of the correct type (that is, in quotes for strings), for each column of data. Named columns can be used instead, but to do this you must set each column explicitly (unless the columns contain automatic data).

```
INSERT INTO <table> SET <column>=<value> or DEFAULT, ...;
```

The DEFAULT keyword simply assigns the default value that has been specified in the definition of the table. When using the VALUES clause rather than the SET clause, you can also use DEFAULT or simply a space to indicate that there is no value for this entry. However, that cannot be performed if column has been set to NOT NULL (meaning it must always have a value set) in the table-creation phase.

You'll see examples of automatic values—DEFAULT and NULL/NOT NULL—in the section detailing the setup of tables using phpMyAdmin.

Once data has been inserted, it can be retrieved, updated, or deleted.

In order to change data with either the UPATE or DELETE FROM commands, it is usually a good idea to issue a SELECT command from PHP in order to determine that the query can be satisfied. The reason for doing this is twofold—to make sure that you are updating the correct data, and to make sure that the selection criteria are well formed.

This might seem unnecessary, and it is quite possible to omit this step entirely, as long as you are confident about the query that is going to be issued. The UPDATE command is in two parts: the items to be updated and the new values, and the WHERE clause that selects the rows that are going to be operated on.

Multiple rows can be updated at once, so some care must be taken to make sure that the result is what you think it is going to be. The general form for the UPDATE command is as follows:

UPDATE <table> SET <column> = <value> WHERE <query>;

So, if you wanted to increase all the prices in the Products table by 10% where they are less than 0.9, you would issue the command:

UPDATE Products SET Price = Price * 1.1 WHERE Price < 0.9;

(This example assumes, of course, that none of the prices are set to 0.)

The usual forms of WHERE clauses can all be used, and multiple columns can be set using a comma-separated list of column = value pairs.

You can delete data from the table using the DELETE FROM command. Similar to the UPDATE command, it requires a WHERE condition in order to select the rows to be deleted.

DELETE FROM <table > WHERE <condition>;

So, to delete all the products from a table where the price is less than 1.00, you could issue the following query:

DELETE FROM Products WHERE Price < 1.00;

These are the simplest forms for the three modification commands and are more than enough to get you started. As you examine and encounter more complex situations, you'll naturally expand your knowledge through experimentation and frequent trips to the user guide. For those needing only simple table management, this discussion will suffice.

ROLLBACK *and* COMMIT

Databases are transaction-based. This means that until the changes are committed to the database, they can be undone. The ROLLBACK command will undo the changes in some circumstances, but the documentation should be checked to see exactly what those are. Generally, it is accepted that changes are committed upon logout from the database system.

Until that point, they can be undone by using the ROLLBACK command. If you are sure of the changes and want to commit them immediately, you should issue the COMMIT command to be sure that the changes take hold immediately. This can be quite important for high traffic sites, but check your documentation before you rely on the COMMIT and ROLLBACK mechanisms.

Creating and Altering Tables

For those not using phpMyAdmin, or for those who are curious about the SQL that it generates in order to manage tables, here is a brief précis of the table-management system. It centers around two commands—CREATE TABLE and ALTER TABLE—with which it is possible to manage the columns in individual tables.

The first of these commands, CREATE TABLE, takes the following generic form:

```
CREATE TABLE <name> ( <column> <data type>, ... );
```

The ellipsis indicates that there may be many column, data type pairs, all contained in parentheses. So, to create the Customer table from the previous examples, you might execute a query such as this:

```
CREATE TABLE Customer ( Name VARCHAR(255), Customer_ID INTEGER );
```

Any of the valid data types can be used, but you should avoid using reserved words as table or column names, because this will confuse the SQL parser. For example, naming a table "Order" rather than "Orders" is not a good idea, because the parser might confuse the table name with the ORDER BY keyword.

Apart from this restriction, there are very few restrictions on names of entities beyond the usual constraints that they should not contain spaces or start with a number. Respect these rules and you will have no problem managing the tables.

You read about keys in the section that detailed how to use the JOIN function. To create a key on a table to use as a pivot for a JOIN, you use the ALTER TABLE command:

```
ALTER TABLE <name> ADD CONSTRAINT <name>
                PRIMARY KEY (<column>);
```

Other common uses for ALTER TABLE are to add and remove columns. So, if you wanted to add a new column to the Customer table, you would use:

```
ALTER TABLE Customer ADD COLUMN Address VARCHAR(255);
```

You could also add more than one column by using a set of column, data type pairs in parentheses. Similarly, you can delete the newly added column by using the DROP COLUMN clause with the ALTER TABLE command, as follows:

```
ALTER TABLE Customer DROP COLUMN Address;
```

Finally, you can use DROP with two other database entities—tables and constraints. Again, using the Customer table as an example, you can remove the primary key (assuming that you called it `primary_key`):

```
ALTER TABLE Customer DROP CONSTRAINT primary_key;
```

Once you are satisfied that you no longer have a use for the Customer table, you can then delete it with the DROP TABLE command:

```
DROP TABLE <table name>;
```

As noted, it is both more common, and easier, to manage the tables using phpMyAdmin; however, it is worth knowing the general layout of these commands so that you can understand the SQL that phpMyAdmin generates. In this way, if you need to create temporary tables programmatically, the commands will be familiar.

User Management

Finally, a note about user management. It is possible to restrict certain commands to certain users. This is a good idea if, for example, there is a database administrator user and a Webuser. The Webuser performs only basic queries on the database and should probably not have enough permissions to create and drop tables, for example.

The GRANT command performs this assignment of permissions to a given user, and the generic format for it is as follows:

```
GRANT <commands> ON <table> TO <user>;
```

Using the example of a Webuser, you might decide to let such a user only select from a specific table and possibly perform updates with the following command:

```
GRANT select, update ON Customers TO Webuser;
```

Of course, this command assumes that the Webuser exists in the database system. Although this can be done from within the SQL language, you're going to see how to set all this up using phpMyAdmin.

Databases for Websites

This section is all about setting up and using databases on Websites using MySQL and phpMyAdmin. It is not designed to be a general guide to databases but concentrates on getting up and running as quickly as possible with a Web host that offers the required tools.

The section covers setting up and administering a database, as well as connecting to it through PHP to run queries as a server side script. This last point is important, because it is highly likely that a Web database exists to provide an interface to the Web application.

For example, in a content-management system, all the content is stored as text in a database and extracted only when it must be rendered. This makes CMSs flexible and dynamic, because they can display any information from the database in a way that's coherent with respect to what the end user has requested.

So, if the user wants to see all the blog posts with "cat" in the title, a query on the database will return all the relevant rows. These are returned to PHP as a two-dimensional array of rows and columns that can then be manipulated programmatically.

Data can be inserted and updated, too, by building query strings that contain variable values. In fact, any query that can be performed on a MySQL database can be done through PHP, and it is this feature that allows phpMyAdmin to perform all manner of database operations via a Web interface.

First, however, you need to set up the database with the cPanel MySQL Databases tool.

Typical Database Setup

The following steps should usually be performed with the MySQL-provided Databases tool, which installs under cPanel in the Databases section. Whether they are performed using a wizard style interface or manually, the steps are the same.

Note that there are some restrictions on the names that can be used for databases. These are essentially the same as for any other kind of named entity in programming—they cannot contain special characters (beyond the _ character) or start with numbers, for example. They also cannot contain space characters.

The first step is to create the database with MySQL Databases. This is shown in Figure 7.5.

As seen in Figure 7.5, the only option is for the user to enter the database name. The next step is to create the users in the system who are going to be attached to the various databases. This can be seen in Figure 7.6. As you will see, the examples

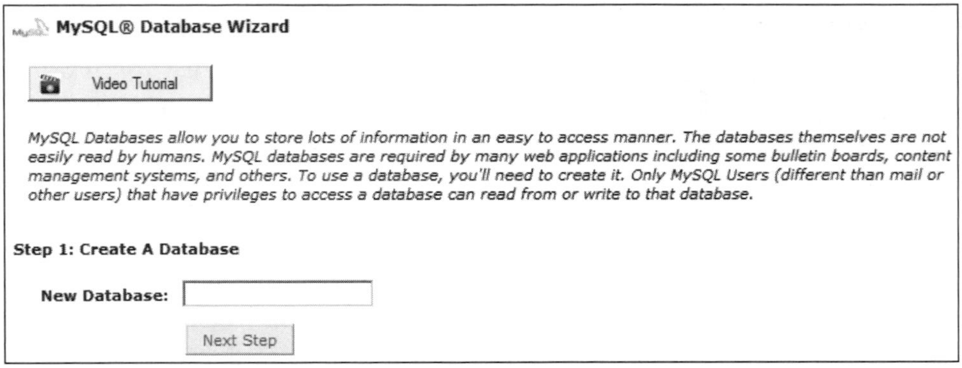

Figure 7.5
MySQL database wizard step 1 (create your database)

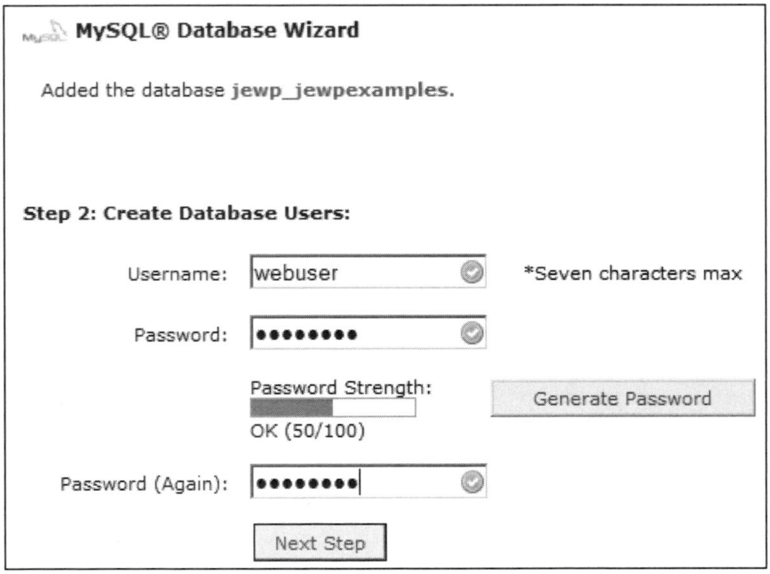

Figure 7.6
MySQL database wizard step 2 (create users)

here use the name jewpexamples, to which the system has added the prefix jewp_, this being the username to which the database is attached.

As you can see in Figure 7.6, each user is created by assigning the user a username and password. Once the users have been created, they can be added to the database that has just been created. The users are created in the system with privileges that are set from the start and applied to the database being built.

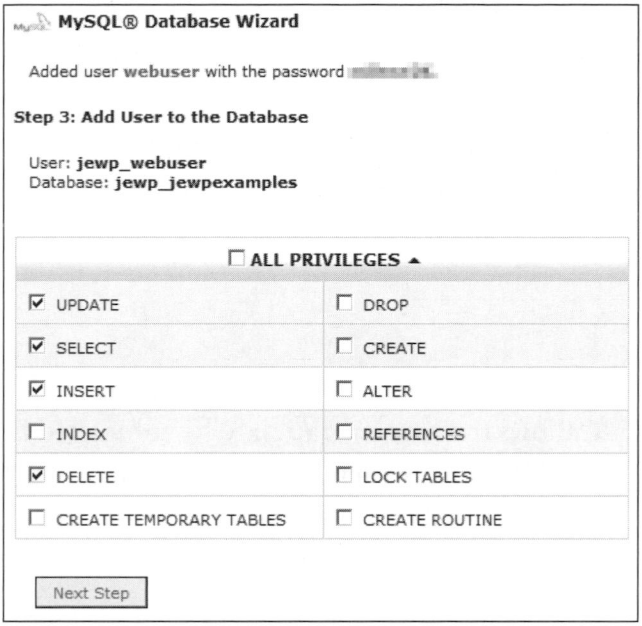

Figure 7.7
MySQL database wizard step 3 (add users)

This example uses a webuser user and password, which is the generic, non-administrative user. For this reason, in the next step, you only select a basic collection of privileges.

The users can pick and choose the privileges that they should have based on the operations that each user is expected to carry out, and then add them with these privileges to the database. This is shown in Figure 7.7.

The privileges that are selected for the Webuser, for example, would be SELECT and INSERT and perhaps UPDATE and DELETE. Once the privileges have been selected, the user clicks on Add, and the user is added to the database domain. Users can be added to multiple databases through the phpMyAdmin interface, if that is required.

The last screen, which confirms the operations, is shown in Figure 7.8.

From here, the user can add another user to the database, a Webadmin user, for example. Such users should have all possible privileges, so long as they are never used in a PHP script. This is for security reasons—the master user should be accessible only from the cPanel interface, which is relatively secure.

If the cPanel implementation does not seem to have the MySQL database wizard, or if the process is too cumbersome, there is another possibility. The MySQL

Figure 7.8
MySQL database wizard step 4 (finished)

database form, shown in Figure 7.9, allows the administration to be completed in fewer steps. This interface will be located in the cPanel Databases section along with the other database administration packages provided by the Web host.

There are still two steps—create the user and add the user to the database—but the form in Figure 7.9 puts all the options in one place and can be easier for advanced users.

One point to be wary of is the names you chose for your users. Most hosts will add the domain or subdomain to the start of the chosen username, to keep it unique. This means that if you type **webuser**, the system will make that

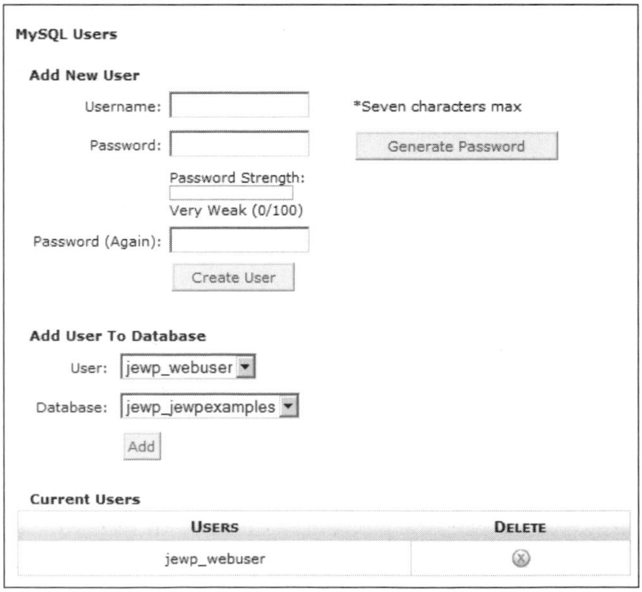

Figure 7.9
MySQL database form (adding a user to the database)

jewp_webuser, if the subdomain is jewp.domain.com. The same usually applies to database names.

These naming conventions are not visible when making queries from phpMyAdmin or PHP scripts, but are added automatically at the system level. They do mean, however, that in the administration panels, the users need to be aware that the names are not the same as the ones that they typed in originally.

Database Tools: Using phpMyAdmin

Having followed the previous steps, you should now have a Web database installed on your host. The next phase is to start administering it, adding tables and so forth, before it can actually be interacted with using custom PHP scripts and Web pages.

The tool used here to do this is phpMyAdmin. You can also write your own in PHP, but considering that the tool exists, it is better to make use of it. Because any query can be performed from PHP, some packages make use of this to do their own database administration.

When you first enter the phpMyAdmin system, the page is broken into two panes. In phpMyAdmin, there are several levels of administration, and the menus in the main frame are context-sensitive.

When phpMyAdmin first opens, it shows the first level of administration. Here, no databases are selected, so operations are performed on the whole cluster. This is shown in Figure 7.10.

The second level allows administration on the database level. Here, you can create tables in the database. On the left side of Figure 7.10, note that the database you created previously appears (jewp_examples) and it is currently empty—the number in brackets indicates zero tables.

You can select the database by clicking the name on the left side, which will then change the context of the administration system to the database level. From here, you can create a table.

Creating a Table

When an empty database first opens, the screen looks like one shown in Figure 7.11. Note that there are additional menu items across the top of the main window frame. These menu items indicate a number of operations that can be performed on the database and the tables contained within it.

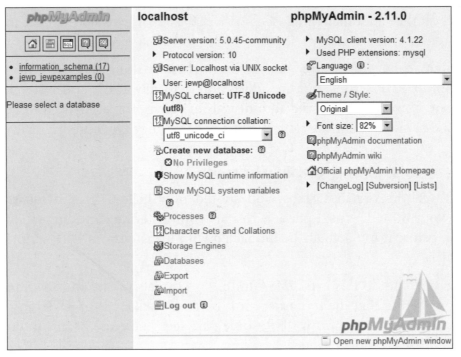

Figure 7.10
phpMyAdmin main page

One of the most common uses for a Web database is to store a Weblog or blog. So, this section shows how to design a very simple Weblog storage system that you can use to store your thoughts about the world. At this point, you need to design a table to contain the data that the blog is to contain.

Blogs usually have space for the date, a title, some kind of summary that can be submitted to RSS clients and search engines, the actual content of the blog, and a unique ID to identify the blog entry. Each of these will have different data types; notably, the blog content should be a TEXT object (with no size limit), and, for efficiency, you should limit the size of the title and summary.

This might lead to a set of fields, as follows:

```
date      Stores a DATE data type
title     VARCHAR; could be limited to 30 width
summary   VARCHAR; limited to 255 width
content   TEXT object
id        BIGINT; assuming that you will do a lot of writing!
```

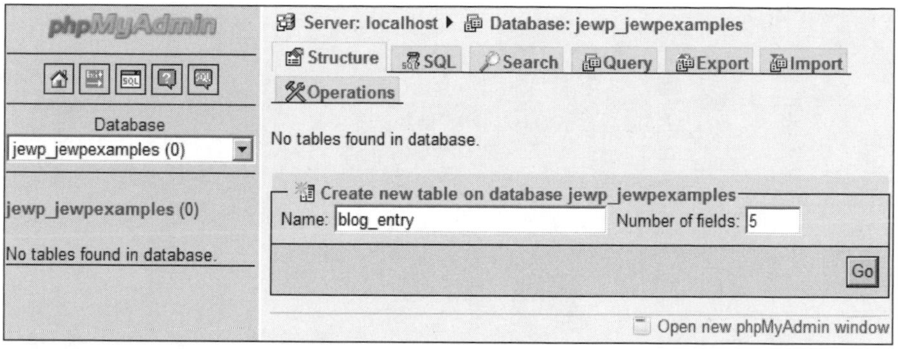

Figure 7.11
Create table page

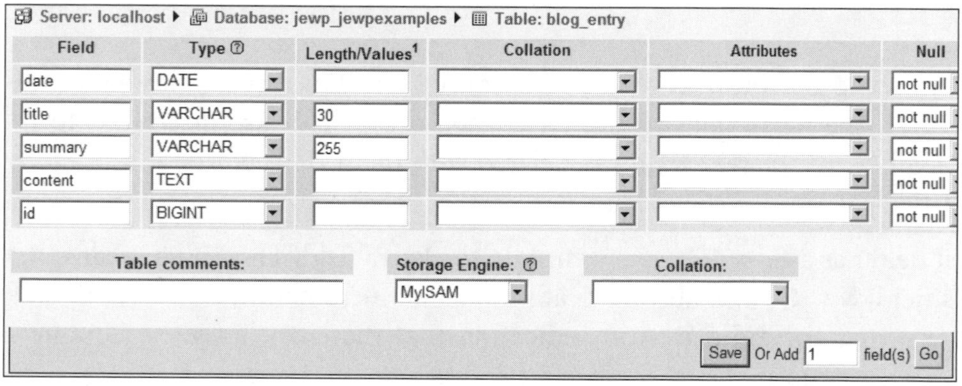

Figure 7.12
Adding column attributes (1 of 2)

The first step is to create the table name, blog_entry, and tell phpMyAdmin how many fields it should have, as shown in Figure 7.11.

You can fill in the table name and the number of fields and then click the Go button. This will create an empty table and open a page where you can set the field names and attributes. Figure 7.12 might look intimidating, but it is really quite straightforward.

Of the first set of attributes, seen in Figure 7.12, you are only going to concern yourself with the name, type, and length. From top to bottom, you can see some familiar data types and length information. In this case, all that the lengths do is limit the field title to 30 characters and the summary field to 255 characters.

In the second half of the screen, shown in Figure 7.13, you need only be concerned with the Null and Extra columns and the set of radio buttons on the right side.

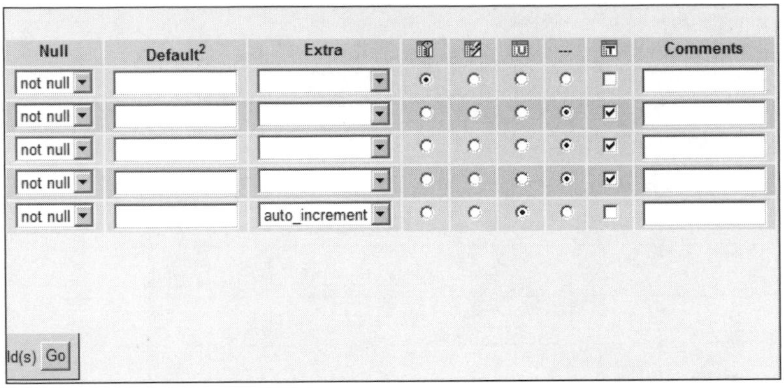

Figure 7.13
Adding column attributes (2 of 2)

Again, working from top to bottom in Figure 7.13, you can see the "not null" entry for all the fields. This means that when these fields are inserted into the database, they must have a value associated with them. This is true for all except the last field.

The last field has a `auto_increment` entry in the Extra field. This value means that, for this field, MySQL will automatically assign an incrementing number as data. Note here that the radio button indicating that the entry must be Unique is selected. This is normal and a side effect of using `auto_increment`.

The other key radio button selected is on the first field, which is the date and is identified as the primary key. So, if you were to perform a join on this table with another that contained news events by date, you would be able to produce a list of blog entries for those dated news events using the `date` field as a pivot.

After all the fields are filled out and the attributes set, you can click the Go button, and the SQL query will be built by phpMyAdmin and then sent to MySQL. The result of this is seen in Figure 7.14.

Any time that the Structure menu option is clicked, the fields will be listed as they are at the bottom of the screen in Figure 7.14. The top half shows the SQL statements that were used to create the table. The same layout is used for the results page of any administration tasks that are executed via SQL statement.

Once the table has been created, it appears underneath the database name in the left menu and can be selected just by clicking on it. All the tables that belong to a database are listed in this way.

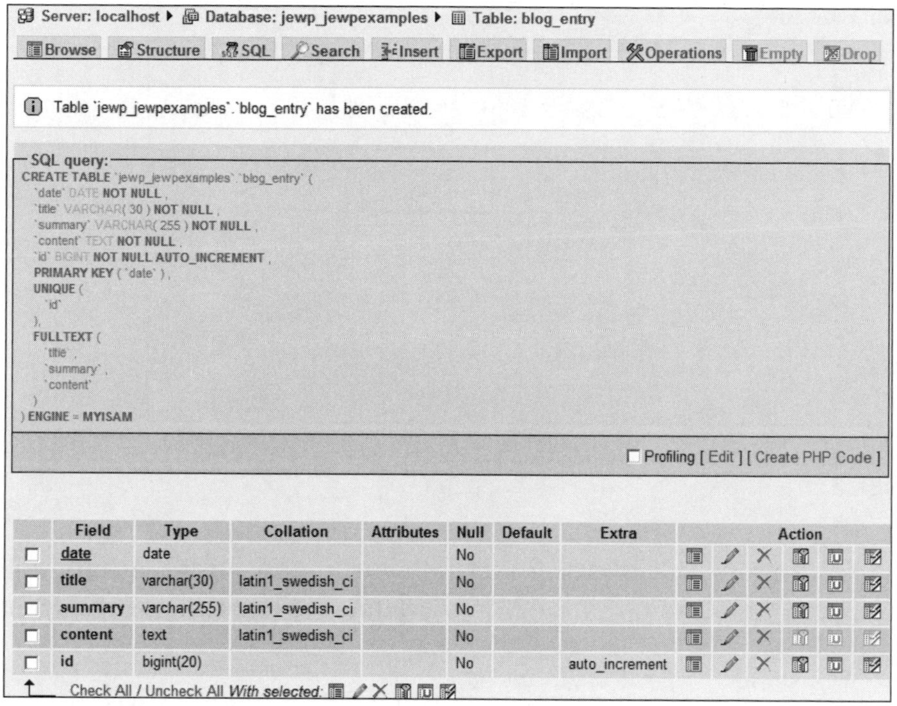

Figure 7.14
Creating a table: the SQL statement and result

Now that the table exists, you can populate it with some initial data (for test purposes) by using the Insert tool available from the menu strip along the top of the main window frame.

Inserting Data

Inserting data through the phpMyAdmin interface is not something that is terribly common. However, it can be useful to be able to insert data from time to time, and the interface provided is flexible and straightforward to use. The initial view is shown in Figure 7.15.

Note that there are two ways to enter data—via a function or by typing in the value. The date field, for example, has been populated using the NOW function, which will place the current date into the field.

The id field has been left blank, because you know from the table definition that it is an auto_increment field. This is where the Data Dictionary comes in useful, because there is no evidence from the interface that this field may be left blank even though the null column is empty, indicating that a value is required.

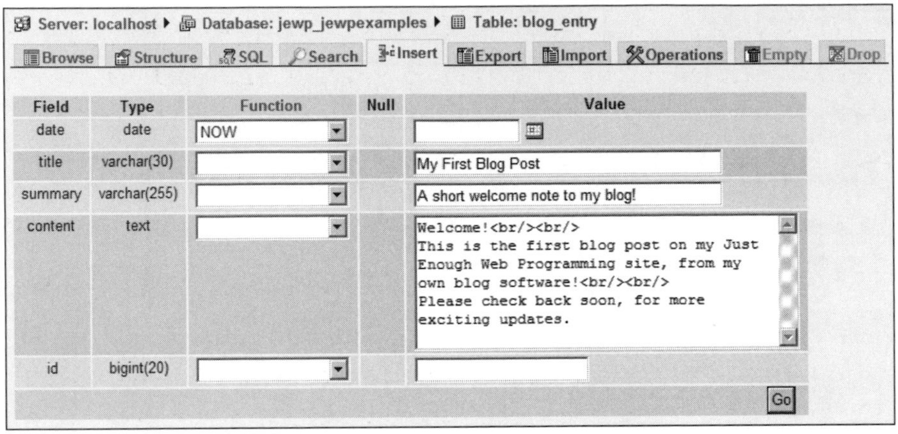

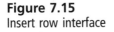

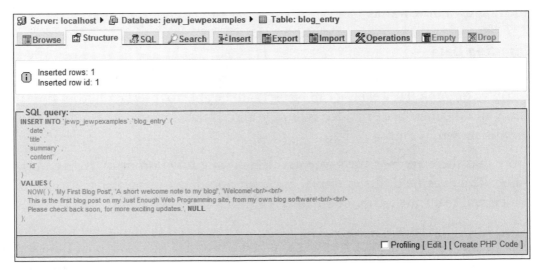

Figure 7.15
Insert row interface

Clicking the Go button will submit the HTML form, and phpMyAdmin will construct and pass the query on to the MySQL database. The result is shown in Figure 7.16.

In Figure 7.16, note the information area at the top of the frame, which shows the status of the INSERT query. The query itself is expanded below that. The query should look familiar, except that the columns have all been individually named (which is a slightly different usage to the one previous). The VALUES list appears in parentheses after the INSERT INTO clause.

Figure 7.16
Inserting a row: the SQL statement and result

You can also use this method to construct sample queries that can be used as a base to create your own queries in PHP code. Having thus inserted some data, you can now use the Browse interface to look at the data.

Browsing Your Database

You access the Browse interface by clicking the Browse menu option. The initial view can be seen in Figure 7.17.

At this point, you only have one record in the database, and you know that it is there, so this is a fairly useless exercise. However, it illustrates one of the interfaces available in phpMyAdmin: the ability to quickly examine the contents of the database through a Web browser.

If the resulting information is insufficient (it is usually limited to 30 rows), keep in mind that it is possible to adjust the quantity and display options. The first two boxes in the input area (under the query expansion) allow the users to adjust which rows are shown.

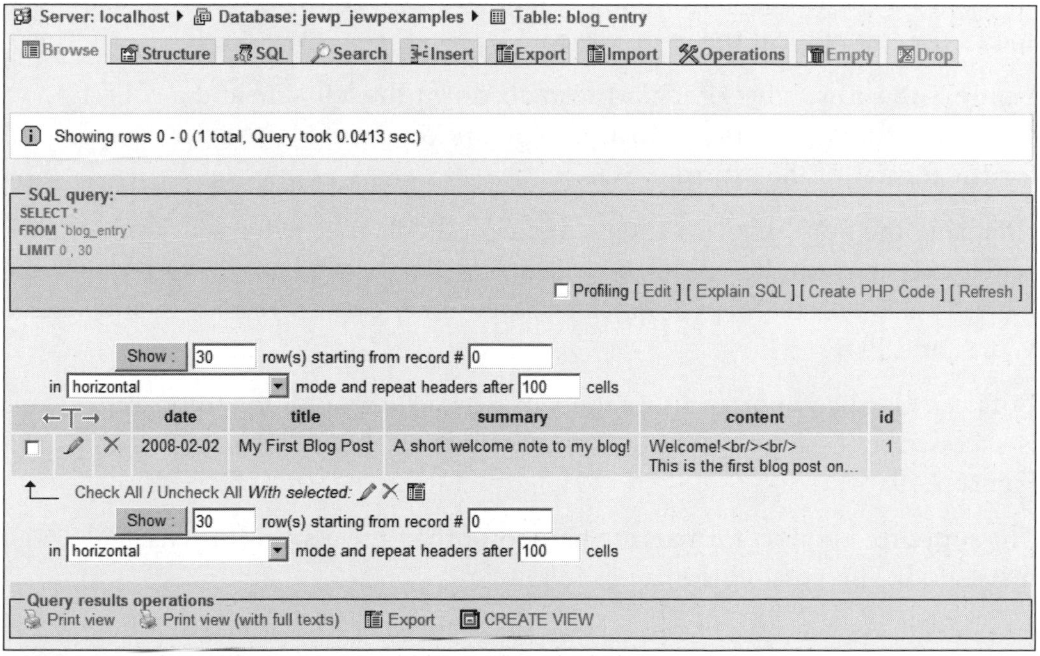

Figure 7.17
The phpMyAdmin Browse interface

If you wanted to view rows 31 to 60, you would enter 31 in the far-right box. This would then change the LIMIT clause in the query to LIMIT 31, 30 instead of 0, 30. You can also change the display mode and point at which the headers (column names) are repeated.

The query can be copied and pasted into the SQL box accessible through the SQL menu option and then run as a SQL query. This is an alternative way to look at data in the database, and also a good way to practice using SQL SELECT statements. You're encouraged to play with the Browse and SQL tools until you're familiar with them. When you're prototyping your database, you'll likely spend quite some time trying out queries and testing the database before you write the actual PHP code to access it.

Exporting/Importing Data

There are two useful tools that the phpMyAdmin collection offers for processing blocks of data. The first, Export, is useful when you want to extract the data into a variety of formats. This section doesn't go into great detail, but it is useful to make a few comments about the interface.

You can access the Export tool by clicking the Export menu option; Figure 7.18 shows the initial form that's displayed.

Figure 7.18 shows a list of export formats down the left side and a collection of options in the main frame. Most of these options relate to the default selection for the format of the export—SQL.

Choosing the SQL export format will create the data schema as a series of SQL statements that can be re-run on a different database platform to recreate the table. This is a useful form of quick backup. Other export formats include Excel, Word, and PDF.

Data can also be imported in a variety of formats, through the Import tool. This is accessed by clicking the Import menu option. The initial screen is shown in Figure 7.19.

The supported import formats are far poorer than the export formats, and are all text-based. The possibilities are as follows:

- CSV—As an export from a program such as Excel, for example

- SQL—As a series of SQL statements

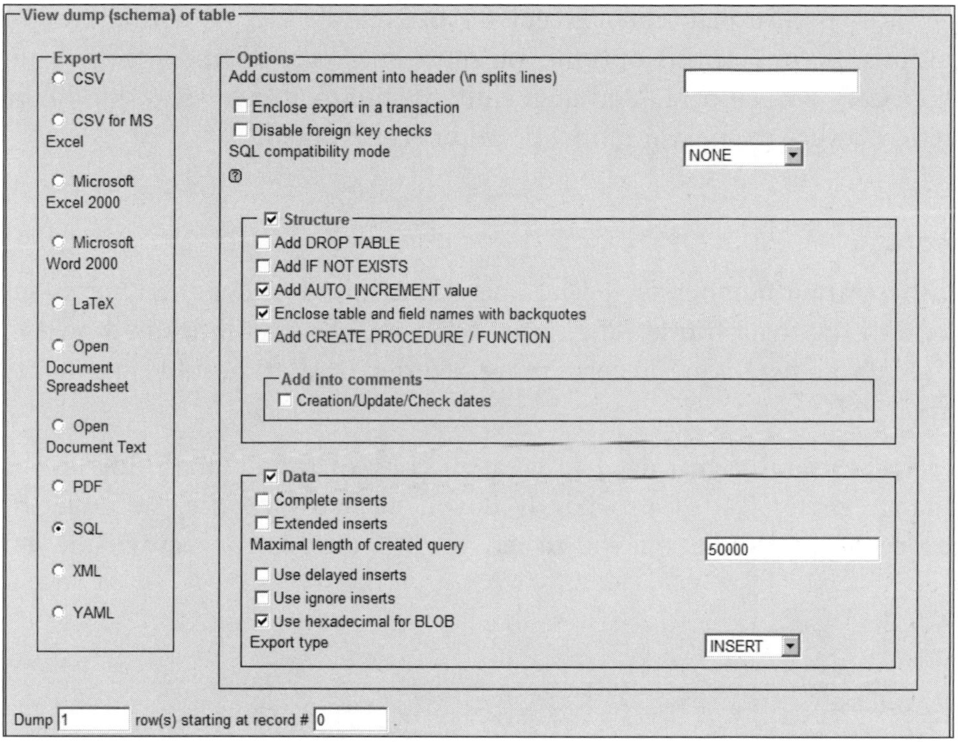

Figure 7.18
The phpMyAdmin export interface

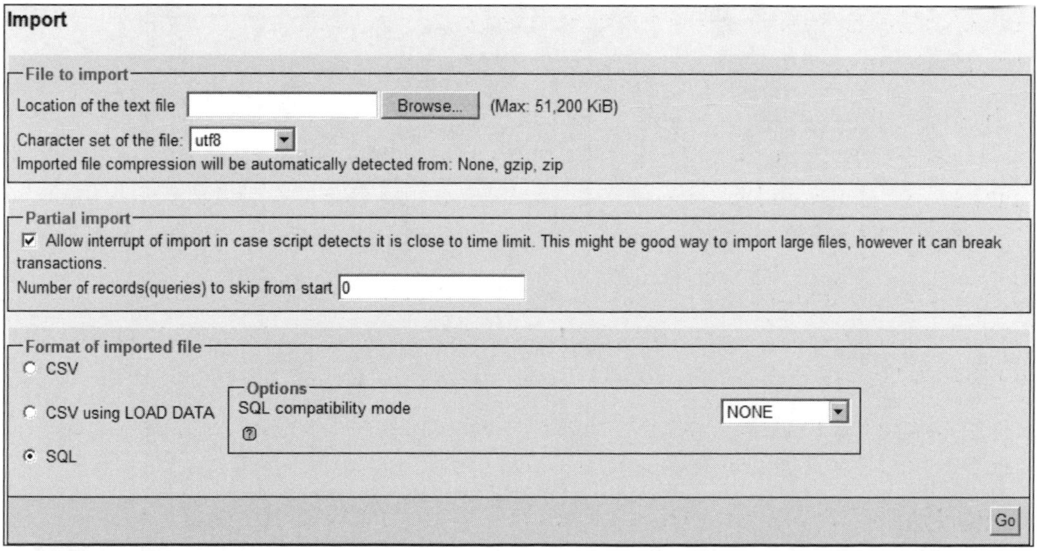

Figure 7.19
The phpMyAdmin import interface

The interface is self-explanatory, except for the middle box, which allows for interruptions. If you use this option, you must query the database to find out how much data was imported and then enter the number of rows to skip in the relevant box before the next import operation is attempted.

Operations

Finally, there are a number of special operations found under the Operations menu tab on the main frame. The initial selection of possibilities is shown in Figure 7.20. From here, you can copy, move, reorder, or alter the table in a variety of ways.

This screen is useful if you need to create a copy of the database for test or maintenance reasons. It is also handy if you need to rename the table for any reason. Beyond these specific issues, the Operations tool should be left alone.

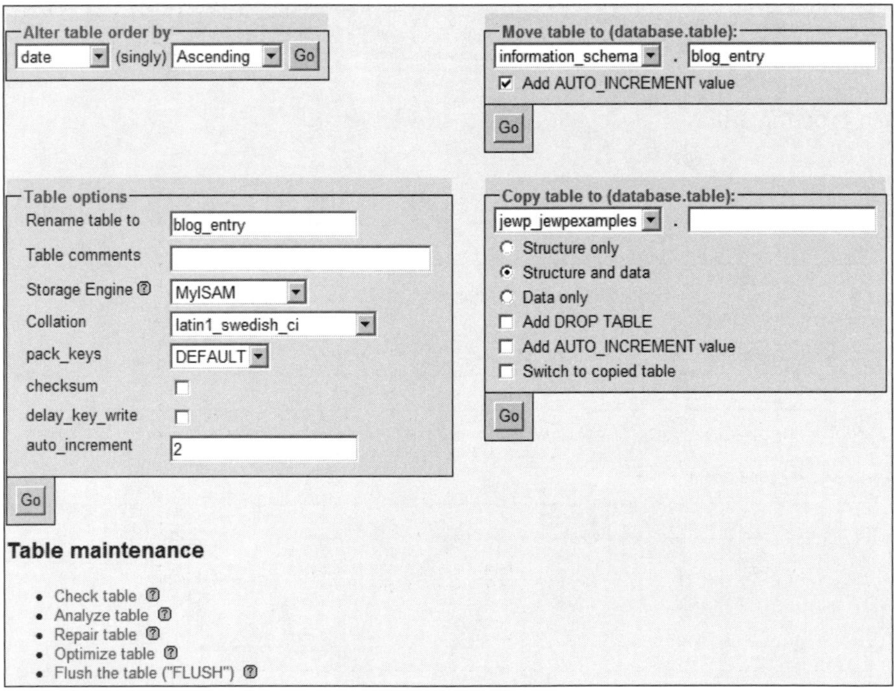

Figure 7.20
phpMyAdmin operations main screen

Indexing, Backing Up, and Maintenance Issues

Before you look at connecting to the database, I need to mention a few points about maintaining databases. A database is a piece of living software in a living data space and will benefit from the occasional bit of maintenance.

Maintenance in this case just involves taking a backup, occasionally cleaning out the data storage area, and rebuilding the indexes. Again, phpMyAdmin makes this process incredibly straightforward.

Backing Up

The easiest way to do this is just to export the data from time to time, as you saw in the analysis of the Export tool. This is an essential part of the chores that you need to do as a Website owner—because if the data is ever lost, a large part of your business goes with it.

So, you should make a backup schedule and stick to it rigidly. You can refer back to the Export option in phpMyAdmin to remind yourself about the options that are available. If you are using cPanel to administer databases and the underlying Website, it's likely that there is a backup option in the Databases section.

This is shown in Figure 7.21.

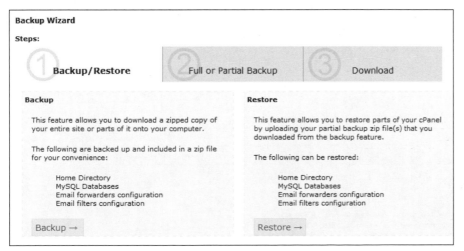

Figure 7.21
The cPanel backup main screen

Now, the Web host should take some of the responsibility, and will hopefully have set up MySQL to prevent data loss. In addition, the Webhost should make file-level backups for you, but there is no sense, given the availability of an easy tool, in ignoring the possibility to make your own backups on a regular basis.

If you're running your own database on your own server, there are quite a few additional things that you can do. For example, it is possible to have MySQL schedule its own backups. The set and forget feature that this offers makes it easy to make sure that the system is adequately protected.

Otherwise, a timely manual backup will just have to do.

Rebuilding Indexes

If you're constantly removing data and adding new data, your tables will become un-optimized. In the worst case, queries will start to take a long time to execute. If this happens, the database can be optimized.

All that the optimization involves is periodic rebuilding of the index. Without going into too much detail, this will improve transaction speed and lookup efficiency as the SQL platform organizes its data in an optimized fashion.

Again, this is best done from the phpMyAdmin interface, the result of which is shown in Figure 7.22. If you look back at Figure 7.20, as part of the Operations menu option you will see a small section at the bottom called Table Maintenance.

Clicking the Optimize Table option causes the system to re-index the database and display the screen shown in Figure 7.22.

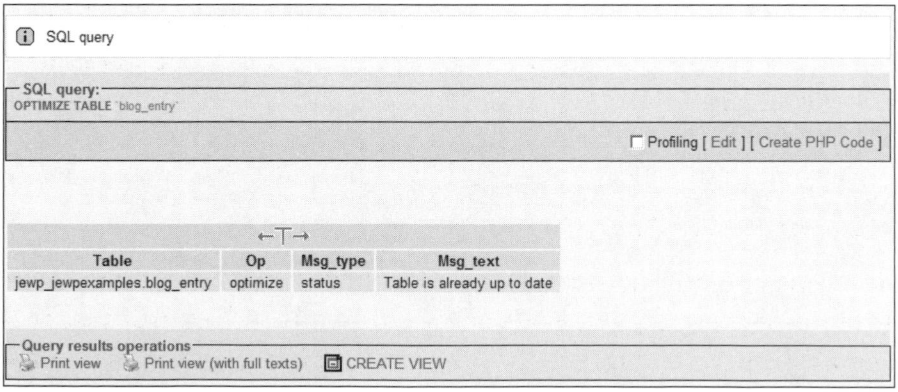

Figure 7.22
The phpMyAdmin optimize screen showing operations

As you can see in Figure 7.22, this can also be done using a SQL query on the database. One way to do that is through the phpMyAdmin Query tool, for example. Be sure to select the table first; otherwise, the option does not appear in the menus because of the context-sensitivity of the menu system.

Connecting to Databases with PHP

Finally, with the database up and running, it is time to look at how you can interface with it from PHP. The following code represents the bare minimum that is needed while still being fairly robust. Luckily, PHP makes it very easy to integrate with MySQL, offering a whole collection of mysql_ functions that are installed as standard.

Once everything has been set up, it's a good idea to test before doing any actual development. The code that is developed in the testing process, for making connections and tidying up, can be abstracted into an external PHP file that can be reused for the same host.

Before starting to create the code, you need to have your connection parameters at hand. This includes the username and password (remembering that the username will probably have the subdomain prefixed to it—that is, jewp_webuser) as well as the IP address of the server.

The first part of the conversation with MySQL is to create a connection over which to communicate.

Making the Connection

The PHP documentation calls the connection a link, and I've used this convention in the code examples. The best way to connect to a MySQL database is with the following stanza:

```
$link = mysql_connect('mysql_host', 'mysql_user', 'mysql_password')
    or die('Could not connect: ' . mysql_error());
echo 'Connected successfully';
```

There are a few things to note about this code. The first point to note is that this code introduced a new concept in PHP, the or keyword. All that this does is perform the equivalent of a test against the return value of the function, and is the equivalent of:

```
$link = mysql_connect('mysql_host', 'mysql_user', 'mysql_password');
```

```
if ($link == null ) {
  die ('Could not connect: ' . mysql_error());
}
```

The or keyword is just a little bit more convenient. It can only be used in this case because the die command, as you might remember from Chapter 6, stops the script immediately.

The next thing to note is that the example has hard-coded the connection parameters. If the file is to be included globally, this is not a problem, but it might be better to use global variables to store the connection parameters under certain circumstances.

The mysql_error function returns a text-printable description of the error from the database server. If the code is to be deployed in a public access environment, it might be a better approach to use the if construct so that contact details can be posted to allow the visitor to alert the development team that there is a problem.

If there are any issues relating to usernames or passwords, check with your Web host, which might not set up cPanel and MySQL according to the book. If all else fails, you can use your cPanel username and password to log in to the server, but be aware that this combination will probably have superuser status and be able to do any operation on the database.

One final point is that the mysql_host parameter can probably just be set to localhost for the vast majority of installations. If this fails, use the IP address of the server, which will usually work just as well.

Having created a link to the database host, you can now proceed to select a database, again remembering that it will probably have a name that has been made unique by adding the subdomain or domain to the start of it. The code to select a database is as follows:

```
mysql_select_db('my_database') or die('Could not select database');
```

Again, note the or keyword, which tests the result of the mysql_select_db function that takes the name of the database that you want to connect to as its only parameter. This name will also probably be one that has been created by the system to be intentionally unique across multiple domains.

Once the link has been established and the database selected, the next step is to try querying for data and retrieving the results.

Querying for Data

This is a two-step process:

1. Create the query string.

2. Send the query string to the server and test the result.

There are a few things to note. First, the query string can be built using PHP variable substitution and string combination, so any user-entered data can be taken into account. Second, the success of the query does not have any connection to the data that it might return.

Having said that, here is the very simple code to perform the query operation:

```
// Create the query
$query = 'SELECT date, title, summary,
            content FROM blog_entry ORDER BY date';
// Send the query
$result = mysql_query($query, $link)
            or die('Query failed: ' . mysql_error());
```

I used a SELECT query here, but you could use any of the queries accepted by MySQL instead. The query is built in the $query variable and then sent to the database server using the mysql_query function. The result is tested and an appropriate error message printed out if it fails.

It really is that easy. Of course, in a live installation, you'll want to do more elaborate testing and catching of errors, but this example will work and is more than enough to get started with.

Assuming that the query has been successful, you can access the result through the $result variable.

Moving Through Records

There are many ways to retrieve the result of a query. The easiest is just to use the built-in PHP array processing functionality to fetch the result from the database as an array. This can be achieved in a loop, as follows:

```
while ($row = mysql_fetch_array($result, MYSQL_ASSOC)) {
  // Do work here
}
```

The curious reader can go ahead and look up MYSQL_ASSOC in the PHP manual. The rest can just use it as is. The mysql_fetch_array function continues to return valid rows until there are none left. Each row that it returns is an array of values that can be accessed using the array operator, []:

```
$current_title = $row["title"];
```

This snippet assumes that you are operating on the blog_entry table created in the previous sections. If you have placed no limit on the SELECT statement, all the data will be returned, row by row, in the $row variable.

However, using the LIMIT keyword in the SELECT statement, you can page through the results, ensuring that the page is returned within an agreeable length of time. This will, of course, reduce the data processed by the while loop as well.

To implement this limit, you need to keep track of the current page and page length, and make sure that sure you pass the values through GET or POST requests. Assuming you are building a GET-based interface, this is really very easy.

First, the SQL statement becomes:

```
$query = 'SELECT date, title, summary, content FROM blog_entry
    ORDER BY date
    LIMIT ' . $page_length * $page_number . ',' . $page_length . '';
```

I have split the line across three lines for the sake of clarity. Assuming that the current page is 0 and that the page length is 10, this will create a query, thus:

```
SELECT date, title, summary, content
    FROM blog_entry ORDER BY date LIMIT 0, 10
```

The query is executed and the while loop processed as normal. It will print ten lines, if there are ten records (or more) in the database. If there are fewer than ten, then, naturally, it will print fewer than ten lines, but ten lines is the maximum.

Once it has finished, you need to allow for the paging to take place. The following code needs to be augmented with testing to check for the first and last page, but the general form for creating the URL to be sent to the server is as follows:

```
echo '<a href='http://mysite.com/record.php?p='
    . $page_number - 1 . '>Prev</a>';
echo '||';
echo '<a href='http: //mysite.com/record.php?p='
    . $page_number + 1 . '>Next</a>';
```

Again, the longer lines have been split to improve readability. When the page is submitted, using one of the URLs printed by the code, the page number can be extracted from the GET variable:

```
$page_number = $_GET["p"];
```

This can then be used to populate the query. To prevent errors, it should be tested against negative numbers before the query is submitted. In addition, in order to establish the number of pages, a COUNT query can be executed against the database:

```
$query = 'SELECT COUNT(*) FROM blog_entry;'
```

When this is executed, a single row will be returned. In the array that can be accessed using the mysql_fetch_array function, the value of the count can be extracted with:

```
$total_records = $row[0]; // also could be $row['COUNT']
```

From this and the page size, the number of pages can be calculated and passed in the GET query from page to page. Thus, a fairly robust paging mechanism can be installed for the underlying data.

Finally, a Web application will also need to insert and update data in the database from time to time. Because this is no more difficult than selecting, you can probably guess how it is achieved.

Inserting and Updating Data

The PHP interface allows you to build an advanced query using values from forms and other HTML interfaces. If you assume that the PHP scripts are stored in a password-protected area of the site, you might be able to process a blog update form in the following manner:

```
$query = "INSERT INTO blog_entry VALUES
    ( NOW(), '" . $_POST[blog_title] . "', '".
        $_POST[blog_summary] . "', '" .
        $_POST[blog_content] . "', NULL);
```

Once again, the line has been broken up to improve readability, but should ordinarily be a single line. Of course, you could also write these using separate statements in PHP as follows:

```
$query = "INSERT INTO blog_entry VALUES ";
$query .= "( NOW(), '";
```

```
$query .= $_POST[blog_title];
$query .= "', '";
$query .= $_POST[blog_summary] ;
$query .= "', '";
$query .=  $_POST[blog_content] ;
$query .= "', NULL);
```

However, some people find this broken-up format more difficult to read and write. From this code, it should be self-explanatory what the query is going to do. However, remember two things—the result needs to be tested (to check that the query is valid) and it's good practice to check the rows returned for additional status information.

By a similar token to the INSERT query, the UPDATE query is as follows:

```
$query = "UPDATE TABLE blog_entry SET content = ";
$query .= "' . $new_content . "' WHERE id = " . $blog_id;
```

Again, the query is executed and the result verified in exactly the same way as before. The same approach can be used for any database access that is required. As long as the query works in the SQL mode of phpMyAdmin, it will work from PHP.

Recap

Web databases are an integral part of knowing how to program for the Web because they manage most aspects of a modern Website. For this reason, you should work through the steps outlined in this chapter to create your own Web database, connect to it, and practice inserting and retrieving data.

In essence, this chapter pulls together all the parts of the Web programming paradigm—HTML, SQL, and PHP—and you should now be well prepared for the next chapter, where you look at how to create Web applications.

Most of the tools that you are going to look at in the next chapter use Web databases and will be installed with Web databases from the cPanel interface. They are also generally extendable with PHP and HTML (and styles in many cases). So knowing how these pieces interact is vital.

Using databases also makes your Website much easier to use, extend, and maintain, especially when it comes to adding content. Instead of having to build Web pages, you just put the new content in the database and it is automatically inserted where the PHP code extracts it—much like the `blog_entry` paging example.

There are several levels that you can insert the data to be displayed into the database—with a SQL query, through the insert row phpMyAdmin tool, or using a custom PHP front-end that is protected by username and password. The CMS that you'll see in the next chapter uses a third option—testing the username and password against the database and maintaining a login session.

However, it is possible, as you've seen, to start building a simple CMS without needing to use a third-party Open Source solution such as the one presented in the next chapter. However, the reality is that it is often more efficient to take such a third-party application and customize it for your own use. This will require knowledge of the database that it is built upon.

This approach is also not always straightforward, but now that you know about databases and how they are manipulated, the next chapter will show you how they are deployed. Therefore, you're now adequately prepared to make sense of an off-the-shelf CMS, with a little help from Chapter 8.

CHAPTER 8

CONTENT MANAGEMENT SYSTEMS

Websites are built on the basis of interconnected pages, but the days when these were static are long gone. As you discovered in Chapter 1, the Web is created from dynamic pages, commonly known as *content*.

Some of this content is built on-demand, some is just served on-demand, and yet more is interlaced with content that is static, surrounded by context- and experience-sensitive dynamic content. Much of this content is also interactive—either directly or after a conversation between the users and the page-generation software.

The so-called *content-management* process is a new paradigm (at least in Web publishing circles) for providing publishing capabilities to the end users. These users can be the surfers or the content managers themselves. The content delivery system creates dynamic pages based on the requirements and the context in which the pages are created. CMSs (Content Management Systems) also pave the way for more specialized delivery and editing systems such as article repositories (About.com, Suite101.com, AssociatedContent.com, and so on). They also provide blogging, feedback, and product commenting (on Amazon.com, for example) to the end users.

Prior to the widespread adoption of CMS for online publishing, the usual way to update a Website was to create the content offline and then upload it. Each page had to be created as a single static entity, which led to some great offline Web page-creation software.

Unfortunately, it remained both cumbersome and error-prone (features in, for example FrontPage, were simply not available in online servers), and using a CMS to deliver dynamic content is a great step forward.

Coupled with these applications are the sites dedicated solely to user-editable and user-generated content (such as forums, Wikipedia.com, and so on). These have grown out of the marriage of several technologies, applied on the client and server.

Today's dynamic Web spheres are made possible with the integration of the basic description and presentation language (HTML), coupled with dynamic documents and presentation (CSS and JavaScript), and the server interface (PHP). Finally, the integration of some persistent editable storage (database such as MySQL) allows such sites to have the appearance of a static medium, while remaining dynamic. These sites are tailored to the surfers and their context.

Note that some of these concepts are part of the Web 2.0 experience, which is expanded in the next chapter. Before you tackle that topic, you need to understand a few things about content-management systems in general.

The typical content-management process has to satisfy many tasks:

- Deliver content

- Allow editing

- Organize into topics

- Allow feedback

- Be easy to use

- Be extensible

These last two points are important because most content creators are not programmers. However, they also want to be able to add more features (advertising, affiliate and product links, and so on) and stay in touch via RSS syndication, mailing lists, and so on. In short, the site owners, like you, want to extend the Web 2.0 experience to users, but without needing a degree in programming.

In essence, that is part of the aim of this book—to learn just enough about Web programming to be able to extend existing content-management systems and create a few bells and whistles of your own. This requires knowing a little about content-management systems, programming, and what Web 2.0 tools are available to model your own services on.

The approach that I advocate in the next few chapters of the book adheres to the "Just Enough" concept of working only as hard as you need to in order to deliver the results that you require. So, the easiest way to approach this is to build the site up, slowly, over time—adding features as necessary.

If you want to approach it as a piece of software that has all the bells and whistles up front, the best approach is to find something that works and then adapt it. In both cases, you should write only as much of your own code as is strictly necessary and reuse other people's efforts wherever possible.

This chapter is the first step on the road to your first Web 2.0—enabled content delivery system—what, in the 1990s, used to be called a Website.

Introduction to CMS

A content-management system is a way to deliver content to visitors in a way that is search engine friendly, easy to manage, straightforward to edit, and so on. From now on, I refer to such a piece of Web programming as a CMS.

I have broken the system model down into several parts:

- Content delivery

- Content creation/editing

- Feedback

Even a basic blog is a kind of CMS in that it allows all forms of content to be delivered and edited, and even provides a way for the visitors to give feedback to the site owner. Even if you have a blog hosted on Google's Blogger or WordPress.com, you are using a CMS, and, furthermore, it can be programmed and customized to serve more than just content.

However, this in turn requires some specialized knowledge that you'll read about in this chapter.

Caution

> Blogger.com allows you to customize your delivery channels and format as well as your content. WordPress.com does not, at least not when it serves the blog. To customize a WordPress blog, you need to install and run it on your own hosted site; you'll learn about this process later in the book.

Besides blogs, online catalogs and ordering systems are also special kinds of CMSs. Like blogs, they serve static information that can also solicit feedback from visitors, provide a communications conduit to the site owner, and process orders and payments.

Mostly people use off-the-shelf Open Source solutions, which they then customize by using the built-in features or by adding their own modules. This turns a standard CMS into something more powerful and adds advanced functionality to an existing online catalog and ordering system.

Tip

The ability to extend the publishing and delivery system by adding modules is key to the CMS principle.

The basic model of a CMS is as follows. The database contains the content, unformatted (except for basic HTML and/or abstract style information). It is important to keep the content that is stored in the database as free from concrete style data as possible. For example, the following is inappropriate:

```
This is the regular text.<br/>
<div style="color:red; background-color:white;
            border:solid double 2px;">
Warning: This is too much style information!!
</div>
```

Although the HTML and CSS statements above are correct, if they are stored in the database, the warning box will only be red on white with a double 2-pixel border. This runs contrary to the CMS paradigm—it might as well be a static page.

Something along the following lines is much better:

```
This is the regular text.<br/>
<div class="warning-box">
This is better!!
</div>
```

In this code, the warning-box class can be dynamically allocated. If, for example, the style information is stored in the database as a user preference, you can use PHP code to include the appropriate style sheet:

```
<?php
  echo '<link href="';
  echo ' . $style_name . '.css"
         rel="stylesheet" type="text/css" />';
?>
```

In this snippet, the resulting line of HTML links to a style sheet. The content can be stored in a table, where each entry has, for example, a title, content, and category. This is then passed to the next layer up where style information is added, and then this is passed to the presentation layer, which generates the page.

The core of the CMS is the page-generation code, which is simply a Web page organized into blocks that are added by the programmer using lines of PHP. Each piece of PHP is essentially a function call that's defined globally in the PHP libraries that represent the CMS's implementation.

To change the layout or to add new content, the Web programmer usually just needs to rearrange the blocks in the presentation layer. To change the graphics, colors, and other elements of style, you simply change the style sheets associated with the site.

These points are vital to the low maintenance, highly customizable, yet easy-to-deploy principles of content-management systems.

Content Delivery

The delivery part of the equation is not as simple as it might at first seem. It is broken down into two main kinds of sites:

- Public access—Everyone can potentially see everything.

- Membership sites—Some or all of the content is restricted based on credentials.

The public access kind of site is easy to set up and maintain. After all, it treats all users as equal and delivers content to them all in the same way. The membership site might require a reasonably advanced level of knowledge of the content-management system.

Most off-the-shelf Open Source solutions provide an easy interface to restrict such information as well as the appropriate pages to manage the membership process and information. Again, all that is required is a simple snippet of PHP code:

```php
<?php
if (logged_in($username) {
  echo '<a href="main_page.php?user='
          $username .'">My Account</a>';
  if (is_admin($username) {
```

```
        echo 'a href="main_page.php?module=admin"
                     >Administration Console</a>';
    }
}
else {
  display_login_block();
}
?>
```

This code snippet is a sample from a fictional CMS, based loosely on the PHP-Nuke system. The code is executed on the server, which means that there is no danger of the visitors being able to circumvent the security and access the My Account or Administration Console.

The logged_in function tests the global variable $username to check if the user has been logged in. Because most CMSs are based around processing a single PHP page coupled with HTTP GET requests and uses PHP's own session management, it becomes easy to build URLs with specific features.

Using the built-in PHP session management, the session data that identifies the users and their credentials is kept hidden and is not made part of the URL. Similarly, the is_admin function tests the $username to see if the user in question is allowed access to the Administration Console.

So, either the My Account menu option, coupled with the Administration Console menu option, where appropriate, would be displayed, or the system would call display_login_block to show the form containing the username and password data entry fields and possibly a link to the signup page.

The is_admin script can be quite complex, but the core functionality is as follows:

```
function is_admin($username) {
open_database() or return false;
          // if cant' open database, die gracefully
if (!logged_in($username)) return false;
          // double check
$query = "SELECT username FROM AdminUsers WHERE ";
$query .= "username =" . $username;
$result = mysql_query($query, $link);
if (mysql_num_rows($result) > 0 ) return true;
return false;
}
```

Note that you should never store the fact that the user is an administrative user, but always use the is_admin function to establish credentials. This is for security reasons.

So, the previous examples combine HTML, PHP, and SQL to produce a result that is essentially dynamic content. This simple example, therefore, successfully draws on all the knowledge that you've learned from previous chapters.

Membership sites, where some part of the site is restricted, follow the same flow. They require some form of authentication and session management layer on top of the basic delivery system. The content that is delivered is based on the user's access level and possibly the user's own preferences, all stored in a Web database.

For both kinds of sites, delivery may also need to be broken into different areas. In addition, there may be different kinds of content (downloads, forum posts, and so on). These might also need to be searchable and grouped, and will therefore be stored in a database, and not as static pages.

One example is the Web 2.0 feature known as *tagging*, where users attach tags to content that they feel represent, in a single word (or phrase), the subject of that content. Multiple tags may be attached to a piece of content, and multiple pieces of content will inevitably be assigned some tags in common.

It is the underlying relational database system that allows this level of richness to be offered, and the result is that individual terms can be selected by the visitors, and all relevant content returned, organized by the proportional importance of a specific tag for each item. This might sound complex, but it is relatively straightforward to implement.

In addition to the restrict-and-deliver model, there are a few other points that the CMS designer and user has to bear in mind.

First, the presentation to the search engines must be such that they see the content and the keywords that the content revolves around. For all the bells and whistles that the Web programmer might be tempted to add to a Web page, they must not violate the principle that the work is wasted if the content cannot be found.

Subsequently, the CMS is delivering content dynamically as much for the convenience of the search engine as for the end users. There are a few things that can be done in this respect:

- Dynamic or meaningful content URLs

- Appropriate meta tags with dynamically allocated keywords and/or tags

- Correct placement of content that represents those keywords/tags

A meaningful URL takes the form:

```
http://mysite.com/articles/mainpage.php?
            content=how-to-write-php-articles
```

This is good, but a permanent link to the article would be better. Something in the form of the following would be more search-engine friendly:

```
http://mysite.com/articles/how-to-write-php-articles.php
```

This might not be possible. What is always possible is building a set of meta tags that contain the keywords that appear in the title. Recall that you built meta tags for search engines that were similar to the following:

```
<meta name="keywords" content="php, article, write,
    web, programming, HTML" >
<meta name="description"
    content="Articles on writing PHP and HTML." >
```

These can be dynamically created by PHP by placing the appropriate code in the head part of the served HTML document. The keywords can be the tags that users have assigned or they can be assigned by the author of the content. Similarly, the description can be a snippet from the content or something that has been assigned by the author.

Both of these can be introduced by the Web programmer via PHP:

```
<?php
echo '<meta name="keywords" content="';
open_database() or echo $default_category_keywords;
$query = "SELECT Keywords FROM TagTable
            WHERE ContentID = " . $content_id;
$result = mysql_query($query, $link);
$row = mysql_fetch_assoc($result);
echo $row["Keywords"];
echo '">";
echo '<meta name="description" ';
echo 'content="';
echo $content_summary;
echo '" >';
?>
```

The second line in this snippet is particularly interesting, because it enables the script to display the categories' default keywords gracefully in the event that the database cannot be opened. It is this kind of flexibility that makes the CMS approach very powerful. A real implementation might use the same approach in the event that no rows were returned from the database to generate content in place of the other fields.

So, the CMS is a great way to make the served page more search-engine friendly by populating the keywords properly. It also needs to place the content high up in the page too, so that the search engine can reconcile the keywords with the content—this is vital to make sure that the engine can confirm that you are not trying to spoof it in any way.

Aside from making the page search-engine friendly, the CMS also has a role in making the content friendly for the end users. The presentation to the end users must be easy to navigate and users must be able to locate the exact information that they need. For a simple article or blog delivery service, this means offering browsing by category, or tag, as well as search facilities.

Most CMSs offer this kind of functionality, but it is also very easy to add in situations where it does not already exist. The key, as usual, is in the database design, which has to take into account the category hierarchy, if there is one, and deliver menu options to allow the visitors to navigate them.

Having all the content in the database also makes it incredibly easy to search, either by keyword, content, or a combination of a few search paradigms. The more complex paradigms are best left to the default CMS offering.

For shopping-oriented sites, the presentation must enable quick searching and shopping. In addition, the delivery system needs to be integrated with shopping systems so it's a straightforward process for visitors to pay for their goods and track their purchases.

The content delivery part of the CMS is responsible for all these aspects. Your specific needs largely influence how you put your content-management system together and whether you use off-the-shelf Open Source systems (which you'll look at in this chapter), build your own system from scratch, or combine the two approaches.

Whichever approach you use, there are also additional delivery mechanisms possible—via RSS, for example—to keep your visitors updated even when they are not on the site. Mailing lists and newsfeeds are the two most popular ways to implement this kind of delivery mechanism, and the latter requires that your Web host allows access to the sendmail system (which is usually the case).

Content Creation and Editing

With the advent of the faster Web and more advanced interaction possibilities through dynamic HTML (HTML, JavaScript, and CSS), content editing has become somewhat easier to offer. From Google's sheets to online article editing systems such as those provided by Squidoo and Hubpages, arranging using drag and drop and editing with interactive style formatting have become the norm.

Although you might not need to offer this kind of functionality straight away, you'll likely need to offer some kind of editing facilities. These can be broken into three broad categories:

- Single author editing

- Multi-author editing

- Open access editing

This last category covers systems such as Wikipedia, and can be quite dangerous in that there is very little moderation of the content that is being offered. It can quite easily bring an otherwise reputable information platform into a less reputable situation.

The second model is a good halfway point and is used by many article repositories. It balances moderated content with a membership system, possibly with some form of compensation for the authors. Here again, the CMS can be very helpful, for example, by allowing authors to specify their Amazon Associate ID or Google AdSense ID, and by displaying a certain proportion of the time inline with the content they have created.

This ensures that the site owner as well as the content creator generates income from visitors' actions. Again, with PHP and a database, the solution becomes trivial. In addition, the database can contain links to products that match the content, or, in the case of Amazon and Google AdSense, these links can be chosen context-sensitively.

The generated HTML code does not need to change; all that is required is that for a certain percentage of the time, the correct ID is placed in the URL. This can be achieved very simply (assuming that the ID has been pulled from the database):

```php
<?php
if ( rand ( 1, 10 ) > 7 ) {
  $aff_id = $user_aff_id;
```

```
}
else {
  $aff_id = $owner_aff_id;
}
echo '<a href="http://affiliate.site.com/
          product.php?id=1011&aff=';
echo $aff_id;
echo '">Product Link</a>';
?>
```

Of course, the Amazon and Google codes are more complex, often including JavaScript, but this snippet gives a good idea of the approach, if not the exact code required. The if clause simply swaps the user's affiliate ID for the site owner's 30% of the time that the page is displayed.

A single author system is one where the site owner and creator is also the sole publisher. This is probably the starting point for most of your projects. It is the easiest to set up and maintain, and possibly, if you're planning to custom-build your CMS, the best approach because it allows you to get up and running very fast.

You learned in the last chapter how a very simple, feature-less content storage and delivery system could be created. However, with a little expansion, you can transform it into a good blogging-delivery system. The editing is a painful experience, because it is based on a manual insertion into the SQL database.

This editing process can be made much better, by using HTML forms to provide the data entry area. However, you need to bear in mind that if online editing is to be allowed, you must consider the authentication issue.

Leaving that to one side, you might envisage a PHP script that allows adding and modifying actions in order to build an HTML form as follows:

```
<form action="post" name="content_editing"
            action="update_content.php">
<input name="action" type="hidden" value="add">
Blog Entry Title: <input name="title"
                   type="text" value=""><br/>
Blog Entry Content: <textarea name="content"
                     rows="10" cols="25"></textarea>
<br/><br/>
<input type="submit" value="Submit">
</form>
```

I have left out the keywords and summary data areas for the sake of clarity. The update_content.php script can then be created to provide the required actions, which are communicated via the hidden control. Such a script might look like this:

```php
<?php
switch ($_POST["action"]) {
  case "add" :
    update_content_add();
  break;
  case "modify" :
    update_content_modify();
  break;
  case "delete" :
    update_content_delete();
  break;
}
?>
```

In the update_content_add function, the script needs to prepare the SQL statement, submit it, and make sure that the data is stored appropriately. The INSERT statement would look similar to the following:

```php
$sql_insert = 'INSERT INTO content_entry VALUES ( "';
$sql_insert .= $_POST["title"] . '", "';
$sql_insert .= $_POST["content"] . '", "';
$sql_insert .= '", null);';
mysql_query ( $sql_insert, $link );
```

Of course, this leaves out the error checking, which might be considered optional in a single author environment, given that the author is also the site administrator and can just check the error logs to see what went wrong. The other issue is that, as it stands, there is no authentication whatsoever in the system.

There are various solutions to this, of varying complexities. The two easiest are to require the users to enter a username and password when they want to update data, and to password-protect the directory holding the update PHP scripts.

In addition, PHP supports the notion of *sessions*, whereby a unique session identifier can be assigned to a login session, and then is used to ensure that the user is authenticated whenever he or she tries to access a restricted function.

In a single author environment, where the site administrator is the content creator and is using his or her own CMS, restricting access to the scripts by password-protecting a directory via cPanel is the easiest option.

There are issues with password-protecting directories, but it is quite a secure way to protect these areas of the site.

An additional layer of security could involve asking for a password before actually publishing the content. This would allow the authors to pre-edit their content and give a username and password only when they want to publish the content. This username and password combination would be checked against the user database before the changes were actually made live.

This solution would scale up to a multi-author system, but might prove to be cumbersome, if more secure. It would only be a small step from this solution to a session-based solution that uses the $_SESSION superglobal.

If this level of security/usability is required, you should generally be using an off-the-shelf content publishing and editing system. There are many solutions, but out-of-the-box CMSs usually have a pretty good wizard for setting up all the aspects of security and content editing.

One additional feature in a multi-visitor environment is different from plain content creation and editing, and that is the ability to allow visitors, whether they are registered users or not, to add informal content.

So, a skeleton CMS must provide the following:

- User management (for editing and publishing)

- Content delivery (serving up articles and other resources)

- Content creation and editing (to allow users to change content)

- A front-end (menus, organization, and so on)

- Keyword storage and management (to allow visitors to find what they are looking for)

This governs the content, which is the main purpose of the CMS. However, there is also ample scope for making it more sophisticated, such as by allowing the visitors to add feedback into the system and help provide content.

Feedback and Visitor Interaction

A successful CMS-based Website should allow visitors to give feedback about what they have read or experienced. This is a Web 2.0 concept, in some ways, but the idea of feedback has been around for a while. The Web 2.0 paradigm, which you'll read about in the next chapter, just makes it more interesting.

Although some sites might not benefit from direct feedback, they might benefit from a forum system. Also known as a *bulletin board,* this type of setup allows a conversation to take place between registered users. For example, a forum can be used to provide support to end users or purchasers of products and services.

The simplest CMS, like blog software, usually offers easy things like the ability to add and moderate comments. These are typically attached to the end of blog posts and allow direct feedback on the content.

Some sites are nothing more than a forum, which is perfectly acceptable for certain kinds of sites. However, most content creators will want to integrate the two aspects—for example, mixing a blog and forum.

Luckily, this is moderately easy if you use a CMS and forum package. Trying to create such a system from scratch would be quite a tricky proposition, but most cPanel/Fantastico-enabled hosts offer phpBulletin, or something similar, for adding forums to sites. (Fantastico is a software management service that integrates with cPanel, allowing its users to install various pieces of third-party software. In the same way that phpMyAdmin lets you manage databases, Fantastico lets you manage applications created in PHP.)

One point to remember is that the forum will also take up an additional database from the database allocation on your account. If your number of databases is limited (usually it is), this will clearly affect your decision about how and if to interact with the site's visitors.

CMS Systems

Now that you've read about CMSs, you're ready to look at a few specific implementations and consider how they can be integrated into a Website in the best way.

The general requirements are to have a Web server, some kind of server side scripting mechanism such as PHP and a database system such as MySQL. Once all these are in place, you can begin to set up your CMS.

The first step is to download the chosen install package or use to cPanel/ Fantastico to install the CMS. The CMS is simply a set of PHP scripts that is used to install the package, set up the database, and get the initial page (which will just confirm installation) to display when the visitor types in the appropriate URL.

The choice of CMS will depend on what your site is trying to achieve. For example, you can easily set up a simple blog using a package such as WordPress. Such a package is also expandable with a little bit of knowledge—adding content panels around the simple blog entries to do everything from sell books to display advertising or allow users to rate content.

The clear advantage of using these Open Source packages is that they can be extended by a Web programmer. This book provides enough detail about PHP and MySQL to be able to do just that, coupled with the generic CMS programming information from the previous section.

There are different ways to do this—either edit the page code itself or make user-defined modules that can be added. This latter approach is the one that is most advisable because the Open Source packages tend to get released fairly often with changes. If the page code is modified directly, this change-management process becomes much more complex, because the user-defined features must be reinstated in the new CMS pages.

The added advantage of Fantastico (for example) is that new versions can be easily installed. Again, though, if you have made changes to the underlying code and not just added modules, the choice is stark—lose your customizations or keep the old version and risk incompatibilities.

You'll see later on that a JavaScript version based on static pages is also possible. This has the advantage that it doesn't use a database, which might be necessary if your database resources are limited.

Another approach, if you're short on resources but have the time and skill to implement it, is to use text files (CSV) that are updated remotely and uploaded. To do this, you need PHP but don't need a database. To display the content, the PHP parses the CSV files, using the built-in data processing capabilities of the language.

The end pages will also need to include a mechanism such as JavaScript to provide the user interface. So, without a database, it is possible to create a whole CMS, but it is hard work.

Databases also allow content to be categorized and therefore delivered in a context-sensitive way, based on search terms, tags, ratings, and so on. The content can also be sorted or otherwise filtered.

Finally, if no scripting is available at all, do not fret, because a CMS is still quite doable; it just takes a lot more time to build the pages. By now, you should be well aware that this update time can be whittled away by using programs such as CSS and JavaScript to help manage the content delivery.

CMS Management

Managing the CMS is all about the way that you decide to follow updates and keep up to date with new releases. If the CMS is not kept up to date, there are risks in:

- Security—Publicized loopholes are closed by software updates.

- Lack of features—New features will be available only in more recent versions.

- Limited community support—The community generally only helps support new versions.

If you are the site administrator and are keeping the CMS up to date, which is clearly good idea, you also need to consider how to keep track of all changes that you might have made. The best way to do this is to keep a log of all changes made to the system and isolate a series of steps to follow that ensure that there are no problems doing the update.

In addition, when upgrading the CMS, there is the question of making sure that the site will still operate correctly afterwards. For this reason, as well as the others, it is worth establishing the correct process to manage the upgrades:

1. Keep a backup of all modifications and other pieces not modified, as well as a complete backup of the database.

2. Try to test the installation on a separate server/directory first to make sure that everything is still working. The last chapter noted that common mistake when creating databases is that not enough testing is done; this goes double for software.

3. Have a rollback plan for when it all goes horribly wrong, which at some point it probably will.

4. Always read the documentation about changes and decide whether the upgrade is worth the risk as well as what parts are being changed.

This last point—about changes—is slightly contentious because there is an additional danger that a future upgrade will not be possible if you skip a version. In general, it is best to keep completely up to date.

If these precautions are followed, your involvement with CMS ought to be somewhat easier and catastrophes will be avoided. Again, having a log book will ensure that the changes can be unraveled if need be.

An additional area of management, a subcategory of CMS management, is user management. This requires that certain content blocks are restricted by user access level, which most CMS will handle by restricting the appearance of a login block by session credentials.

This often leads to the same block metamorphosing between login link and link to (for example) a My Account page. Managing the users is normally left up to the CMS, but it is worth knowing how it is handled in case you ever need to adjust it in some way.

Bulletin Boards (Forums)

A bulletin board used to be a place where users interacted in a kind of notice-board-plus-comments environment. Users would post their questions or comments, and other users would reply by posting comments, and the whole conversation would be managed as a single thread.

These days, forums are a little more sophisticated, but the basic principle hasn't changed. A forum is still a place to communicate en masse, and site owners still have the usual problems of boards being hijacked for personal gain, and of flame wars where users bombard each other with negative comments and insults.

Forums are, by nature, multi-user and cannot be extended easily by the Web programmer because they're not designed to do anything more than provide a forum for discussion. Customization can be performed to change the look to match the main site, but adding features is not possible in the same way as, say, for other CMSs.

Each forum is split into boards, and each board is sub-split into threads. It is customary to present the boards, and then let the users drill down to see the threads where they can see how many people have commented on, or joined, each thread.

Each page is dynamically created and provides a snapshot of the database. There are usually pages that allow for the following:

- Searching

- Viewing the most popular threads

- Viewing threads with the most activity

Member-based systems are often the best because anonymous use promotes behavior that is usually not in keeping with the forum ideals. It's therefore easiest to take an off-the-shelf forum package rather than try to build one from scratch.

phpBB

phpBB is one of the most well-supported and popular forum packages, and is more or less plug and play. In addition, it integrates well with CMSs such as PHP-Nuke, often to the point that the transition between the two is seamless.

phpBB uses a MySQL database, and the content is delivered via PHP scripts. These PHP scripts can, to a certain extent, be customized to change the appearance and add little gimmicks such as top ten contributors, which might not have been perceived by the phpBB creators.

You can learn a lot from examining the code, and among the many customizations possible, some are necessary before you can use the system.

For example, there is a security mechanism that checks to see if the person signing up is real, by having the visitor type in a series of letters from an obscured image. This usually requires the GD package to be installed, but this might not the case on all systems.

Therefore it's sometimes necessary to dig into the code and remove this facility, or adjust it to use a slightly different mechanism.

These kinds of customizations are actually very easy to do because the authors of phpBB have included them in a list of global variables in one of the PHP files.

These global variables can be used to adjust all kinds of user interface elements and change the look and feel of the forum.

The interface is almost completely managed by styles, which can be created by the Web programmer and used instead of the defaults. The changes possible include placement of content as well as the general color and graphical theme.

One part of this is changing, for example, the identifiers (that is, the variables) that contain the URL for the logo. This is an easy change and helps customize the forum so that it matches more closely the main site.

In addition, there are features that can be changed directly in the database that are then reflected in the forum front-end. All in all, it is well worth the time to get to know the system and practice making changes to see what extensions and customizations are possible.

These customizations extend to the look and feel of the CMS—the logo, color scheme, descriptive text, and so on. These items can often be manipulated using the database (through phpMyAdmin) without having to touch the underlying code. To clarify: managing a CMS often requires retouching database entries or adjusting simple definitions in the code to change the look (and sometimes feel) of the CMS without re-writing it or without changing the underlying functionality.

Weblogs

A Weblog, or blog, is just a place where the content producers can post their thoughts. They can also add links, organize their posts by category, and allow visitors to search, sort, and sift through the content to find what it is that they want to read.

There are two kinds of blog solutions—hosted by a service or hosted by the content creator's hosting service. The latter one requires that the platform code is downloaded and configured. If a service is hosted elsewhere, the site owner does not have to worry about the content and user management, for example, because it's managed by the service provider.

Just because a hosted service is used doesn't mean that the interactivity and ownership is lost, as you shall see. It is quite possible to use someone else's database and user management while causing the blog entries to appear on your own Website—thereby gaining a database, removing the need for scripting, and so on.

This means that there is actually also a third type too—that doesn't use a database on the reader's Web host at all. This kind of roll-your-own solution relies on using external services and then deploying techniques to relay the content onto your own site. With a little programming knowledge, you can create a professional blog (for example) on your site by making use of free services.

The principle of a Web log is that once the content is introduced and updated, it is immediately visible. One good thing about Web logs is that the search engines tend to pick them up very quickly. Web logs are also easy to:

- Syndicate onto other Websites.

- Update very quickly, which means you can easily propagate those updates to your readers.

This makes them ideal for forming part of the general marketing strategy of a site, as well as a good way to provide up-to-date content. However, a little programming and Web design knowledge goes a long way in making the connection between the blog host and the user's own Website, which will end up as a container for remotely hosted services.

One of the key features of a blog is that the content is stored without formatting. You can change the complete look and feel of a site by changing a couple of files. More importantly, even the old entries will adopt the new style, without additional updates. This is sometimes called *one-click publishing*.

One such service is Blogger.com.

Blogger

Blogger is now owned by Google. It is a blogging solution, only available as a hosted service, where users update the content on the Blogger server. This could change at some point, but although the service is open, it is not really Open Source as such.

What is Open Source is the API that allows the Web programmer to interact with the content that is provided on the blogs that are under Blogger's control. Essentially, Blogger provides an open way to pull content from the server via a well-defined series of interfaces.

You'll learn about this in more detail in the next chapter, when you look at making use of Web 2.0 features such as XML and RSS. For now, you just need to be aware that the possibility exists.

When building a site, it is easy to leverage Blogger's powerful API by creating the content on the Blogger database and then using the API to extract it and place it on your own Website. This is known as *syndication.*

One benefit of this mechanism is that it reduces traffic to the pages under your control, and at the same time means that you do not use up a database for the blog. After all, it is a shame to waste a database on storing blog entries when you might need to store Web catalogs and more on the database instead.

Many CMSs also have built-in support to fetch the Blogger updates for a specific blog, making the integration with an off-the-shelf system very easy. Yet another advantage is that the blog will have high visibility in Google, the world's leading search engine.

The Blogger API for PHP requires knowledge of the Zend engine, which takes it slightly beyond the "Just Enough" programmer. In addition, there is the possibility that the site owner would have to set Zend up correctly if the Web host has not done so.

All in all, this makes using the Blogger API more difficult. Therefore, the examples in this book all work by exchanging HTTP GET requests to obtain documents and then parsing the XML that comes back. You've seen both of these techniques in other chapters in the book.

For example, you might like to look back to Chapter 6 for details about using the DOMDocument object in PHP. This enables you to create simple statements such as:

```
DOMDocument->loadFile('http://www.blogger.com/
                       feeds/blogID/posts/default');
```

This code will return an XML document that can be accessed using the DOMDocument class members. An even easier solution, if you don't need advanced XML processing, is to use the simpleXML interface:

```
$xml = simplexml_load_file('http://www.blogger.com/
                           feeds/blogID/posts/default');
```

Given that the XML structure provided by Blogger is both static and well defined, this gives you many possibilities to syndicate your own content. In addition, query requests are also allowed, so by attaching REST data (such as &post=id), you can be very selective about the data that is returned.

Publishing The easiest way to publish is through Google's own Blogger interface. After all, you'll need an account anyway and the "Just Enough" approach is to get what you need with a minimum of work. So, content management will be via the standard Blogger login and edit cycle, which is stable, well documented, and offers more features than you'll likely be able to create yourself.

Using the GData API, it is possible to authenticate, update, and manage content. The GData API is offered by Google to access all of the various services that are under its control, from AdSense to Blogger.

However, deploying the GData API requires using PHP features that you might not have, depending on who is hosting your site. At some point, you might want to make use of this, but for now, the Blogger supplied interface is adequate.

Another good thing about Blogger is that the template can be edited and displayed. This means that blog owners can put in their own little bits of markup to change certain aspects of the process. You'll look at this in more detail in the next chapter.

Retrieving Content After the blog owner makes changes, content creators no doubt will need to integrate those changes into their sites. After all, while leaving the blog updates on the Blogger site will attract traffic, part of the power of this approach involves syndicating the posts onto your own site.

Luckily, in the spirit of cooperation with the publishers, Google has made its interface transparent, so you do not have to guess what the code might be to retrieve the posts. The URL, for the technical-minded reader, is as follows:

```
http://code.google.com/apis/blogger/developers_guide_protocol.html#RetrievingPosts
```

Retrieving the posts is really easy because Google has given a great interface that is available in a single HTTP request, using the author's blog ID. This is the ID number that can be found on any of the options pages connected to the blog on Blogger.

The code to extract the first post, using DOMDocument, is as follows:

```
$blogger_feed = new DOMDocument();
$blogger_feed->load('http://www.blogger.com/
                     feeds/25130512/posts/default');
```

```
// Get the first post
$feed_entry = $blogger_feed->getElementsByTagName
                            ('entry')->item(0);
$feed_title = $feed_entry->getElementsByTagName
>                           ('title')->item(0)->nodeValue;
$feed_text = $feed_entry->getElementsByTagName
>                           ('content')->item(0)->nodeValue;
```

Notice that you first obtain a reference to the feed that you're interested in, using the getElementsByTagName method to locate the array of the entry tag in the XML document. Each entry then has title and content tags, which contain the actual post text.

This last might be a bit difficult to appreciate, so it's worth checking the document structure. In XML, the most useful parts of the feed available at the Web address used in creating the $blogger_feed instance of the DOMDocument object are:

```
<feed>
<title>title</title>
<link>link to blog</link>
<author>author</author>
<entry>
  <title></title>
  <content></content>
  <link></link>
</entry>
</feed>
```

Obviously, the entry is multiplied as necessary—there will be one entry per post—and the first three tags at the root level contain specific details about the blog. These tags can be useful when mashing up several XML feeds, which is a technique you'll at in the next chapter.

For those readers familiar with DOMDocument and XML layouts, this might seem fairly easy to appreciate. However, it is complex for many Web programmers, who much prefer the interface offered by the simpleXML library.

The advantage of simpleXML is that the object created by loading a feed takes on the structure of the feed. So, if you know the tag names, the data is easier to extract. For feeds where the tag names are not known, the array structure offered by DOMDocument can be a little more flexible.

So, the equivalent of the DOMDocument example, but using the simpleXML interface, is as follows:

```
$xml =
  simplexml_load_file('http://www.blogger.com/
                        feeds/25130512/posts/default');
$feed_title = $xml->entry[0]->title;
$feed_text = $xml->entry[0]->content;
```

Given that you can, in both cases, create a reference to the entry object using PHP, you can even do something like the following:

```
foreach ($xml->entry as $entry) {
  echo $entry->title . "<br/>" . $entry->content;
}
```

Clearly, the HTML that this generates will need to be padded out with some style statements to adapt the look and feel of the posts to the host Website, but the core PHP code remains the same. There are also a few other things that you can do with these simple REST requests, which is the subject of the Web 2.0 discussion in Chapter 9.

Given that Blogger is not the only platform available for this kind of content creation, the next section looks at one of the other Open Source solutions: WordPress.

WordPress

WordPress is a curio in blogging terms. It is available as a paid service on WordPress.com or it is available as an Open Source publishing platform. The latter can be installed on a Website as a simple PHP install through cPanel's Fantastico or it can be downloaded and installed manually.

If you choose this route, you can then update it with plug-ins, but it does take (yet another) database away from the allocation for the site. Once WordPress is installed, you can access the functionality of the system via a well-documented development API.

You'll read about the API later on in the chapter, because it is important for Web programmers who have decided to install their own WordPress. It is also available as both a free and paid service, hosted on WordPress.com (WordPress.org being the site for the Open Source version).

Sadly the hosted version is very limited. It does not allow much in the way of customization beyond a selection of templates offered by WordPress. These are professionally produced, however. Happily, the editing interface and content delivery system gives you enough to get started.

In addition, if the content creator is going to cross feed (syndicate) the data anyway, as you saw with the Blogger feed, this might not matter.

Publishing   Again, the easiest route is to use the WordPress main content creation and publishing system because of the issues surrounding authentication against the database. There is an interface for Web programmers to create their own content-editing environment, and in some multi-author publishing models, this might be an advantage, but as far as creating a blog is concerned, the default is more than adequate.

The interface and connection to the main system is the same whether it is being used in a local or remote fashion. There are also other ways to do it such as inserting entries directly into the database that might be appropriate under certain circumstances, such as automatic content creation or blogging from an unsupported platform.

The downloaded version has much better publishing possibilities, because you're not limited to specific templates as you are in the hosted version. In addition, the templates and schemes can be edited in PHP to get the right look and feel, but be aware that future updates may negate some of the changes if they are made in the core WordPress files.

In fact, you can even pay an upgrade fee to allow customizations to the Word-Press templates to be made on the WordPress.com site, and it is always possible to experiment with the CSS behind the templates for free. This makes it a great playground on which to test ideas.

Tip

Always be sure to test layouts in the CSS Editor on the WordPress Website before distributing your own implementation.

Given the restrictions on the publishing side, it makes even more sense to extract the feed for use with another site where styles can be applied. However, remember that these feeds contain only a snapshot of the blog, whereas the Blogger feed contains the *whole* article.

With that said, it is equally easy to extract and republish the feed containing the summaries.

Retrieving Content   WordPress provides feeds in several formats, each accessible through a special syndication URL. Each theme might have slightly different feeds available, so it is worth experimenting to find that one that fits the target site the best.

Again, you'll look at various ways that feeds can be mashed together to produce Web applications in Chapter 9, but the basic structure of the feed is very similar to Blogger's, and other blogs will likely have very similar layouts too.

The WordPress layout is as follows (having removed some of the extraneous fluff):

```
<channel>
<title></title>
<item>
<title></title>
<content></content>
</item>
</channel>
```

As before, this can be accessed with a DOMDocument or simpleXML object. Pick the solution that offers them the level of flexibility that you need. One point to note is that the content tag contains information that is bracketed by HTML CDATA statements.

This may have been stripped out by the DOMDocument (or simpleXML) processing, but if not, it needs to be removed before it is displayed. The alternative is just to restrict the feed to the description and leave the preview snippet out of the display, because it only contains a small part of the whole post.

Assuming this is the path that is taken, the following will extract the first title from the DOMDocument object created by loading a WordPress feed:

```
$wordpress_feed = new DOMDocument();
$wordpress_feed->load('http://leckyt.wordpress.com/feed/');
  // Get the first post
$wordpress_item = $wordpress_feed->
                 getElementsByTagName('item')->item(0);
$wordpress_title =
  $wordpress_feed->getElementsByTagName('title')
                 ->item(0)->nodeValue
```

More work is obviously needed get the posts themselves. This will include getting the number of posts with the DOMNodeList->length property and then using the PHP foreach construct to iterate through them.

Again, for those who don't need the DOMDocument flexibility, simpleXML can be used and represents a much easier route, assuming that you know in advance the name of all the tags in the XML document. The following code will print all the titles:

```
$xml =
  simplexml_load_file('http://leckyt.wordpress.com/feed/');
$feed_title = $xml->item[0]->title;
$feed_text = $xml->item[0]->content;
foreach ($xml->item as $entry) {
  echo $entry->title . "<br/>" . $entry->content;
  echo "<br/><br/>";
}
```

In addition, the simpleXML interface supports XPath. This means that you can, if you know that the title tags are unique, extract them all with one loop:

```
foreach ($xml->xpath('//item' as $entry) {
  echo $entry->title . "<br/>" . $entry->description;
  echo "<br/><br/>";
}
```

All that the XPath functionality does in this case is search along the entire simpleXML object tree, looking for nodes whose tag is item. The // indicates that you want to have all from the root—if you wanted to restrict the search, you would have to give a path to the root that you required (/channel).

The references that are returned are simply an array of title elements, from which you can extract the title and description, as before. This approach works equally well with Blogger posts as it does with WordPress feeds.

Where using WordPress comes into its own, however, is when it is deployed as a locally based CMS hosted by the content creator or your chosen Web host provider. Providers will usually provide the option to install WordPress via Fantastico or a similar mechanism.

Development API   One great aspect of WordPress is the API that has been provided for CMS development. It allows the Web programmer to tap into the WordPress publishing mechanism while also allowing you to customize both the functionality and the output.

The WordPress.org Website distributes the Open Source version. This site includes downloadable installs for those not using Fantastico and also provides some great plug-ins. Part of the power of WordPress is that users can add their own modules (plug-ins) to expand the functionality.

This is probably outside the scope of the "Just Enough" Web programmer, but the site also contains a documentation section, which contains all the developer documents. Depending on what the programmer wants to achieve, this can get quite complex quite quickly, but the aim here is to give an overview so that you at least know where to look when you need to get started.

Customization of WordPress is basically split into two categories:

- Themes

- Plug-ins

Themes are layout oriented and use a CSS-aware template that calls specific PHP scripts to fill out the content. The PHP renders the content decorated with style information, and the CSS files that are linked to the generated HTML provide the visual formatting.

So the CSS and HTML together give the layout (HTML) and style (color, images, and so on), and on top of that the PHP scripts fill out the actual content. Depending on where the PHP writes in that content, it will appear at different places on the page.

The easiest way to get started building a PHP theme is to use one that is based on the default theme. The overall structure is very easy to understand, and therefore easy to customize. The starting point is the `wp-content/themes/theme_name` folder under the WordPress installation tree, where the theme data is stored.

This folder will contain, among other things, two files:

- index.php

- style.css

The PHP file contains the structure, and the CSS file contains the various definitions of style that manage the look of the resulting page. The folder also contains some other PHP scripts called *modules*. Each module contains a function that will be called by the index.php script to create the content that surrounds main blog.

The bare minimum modules used to generate a page are as follows:

header.php	Generates the header
sidebar.php	Generates the sidebar (usually left)
footer.php	Generates the footer
comments.php	Contains the comments if comments are allowed on the blog
comments-popup.php	Provides a pop-up version of comments.php

The index.php file contains references to these files through functions that have common names throughout the system. This ensures that any theme is compatible with the system. If a user changes the themes, he or she can be sure that the new theme will display the content in a reasonably standard way.

The reason for the standard is just to make the customization process easier. Once the modules are written, the functions could have any name, but importing a new index.php file from a default installation (for example) would not work because the function naming would follow the standards.

The standard function names are as follows:

```
get_header();
get_sidebar();
get_footer();
```

These three functions, if called from index.php, will create a basic page with no content. The functions in the header.php, sidebar.php, and footer.php scripts will fill out whatever content they have been scripted to do. For very basic modifications, only the index.php file needs to be changed—usually to add content to the existing page—perhaps from other sources or by using Web 2.0 techniques that you'll look at in Chapter 9.

Tip

Always make a copy of the existing Theme directory and edit that copy so that you do not disturb a working WordPress setup.

The way to proceed is to take the Default (Kubrick) theme and copy it to a new folder. Then you can start editing it, being careful to leave the default setup alone in its own folder. Use the default setup as a reference point when the customization goes wrong—as it will from time to time.

The index.php file contains something the official documentation calls the WordPress *loop*. This is the mechanism that actually displays the posts—either all of them or a subset.

Note

If you're creating a index.php file from scratch (or from a copy) and not using templates, be sure to set the WP_USE_THEMES global constant to false:

define('WP_USE_THEMES', false)

Otherwise, WordPress will substitute the loop for its own, or worse, you'll get two loops of data!

A WordPress loop uses the following functions, as a bare minimum:

```
have_posts();
the_post();
the_title();
the_content();
```

The have_posts() function returns true while there are still posts to be displayed. Each time that the_post() is called, the data for the next post in the collection is gathered. WordPress maintains its own pointer into the collection of posts, so that if the administrator has deemed that only five are to be displayed, have_posts() will return false once there are no more to be displayed.

The the_title() and the_content() functions output the title and content of the current post; the value returned will change on each iteration of the_post(), automatically.

These functions all go in a PHP while loop, which could look something like the following:

```php
<?php
while (have_posts()) {
  the_post();
  // Other things here for this particular post
  the_content();
}
?>
```

Obviously, the result from this code will not be terribly pretty—after all, you have not added any style information. However, before you look at that aspect, you need to first look at a few other commands. One of the most useful is:

```
rewind_posts();
```

All that this does is reset the current query such that the next call to the_post() will retrieve the first in the set. Sometimes the while loop is expressed as:

```
<?php while (have_posts()) : the_post(); ?>
<!-- The other HTML Code -->
<?php the_post(); ?>
<?php the_content(); ?>
<?php endwhile; ?>
```

This is the same as the previous format, but without the { and } that enclose the PHP script. This makes it easier to write manageable code that breaks out of the PHP and inserts HTML. This is necessary to combine the CSS with the PHP to obtain the correct display.

For example, WordPress identifies a collection of classes, such as the following, which are common to all themes:

```
<div class="post">            For the post
<div class="storycontent">    For the content of the post
<h3 class="storytitle">       For the title of the post
```

These, and all the others, can be found in the index.php and style.css files available in the template folder. Experimentation will be most likely to lead to the desired results—you'll have to play around with both index.php and styles.css to get the mix of placement and visual formatting just right.

It is also possible to search through a collection of posts and return them as a subset of all the posts in the database, by using the following function:

```
query_post('query');
```

This function will start a new query based on the contents of the query string. The loop and display functions are the same as before—that is, have_posts() still returns true as long as there is a post to display, and the_post() advances through the selected collection.

An example of a query string might be as follows:

```
category_name=my_category&showposts=10
```

This would restrict posts to the `my_category` category and override the globally defined default number of posts to show in the `have_posts()` loop to 10. Categories are created at the management (admin) level through the WordPress administration panel, which you should explore once you have installed the WordPress system.

The general principle is to use the query outside of the WordPress loop, so that the `have_posts()` and `the_post()` functions will behave as expected and return the results of the query. There is one last function related to post navigation:

```
posts_nav_link();
```

This function displays the navigation bar that allows the visitors to scroll through the remaining posts (should there be any) or review the previous set of posts. Again, this aspect is managed by WordPress behind the scenes. Obviously, the `posts_nav_link()` function should be placed outside the WordPress loop.

The WordPress documentation calls these PHP functions used in the index.php file *template tags*. A whole book could be written on WordPress alone, but the most useful tags can be used anywhere in the index.php file.

For information about authors:

`the_author()`	Displays the author's WordPress ID
`the_author_email()`	Displays the author's email address
`the_author_url()`	Displays an URL to the Website
`the_author_posts_link()`	Gives a hotlink to the author's posts in the system

To retrieve category information:

`the_category()`	Returns a link to the categories to which a post belongs
`category_description('cat_id')`	Displays the description of category cat_id
`wp_dropdown_categories()`	Creates a drop-down list containing the categories
`wp_list_categories()`	Displays a list of categories as links

For the last two, there are multiple options available, all listed in the WordPress online documentation. Primarily, they are used with the drop-down generator to provide a Submit button so that the visitors can select and submit their choice. This emulates the point-and-click interface of the list generator, but saves space.

There are also some other useful category information functions:

```
in_category('cat_id')    Returns true if the post is in the cat_id category
get_the_category()       Returns a list of the current post's categories
```

Finally, it is possible to use the following function to display a crumb trail of categories to a given category:

```
get_category_parents('cat_id', link, separator)
```

In the `get_category_parents` argument list, the first parameter is the category identifier as returned by, for example, the `cat_ID` member variable of the first element of the list of objects returned by the `get_the_category` function. The `link` is a `TRUE/FALSE` value that indicates whether links to the categories in the crumb trail should be displayed.

Finally, the separator allows you to choose a suitable separator to be displayed between the categories. So, you could construct code such as:

```
$cat = get_the_category();
get_category_parents($cat[0]->cat_ID);
```

These functions can often only be executed in the WordPress loop. It is important to remember that, generally speaking, only those functions that are not tied to a blog entry can be used outside the loop. All other ones must be used inside the loop.

For date and time handling, there is a collection of interesting functions:

```
the_date()              Displays the date when the post was created
the_time()              Displays the time when the post was created
the_modified_date()     Displays the date when the post was modified
the_modified_time()     Displays the time when the post was modified
get_calendar()          Displays a calendar with today's date highlighted
```

In addition, there are some functions that are part of the post itself, and which, again, can only be used inside the WordPress loop:

```
the_ID()
the_title('before_text', 'after_text', display)
```

In the_title, before_text and after_text are simply strings that contain any text to be placed around the title. For example, before_text could contain a header or bold text tag, with the closing tag in the after_text parameter. Setting display to TRUE will print the title, whereas setting it to FALSE will just return the text for use in the PHP code.

To display the content or excerpt of the blog entry, you use the following functions:

```
the_content()
the_excerpt()
```

Finally, two navigation functions are useful when generating relational chains of posts. The both take the same number of parameters:

```
previous_post_link('%link', 'link text', same_category)
next_post_link('%link', 'link text', same_category)
```

It should be obvious that the first will create a link to the previous post (if any) in relation to the current one, and the second creates a link to the next one, if any. The %link is a formatting string that allows you to enhance the display with text around the actual link (< link to put a ≤ before the link).

The link_text is just a string that is displayed as the anchor text for the link. If same_category is set to TRUE, only posts from the same category as the one in focus are allowed.

With these few functions available to Web programmers using WordPress, you'll have enough to build your own templates. In the WordPress documentation, all of these are referred to as *template tags,* which is a slight misnomer, probably designed to mask the fact that the Web designer has turned into a programmer somewhere along the way.

A Note on WordPress Plug-Ins   Although you've concentrated on developing themes for WordPress, it is worth giving an overview of plug-ins, just so you'll be aware of how they fit into the model. This is not so much so that you can develop your own, but more so that you can deploy other people's plug-ins.

WordPress plug-ins are little modules of code that can be developed by the end user and then put into the blog at the appropriate point. Usually, they are included in sidebars or other parts of the blog, although there are a few that manipulate the main content as well.

If a developer is developing a plug-in for a wide market, there are many guidelines to follow. However, for plug-ins for personal consumption only or a limited user base of known users, the following is a fair getting started guide.

The simplest approach is to create a so-called template tag (function), which is then called from within the appropriate PHP file (sidebar.php, for example). This template tag function will exist in a PHP file that is included in the plug-ins folder.

These plug-ins can have options set for them that allow the users to set specific values and can be accessed by the plug-in itself, because the plug-in processes its template tag. This processing is part of the PHP script that makes up the plug-ins description. These functions are as follows:

```
add_option($name, $value, $description, $autoload);
```

The `add_option` function allows the plug-in designer to add an option, with a specific `$name` and a current (default) `$value`. In addition, the programmer can specify an option to autoload the value each time the plug-in is used. In order to get a specific option value, the plug-in can then use the `get_option` function:

```
get_option($option); // takes string returns value
```

This function will return the string that was set in the `add_option` function call or, alternatively, another value that has been set using the following function:

```
update_option($option_name, $newvalue); // sets option value
```

These are the three basic setting and retrieval functions, which allow communication between the plug-in and the programmer. Beyond this, the functionality is left up to the programmer to implement.

Besides these kinds of plug-ins, which can be created in a PHP file and then referenced from the pages that use them, there are ones that hook into WordPress Actions. This is altogether a more complex way to create extended functionality.

In essence, it is a three-step process:

1. Make the function.

2. Create a hook to action that calls it.

3. Activate the function.

The first step is just to create a simple PHP function, as you've seen before, and this part is relatively easy. It is also the part of the plug-in that does the work—based on the action that is performed in WordPress to which the plug-in wants to respond.

The `add_action` function is then called to hook it into WordPress. This will link a WordPress Action to the function so that it is called in response to that action. In its simplest form, `add_action` is as follows:

```
add_action ( 'hook_name', 'your_function_name');
```

You can find the list of acceptable hook names as part of the WordPress API at `http://codex.wordpress.org/Plugin_API/Action_Reference`.

If the function can receive parameters, these parameters will need to be listed after the function name in the `add_action` call. That is all there is to it—whenever the action is triggered by WordPress, the user-specified function will be called.

Finally, when the action does not need to be linked to the special function (plug-in) any more, the `remove_action` function can be called. This function takes the hook name and function for its parameters, as before.

Using this whistle-stop tour of WordPress programming, you should be able to do the vast majority of the programming that you'll ever need. More specific Websites might require more specific knowledge, but with experience, writing snippets of PHP code into the content delivery system will become second nature.

WordPress is an Open Source CMS (blogging package) and is often available to Website owners through Fantastico. The advantage of this route is that Fantastico will install the PHP scripts, set the default options and themes (the interface), and install the appropriate databases.

Failing that, you can obtain WordPress from WordPress.org for installation on a third-party Web host, or on your own server. In addition, you can take the WordPress system for a test drive at WordPress.com, both as a free user (where template changes can be tested, but are shared with visitors) or as a paid user, where every change can be delivered to your visitors.

Open Source Content Management Systems

We spent a lot of time describing how blogs work because they are the simplest form of CMS. From Blogger to WordPress, the organization and content creation are both based on more advanced CMSs. Understanding how blogs work will help you understand how all CMSs work—Blogger is the simplest example, the discussion of WordPress added some basic page structuring, and now you are going to learn how the rest of the CMSs are generally put together.

There are other Open Source CMSs available for content delivery. They are all built on similar principles, and detailing each one would not be appropriate in this book. Once you appreciate how they work, each one is easy to deconstruct at the PHP level, and you've been well equipped to read the PHP files that make up the CMS itself.

The advantage of using an Open Source CMS is that the beginning programmer has a good base to start from, which you can extend very easily. The development environment that is offered by the developers of the CMS is usually very well supported and open to extension.

Many hosts still support all of the following through the cPanel/Fantastico interface:

- Drupal

- Joomla

- PHP-Nuke

- Post-Nuke

From a beginner's point of view, assuming that you are a not yet familiar with any CMS, the features CMSs offer are relatively equivalent. Pick one that feels comfortable and seems to fit your immediate needs. Each one has its fans and each one its detractors. Given that they all follow a similar theory of operation, as you'll see here, all you need to implement any one of them is a handle on the theory and a quick scan of the documentation that comes with each install.

The analysis of how to extend these CMSs is based on PHP-Nuke, because it is the easiest to come to grips with. By comparison, Drupal is modern and relatively easy and flexible, and has some issues in relation to the available documentation.

By a similar token, Joomla is quite complex and very powerful, and takes some practice to master. It has excellent support and good documentation. In the middle of these two there are PHP-Nuke and Post-Nuke. They both offer a good compromise between ease of use, flexibility, and adequate documentation.

PHP-Nuke is one of the most established CMSs, offering fairly informative but terse documentation, but is a very easy development platform.

General Structure

Like blogs, CMSs generally follow a structure that has a header, a left menu area, a content area, and, in some cases, a right content area. The content is based around categories and types of content to be delivered—articles, downloads, and so on.

Figure 8.1 shows the front-end for PHP-Nuke. Note the header area is highlighted and the three columns below it can clearly be seen.

The content areas on the page are often called *blocks* or *modules*. Figure 8.1 shows, for example, the PHP-Nuke Menu block on the left side and the Site Stats block

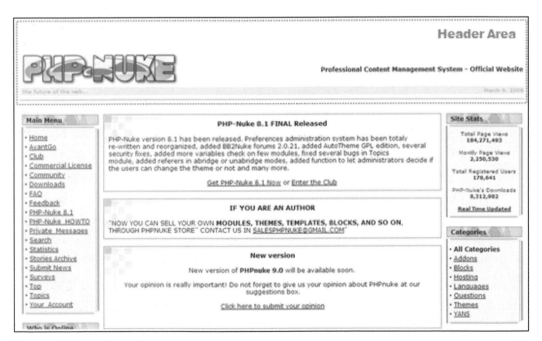

Figure 8.1
CMS interface

on the right. Blocks are the building blocks for the left and right sides, and modules are the bits in the middle that provide actual functionality rather than just the references to that functionality.

So, a block might contain a list of categories, which, when one was chosen, might use the category module to expand that into a set of articles on the category page, once expanded. All of the content is stored in a relational database (MySQL) and can therefore be manipulated easily.

The site is usually split into two or three parts. There is a front-end, where the visitors see the layout that the programmer has decided that they should see. They might also be allowed to see some content that is restricted to their own personal user level.

Then, there is an administration back-end, where the bits and pieces are put together and ordered in a way that makes sense to the programmer. These two areas (three if you count the member-only display) are quite distinct, but any changes made in the admin area will be immediately carried through to the public area.

There are usually some default blocks and modules available to the administrative user, which include the ability to manage the categories that are attached to articles. In addition, there are some interfaces to menus that list the various artifacts that are stored in the system—the administrative user has also a primary responsibility to manage these as well.

In effect, the management of the CMS is a two-tier system, with one part used to build the features that will be used and another used to actually edit the content. These can be fairly transparent, such as in a system with a single content creator, or they can be very opaque. The difference is quite marked between administering the system and editing the content.

So, in most CMSs, there are blocks that are only displayed to the administrator, for example, which allows the administrator to edit the content. Other blocks might be displayed to other users with different levels of privilege within the system.

This implies some kind of user management system and hierarchy, as well as an underlying selective and conditional content-generation platform. The organizational framework is identical to the blog platform, with styles and PHP scripts generating HTML that uses those styles, coupled with a container-based system for templating the content.

PHP-Nuke, for example, has many modules—Downloads, Feedback, Search, Sections, Stories, Submit News, Surveys, Topics, Content (freestyle), phpBB, and so on.

Each module has PHP functions that define what to display and where the data to display comes from. This data is taken from the database, as with any other CMS. The next layer up is the first part of the content organization—the container that places the modules on the page.

There is a collection of blocks that are pre-installed; for example:

- The Modules block—Lists links to the various modules that are active and installed. These can be deactivated by the administrator, at which point they will not appear in the block any more.

- The Administration block—Lists the various administration options available to manage the CMS—from deactivating modules to moving and reordering blocks in the columns or center content area.

- The Search block—Allows site-wide search of the artifacts stored in the content database.

- The Login block—Visible if multi-user is allowed, and when the visitor is not logged in, shows links to user management functions (My Account) page, as well as status (messages, email, and so on) when the user is logged in and browsing the site.

- The Advertising block—Shows advertisements (for example, AdSense or Amazon.com affiliate linked products) or other information that is contextual but not part of the content.

- The Last 5 and Top 10 blocks—Shows, by date or viewing figures, respectively, the last five items to be added or the top ten items that have been viewed.

These can be activated and managed from the admin panel for beginning users. But they can also be altered by adjusting the PHP code that is behind them. This kind of adjustment is endorsed, indeed, encouraged, by the PHP-Nuke developers, and the community has a wealth of information catering to the amateur developer.

Layout and Editing

Again, the layout of the CMS is changed by editing the various CSS files that produce the visual element, which changes the colors and underlying styles. Then, the PHP code can be edited to change the layout further, but this is entirely optional.

Indeed, the system is so structured that the entire CMS can be managed without changing even one line of PHP code. Logos and other interface images adhere to naming conventions that make their use quite clear. Simply swapping them for your own is often sufficient to change the look of the theme to match your own design.

The same goes for the directory structure. It is often possible to copy files into the appropriate places so that the CMS picks them rather than the defaults.

However, if you take the time to become familiar with the PHP scripts that make up the underlying page structure, you can use some contextual scripting to manage the blocks and modules. For example, the container page (index.php) can contain PHP scripts that select blocks to be displayed depending on whether a user is logged in, is of a certain level of privilege, and so on.

This means that, even if a block is enabled and visible, it might not be shown on the page if the PHP code that makes up the index page precludes it. Once you understand this concept, it will be much easier to make sense of the PHP-Nuke documentation.

CMS Management

As always, the CMS system is based on a database with a front-end to edit and display the contents of that database. This means that all the aspects of database management that you've already read about come into play, as well as some way to back up the PHP files that make up the display element of the system.

The CMS usually has a backup function as well, but to be on the safe side, the site manager should get into the habit of copying the theme and the database across from time to time. Copying a theme relies on the Web programmer having stuck with the guidelines laid out by the PHP-Nuke developers regarding naming conventions and locations of key files.

Also, you should be aware that when a new version of the CMS is installed over the existing one, any changes and edits to the modules might be lost. It is therefore a much better idea to clone the modules and alter the cloned modules rather than edit in-place code.

Caution

> Be very careful when making system changes to your chosen CMS. Many of the integral parts offer attractive customization options, but there is usually a better way—introduce the changes in the user-defined theme area as a plug-in, and not in the main code. It might seem like a longer way around, but the advantage is that when the CMS is updated, the plug-ins and structure information are left untouched, therefore preserving your changes.

There is also a set of guidelines that the PHP-Nuke developers have laid down to ensure that any modules developed are picked up by the underlying block level management system. Blocks containing modules can be placed either in a sidebar or main content area, but the system will not know about them or how to communicate with them unless they follow the prescribed format and interfaces.

Roll Your Own CMS

Thus far, you have looked at three CMS or content delivery systems. First, there is the Blogger syndication into a static or server side scripted site, which offers ease of editing coupled with relatively easy content generation.

Next, you saw the WordPress option, which straddled a point between a blog and a full CMS, installed on a Web host and customized with PHP code to change the layout and features available. Finally, you had a brief look at the theory behind the various Open Source CMSs, which offer a much more advanced, yet easy to grasp, approach to content delivery.

The final option is to try to create your own CMS. This is an easier option than you might at first think, but is only valid for single editing systems. After all, you know how to put data into a database and extract it into a format that can then be displayed, and have a knowledge of CSS and HTML to format the content into the way that you want.

However, multi-user systems with authentication should be done from a starting point like an Open Source CMS; otherwise, you will find that it gets very difficult very quickly. Here, there is the additional issue of managing the user's sessions, keeping them secure, and matching them with their content.

So, leaving user management to one side, if you are going to create a CMS, you need a way to display, manage, and edit the data that will become the content. It only becomes content when it is combined with the markup that produces the final Web page.

You still need a database unless you feel that going with a static page version offers enough flexibility and control. Beyond that, you will need some kind of server side scripting, possibly some client side scripting, and a way to deliver the pages.

Given that mix of technologies, this section isn't a complete guide to building a CMS from scratch, but more a list of pointers as to what can be achieved using the information from this book. You'll still have to make the final decisions that take you from a blank page, or a skeleton solution, to your own CMS.

JavaScript CMS

A static page can give the illusion of providing a front-end to a real CMS. By combining JavaScript with HTML and possibly XML, you are essentially copying the navigation options offered by a traditional CMS.

At the same time, you need to find a way of easily including new content without having to re-write pages over and over again. This means that the JavaScript has to contain a collection of scripts to display and link to the various content areas, and each category of content, represented by a single page, has to contain dynamic content.

One obvious challenge is that you would like to achieve all this without a database—and the answer lies in serving XML rather than Web pages, but using a technology called AJAX, which you have met before, to serve the XML within the page in a dynamic fashion.

The issue that this solves is that the content that is being read in still has to be served, and for a really large site, that is going to mean one of two things. Either the text all has to be downloaded to the client system, as JavaScript variables, so that it can be displayed, or multiple files have to be created.

Because you will use style sheets to manage the look and feel of the site, if you want to change that look, you only need to change one file, so that is one problem solved. If you then assume that each page will represent one category of data (or area of the site), you can solve the other channel by using AJAX.

You'll read more about AJAX in the next chapter, but it basically means downloading all or part of an XML file and then displaying the content inside

CSS containers (such as `div` blocks) as if it were served from a database. This only leaves the editing aspect.

Because XML is a plain text format, you can, of course, just edit the files and upload them. You should now have the know-how to do this, but it is much harder work than is necessary.

Because Blogger offers a nice editing interface, importing feeds from Blogger and applying the style sheets to the resulting feed offers the perfect solution. You can mix dynamic content, which is easily edited, with static pages that don't need PHP or a database to make them work.

PHP CMS

One step above the JavaScript CMS is a similar theory applied to dynamic pages. The strength of this approach is that the pages are generated based on a series of XML files. These XML files define the way that the site is put together. All that you need to be sure of is that your decision process matches the `REST` request.

So, how does this work?

In essence, you are replicating the theory of operation of any other CMS, in that the page is generated based on the incoming contents of a `$_GET` or `$_POST` superglobal. Suppose that the incoming URL is something along the lines of:

```
http://www.mysite.com/index.php?operation=show_blog
```

You can test the `$_GET` superglobal to pull out the relevant value for the `operation` variable. Then, you can proceed to populate the variable content on the page, based on the fact that the users want to look at the blog. The posts can be stored in an XML file, which can be easily edited with a text editor or served from a service such as Blogger.

The PHP feature that makes this possible is an XML parser such as the `DOMDocument` or `simpleXML` parsers, which you've already encountered. There are still a few problems with this approach, namely that the DOM can get quite big, especially if you want to be able to search and sort by category, within an individual XML file.

In fact, it is the category management that makes the CMS more powerful and difficult to do without a database behind it. The database enables you to pull up selective collections of data without having to parse a huge text file or one of several text files.

Also, if you want to add games and other interactive modules to a high-volume traffic site, it's better in that case to go with a database solution. So, the last kind of roll-your-own CMS pulls all the technologies together and becomes a PHP plus MySQL CMS.

PHP and MySQL CMS

Here, the main container is a single PHP file which, as before, provides a window on the database based on the operation that the visitor has chosen. Of course, different PHP files can contain different operations, but it makes much more sense to put all the functionality in one place.

The tasks are, as before, very simple:

- Extract data (to build into content) from the database with titles and content text

- Insert data (as text) into the appropriate place in the database

- Provide statistics and feedback to readers

The advantages of this system are that you maintain control of the database and can change the way that data is stored to best match the requirements of the site design. This includes the kind of data that is stored as well as the way that entries are described in the database.

The disadvantages are that it might not scale to a multi-author environment because the authentication system, probably the most complex part of the system, will be difficult to create and manage to make sure that there are no breaches.

Clearly, you're going to have to start simple, with a simple design, and work up to this final system. You might find that the best solution is, after all, to install a CMS like PHP-Nuke and learn how to customize it.

However, equipped with the information in this book, you should be ready to take either solution by the horns!

Recap

This chapter discussed many types of CMSs and how they can be implemented from the point of view of a template-based approach. However the CMS is implemented, it will need to be a combination of technologies that come together to provide the functionality that is required.

Different levels of sites require different combinations of technologies. If all you want to do is embellish a simple blog with context-sensitive advertising and product placements, you can get away with a syndicated blog feed in a static main page.

On the other hand, a full catalog system, or a feedback-based community site, will benefit from having a database-powered multi-user system. Membership sites and sites that offer shopping or other goods or services also need integrated payment management systems, which are delivered as modules that expand off-the-shelf CMSs.

Now that you know the options, challenges, and solutions, it should be clear that the best path is the one that combines the available platforms and technologies in the most efficient manner. The "Just Enough" premise is that the Web programmer should not expend more energy than is necessary to get a site up and running.

This leaves you free to concentrate on what is important—the content. With that in mind, you need to take a look at Web 2.0 and the dawn of Web applications, which are providing an even more powerful way to deliver, share, and manage content in the open multi-user environment that is the World Wide Web.

WEB 2.0 FEATURES

This chapter details the next generation of the Web, or at least the Web that is taking shape after the dot-com bubble burst. With higher Internet speeds, faster servers and better hardware at the client side, the trend is towards Web applications and away from the traditional delivery systems where the interaction between the client and the Web was minimal at best.

The chapter looks at Web 2.0 and how to deploy its features in your own Website creations. In addition, you'll look at the technology that powers Web 2.0 and how it can be harnessed in enhancing your own Website.

The point behind picking up Web 2.0 techniques is that that there are many aspects that you can use to make your site more attractive to visitors while also offering higher levels of functionality than ever before, to keep your visitors coming back.

To date you have learned, in stages, everything that is necessary to start building Web applications—HTML, CSS, PHP, SQL, XML, and JavaScript. This chapter is where they all get pulled together and used, in conjunction with the delivery system that you have learned about in the content-management systems chapter.

The best thing about Web 2.0 is that it doesn't require learning any new technologies, just new ways of combining existing ones. Given the level of standardization that now surrounds these open technologies, this looks like a trend that's set to continue, so a good grounding in the ideas behind Web 2.0 will also future-proof Website designs to a certain extent.

What Is Web 2.0?

The key to understanding Web 2.0 is accepting that it is a combination of existing technologies that allow your visitors to interact, but also provides interaction between Web applications, both at the front-end and the back-end. It is a relatively new term, coined in 2004, that has yet to completely realize its potential.

Tim O'Reilly (`http://www.oreillynet.com/pub/a/oreilly/tim/news/2005/09/30/what-is-Web-20.html`) coined the term and held the first Web 2.0 conference in 2004. O'Reilly had decided that it was more than a flash in the pan and worth exploring further in a formal conference.

However, despite the general acceptance, many people decry Web 2.0 as just another marketing tactic or a meaningless buzzword. The various phrases that get bandied about do sound rather like buzzwords, which can scare some people.

Behind the buzzwords are some very clever ideas about how people should be using the Web—not just to look up information, but to interact, share, and *mash up* different aspects and ideas to create Web applications. This makes the Web act more like a set of interconnected applications and services, and not just a place to look at static Web pages.

So Web 2.0 is the Web as a computing platform (see Google's set of applications, with spreadsheet, word processor, and so on) as well as a way to distribute information. That aspect is still there, and still important, but the interactivity provided by new technologies and better computers has pushed new features to Web surfers.

Part of the importance of this new power also makes Web 2.0 about user-generated content and being able to publish and share information. From YouTube to podcasting, file sharing and collaborative editing, Web 2.0 connects Web users and connects Web services. The driving force behind this is arguably linked to two phenomena:

- Wikipedia

- Blogs

Both of these are about interaction—in the first instance, many authors collaborating towards the same goal, and in the second, one author providing her view to the world, who can then provide feedback through the Website. It is the Web community coming together that provides another key aspect to Web 2.0 and is facilitated by Web programming.

The new Web is also about outreach—how to touch people by marketing and advertising. AdSense, for example, is born of people's newfound journalistic freedoms and the ability to provide advertising space alongside popular online information, be it in a blog or in an article repository.

More than just the ability to push the written word, Web 2.0 is also about interaction through multiple media, including podcasts, video (YouTube.com), and a variety of other ways in which people can project their personality onto the Web. Other aspects include consumers finding content and taking away an experience (sound, vision, written, and so on), as well as being able to contribute to it, in addition to the commercial aspect. Businesses, after all, need to be able to make money from Web 2.0 in order to continue offering Web 2.0 experiences to visitors.

I spent some time discussing what the term Web 2.0 means, because it is useful to understand what the terminology is so that you can understand how it is put together.

This section is about the technologies that are underneath, allowing the *mashup* (connecting together of technologies and/or services) phenomenon to help drive Web 2.0. It's not just about mashup but also about other concepts, such as integrating your site with your Web services, as well as others' Web services, and both principles are built on the same kind of platform.

Many of the ways in which the eventual mashups and APIs will be used rely on an underpinning of communication between the client and the server. This communication happens in one of two ways:

- Synchronously

- Asynchronously

Synchronous communication is like a plain text Web page. The client requests it, and the text comes back to the client, which then has to wait before displaying the result. Asynchronous communication is something different—the client no longer has to wait and can start to display parts of the page even while it is working behind the scenes to update other parts.

More than that, if something changes on the page as a result of interaction with the users, the page can locate and deliver the media without having to refresh the page. Part of delivering that aspect involves AJAX.

AJAX

AJAX stands for Asynchronous JavaScript And XML, simply reiterating the core technologies that provide the underlying base for providing the functionality.

Asynchronous means that there has to be some kind of trigger. The whole page loads and then data is populated behind the scenes. The trigger usually comes from some form of user action that causes more data to be loaded and displayed, without breaking pace with the display of the page to the end users.

The JavaScript is needed to intercept that action (as an event handler) and start communication with the server. Once the communication request is complete, the JavaScript comes in again to retrieve the result. Finally, having received the result, the JavaScript has to work within the confines of HTML and style sheets to assign the data to a visible element on the page.

You are, by now, familiar with some of these technologies. In technical terms, one way to render the information is to insert the formatted data into a named `div` using the `getElementById` part of the DOM interface provided by JavaScript.

Before you look at implementing AJAX mechanisms, there are a few things to watch out for that you'll need to bear in mind when designing an AJAX site.

First, there is an issue with browser incompatibility. The discussion here shows how best to deal with this when it occurs, but it stems from the fact that one of the key mechanisms that has been defined by the W3C for AJAX, the `xmlHttp` object, has been implemented differently by Microsoft than some of the other browser vendors.

The next issue is that JavaScript might not be active on the client's system. There is nothing you can do about this beyond trying to anticipate problems and displaying appropriate HTML code. You saw how to do this in the JavaScript chapter.

Tip

Keep .js files separate for creating and manipulating the XML objects, as well as the functions that process any results that come back from the XML querying process. This way, the programmer will not have to copy the same code over and over.

So, the requirements for being able to provide AJAX functionality are as follows:

- HTML and JavaScript

- Server side scripts (PHP in this case)

- Database—This is optional, depending on what mechanism provides the data

XML fulfils two different roles in the AJAX paradigm. On the one hand, it is a communication conduit, and on the other it is a way to describe the data and the way that it should be rendered on the Web page.

A worthwhile side note for those who are using Microsoft solutions is that ASP offers an AJAX component that works within .NET scripts that operate on the server side. This can also be integrated with the browser. This chapter discusses the more popular PHP/JavaScript XML solution, because it seems to be more widely adopted among Internet publishers.

The Role of XML in AJAX

The `xmlHttp` object provides the mechanism for asynchronous communication and is a standard that has been created to facilitate this communication. The standard is managed by a working group of the W3C.

XML provides both the request/response mechanism as well as a way to describe the data that's retrieved. On the one hand, it can be used to retrieve a plain text (usually HTML) response for display using one variation:

```
xmlHttpRequest. responseText
```

On the other hand, it can be used to retrieve an XML document using another variation:

```
xmlHttpRequest.responseXML.getElementById('id')
```

The only difference between these two is that the data retrieved by the JavaScript, through the `xmlHttpRequest` object, is unstructured in the first case and structured XML in the second.

As mentioned, there are two steps to using the `xmlHttp` object—creating the object and testing for compliance with the standards provided for its deployment.

Creating the `xmlHttp` Object

Different browsers use different kinds of `xmlHttp` objects. In ECMAScript-compliant browsers, the `XMLHttpRequest` object is part of the language. In other environments, it might be contained in an ActiveX object. This latter approach is the one typically used by Microsoft.

In order to make sure that you perform the right actions without causing the JavaScript to crash, you have to use something called the exception mechanism. Logically speaking, you *try* to perform a function and then you *catch* any error that it returns before JavaScript has a change to report the error.

In JavaScript, these two actions are called the try and catch blocks. The *exception* is the thing that is caught. Bearing that in mind, here is the user-defined CreateXMLHttpObject function:

```
function CreateXMLHttpObject()
{
  var _xmlHttpObject = null;
  try {
      // ECMAScript compliant object creation
      _xmlHttpObject = new XMLHttpRequest();
  }
  catch (e) {
        // e is the exception, thrown because
        // XMLHttpRequest does not exist.
    try   { // try something else
        _xmlHttpRequestObject =
                  new ActiveXObject("Msxml2.XMLHTTP");
      }
  catch (e)   {
        // e is raised again, obviously the ActiveX approach
        // is not working either, so try another one:
        _xmlHttpRequestObject =
                  new ActiveXObject("Microsoft.XMLHTTP");
      }
    }
    return _xmlHttpRequestObject;
}
```

If the return value from CreateXMLHttpObject is still null, the last catch block also fails, and there is not a lot you can do about that, so you can just report it and stop the script. Apart from that, the rest of the code should be fairly self-explanatory.

There are some things to remember. First, you need to test whether the global variable that is allocated to the return value of the CreateXMLHttpObject has been set. If it has not been set, you need to reinitialize the xmlHttpRequest object.

If the variable xmlHttp object is still null even after you run the script, you need to set the relevant piece of content to a suitable message on the page. If you do not do that, the visitors are left wondering why their pages do not look quite right.

This can be done using code such as the following:

```
if (g_xmlHttp == null ) {
  document.getElementById("result_area").innerHTML =
    "<b>Your browser does not support xmlHttp requests.</b>";
}
```

There is a better alternative to this last fragment. You can provide, via an interactive form, an alternative way to get the information. This would move the model from an AJAX model to a synchronous HTTP request/response mechanism.

The way that the system detects that an action needs to take place is via the xmlHttp state change mechanism.

xmlHttp *State Changes*

The xmlHttpRequest object has a property that is referenced as follows:

xmlHttpRequest.onreadystatechange

This is a function that can be called whenever the state of the object changes so that it can do some work. A state change can be instigated when data is requested and received or when something else happens.

The function contained in the onreadystatechange property is triggered by a change in an associated property:

xmlHttpRequest.readyState

The states that you're interested in, and the ones that can be values for the readyState property, are twofold:

- 3—The request is in process

- 4—The request is complete

The responseText and responseXML properties of the xmlHttpRequest object will contain the appropriate response for the type of data (text or XML) that was returned by the server to the client when the readyState is equal to 4.

However, before you will be ready to process that information, you first need to make a function to handle the state change. The generic skeleton for such a function might look like this:

```
function xmlHttpStateChange () {
  if ( g_xmlHttp.readyState == 4 ) {
    // Do work here with the responseText or
    // responseXML property
  }
}
```

The next step is to assign the function to the xmlHttpRequest object through the onreadystatechange property. You do it this way so that other functions can be assigned to the object depending on what you want to do with the response when it comes back. This is achieved with a simple line of code:

```
g_xmlHttp.onreadystatechange = xmlHttpStateChange;
```

Of course, you could make the entire solution more object oriented by creating a derived object to put it in, but there is no sense in working harder than necessary to create client side solutions.

Having set up the xmlHttpRequest object, and assigned a function to process the data that comes back in the response, you need to send a request so that you can obtain that response.

Sending the Request

This is a two-stage process:

- Build the URL that locates the data

- Perform the request

The request can be an HTTP GET or POST, depending on what the server script is expecting. These examples use GET because it's far easier to explain and exposes the components that will be used as input. The URL is hidden behind the rest of the HTML via the JavaScript, so it is never exposed to the end users.

The URL is built in the usual fashion for this kind of request:

```
http://www.your_url.com/script.php?first_parameter
         =value&second_parameter=value"
```

The next step is to call the method that makes the actual request. Assuming that the previous URL is present in an appropriate variable, and that you have initialized a global variable `g_xmlHttp` using the appropriate object-creation function, the following can be used to open the URL:

```
g_xmlHttp.open("get", url, true);
```

The `g_xmlHttp` variable is an object that must be created as per the JavaScript/ECMAScript standard discussed in Chapter 5. It can be instantiated with code such as the following:

```
g_xmlHttp = new XMLHttpRequest();
```

Finally, you need to send `null` to the server because you're not providing any additional data (that is, this is a GET and not a POST request, which would contain the form data). This is performed very simply:

```
g_xmlHttp.send(null);
```

The `true` parameter in the call to the `open` method means that the script will continue and not wait for response. If you had used `false`, that would instruct the script to wait for the response. This changes the behavior of the local object, and not the server, so putting in `false` means that the page might not load properly, as the page would become temporarily unresponsive.

Once the response comes back from the server, the state change property will be updated and the `onreadystatechange` function (referred to in the property) will be called.

Processing a Text Response

Due to the fact that you have requested that the data be returned asynchronously, at some point in time, the function assigned to the state change property will be called. This will occur in reaction to the state change of the `g_xmlHttp` object.

At the server side, the response can be either plain text or an XML formatted object. A PHP script will usually return, by default, the text content type, although you can change what's returned using the `header` function (to return HTML, for example):

```
header('Content-Type: text/html');
```

When a text variant is provided in the response, the entire response will be accessed via the following object property:

```
g_xmlHttp.responseText
```

This property contains plain text, but that may contain fragments of HTML, which can subsequently be directly assigned to any named element through JavaScript, as noted. A div element, for example, could be set up that was previously empty and then have its .innerHTML property set to the text (with or without HTML formatting data) returned through the .responseText property.

Processing an XML Response

The xmlHttpRequest object also provides an interface that equates to a DOMDocument style object, which you first encountered in Chapter 5. This allows you to have standard access to a structured piece of data—in this case, an XML document.

This is brought into play when the header is returned from the PHP script running on the server, as follows:

```
header('Content-Type: text/xml');
```

At this point, you can retrieve the XML document from the following member property of the g_xmlHttp global that you set up in the first place:

```
xmlDocument = g_xmlHttp.responseXML;
```

From here, you can access the XML using the usual set of methods through the xmlDocument object, such as:

```
xmlDocument.getElementById('id');
```

To do this, you need to know the structure of the document that has been returned. Otherwise, it becomes difficult to extract the appropriate data to place in the HTML document that is used as the interface with the end users (the visitors).

AJAX with PHP

The previous discussion described the client side processing, so now you need to look at what happens on the server side when the server receives the request. There is, in fact, nothing special about the HTTP request itself; it is identical to any other request for a resource that it might receive.

The PHP script will be called with the HTML GET protocol, and so the query data, if any, will be in the appropriate superglobal variable. As you'll remember from previous chapters, this is accessed as follows:

```
$_GET['parameter_name']
```

All that you need to do on the server side is perform any processing and return the result by using familiar PHP commands, such as echo to send back the data. This data can be returned as if it were a text or XML stream.

The best way to illustrate this is to go through a whole example by starting with a simple HTML document that provides the interaction among the user, the Web, and the server. You'll need a text box, a button, and a div to store the result in.

The core of the HTML document can be written as follows:

```
<form name="table_layout">
Number of Columns : <input type="text" name="columns_entry"/>
<input type="button" onClick="updateColumns();">
</form>
<div id="columns_area">
</div>
```

The important parts of this document are the button and the div. The update-Columns function attached to the onClick handler of the button has to start the AJAX operation by creating the query and submitting it.

The function can be created as follows:

```
function updateColumns() {
   if (g_xmlHttp == null ) {
     g_xmlHttp = initXMLHttpObject();
   }
   if (g_xmlHttp == null)   {
   // not much point continuing
   return;
   }
   var queryURL = "get_columns.php?";
   queryURL += "col=" + document.table_layout.
      columns_entry.value;
   g_xmlHttp.onreadystatechange = columnsChanged;
   g_xmlHttp.open("get", queryURL, true); // Do the AJAX
   g_xmlHttp.send(null); // No data to go
}
```

The first part of the code tests to see if a g_xmlHttp object exists, and if it does not, the code uses the assumed initXMLHttpObject function to create it. If everything is correctly instantiated, the queryURL is built, and the function columnsChanged is attached to the g_xmlHttp object.

The queryURL contains the name of the PHP script you are going to call and a data part that contains col= followed by the contents of the text control.

This columnsChanged function then has to handle the state change once the data is returned and place the data in the div container of the HTML document. The updateColumns function then sends the request.

This function simply sets the contents of the div container to the responseText of the g_xmlHttp object. The code might look like this:

```
function columnsChanged () {
  if (g_xmlHttp.readyState == 4 ) { // We have a response!
    document.getElementById("columns_area").innerHTML
             = g_xmlHttp.responseText;
  }
}
```

This is all well and good, but you also need to create a PHP script that is run on the server. It has to be able to extract the data fed in by the users and return appropriate text with HTML. The script could be as simple as follows:

```
<?php
$num_cols = $_GET["col"];
echo "<table border=1><tr>";
for ( $col_num = 0; $col_num < $num_cols; $col_num++ ) {
  echo "<td>" . $col_num . "</td>"; // Basic work
}
echo "</tr></table>";
?>
```

The PHP script extracts the number of columns from the $_GET superglobal, and uses that to construct a table using HTML code, which is then sent back to the client as the response to the original request.

Of course, you could make refinements to this example, but the general procedure remains the same. If you wanted to produce XML instead, for example, by way of the result, you would have to change the way it was both written and interpreted.

You'll look at this possibility in the "AJAX with Databases" section.

AJAX with CSS

This can be considered as more of a side note than anything else, as well as a kind of best practice style hint. CSS is generally used to provide a consistent user interface, and where AJAX is used, and the response possibly follows a different look and feel, the combination of the two technologies can come into its own.

The main principle is that, when using AJAX, try not to make the server side script produce pure HTML. Otherwise, the JavaScript might have to do some finessing of the HTML to fit it into the look and feel of the page on which it is placed.

Instead, leverage the use of CSS to only change the pure text and let the structure of the document also dictate the style information. That way, if the style changes, the PHP script does not have to change, provided that a consistent use of CSS statements has been established.

Otherwise, it becomes very hard to keep up with the style changes, unless the style information is stored in a database. Because AJAX is built on three different technologies—HTML, JavaScript, and XML—there are potentially three pieces of source code that could change.

Using styles helps to keep these potential changes to a minimum.

AJAX with Databases

Finally, AJAX with server side databases becomes a very powerful tool. It is wise to return the information in a structured way such as XML, rather than as plain text, to cut down on the client side processing.

The reasons for this are that it allows you to keep the client/server interactions down to a bare minimum, and XML can store much more information in a structured manner. It is the mix of AJAX with databases and visitor interaction that is at the heart of many Web 2.0 applications.

If you look at previous example of the blog database, it has the following basic schema:

```
date, title, summary, content
```

When you first produce the page, you might populate a form control that contains the dates of all the blog entries. You can do this using AJAX (but this might be overly complex) or using straight PHP to build the Web page. The latter implementation might be coded in a PHP script as follows:

```
<html>
<head></head>
<body>
```

```
<form name="blog_search">
Date : <select name="blog_date"
        onChange="listBlogs(this.value)">
<option value="">
<?php
$db_link
  = mysql_connect('mysql_host', 'mysql_user',
                  'mysql_password');
mysql_select_db('site_content');
$query = 'SELECT DISTINCT date FROM
         blog_entries ORDER BY date';
$result = mysql_query($query);
while ($line = mysql_fetch_array($result, MYSQL_ASSOC)) {
  echo "<option value='" . $line["date"] . "'>";
}
?>
</select>
</form>
<div id="blog_list">
</div>
</body>
</html>
```

This code leaves out any non-essential information, and of course, the final version would have to be better formed, using more correct HTML. However, in the interest of clarity, I have kept the code to a minimum. The core of the page is the SQL query that is used to populate the HTML select control with a series of option drop-downs—one for each date in the fetched result.

Attached to the select control is an onChange handler, which calls a function, listBlogs. Given that you have a range of dates, the listBlogs function becomes easy to implement:

```
function listBlogs (var blog_date) {
  if (g_xmlHttp == null ) {
    g_xmlHttp = initXMLHttpObject();
  }
  if (g_xmlHttp == null)   {
  // not much point continuing
  return;
  }
  var queryURL = "get_blogs.php?";
  queryURL += "date=" + blog_date;
  g_xmlHttp.onreadystatechange = blogListChanged;
```

```
    g_xmlHttp.open("get", queryURL, true); // Do the AJAX
    g_xmlHttp.send(null); // No data to go
}
```

This code should be reasonably familiar by now, and does nothing really different except to build a slightly different URL. Finally, the blogListChanged function can be created so that when the xmlHttp request returns, the appropriate HTML code can be built based on the data that is returned by the get_blogs.php function.

Because this data will be XML, you can use the following implementation:

```
function blogListChanged () {
  var html_out = "<table>";
  if (g_xmlHttp.readyState == 4 ) {
              // We have a response in XML!
    xmlDoc = g_xmlHttp.responseXML;
    // For each entry, print the date and summary
    var blogItemList = xmlDoc.getElementsByTagName("item");
    var numBlogItems = blogItemList.length();
    for ( var blog_item = 0; blog_item
        < numBlogItems; blog_item++) {
      var curr_item = blogItemList.item(blog_item);
      // curr_item is an entry in the NodeList
      html_out += "<tr><td>" + curr_item.childNodes[0].
                        nodeValue + "</td>";
      html_out += "<td>" + curr_item.childNodes[1].
                        nodeValue + "</td></tr>";
    }
  }
  html_out += "</table>";
  document.getElementById("blog_list").innerHTML = html_out;
}
```

Note that this example uses the DOMDocument object in JavaScript to access the XML data returned by the PHP script. Note also that I left out the PHP script that generates the XML data based on a query from the database.

It really is not that different from returning a piece of text, except that the header needs to be changed, as previously noted, with the header function. The general layout of the XML should look something like this:

```
<bloglist>
<item>
```

```
  <title>Title</title>
  <content>Content</content>
</item>
</bloglist>
```

Really, that's all there is for AJAX. This discussion is just enough for you to get started using it on your own site. The rest of this chapter is dedicated to showing you a few Web 2.0 applications that you can create using AJAX and some other techniques that are already in existence—why work harder than you need to?

RSS

RSS stands for Really Simple Syndication. Syndication is a way to share regularly updated content, such as that of a blog, with other Web users so that the content spreads around the Web creating a following for your output.

RSS is an open standard for exchanging syndication information. There are many flavors of RSS and there is not space here to describe them all, but each service uses one flavor of RSS, so it is worth checking the result of an RSS request to see what data is returned.

Each RSS document is known as a *feed* and has a structure that is well known and publicized, even if it does follow one of several conventions. The good thing about RSS is that, despite this clash of different standards, it facilitates the sharing of information through the Web.

AJAX with RSS

Due to the fact that RSS feeds are returned from the HTTP request as XML documents, it becomes easy to integrate feeds of data sources with AJAX on the page, as long as they support the HTTP GET protocol.

This means that a request for a feed will result in an XML object being created that is accessible through DOMDocument in JavaScript and PHP. The latter might make use, for example, of the SimpleXML interface to access the feed, filter it, and return a modified version to the AJAX request object, which then uses JavaScript DOMDocument operations to render the result.

In this way, you should begin to see the power of so-called mashups and Web applications. They reuse lots of different existing technologies and services, one of which is called Yahoo! Pipes.

Yahoo! Pipes

Yahoo! Pipes is an RSS mashup available at pipes.yahoo.com that allows the users to build applications that are solely centered around processing one or more feeds. The principle is that the pipe starts with a data feed, operates on it, and returns a data feed.

Those familiar with UNIX command-line (csh/bash) programming will realize, of course, that the terminology has its roots in UNIX pipes, which are used to redirect output from processes as input to other processes, all from the command line. This technique is also available in MS-DOS-like operating systems, using, like the UNIX/Linux counterpart, the | (pipe) symbol.

The core of Pipes is a process that enables the users to get a variety of XML feeds and build a set of operations around the data in a visual way. It combines dynamic HTML (JavaScript and styles) and AJAX to provide intermediate results.

One of the uses for Pipes is to integrate the result into your site through AJAX, by requesting the URL that the pipe can be accessed through. The Yahoo! Pipes system then runs the pipe and returns a feed that can be freely used.

The underlying Web 2.0 principle is to obtain one or more feeds, combine them, filter the data or use the feed data for something else (a Web search, for example), and then return a result as a feed. There are many different building blocks allowing the users to enter data, services to be queried, and results manipulated.

For example, one use could be to look for open hub requests on HubPages.com, which is a public feed. Then, you could use one of the Pipes functions to extract the search terms from each of the HubPages.com Request titles. The resulting stream of search terms can then be passed to Google.

The result of the Google search is a Web page, for which there is also a Pipes widget, which enables the users to break the page down into tag values. The results of the search could then be returned as an XML feed. This XML feed can then be embedded, using AJAX, in a static Web page, making it dynamic.

Social Networking

Another Web 2.0 phenomenon has been the rise of social networking. Although you might not realize it, many of the social networking activities such as messaging and tagging (not to mention rating, reviewing, and recommending) would not be possible without the underlying technologies discussed in this chapter.

A site such as Facebook, for example, uses many of the technologies discussed here—from HTML, CSS, and AJAX to server side scripting and RSS—to deliver a rich interface for its users and developers. The extensibility of such networks makes them attractive for both content creators and Web programmers.

With this popularity comes better applications and a more attractive platform.

The key to it all is allowing people to present their information online and other people to search and view it. But that's only part of the interest. The other part is allowing like-minded users to connect with each other and share their own information and experiences.

All of this takes Web programming.

Integration with Web Services

The final component of Web 2.0 programming is being able to integrate with many services available on Web capable of fulfilling a variety of uses.

This section looks at three categories—Amazon representing the shopping services, eBay representing auctions and, very briefly, Google—representing data sharing and publishing.

The idea is to show you how to integrate your site, static or dynamic, with these services to create Web applications in the easiest possible manner, using your newfound knowledge.

This interface to an online processing system is known as a *Web service*. There are many kinds of Web services, from shopping services (such as Amazon) to search services (such as Google). Usually, the Web service provider offers:

■ An API (application programming interface)

■ Documentation

■ Processor resources

The API is required to enable the Web application to communicate with the Web service; Google, for example, provides the GData API to allow interaction with everything from Froogle to Google Search.

The documentation enables programmers to make sense of what is usually a reasonably complex proprietary API. Finally, the processor resources actually service the requests. It is very important to note that these are not infinite—the service provider will usually put some kind of cap, or threshold, on resource use.

For this reason, the developer usually has to register with Web service providers in order to start using their services. This enables the user's processor and other resource use to be monitored to make sure that the user doesn't exceed the predefined limits.

Amazon Web Services (AWS)

Amazon Web Services give the Web programmer access to the Amazon catalog, shopping cart, and fulfilment process. Using AWS, you can integrate Amazon into your site, offering better services, for which you can also earn a commission.

These services use familiar POST requests (otherwise known as REST) over HTTP and result in XML being fed back to the browser.

The following PHP code is taken from one of the official articles covering AWS, on the Amazon Website available at http://developer.amazonwebservices.com/ connect/entry.jspa?externalID=636&categoryID=12:

```php
<?php
$request = 'http://ecs.amazonaws.com/onca/xml?
Service=AWSECommerceService&' .  ' AWSAccessKeyId=[YourKeyHere]
&Operation=ItemSearch&SearchIndex=DVD&' .
   'Actor=Brad%20Pitt';

$response = file_get_contents($request);
echo htmlspecialchars($response, ENT_QUOTES);
?>
```

As you'll note, the query is built up in the usual way as an HTTP request string. This is then sent to the Web server using one of the standard GET functions. The get_file_contents function is part of PHP and just returns the entire contents of a file from the source—local or over the Web—using HTTP.

Of course, this could be an xmlHttpRequest object as well, especially since the result that comes back is actually XML, but the key is to keep it as simple as possible. There are a few things to note.

First, an ID key is needed to use AWS, and this goes in the AWSAccessKeyId part of the request. Second, to deploy AWS efficiently, you need to know the various Operation codes. These are well documented, however.

Processing the XML data is easy, as you have seen in previous examples. It is a good idea to try to access the URL with a browser first to see the structure of the XML before coding a solution that navigates the object tree to obtain the data that the programmer requires.

There are also functions provided by Amazon to interface with shopping carts. For example:

```
http://ecs.amazonaws.com/onca/xml?Service=AWSECommerceService&
AWSAccessKeyId [YourKeyHere]&
Operation=CartCreate&
Item.1.ASIN=[An ASIN]&
Item.1.Quantity=1&
Item.2.ASIN=[An ASIN]&
Item.2.Quantity=1&
Item.3.ASIN=[An ASIN]&Item.3.Quantity=1
```

I have broken the URL up so that you can see the various components. Note that a shopping cart that is reasonably full can result in quite a long URL.

The only other issue with this example is that the programmer needs to keep track of the shopping cart and its contents. However, because you can also use Amazon for accepting payment and adding items once the cart has been set up, this is relatively easy.

The CartCreate operation, which returns a cart ID, for example, is provided by AWS. In addition, there are operations to add and remove items, which make it easy to manage the cart, even if the developer has to provide the code to actually show the end users what they have in their carts.

There are many other operations supported by the AWS API for Associates (which is the ability to look up items and include the Associates ID—affiliate ID—to get paid), and each operation returns different data. You'll become quite intimately acquainted with the AWS documentation once you start building AWS-aware Web applications—but it is worth the effort.

There are several layers possible, but the easiest is to use HTML+CSS as the presentation layer. The presentation layer can then be deployed within PHP scripts, which provide the application layer, responsible for creating the display and communicating with Amazon behind the scenes. This communication will usually take the form of XML HTTP requests that yield data that can then be processed and turned into HTML and CSS for presentation to the users through the browser.

The result, therefore, is a standard HTML page that belies the enormous amount of work, and mashing up of services to produce a result that combines the best aspects of several online services. The term *mashup* means exactly that—the combination of existing services to produce something new.

You also could include AJAX at the interface level and embed some of the AWS functions in an otherwise static page. However, it is tricky to use at the cart level, because of the way that the page is updated and that data is passed around. It is possible; it, just some work, and probably would involve cookies to handle the cart contents.

In some cases, this might be the only option because the Web host might not allow `get_file_contents` to work over the Internet. This is something that you'll have to check for yourself.

Of course, AJAX can be used and the data passed back to PHP to get around this, but this introduces a two-tier system where data has to be relayed from the client to the server and then back to the client again. The logic will then be split across two interfaces, which will make the end result more complex.

Finally, services such as Yahoo! Pipes can be leveraged too, because they can create and process XML/RSS data feeds. This is an advanced mashup, and will require an in-depth knowledge of the Yahoo! Pipes system. However, because it simply passes URLs (with `REST` data) around, the AWS interfaces can be deployed with Pipes without technical problems.

eBay

Again, eBay uses `REST` to deliver services, and again, a user ID and developer token are required to get up and running. These are then used in the URL that provides the `REST` request to authenticate the programmer with eBay. This also implies that there are some usage limits in place to avoid abuse.

Of course, AJAX can be deployed, and even Yahoo! Pipes and similar RSS/XML processing platforms can be deployed, because they are all based on the same underlying communication and data sharing technologies.

An example of this might use Amazon's XML feeds services to pull down the top ten books and then use this data to look up eBay auction items. These auction items can then be returned as an RSS feed with the affiliate ID of the site owner inserted using some of the Pipes processing functionality for manipulating strings.

An eBay service query string looks similar to the following example:

```
$apicall = "http://rest.api.ebay.com/
            restapi?CallName=GetSearchResults&" .
"RequestToken=$RequestToken&RequestUserId=$RequestUserId&" .
"SiteId=$SiteId&Version=$Version&Query=$SafeQuery&" .
"EntriesPerPage=$EntriesPerPage&PageNumber=
              $PageNumber&UnifiedInput=1";
```

The official eBay developer guide uses the `simplexml_load_file` PHP function to execute the `$apicall` and resolve the result. The following is taken from the online documentation:

```
$xmlResult = simplexml_load_file ( $apicall );
foreach ($xmlResult->SearchResultItemArray
          ->SearchResultItem as $searchitem) {
    $link  = $searchitem->Item->ListingDetails->ViewItemURL;
    $title = $searchitem->Item->Title;
    // For each SearchResultItem node,
    // build a link and append it to $results
    $results .= "<a href=\"$link\">$title</a><br/>";
    }
```

As you can see, the power of `SimpleXML` is very useful when you're applying it to documents for which the structure is well known. This code can be deployed in any CMS to provide auction listings, something that's almost guaranteed to provide lasting interest for visitors.

Google

Finally, Google has many developer APIs that you can use to interface with the Google services, including specific ones for Data, Calendar, Spreadsheets, and Gadgets. Each of these APIs is a well-documented set of REST requests that can be deployed with any of the previous technologies to consume the available Web services.

You read in the last chapter how to do this with the Blogger API, which is used to display a blog using PHP. Of course, you now know that the same effect can be achieved with AJAX, thereby turning a static Web page into a dynamic one.

If you assume that you have a single page divided into three columns—navigation, content, and advertising or product placement—you can see how, with a little ingenuity, you can build a whole CMS without needing a Web host that supports PHP.

JavaScript can be used to display data conditionally in the left and center panes. The content can be pulled from Blogger using AJAX, which means that the Blogger interface is used for editing.

Then, the right pane can be populated with AdSense adverts, another Google invention, with AWS and eBay API calls providing additional placement, again via AJAX.

And there are plenty of other possibilities—so you have no excuse not to be able to build a great site.

Recap

Note that the vast majority of the examples of Web 2.0 technologies in this chapter have been built on extensions to HTML and XML. In addition, developers can use private extensions and modifications, using JavaScript, XML, and CSS together to do new things with the underlying technologies.

It is the client technology driven by interaction with the visitors, combined with server side technology, that provides the illusion that not only is each Web user interconnected in a communication Web, but also that the Web page is an application that runs over the Web and connects the users to the back-end.

That is what Web 2.0 is all about—more interactivity, and better and more powerful applications making ever better use of the information and opinion distributed through the information superhighway.

CHAPTER 10

SETTING UP WITH OPEN SOURCE

Now that you have all the knowledge, it is time to see how to put it into action. Whether you want to build a blog, create an online catalog, or just show a static collection of pages, the chances are good that you can get everything done almost for free.

The key is in something called Open Source software. Generally speaking, Open Source software is software that has been placed into the hands of end users for free, subject to licensing restrictions. These licensing restrictions exist to protect the intellectual property of the original authors and not to restrict the use of the software.

This has two effects:

- Setting up Web servers has become very cheap.

- A lot of good server scripts have become available.

The result of these two effects combined is that Web hosting solutions are usually based on Open Source packages. When they are not (where proprietary, non–Open Source solutions are chosen such as Microsoft Windows), you can expect to pay a higher price—sometimes even to the point that a host will give you a Linux-based account for free but charge for a Windows equivalent.

This book has been created with Open Source solutions in mind:

- The JavaScript (ECMAScript) specifications are Open Source

- PHP (the language) is Open Source

- MySQL is an Open Source database system

- HTML, XML, and related standards are all Open Source

Luckily, it is not necessary to actually own or operate the hardware or software (except for the PHP scripts that might be needed) that the hosting solution is based on. This chapter assumes that you're going to build one of several kinds of sites, using generally available technology and services.

It is split into two sections. The first is designed to help you to establish what it is you actually need, and the second gives some basic configuration examples and clues as to how to get started.

Never forget that for each project you undertake, it is very likely that there has been a solution already created that you might easily adapt to your needs. This being the case, if it can be downloaded and adapted, you will save yourself a lot of hard work.

What Do You Need?

The first question to ask when getting started is to determine what you want to do, so that this can be translated into a checklist of things that are required to get up and running as fast as possible. Generally, building a Website is all about getting started—once the site is up and a flow of visitors is established, it becomes easier to justify bolting on new features along the way.

However, different kinds of sites have different needs and it can be costly to change Web hosts if you find that something that you later need was not planned for when you first chose your host. This means that the initial checklist has to allow for growth.

In other words, the aim is to plan for the future as far as is possible while staying in line with the emphasis of this book—doing just enough to satisfy your short-term goals.

If cost is an issue, consider free hosting or hosting that comes free with a domain name registration. This is not really the place to cover the ins and outs of free versus paid hosting, but with the advent of Open Source solutions, more providers are changing their models as the cost of technology comes down.

Free hosting is not always the bad experience that people might believe. For those just starting out, it can be a better solution than trying to host a site on your own hardware, as long as a paid upgrade is available.

One thing to think hard about is where the site will be hosted, because if you choose to install everything on your own hardware, there are additional points you have to consider. If you host the site yourself, you have to contend with all the vagaries of hosting support such as backup facilities, a permanent fast Internet connection, and so on.

Besides these aspects, there is the software side. You would need to install a piece of Web server software, a database, and PHP. For Windows servers, this means the .NET framework for Windows servers, plus the database and PHP. For Linux systems, this usually means a LAMP setup: Linux Apache MySQL PHP. Apache, in this case, is the Web server software.

The first step is to decide what your site has to do.

What Do You Want to Do?

What the site has to do—the facilities it has to provide—will depend entirely on what the goal of the site is. This will, in turn, dictate how the content is served, which will have a bearing on the features that the site host must support.

Once you've decided whether the site is static, dynamic, open access, or a special features site containing membership areas or user-based sensitive information or services (like Facebook, for example), you can then start narrowing down the kind of features you'll need.

One of the decision points revolves around how the information is presented and delivered. For example, the site could offer a service (paid or not) that results in the distribution of the information (a mailing list, an expert system, basic search, and so on) or it could just provide a hierarchical set of articles.

If you decide on a dynamic site, perhaps offering services or just generating content on demand, this opens up a separate set of decisions. This starts with the question as to whether you have to store and manipulate large amounts of data.

Given that this might be the case, you have to consider whether you'll need a database to store the content instead of simple XML or text files. This, in turn, means that the database has to be designed and that, above all, the chosen Web host must support database access.

Even if the Website will (at first) only contain essentially static pages, you still might need, due to the complexity of the hierarchy, to have a CMS that manages the content. Depending on the kind of CMS you choose, this might require a database and will certainly be likely to require some PHP scripting.

On the other hand, you might ascertain that the pages can be entirely static, and rely on technologies such as AJAX to populate them from the outside. If your pages are created on your own hard drive and uploaded to the Website, they can be tested locally before a new version of the site is made live.

This might be more work in the beginning, but always remember that testing a site is necessary and that uploading while you're still testing can disrupt a working Website. Hence, an HTML and JavaScript solution might be the best approach for the simplest mashup or blog-based sites.

(Clearly for a forum site, or one where collaboration between visitors is encouraged, this approach will not work quite so well.)

Once you've decided what your site needs to offer, you can begin with the next step—making a checklist of required features so that you can select a Web host.

Choosing a Web Host

Once you decide what your Website will do and determine what features you want to provide, you can create your own feature checklist, like this one:

- PHP

- FTP

- MySQL

- Fantastico

- CMS

- Password-protected areas

- Email/WebMail

- Integrated search

This is only a subset of what you might put together, and for each of the more complex items, such as the database, you should include some sizing information. For example, one blog, one forum, and one Web catalog typically mean you need three databases. Coincidentally, three databases are often the limit established by many Web hosts.

From here, it's a simple matter of tabulating the hosts and what they offer before choosing one. For the most part, this will be easy, but there are a few sticking points, usually related to bandwidth and storage space.

Bandwidth is the amount of data that you are allowed to transfer, both up to the server and down from the server, in a given time period. Once you have exhausted the available bandwidth, the site can become inaccessible unless you purchased more.

For example, you should make sure that if your site is designed to be used in conjunction with popular services such as Facebook (as a Facebook application server for an application offered to Facebook users), the site will receive a lot of traffic. This translates into two consequences:

- High bandwidth usage

- High server processor usage

For this reason, some Web hosts have a "no Facebook" policy, so that their servers aren't run ragged with a high volume of requests. Also the amount of data that can be stored on a Web host is important. If there are many pages or scripts creating dynamic pages, quite a lot of space might be used.

If you install an off-the-shelf CMS, you need to check that the available disk space is not eclipsed by the high requirements of the more complex systems. You'll also be adding your own media, such as images and music, which might push the storage requirements a little higher.

You can't neglect the database, because this will also add to the space that is being used to host the site. Admittedly, space is not such a big problem these days, unless you're using the site as a movie host or something like that. These sites come with their own technical challenges, such as finding a host that allows streaming media—it adds to bandwidth in a serious way!

Finally, choosing the right kind of scripting interface is also quite important. The reason for this is that there are some features that might not be available on the

Web host, such as some PHP libraries that the host might not allow their sites to use. One such feature is access to the sendmail program for sending email.

Over the years, the fear of being shut down because of one unscrupulous user sending spam through the sendmail program, coupled with a number of possible security flaws, has led to hosts starting to restrict the use of this program. They often offer an alternative, but sometimes they remove this functionality altogether.

However, some CMSs require registered users to confirm their registration by email (for security reasons), which will need use of a PHP facility to send email. It is not a big issue, but something to be aware of.

Once you've satisfied your feature list and chosen a Web host, it is time to move on to the next phase and install your site.

Installing the Site

The first thing to do once the site has been set up is install the first version to make sure that everything works. Even if it is just a test page to check that the CMS is in place and that the database is connected, it is worth doing before you spend hours creating content and placing it in the database.

For a basic sites made just with HTML, this is an easy process. You simply need to FTP everything up or use the host's built-in site upload tool, and then view the main page. This is not always as straightforward as you might think, because there are many possibilities for the all-important index page:

- index.php

- index.htm

- index.html

So, if the first page does not come up as planned, you should check to see if the Web host has left your own index page lying around, which is then being served instead of the new one that you have just uploaded. It's small things like this that force you to test installations regularly when you make changes.

Some hosts will even offer site builder tools, whereby you can put your own HTML in as well as accept their default layouts. Provided that they also allow JavaScript and the possibility to extend your site with your own files once your confidence grows, this is probably the best way to get started.

Otherwise, if the simple file upload mechanism does not give enough control over the resulting site, it is time to use a tool such as cPanel.

Using cPanel

You've read about cPanel a few times now, as a way to help manage various aspects of a Website. In my experience, every cPanel I have used has looked different, but they have always had two things in common—a list of installed resources and measure of current usage on the left, and groups of programs in the middle designed to help manage the various aspects of the site.

A word of warning—if you do not understand the nature of a change that you are about to make in cPanel, don't do it. Generally, the documentation is good enough that clicking the little yellow question mark and consulting the manual is sufficient to ascertain *how* to do something, but it doesn't always elaborate on the *why*, because it assumes that the person using the tool knows what he or she is doing.

Usually, cPanel is accessed on port 2082, typically through an URL such as `http://www.mysite.com:2082`.

However, some ISPs might block this port, and so an alternative is sometimes offered at `http://www.mysite.com/~cpanel`.

If neither of these URLs works, you need to contact the Web host and ISP to resolve the issue. Without cPanel, it is impossible to set up databases or install packages. This might not be an issue if the site can be uploaded through FTP, but it is certainly an issue if the site has to host a database for a CMS.

Essentially, cPanel is basically an Open Source configuration package for Web hosts. Through it, you can manage the email settings, databases, and various other aspects. This includes the ability to access raw and treated statistics, consult logs that might give clues as to why a certain PHP script is failing, and provide an interface to manage files.

Directory permissions and password-protected areas can also be managed using the cPanel interface, although there are better methods of protecting areas of the site, such as using proper PHP session authentication.

The only things that you really need to use straight away are the email and database setup tools, as well as the file manager and perhaps Fantastico—the package manager. Once these are located, you are ready to get started.

The Web host that you have chosen, based on the feature checklist, will have installed all these tools already. So, you don't need to worry about them; because these tools are Open Source, however, if you did want to download and install one of the script sets that make up an application, you can do so.

In addition, some Web hosts might use a different package manager than Fantastico, but it seems to be the most popular. Package managers all tend to work in roughly the same way, so you are bound to find parallels in the discussion here.

Using Fantastico

Fantastico is a cPanel application plug-in that is used to manage third-party Open Source packages that are used for a variety of different purposes. The list of packages that are supported grows all the time.

Figure 10.1 shows the Fantastico DeLuxe logo, and the usual software group that it can be found in. Note that different cPanel versions (this one is from cPanel 11) will place the Fantastico program in different areas.

In Figure 10.2, you can see the various options that are available for this specific Web host (x10Hosting.com).

You will see that the programs that can be installed are listed on the left side (the list is much longer than what's shown here), with the currently installed packages in the middle. In this case, only WordPress is installed (with an upgrade available).

There is also a little note in red at the top of the page for warnings. In this case, I appear to have run out of available MySQL databases!

The scripts that Fantastico uses to install a specific piece of the Website are wizard-based, so you're taken through the stages step by step. This includes setting up the initial administrator accesses, setting up databases (if any), and emailing a confirmation message at the end that contains all the settings.

Figure 10.1
Fantastico software group

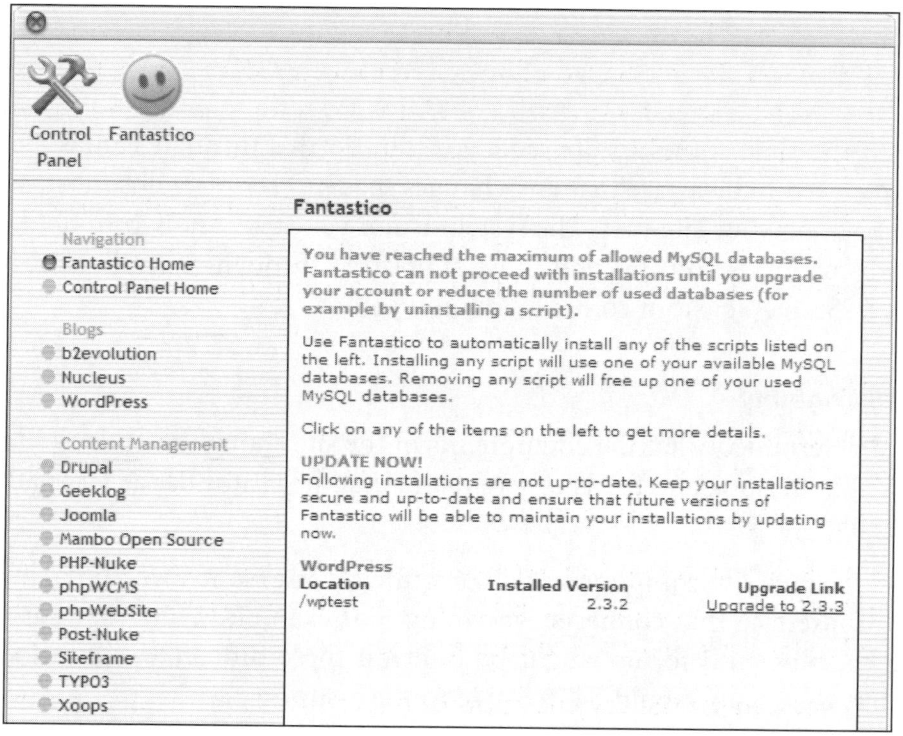

Figure 10.2
Fantastico interface

It is a much better approach than downloading the PHP files, trying to set up the database by cutting and pasting (or uploading) SQL scripts that recreate the environment, and then finding that there are a hundred settings to make in the PHP scripts.

So, if the Website needs a CMS, it will probably be installed though Fantastico, which creates all the databases for you and picks the optimal settings for the startup package. Of course, once the system has been installed, you still have to go and customize it, but Fantastico saves a lot of time.

Because Fantastico and the packages that it installs are Open Source, it usually is available where a host allows PHP access and databases. Some common applications include the following:

- WordPress

- PHP-Nuke

- phpBB

- Drupal

- Joomla

Finally, when the time comes to upgrade, you can do this through Fantastico. However, you need to be aware that any changes made to scripts will be lost, so you should back up your site first. The system is not yet clever enough to detect and integrate customizations beyond those supported through generally accessible means (CSS files, custom colors/logos, and so on).

Gluing It All Together

Once you've determined what the components of the site should be, it comes to making sure that the look and feel is coherent and that the visitor has a clear path around the site.

It is possible that the site components will be quite diverse, so it's worth having some kind of interface that connects everything. For example, a site that has a shopping area, blog, and forum might be built on three different application platforms, but this setup should be invisible to the visitors.

Consequently, you'll need to create glue code to attach everything to the main page.

This will usually be part of the CMS, but there also needs to be a main index.php page that's accessed from the outside world via the Website URL. Now, on most hosts and some CMS, the package is stored in a subfolder of the main site, and so the index.html page that is served from the default folder needs to redirect to the main page of the CMS (or blog, or catalog).

If you are following this discussion step by step, you'll remember that you already read about the index.html page that was uploaded by FTP. This will sit in the root of the Website as `http://www.yourURL.com/index.html`.

However, when you install a CMS, it is usually placed in a subfolder called `http://www.yoruURL.com/wordpress/index.php`.

Subsequently, you need to make sure that the CMS index page (WordPress, in this case) is visible from the root index or that the root index.html page redirects automatically to the CMS index page. You do this with a simple redirect statement in the `HEAD` element of the HTML page:

```
<html>
<head>
<title>Your Title Here</title>
```

```
<meta http-equiv="refresh" content="0;
        url=http://www.redirecthere.com">
</head>
<body>
  <a href="http://redirect to this url">
          Click here if not redirected...</a>
</body>
</html>
```

The `content` of the `refresh` `meta` tag just tells the browser not to wait before redirecting to the new page. It is also a good idea to leave people with the option to click in case their browsers do not support the refresh `meta` tag.

Once you've set up and tested all the individual components, the gluing together begins. For example, if the WordPress blog package has been installed alongside the PHP-Nuke CMS, it makes sense to integrate the blog entries into PHP-Nuke, either at the database level or through a PHP script that can access the blog entries and display them.

You've so far looked at many ways to do this, from using AJAX to leveraging the WordPress API to retrieve the XML data and using it directly. In the end, only your imagination will limit how the mashups of different services can be performed to create your own unique online identity.

Examples

The following are some examples of very basic solutions, along with discussion about how to get started as soon as possible, using "Just Enough" principles. They are provided as a kind of cookbook of solutions to common questions and as a way to help you overcome feeling overwhelmed when you think about how to create your online service.

Static Site

This is the easiest way to get going, and a good way to test the water and practice newfound skills. That is not to say that nothing useful can be built with static pages, just that you have to know what the limitations are.

The minimum that a static side will need is an index.html page, which can be created with a text editor. Once it is created, you can start to build up the content page by page. It is probably a good idea to try to use some JavaScript to create things like the site navigation menus; otherwise, whenever they need to change (when a page is added), the menus have to be updated in many places.

There are Open Source scripts available on the Internet to make this more manageable—they run as client side scripts and can be customized by the Web programmer.

However, because the site can have only static pages, there is no interaction with the server beyond the fact that the server serves the pages to the client. This means that there is no possibility to access a database or have server side scripting to perform tasks that deliver HTML.

The site requirements are modest, so it should be possible to find a free Web host that is ad-free and possibly buy a domain name to park on it. This will mean that your domain name points to the Web host so that it looks as if the site exists under that domain when it really exists under a subdomain of the free hosting provider.

This approach works well for blogs where the editing is done off-site, that is, where a local piece of software builds the site each time that content is updated and provides a set of HTML pages for the content creator to upload.

It is also valid for blogs that take their content from a blogging site (see Chapter 8, "Content Management Systems") and can use AJAX to retrieve the blog. In fact, any site that makes use of externally hosted content that is delivered as XML can be based on a static page model.

Therefore, there is no need, if a blogging site is all you require, to waste time putting blog software on the Web host and paying for bells and whistles. The Web 2.0 mashup principle lets you set this up very easily with a few lines of JavaScript.

Adding a Bulletin Board

Going beyond the static site and offering a bulletin board (forum) means that the Web host will need to provide some server side functionality. At the very least, you'll need a database and access to PHP in order to manage and store the content, house posts, and store user identification.

Assuming that you've chosen a host that supports cPanel, the process is easy. From the main cPanel account management page, select the Fantastico application. From there, you can choose from several different forum packages—

phpBB is perhaps the most well known and also integrates well with CMS packages.

Once you select a forum package and begin the installation, the database will be created and you'll be asked to provide the credentials for a forum owner (or moderator). This is the person with responsibility for the forum and all the conversations in it.

The initial setup will not include any real content, just some default boards. So, the next step is to set up user groups, boards, and possibly categories. The general membership structure should be worked out ahead of time so that this creation process is easier.

For example, sometimes you will need to limit what users can see by introducing rules in the structure of the forum. Although phpBB makes this easy, it is almost impossible without some kind of plan as to how the boards should be divided up.

In most cases, you'll also need to alter the PHP code to change the look and feel or terminology of the forum by adding a theme. This follows the same kind of customization route as a CMS, but the PHP code that manages the forum should not be changed—only the pieces that manage the look and feel. They are easier to break than a standard CMS.

Basic Content Management System

A step up from having static Web pages with a forum is to start working with a CMS that is integrated with the forum and static content. The biggest part of the move will be migrating the static content to the database of the CMS.

It is assumed that the static site has been built, and that the CMS is an upgrade. If you're building the site on a CMS from scratch, you need to build an index page and then keep the CMS under development in a locked part of the site until it is up and running.

It is not possible to do local debugging in many cases because, unlike with normal Web pages, it is not possible to run the server side code on your computer. If you have access to a copy of Apache (a Web server software package) and a database, you can do some local debugging, but this is not likely the case for the vast majority of readers.

If you're not planning to use an out-of-the-box CMS solution, all you need is a database and some PHP code to set up a simple single user content-delivery system.

This should be relatively easy to upload and test. Some PHP scripts can also be tested locally by installing the PHP software; however, you must make sure that the version matches the one available on your Web host.

Online Brochure

The final kind of site that you'll look at is easy—it's simply a collection of pages that contain images and details as well as a way to order products. All of these elements are available as off-the-shelf Open Source installable modules.

The behavior is actually just a subset of a CMS, so that is the model that is required. Picking an easily customizable CMS such as PHP-Nuke or Drupal will reduce the development time.

The Web programmer needs to create a module for displaying the pictures and the description, as well as for maintaining some session data. For example, the simplest way to do this is to use the authentication from an out-of-box CMS. This will require that visitors join the site before they can order, but this is the general model of most online shopping sites.

Next, the database has to be populated with the images and textual descriptions so that they can be reproduced in the pages of the CMS. There might be a module available for download that can plug in to the chosen CMS, so check the main support site to see if there is one available.

At the same time, you might also like to find a shopping cart that has already been implemented for the CMS in question. These shopping carts usually integrate well with the authentication system, thus tying it all together.

Finding pre-built modules will save time in long run, because all you need to do is glue them together using your PHP skills, and a site can be up and running in hours. As soon as you need to start implementing your own modules, it can take weeks before you're ready for production.

The final step is to add a forum. This will also be based on the CMS solution you've chosen, as it needs to integrate. This forum will be used for customer feedback, questions, problems, and so on. It is a far better mechanism than having a support email because it allows other customers to collaborate and help solve the problem, which fosters a sense of inclusion.

The icing on the cake is to deploy your XML skills to obtain a live feed of urgent questions so that you can stay in touch. All of this uses technology to solve problems and present solutions where, in the days before Web programming, the only tools a site owner had were an email address, some Web forms, and their time.

Recap

This chapter provides some basic guidelines on how to get up and running, but it essentially contains everything that you need to know before you choose your exact site building path. It has been mentioned many times in the book, but it also bears mentioning just one last time—mashing together existing solutions is easier than building them from scratch.

If you want to build a site that has a blog, but do not find a Web host that will let you install WordPress, the easiest option is to use AJAX in the Web page and connect to a Yahoo! Pipes, or Blogger blog feed.

In fact, even if your Web host will let you install WordPress, if you are adept at writing HTML, the AJAX option will probably give you far more flexibility. The reason for this is simple—it is easier to lay out a table with three columns, and put a menu on the left, content in the middle, and adverts on the right, than to use a real content-management system.

On the other hand, if you want to implement an online game of some kind, you will need to pull all your skills together—HTML, CSS, JavaScript, and PHP, probably coupled with SQL and XML to boot!

But here again, leveraging an Open Source CMS such as Drupal or PHP-Nuke to create the framework and authentication systems will save you hours of time when creating the final system. It's all time you can spend on other, more worthwhile, activities.

The next chapter in the book (and the last one) provides a list of some of the best places to go when this book doesn't have the detail that you need. It also lists some great Web resources that give every indication of being around forever. That's a rare commodity in this online world, so they must be of high quality.

Hopefully, though, the book, along with this getting started chapter, has given you enough of a head start that you can begin to build your Website straight away without any additional information.

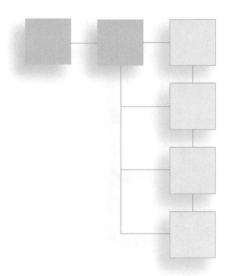

CHAPTER 11

WEB REFERENCES

The goal of this chapter is twofold—to give you a collection of starting points that you can refer to when you need to find out about one of the official standards or when you need to find a piece of standard documentation, and also to annotate those references so that you know what to look for when you get there.

The World Wide Web is a great repository of information, but it can take some research to get to the individual nuggets of useful information. Luckily, most of the standards-related sites are very well laid out, and navigation is a snap, yet they can be quite technical.

Anything that can help direct readers to specific documents and help them understand what they are looking for, and why, is helpful. That is what this chapter is all about.

Authoring Standards

By and large, the body responsible for maintaining the authoring specifications that are used by Web programmers is the World Wide Web Consortium, or W3C. This organization sends out for comments, and then updates and publishes the standards that the browser manufacturers agree to support when rendering Web pages.

The W3C's mission statement, laid out on the "About Us" Web page (located at `http://w3.org/Consortium/`), is as follows:

> "To lead the World Wide Web to its full potential by developing protocols and guidelines that ensure long-term growth for the Web."

Not only does the WC3 maintain and publish the HTML, XML, XHTML, and CSS standards, it also provides a collection of tools that can be used to validate pages. These are very useful when trying to ensure compliance with the ever-evolving standards behind the World Wide Web.

There seems also to be an ongoing commitment by browser vendors to maintain backwards compatibility, so it is likely that the standards mentioned in this chapter will be with us for some time to come.

Before reading any individual standard, you're well advised to take note of the following:

> "The DOM5 HTML, HTML5, and XHTML5 representations cannot all represent the same content."
> `http://www.w3.org/html/wg/html5/#html-vs`

This brief statement indicates one of the underlying principles of the Web standards—different representations can address different kinds of content. You met the DOM (Document Object Model) previously as an abstraction of an HTML (or XHTML) document. The DOM5 HTML standard is the abstraction that caters for HTML and allows browser developers and Web programmers to manipulate it.

HTML5 is just an improvement of the current recommended incarnation of HTML (which is HTML 4.01, introduced in 1998). XHTML5 is the XML-compliant representation of the next HTML standard. In other words, it is HTML5 represented using the XML standard.

The thrust of this is that Web programmers need to choose, and possibly mix, their choice of standards depending on what they are trying to achieve. Being aware of the constraints and differences between the standards is half the battle in understanding them.

A complete list of the current W3C recommendations can be found at `http://www.w3.org/TR/`.

This list contains everything that the W3C is working on, but the following were used in preparing this book.

HTML Standards

The main HTML working group entry page can be found at `http://www.w3.org/html/`.

It contains links to the most recent published drafts of the HTML standard, as well as links to tutorials, validation services, and conformance checkers for all currently supported versions of HTML.

The currently stable version of HTML is HTML 4.01, with work on HTML 5 being drafted on the 31st of January 2008.

HTML 5.0

Source: `http://www.w3.org/TR/html5/`.

One of the major improvements in the new HTML standard (which, as of 2008, was still only an editor's draft) is the stance taken by the W3C on Web application standards. It is now accepted by the standards body that Web applications and developers need a single document that represents the capabilities of the Web application language rather than having to mix different standards, as they do today.

One of the key differences is the incorporation of the Document Object Model into the HTML draft, and the provision of editing markup to facilitate dynamic document creation.

HTML 4.01

Source: `http://www.w3.org/TR/html4/`.

The current W3C recommendation for static HTML documents, designed to be enhanced by style sheets, uses the incorporated CSS standard.

The W3C HTML working group also works on CSS standards for defining style sheet languages, and the current CSS standard can be found at `http://www.w3.org/TR/REC-CSS1`.

HTML 4.01 has been the standard since 1998, despite the ever-changing nature of the Web, and HTML 5.0 is backward compatible. Given that artifacts on the Web are designed for longevity, 4.01 is a safe standard to use when authoring pages.

It also has the advantage of being stable, whereas, at the time of writing, HTML 5.0 is only a draft document at the W3C.

XML Standards

The XML specifications are maintained by the XML working group. The main page can be found at `http://www.w3.org/XML/`.

The latest W3C recommendation for XML specifications can be found at `http://www.w3.org/TR/xml`.

Because XML is essentially a language for describing communications and other languages that are self-describing, almost all third-party scripting languages (such as XUL, Silverlight, and so on) are based on the XML standards published by the W3C.

Advanced Web 2.0 technologies and techniques such as RSS and AJAX also make use of XML, so it is worth taking the time to become familiar with the structure and terms of reference of the standard, if not to actually read it cover to cover.

XHTML Standards

The XHTML standard is maintained by the XHTML working group, whose home page can be found at `http://www.w3.org/MarkUp/`.

This page contains many useful links—not just to existing standards, but also to test suites used to validate XHTML implementations. The working group's mission is clearly stated:

> "The mission of the XHTML2 Working Group is to fulfill the promise of XML for applying XHTML to a wide variety of platforms with proper attention paid to internationalization, accessibility, device-independence, usability, and document structuring." `http://www.w3.org/MarkUp/`

This includes new standards for rendering rich Web content that goes beyond the simple document plus images model of HTML.

Programming Documentation

This book references three programming languages and several software packages. The following is an annotated list of the official documentation that supports the Web programming languages:

- JavaScript

- PHP

- SQL

Most of the organizations concerned also have forums where users can ask questions and pick the brains of the community.

JavaScript and ECMAScript

The official ECMAScript standard can be found at `http://www.ecma-international.org/publications/standards/Ecma-262.htm`.

In addition, there are a number of extensions that can be found listed in the ECMAScript section of the standards index at the previously mentioned site. This index can be found at `http://www.ecma-international.org/publications/standards/ Stnindex.htm`.

Most JavaScript implementations will be compliant with the ECMAScript standard, or be based on Sun Microsystems own JavaScript implementation. The Sun document can be found at `http://docs.sun.com/app/docs/coll/S1_Javascript_13?l=en`.

It is a PDF download, and is well written and extremely complete. If you have read Chapter 5 of this book, there's no reason why you should not understand the "Client-Side JavaScript Reference Guide."

PHP Documentation

The main PHP documentation page can be found at `http://www.php.net/docs.php`.

From here, it is possible to select a specific language and format. You can download the manual to a PC or review it online.

MySQL Reference

The MySQL Reference manual, from MySQL, can be downloaded in a variety of formats—from PDF to HTML archives and compiled HTML files—from `http://dev.mysql.com/doc/#manual`.

However, be aware that it is an extensive and technical document and goes far beyond the basic Web programming as presented in this book. This book has treated databases as somewhere to store data, which is adequate for most needs.

The manual is useful only if your site has very high traffic, has a complex data model, or is installed on a system to which you have complete access. A lot of the manual is dedicated to the setup of MySQL, which goes beyond regular usage.

The SQL language itself is an ANSI standard, and as such must be purchased from the organization at http://webstore.ansi.org. However, there are free versions available, and checking www.sql.org is a good place to start.

Most SQL database vendors (including Open Source vendors) tend to develop products that have SQL implementations that are closely compliant with the commercial leaders, such as IBM and Oracle.

Open Source References

The home of everything related to Open Source is the Open Source Initiative home page, which can be found at http://www.opensource.org/.

Its chief activities are in approving licensing models and maintaining discussions and resources for the various OSI license holders.

Licensing

The Open Source Initiative maintains a complete list of licenses that it holds as being acceptable to the provision of Open Source resources. This list can be found at http://www.opensource.org/licenses/category.

The licenses that are most commonly applied are the GPL and LGPL, which are applied to most of the software packages referenced in this book.

Software Repositories

These are places where Open Source software and free scripts for PHP and JavaScript can be downloaded.

SourceForge.net (also www.sf.net)

This is a large collection of projects that are written in a variety of languages, including PHP and JavaScript. Each project is rated according to its activity and the downloads that are available, as well as a categorization by both topic and product maturity.

It is the best place to look for cutting edge solutions, as well as specific libraries designed to solve a specific problem. All the source code is available under one of the OSI licenses, and projects have specific bug tracking and release management responsibilities.

PEAR and PECL

The PEAR (PHP Extension and Application Repository) contains many reusable PHP components that can be glued together to make exciting applications. Make it your first place to look for something that might, at first glance, seem to be a unique solution for a unique problem. (PECL refers to the extensions available for PHP, and stands for PHP Extension Community Library. The community is all the people contributing to making PECL better and better.)

Given the size of the PHP user community, there are very few truly unique problems left to solve, and even if the code requires some reworking to fit exactly with your problem, considering that the source is available, you can still save a lot of time.

Caution

Do not change PECL or PEAR sources directly, as future updates of these modules will cause the local copy to be overwritten so that you will lose any customizations that you've made.

The main PEAR home page can be found at `http://pear.php.net`.

For the PECL (extensions) collection, the main address is `http://pecl.php.net`.

Although the standard PHP install contains the vast majority of extensions that any Web programmer might need, advanced users might occasionally want to add an extension that has functionality not covered elsewhere.

Note that anything from the PEAR or PECL collections that needs to be built and installed as a *shared* extension must be done by the administrator. This does not generally apply to solutions made available as PHP scripts only.

General Repositories

The following is a list of places that have useful code snippets that can be downloaded and used under the Open Source license.

- `http://www.phpfreaks.com/quickcode.php`—This is a collection of categorized code snippets that are very useful for learning intermediate and advanced PHP programming tips and tricks.

- `http://www.opensourcescripts.com/`—This site has a collection of categorized JavaScript, DHTML, and PHP source code files, as well as code written in other programming languages.

- `http://www.devshed.com`—This site is geared towards a tutorial-style discussion of specific coded solutions and covers DHTML, JavaScript, PHP, and MySQL topics, as well as specific examples from other Web programming products.

- `http://thefreecountry.com`—The Free Country is an interesting and reliable resource site. In particular, it contains references to many of the best freely available solutions for all kinds of Web programming problems. It covers specific subjects (shopping carts, content-management systems, and so on) and a variety of languages. Of particular note are the following:

  - `http://www.thefreecountry.com/php/index.shtml`
  - `http://www.thefreecountry.com/javascript/index.shtml`
  - `http://www.thefreecountry.com/scripthosting/index.shtml`

The script hosting page is very useful for readers wanting somewhere to try out their scripts or wanting to find a pre-built solution, hosted elsewhere, that they can mash together with their own sites.

INDEX

Symbols

{ } (curly braces), 109, 166
< > (chevrons), 3, 55
| (pipe) character, 385
; (semicolon), 153
symbol, 93, 97
_ (underscore) character, 288

A

<ABBR> tag, 73
abbreviated text, 73
absolute positioning, 115–116
<ACRONYM> tag, 73
acronyms, 73
Active event, 123
Active Server Pages (ASP), 214
addresses, 28–29
Administration block, Open Source CMS, 362
Advertising block, Open Source CMS, 362
advertising, Internet, 30–32
AJAX (Asynchronous JavaScript and XML)
    with databases, 381–384
    discussed, 47
    functionality, 372
    with PHP, 378–380
    role of XML in, 373
    with RSS, 384–385
    with style sheets, 381
    xmlHTTP object
        creating, 373–375
        sending the request, 376–377
        state changes, 375–376
        text response processing, 377–378
alert method, 184

alignment
    bottom, 87
    center, 75, 77, 87
    left, 75, 77
    paragraphs, 76–77
    right, 77
    table, 85
    text, 75
    top, 87
    vertical, 87
ALTER TABLE command, 297
Amazon Web Services (AWS), 387–388
anchors, 92–94
API (application programming interface)
    Blogger, 343
    defined, 47
    WordPress, 349–356
arguments, variable, 167–168
array data type, 224–225
Array object, 193–197
array operators, 234–235
array_diff function, 259
array_merge function, 257
array_pop function, 259
array_push function, 259
array_rand function, 259
arrays
    array related functions, 256–259
    defined, 155
    forms, 156
    mixed, 156
    multidimensional, 157
    one-dimensional, 157
    self-sizing, 196
array_search function, 257